Political Thought of the Ukrainian Underground

1943–1951

Political Thought of the Ukrainian Underground 1943–1951

Edited by

Peter J. Potichnyj

and

Yevhen Shtendera

Canadian Institute of Ukrainian Studies
University of Alberta
Edmonton   1986

THE CANADIAN LIBRARY IN UKRAINIAN STUDIES

A series of original works and reprints relating to Ukraine issued under the editorial supervision of the Canadian Institute of Ukrainian Studies, University of Alberta, Edmonton.

Copyright © 1986 Canadian Institute of Ukrainian Studies
            University of Alberta
            Edmonton, Alberta, Canada

Canadian Cataloguing in Publication Data

Main entry under title:
Political Thought of the Ukrainian
    Underground 1943–1951

(The Canadian library in Ukrainian studies)
English translation of extracts from the
series: Litopys UPA.
    ISBN 0-920862-45-4

1. Ukraïns'ka povstans'ka armiia – History –
Sources.   2. Ukraine – History – Autonomy and
independence movements – Sources.   3. World
War, 1939–1945 – Underground movements –
Ukraine – Sources.   4. National liberation
movements – Ukraine – Sources.   I. Potichnyj,
Peter J., 1930–   II. Shtendera, IEvhen.
III. Canadian Institute of Ukrainian Studies.
IV. Series
DK508.79.P64 1986   947'.710842   C86-091329-5

Cover design: Sherryl Petterson

Printed in Canada by Hignell Printing Limited
Distributed by the University of Toronto Press
                5201 Dufferin St.
                Downsview, Ontario
                Canada M3H 5T8

Contents

ACKNOWLEDGEMENTS

The editors wish to express their appreciation to the many people who helped them in the preparation of this volume.

To Mr. M. Lebed go our thanks for access to the archives and background information on the members of the Supreme Ukrainian Liberation Council. Dr. M. Prokop kindly shared his knowledge about individual events, authors, and members of the UHVR. Dr. V. Potishko offered information about K. Osmak; Mr. R. Petrenko about P. Chuiko; and Rev. Dr. Iu. Shumovsky about his brother P. Shumovsky. Dr. M. Ripeckyj and Mr. V. Makar were very helpful in tracing various difficult and obscure details, and Mr. J. Majiwskyj helped with archival problems and other technical questions. Mrs. H. Malyk had the onerous job of retyping often illegible texts, and Mrs. Z. Keywan did the translations often as a personal sacrifice. Mr. M. Yurkevich deserves our profound thanks for his work both as advisor and as copy-editor. We are grateful to them all.

Dr. M.R. Lupul and the Canadian Institute of Ukrainian Studies deserve our special thanks for the research grant that made this volume possible, as does McMaster University for handling so efficiently the financial problems connected with this enterprise.

INTRODUCTION

This anthology of political writings of the Ukrainian underground during and immediately after the Second World War (1943–51) includes the works of the leading underground publicists who made a significant contribution to the development of Ukrainian political thought. The articles and documents collected here also mark several points at which important ideological shifts took place and changes were made in the organizational structure, strategy and tactics of the Ukrainian underground.

The underground struggle in Ukraine occurred in two stages, each with its own strategy and tactics and each determined by the specific conditions of the time.

The first stage (1941–4) was the period of German occupation. This period was characterized by the vigorous, large-scale development of partisan warfare waged by the Ukrainian Insurgent Army (*Ukrainska povstanska armiia*, UPA), which was created in 1942. The army's foremost task was to defend the population against the racist, destructive policies of the Nazis and against the marauding bands of Red partisans, which often behaved in the most callous and provocative manner toward the Ukrainian population. At this time the UPA grew into a major force (its peak strength was approximately 40,000)[1] capable of clearing large regions of Ukrainian territory of the enemy and administering them on its own.

The underground writings of this period fully reflected the conditions of the struggle. They exposed the criminal policy of the Nazis toward Ukraine and neighbouring countries. They discussed the hostile attitude of the Ukrainian population to the occupiers. They indicated the need to develop proper countermeasures against the forcible conscription of young people for work in Germany and advised how best to resist the enemy. The writings of this period, which are full of optimism, express the belief that in the cataclysmic confrontation of the two brands of imperialism, Nazi and Soviet, both would perish, and that all the subject peoples of Europe, including the Ukrainians, would win a free and independent existence in their sovereign states.

The second stage (1945–51) is marked by a shift to new forms of struggle under conditions of renewed Soviet control. The years 1945–7 may be considered a transitional period characterized by large-scale armed resistance as heretofore, as well as intensive underground organization and activity of small conspiratorial groups.

During this second period the underground writers exhibited a more judicious and sober evaluation of the prospects for the liberation struggle. They were fully aware that the contest would be very long, complex, difficult and full of sacrifices. Nevertheless, they concluded that in the conditions of Soviet totalitarianism underground warfare was the only viable form of political struggle available to them. This activity was to be undertaken by small guerrilla detachments for purely political purposes. However, underground work in general was to be conducted in highly conspiratorial fashion with a view to the political education and mobilization of the masses.

This change of tactics and development of new forms of struggle represents only one side of the coin. The other side—much more important, in our opinion—manifested itself in the changes brought about within the ideological sphere. Organized Ukrainian nationalism had developed during the inter-war period as a reaction against the socialist and democratic-populist currents which dominated the revolution of 1917–20. Before the revolution, the leading Ukrainian intellectuals in the Russian Empire favoured a decentralized federation with broad political and cultural autonomy for Ukraine. It was only after the Provisional Government and the Bolsheviks had demonstrated their hostility to the federalist concept that the independence of the Ukrainian People's Republic was proclaimed in January 1918. In the western Ukrainian lands under Habsburg rule, where the national movement was much farther advanced than in the Russian Empire, Ukrainian independence was seen as an ultimate goal to be achieved after a period of federation with Austria. The Western Ukrainian People's Republic was not proclaimed until November 1918, when Austria was on the point of collapse. The united Ukrainian republic, established in January 1919, was over-whelmed by the invading Russians and Poles.

The failure of the struggle for independence radicalized many who had taken part in it. For the ex-officers and soldiers of Ukrainian ar-mies who formed the underground Ukrainian Military Organization (*Ukrainska viiskova orhanizatsiia*, UVO) in 1921, it was axiomatic that the national identity of the Ukrainian people could find expression only in an independent state. Operating on the Ukrainian lands under Polish rule, the UVO carried on a terrorist campaign intended to dis-rupt the functioning of the Polish administration. In 1929, the UVO combined with representatives of student nationalist organizations to found the Organization of Ukrainian Nationalists (*Orhanizatsiia ukrainskykh natsionalistiv*, OUN). Ievhen Konovalets, a prominent military commander during the revolution and head of the UVO, be-came the OUN's first leader.

The OUN adopted as its overriding political goal the attainment of an independent Ukrainian state—a goal for which the organization's mem-bers were enjoined to struggle to the death.[2] According to the pro-gramme adopted at the founding congress, political sovereignty could be attained only by means of a national revolution. Consequently, the OUN was strongly critical of all legal Ukrainian political parties, since they proposed to attain independence by evolutionary means.[3] The OUN's corporatist social program, which emphasized state supervision of every aspect of national life, was inspired by the example of Mus-solini's Italy. Ievhen Onatsky, a journalist and former diplomat of the Ukrainian People's Republic who had taken up residence in Rome, wrote enthusiastically about Mussolini's regime, which, in his view, had brought about the political rejuvenation of Italy.[4] After becoming a member of the OUN leadership, Onatsky lobbied tirelessly with the Italian government for support of the Ukrainian national cause. Another leading OUN theoretician, Mykola Stsiborsky, proposed the establish-ment of a national dictatorship, a State Council, and corporate social organization on the Italian model in his work *Natsiokratiia* (Natio-cracy), which appeared in 1935.[5]

For all its advocacy of revolution, there was a strong conservative streak in the OUN leadership. Ukrainians were still overwhelmingly a peasant people, and the OUN leaders continued to think of Ukraine as a traditional agrarian society, assuring peasants that they would become landowners in an independent Ukrainian state.[6] Stsiborsky devoted two pamphlets to the land question.[7] Although he planned a brochure on Ukrainian workers, it was never published. The leadership's conserva-tism was also reflected in a resolution of the 1929 programme which declared that the government of an independent Ukraine would co-operate with the church to foster the nation's moral education.[8]

Thus, when Hitler took power in Germany, the OUN leaders were not prepared to endorse his ideology. In two outspoken articles, Onatsky insisted on the differences between Italian fascism and German Nazism, condemning the latter as imperialist, racist and anti-Christian.[9] Stsiborsky devoted a chapter of *Natsiokratiia* to a critique of the Nazi dictatorship.[10] Still, Germany was the most militantly anti-communist power in Europe and the only one that could be expected to go to war against the Soviet Union. Therefore, in spite of its reservations about Nazism, the OUN leadership maintained contacts with German military and intelligence circles, providing information about Polish government activities in order to finance its operations and attempting to interest the Germans in Ukrainian independence.[11]

The OUN's integral-nationalist programme and its tactical cultivation of the Germans had far-reaching ideological consequences. Even though the leadership was at pains to emphasize its political and ideological independence,[12] it was hard put to resist the conviction that the Ukrainian nationalist movement was part of the fascist "wave of the future" which was sweeping Europe. This feeling was encouraged by the nationalist ideologue Dmytro Dontsov, who indiscriminately praised Hitler, Mussolini, Franco, Salazar, La Rocque and Degrelle.[13] Although Dontsov was never a member of the OUN, his writings exercised considerable influence on its younger members.[14] Writers for the extensive nationalist press (frequently suppressed by the Polish authorities) often took positions compatible with Dontsov's; the few who polemicized with him, such as Onatsky and Stsiborsky, did not match his stature.

It was the younger nationalist cadres who shouldered the burden of OUN activity in Western Ukraine, organizing boycotts of Polish monopolies and state schools, distributing propaganda, and assassinating government officials and Ukrainians considered to have betrayed the national cause. The OUN leaders, meanwhile, lived in various cities of Central and Western Europe in order to escape arrest. When the Polish authorities penetrated the OUN in 1934 and sentenced many of its activists to long prison terms, the younger men's resentment of the older leadership became intense.

In May 1938 Konovalets was assassinated in Rotterdam, almost certainly by a Soviet agent. In order to forestall a challenge from the younger members, the leadership appointed an associate of Konovalets, Andrii Melnyk, as his successor. This was done on the basis of what was claimed to be Konovalets's verbally expressed will.[15] Attempting to outdo the younger men in decisiveness, the leaders changed the OUN constitution to give the head of the organization absolute power.[16] The manoeuvre backfired: in 1940, after the younger men had been released from prison, they formed a Revolutionary Leadership headed by Stepan Bandera, who had earlier served as leader of the OUN's Western Ukrainian Territorial Executive. Most of the membership acknowledged Bandera's authority, and the split became irrevocable.

The OUN's position in Western Ukraine was made virtually untenable by the Soviet occupation of this territory, which was carried out under the terms of the Molotov-Ribbentrop pact. The Soviet army and secret police destroyed all independent institutions, killing or deporting as many politically active Ukrainians as they could find.[17] Hitler's acquiescence in the occupation was the second blow that he dealt the Ukrainian nationalists: earlier, in the spring of 1939, he had allowed the Hungarians to destroy the short-lived Carpatho-Ukrainian Republic, whose defence force the OUN had helped organize. Nevertheless, both factions of the OUN continued to hope for a Nazi-Soviet conflict that might give them an opportunity to assert Ukrainian independence. They formed expeditionary groups (*pokhidni hrupy*) whose task was to follow the Germans into Ukraine and seize power. The Bandera faction organized two battalions which trained with the German army.[18] When the invasion took place, both OUN factions issued statements supporting the Germans, hoping that they would recognize Ukrainian independence in return for assistance against Russia.[19] Still, it was recognized that the Germans might be hostile: the expeditionary groups were instructed to organize anti-German resistance if this should become necessary.[20]

Hitler immediately showed that he had no intention of co-operating with the Ukrainian nationalists. He saw Ukraine exclusively as a territory for German exploitation; its "racially inferior" population was to be enslaved and exterminated. Thus, when the Bandera faction proclaimed Ukrainian independence in Lviv on 30 June 1941, the Gestapo arrested Bandera and his followers, imprisoning them in concentration camps for the duration of the war. Representatives of the Melnyk faction who planned the proclamation of a Ukrainian National Committee in Kiev were arrested and shot. Melnyk was kept under house arrest and sent to the Sachsenhausen concentration camp in 1944. The Gestapo began to round up and kill members of both nationalist factions.[21] German policy toward the general population was equally ruthless: the Soviet collective farms were maintained in order to extract as much food as possible for the war effort, and hundreds of thousands of Ukrainians were deported to Germany as slave labourers.[22]

The nationalists who escaped the Gestapo's dragnet no longer had any reason to identify themselves with a fascist or Nazi "new Europe."

The process of ideological revision was given strong impetus by the expeditionary forces' contacts with eastern Ukrainians. Having survived the horrors of forced collectivization and Stalin's political purges, which had claimed millions of Ukrainian lives, these people flatly rejected the idea of a national dictatorship and one-party rule. They also obliged the nationalists to pay greater attention to social questions, for which the attainment of national independence had earlier been seen as a panacea.[23]

The new situation gave rise to intense political debate among the OUN membership, which is reflected in the writings published in this volume. Among the most important publicists of this period were O. Brodovy, Ia. Busel, the Rev. Dr. I. Hryniokh (Kovalenko), Iu. Khersonets, V. Mudry (Borovych), M. Prokop and M.V. Radovych. A leading role was played by D. Maivsky, who, as editor-in-chief of *Ideia i Chyn* (Idea and Action), the official organ of the OUN, strongly promoted the cause of ideological revision. The OUN publicists launched a powerful critique of Nazi and Soviet imperialism. Rejecting the political model of one-party dictatorship, they began to put forward the conception of Ukrainian nationalism as a revolutionary democratic force that would lead the struggle against both totalitarian powers. Ukraine was to rely primarily on her own forces, but these would be linked with the revolutionary strivings of other subject peoples. The nationalists' previous ideological distaste for the socialist and populist leaders of 1917–20 gave way to a recognition of the fundamental continuity of their struggle with the national revolution of that period.

The debate culminated in the convocation of the Third Extraordinary Grand Assembly of the OUN (Bandera faction) in August 1943 and the creation of the Supreme Ukrainian Liberation Council in July 1944. It was at this time that the OUN adopted a collegial leadership and accepted significant elements of pluralism into its programme,[24] the UPA was recognized as a military formation representing the whole Ukrainian people,[25] and the Supreme Ukrainian Liberation Council was constituted as a non-partisan representative body co-ordinating the liberation struggle.[26]

This reorientation did not come easily. For many members of the OUN, especially those with no first-hand experience of the wartime evolution, the OUN remained a monolithic revolutionary vanguard whose leadership was entitled to impose its policies both on the organization and on the Ukrainian people. The debate between proponents of centralism and pluralism raged for several years and was ultimately to split the Bandera faction of the OUN in the post-war emigration.[27]

In Ukraine, however, the pluralist current triumphed. Beginning in 1944, a new group of highly talented and dedicated publicists began to assert itself in underground publications. O. Diakiv (Hornovy), U. Kuzhil, R. Mokh, A. Panasenko, P. Poltava, R. Shukhevych, Ia. Starukh (Iarlan) and others produced a substantial number of articles, pamphlets, appeals, leaflets and declarations in which they succeeded in defining and deepening the main tenets of the revised political program. Their writings, of which a generous sample appears in this volume, represent the "culmination of the development of the Ukrainian nationalist ideology towards greater emphasis on economic and social welfare, and upon securing individual rights."[28]

This volume is divided into four parts. Although the editors did not attempt to organize the material in chronological order, most of the articles—with the exception of the programmatic documents in the fourth section of the book—do fall naturally into a rough chronological order.

The first section, "Ukraine in Imperialist Plans," is composed of articles which view Ukraine as the key political problem of Europe, with various imperialist powers (Russia, Germany and Poland) waging a struggle for control of her natural resources.

The article by O. Brodovy discusses the political tendencies that existed in Ukraine in the period between the world wars and explains why the principle of reliance on one's own forces, which came so strongly to the fore in 1917–20, was replaced by an orientation on foreign powers, especially on Germany. This orientation was undermined by German repression, which brought about the Ukrainian-German conflict and the establishment of the Ukrainian Insurgent Army.

In an article written in 1942, here translated in abbreviated form, I.M. Kovalenko (I. Hryniokh) analyzes the ideological basis of the Nazi occupation of Eastern Europe, with emphasis on Ukraine. The article points out that Hitler and other Nazi theorists defined Ukraine as *Lebensraum* for the German race; the original inhabitants were to be killed or turned into slaves. Despite its interference with the war effort, this plan was put into effect immediately following the German military occupation. In the author's view, German imperialism is the enemy of all European nations. The Russian Bolsheviks, for their part, carry on the war against Germany purely as imperialist competitors. All conquered peoples are therefore faced with an inevitable decision on which their liberation depends: to unite in a single revolutionary front against the rapacious imperialism of Berlin and Moscow.

The article by Ia.V. Borovych (V. Mudry) examines the conflict-ridden history of Polish-Ukrainian relations and calls for a common front against the Russian and German imperialists. The author, who was deputy speaker of the Polish parliament in the 1930s, is rather pessimistic about the prospects for such co-operation. As he puts it: "The entire history of our mutual relations and all the experience garnered over centuries teach us that even when its own people is undergoing the greatest tragedies and sufferings, the Polish ruling class is unwilling to renounce its plans to subjugate other peoples, particularly Ukrainians . . . ''[29]

The work by U. Kuzhil surveys the growth of the Russian Empire from the time of Ivan III (1462–1505) to the Second World War. The author describes the main goals of Russian expansionism and shows how this policy was implemented in different periods, whether by means of military invasion, penetration by agents, annexation, treachery, deceit, or straightforward conquest. He also examines the foreign policies, diplomatic maneuvers, propaganda campaigns and other activities that formed part of Russian imperial policy. The author considers the Bolsheviks true successors of the tsarist imperialists who falsify history and depict Russian conquests as voluntary unions, ''progressive'' and ''noble'' events that abetted the economic and cultural development of the conquered peoples, when in fact the exact opposite is true.

The last article in this section, written by P. Duma (D. Maivsky), reads like a continuation of the preceding article. The author underscores the fact that the USSR is ''not 'the bastion of the world proletarian revolution,' but a *Russian imperialist state* which uses the slogans of socialism to implement its imperialist concept.''[30] To prove this contention, the author describes in detail the structure of the socioeconomic, political and military system of the USSR. But most of the article is devoted to the brutal methods used by the Kremlin in Albania, Bulgaria, Czechoslovakia, Poland, Hungary and Yugoslavia, which are camouflaged by Soviet propaganda as the ''democratization'' of these countries. The essay, offered as a warning to European nations against the Soviet threat, nevertheless ends on an optimistic note. The Russian Bolshevik empire will be destroyed from within by a united front of subject peoples.

The second section of the book, which is devoted to ''Ideological Questions,'' contains five articles. In his essay ''Idealism or Materialism: Which Philosophy are Members of the OUN Obliged to Follow?'' O. Hornovy (Diakiv) argues that, ''given that the correctness of either idealism or materialism has not yet been scientifically established,'' it would be harmful for a political organization ''to bind [itself] categorically to one or the other philosophy.''[31]

For the same reason, he continues, *''our organization grants full freedom to its members to profess either philosophical idealism or materialism.''*[32] According to him, *''the full, all-round development of the*

Ukrainian nation in an independent, united Ukrainian state, the creation of a *truly national regime and a classless society, the destruction
of imperialism*, the establishment of international accord among *free
and equal sovereign states of all peoples—these fundamental points of
our ideology do not lose any of their mobilizing power by the fact that
we do not recognize the primacy either of spirit or of matter.*"[33] To
proceed otherwise would be to follow in Stalin's footsteps, with the result that an "ideology can maintain itself only by political force."[34]
Futhermore, "since it is fighting for a truly national regime that will
guarantee all democratic rights and freedoms to the people, the OUN
will not attempt, in a free and independent Ukrainian state, to make its
own ideology supreme."[35]

In "The Scientific Validity of Dialectical Materialism," U. Kuzhil
develops some of Hornovy's assertions even further by pointing out
that the claim of dialectical materialism to scientific validity is severely
undermined by recent scientific discoveries. The insistence of Soviet
ideologues that their policies are based on scientific theory is simply
political sleight of hand. In the author's view, "Marxist 'theory' stands
in contradiction to the most recent, experimentally and theoretically
grounded conclusions reached by physics."[36] Therefore, he concludes,
"if Marx's greatest achievement was to transfer the principles of
dialectical materialism from natural phenomena to society in the form
of historical materialism, then the teachings of historical materialism
about society have as much value as the teachings of dialectical materialism about inorganic nature: that is, the value of fantasy."[37]

In "The Spectre of Fascism," Iarlan (Ia. Starukh) describes and analyzes the fundamental characteristics of the fascist totalitarian regimes
of Europe and, by means of an extended comparison, demonstrates
quite convincingly that the USSR functions according to the same principles. According to him, "Italian fascism, German Nazism, and Russian Bolshevism are identical totalitarian movements and systems that
came into existence and developed in various European countries after
the First World War. They are all typical totalitarian systems and are
so very much alike that *we could call Bolshevism Russian fascism absolutely without hesitation, or, better still, Russian Nazism, whereas
Nazism could equally well be called German Bolshevism.*"[38] It is well
to remember that these words were written in one of the underground
bunkers exactly ten years before the publication of *Totalitarian Dictatorship and Autocracy*, a work which gave a strong impetus to the
concept of totalitarianism and helped shape the thinking of thousands of
Western intellectuals well into the 1970s.[39]

The last two articles in this section are both by P. Poltava. In "Our
Teachings About the National State," he admits at the outset that "our

doctrine with regard to the state has grown out of the ideological and political struggle that we have been waging on two fronts—against the imperialist views voiced by representatives of the great powers and against Marxist views of the state.''[40] In this article he begins by taking issue with the Marxist view of the state, which he considers quite false. In the first place, the Marxists are mistaken in their analysis of the rise of the state. Secondly, while their criticism of the shortcomings of the state during various historical periods is correct, their conclusion that in future nations will be able to manage without states is "utopian, fantastic and deprived of any basis in reality."[41] On the contrary, "a system of free national states of all peoples represents not only the most *just* solution to the problem of international order, but also the most *viable*, the most *suited to reality*."[42] But this is not enough: in order "to prevent the state from being a tool of exploitation and oppression employed by the wealthy classes against their own working masses, *it is necessary to rebuild the present social order on the basis of a classless society*."[43] Only then will the state become, as it was at its very beginning, "*simply a form of organization of the internal economic and cultural life of the nation and a tool of defence against external enemies*."[44] With the establishment of a truly just international order, even the defence function will disappear and the state will "only retain the function of organizing the internal economic and cultural life of the nation."[45]

Poltava's "The Concept of an Independent Ukraine and Current Political Trends in the World" is one of his most important essays, vital to the understanding of the theoretical positions and programme of the Ukrainian national-liberation movement. His concept is that of an independent Ukrainian state on Ukrainian ethnic territory, for he strongly believes that only in its own state can a people be guaranteed all-round economic and spiritual development. Moreover, to ensure the most complete, harmonious development of a nation, the state should have a democratic regime and a socio-economic system that eliminates all exploitation of one person by another. For him, the best socio-economic system is one that combines state, co-operative and private ownership, allowing for a free market and private initiative. Some of the notions presented here manifest a striking resemblance to a number of theoretical propositions developed in Yugoslavia after its break with the Soviet Union in 1948.[46]

In Poltava's view, current political developments are the result of struggles between contradictory forces. Thus, the struggle waged by workers for a fair share of the national product and for social reform fostered an improvement in their economic position, eliminated the need for violent social revolutions, led to more harmonious relations among different social classes, and thereby substantially strengthened the nation. Other contradictions, for example, those among various empires, led to the weakening and even the collapse of some of them and to the birth of new national states. The major contradiction at present is, in Poltava's opinion, between ruling and subject peoples and the attendant revolutions waged by liberation movements, as well as peaceful political struggles waged by colonies for their independence. Sooner or later, these struggles always end in victory for the subject peoples, who gain their independence. "The current period of history," says the author, "is *the period of the emancipation of hitherto subject peoples in Europe and around the world.*"[47]

Proceeding from these basic assumptions, the author offers a rather optimistic view of the international order of the future. He predicts that empires will disappear, to be replaced by independent national states which will work together as equals. The Ukrainian liberation struggle is therefore in accord with current tendencies in world politics and is destined to triumph. "We who struggle for an independent Ukrainian state and for the right of every people to live a free life in its own independent state can say of ourselves, in the words of Ivan Franko: *We are the prologue, not the epilogue!*"[48]

The six essays grouped in Part III, "Strategy and Tactics of the Ukrainian Liberation Movement," address themselves primarily to internal Ukrainian problems in the struggle for independence. In his essay, "At the Turning Point," Iu.M. Khersonets discusses the extent to which Ukrainian youth was socialized into the Soviet system by the Russian Bolsheviks and comes to the conclusion that only a small group really supports the system. The majority are either confused or indifferent. But the war is changing their attitude, and the turning point has been reached. According to the author, more and more of them are beginning to embrace the idea of an independent Ukraine. "*Yesterday, these young people numbered in the hundreds. Today, they number in the thousands, and, when hundreds of thousands and millions take this path, ultimate victory will be ours,*"[49] he concludes.

The essay on "Internal Obstacles to the Ukrainian National-Liberation Struggle" by P.T. Duma (D. Maivsky) is similar in tone. Written, like the previous one, in 1943, it addresses itself primarily to the psychological dilemmas which the Ukrainian nation faces in its struggle for independence. These include an orientation on foreign powers, a lack of faith in one's own capacities, political divisions in the form of small groupings struggling one against another, the lack of a single representative political institution to co-ordinate the struggle and represent the nation abroad, the merely regional ethnic self-identification of the population in Eastern Ukraine, and excessive parochialism in Western Ukraine. These are the internal obstacles which, according to the author, are being overcome in the revolutionary war of struggle against the German and Russian occupiers.

The next two articles are by P. Poltava. In "Our Battle Plan for the Liberation of Ukraine under the Present Circumstances," Poltava discusses the adaptation of battle tactics to the new conditions of Soviet occupation. The tasks facing the nationalists, as he sees them, are: to maintain and extend the underground organization; to conduct extensive political, educational and propaganda activity among all the peoples of the USSR; and to organize large-scale resistance by Ukrainians and other peoples to the Russian-Bolshevik oppressors, both in the form of sabotage and individual initiative and in the form of military action where conditions warrant.

The second essay, "Preparatory Steps Toward the Third World War and the Tasks of the Ukrainian People," written after the outbreak of the Korean War in 1950, analyzes the concepts of war and peace from the point of view of Ukrainian national interests and sets forth the tasks to be accomplished by the Ukrainian people should the Third World War become inevitable. Their principal task will be "to make use of this war for the purpose of attaining their complete national and social liberation and overthrowing Muscovite-Bolshevik rule in Ukraine and in the whole of the USSR."[50] But this is possible only if every Ukrainian is aware of the true political situation in the world and in the Soviet Union and is willing to act in defence of his nation.

The article by D. Shakhai (Iosyp Pozychaniuk), "Our Tactics with Regard to the Russian People," is the second part of a longer work entitled "Problems Relating to the Struggle for an Independent United Ukrainian State." It was a memorandum written in 1943 for use in the discussion that took place among the leading activists of the Ukrainian underground with a view to re-evaluating the political strategy and tactics of the resistance movement. A chapter about the Vlasov movement which was added to this memorandum in 1944 is omitted here, while the first part is missing altogether and could not be located.[51] According to the author, besides adopting a democratic and socially progressive programme, establishing an all-Ukrainian political leadership and creating a strong and creditable political party, the Ukrainian underground must formulate an intelligent policy toward the Russian people in order to bring them into a common front of struggle for the overthrow of the communist regime. This can be achieved only if Ukrainians stop preaching "racial nationalism" and put forward universal ideas which will have the power to mobilize all those dissatisfied with the Soviet regime, including the Russians. These are the ideas of political freedom, social justice and the transformation of the USSR into a group of independent democratic states which will co-operate with one another on the basis of true equality.

The author sees two distinct tactical stages in the struggle: the organization of a revolution in the whole of the USSR and the establishment and consolidation of the Ukrainian state. During the first stage, he advises, all anti-Bolshevik forces (even the Russian monarchists and the Vlasov movement) should be encouraged. At the same time, a democratic front of subject peoples must be organized, but it is to include only those movements that are fully committed to the destruction of the empire. During the second stage, he foresees the possibility of a conflict with those Russians who might wish to re-establish the empire and again subjugate Ukraine. But he does not believe that these forces would be very popular, for the Russian masses have come to realize that the maintenance of the empire denies them their own liberty and requires great material and human sacrifices of them.

The article "Our Attitude Toward the Russian People" by O. Hornovy (Diakiv), written six years later, continues this general theme and follows the line of argument presented by D. Shakhai. Quoting the resolutions of the Third Extraordinary Grand Assembly of the OUN, the author states: "*The OUN's struggle is not directed against the Russian people. It aims at liberating Ukraine from oppression by the Russian-Bolshevik invaders. The OUN maintains that the Russian state should correspond to Russia's ethnic territory and should not extend beyond those boundaries. We aspire to the closest possible co-operation with the Russian people as long as they live in their own national state as defined by their ethnic boundaries, as long as they do not oppose the Ukrainian people's efforts to attain freedom and as long as they renounce imperialism and fight for the destruction of their own imperialist cliques.*"[52]

The articles by D. Shakhai and O. Hornovy are of the utmost importance for the understanding of the theoretical position and programme of the Ukrainian underground on this crucial question.

The fourth section of the book, "Programmatic Documents and Appeals," includes seven documents which span the period between 1943 and 1949. The most important among them are the "Resolutions of the Third Extraordinary Grand Assembly of the OUN" of August 1943, "What is the UPA Fighting For?", also dated August 1943, and the principal documents of the Supreme Ukrainian Liberation Council, created in July 1944, including the council's "General Proclamation," "Platform" and "Provisional Organization." The last two documents in this section are an open letter from Ukrainians living on the territories ceded to Poland, protesting their forcible evacuation to the USSR, and an "Appeal from Embattled Ukraine to All Ukrainians Abroad" bidding them to do their utmost to liberate their homeland.

The "Resolutions of the Third Extraordinary Grand Assembly of the OUN" are remarkable primarily because of the new ideological statements that they embody. The document consists of three sections — a lengthy preamble, programmatic resolutions and political resolutions — of which the second is the most interesting. Its basic principles are as follows. In the sphere of international relations, both the Russian and German forms of imperialism as well as all other imperialist conceptions are rejected. The OUN declares itself in favour of the recognition of the right of every people to independence and self-government on its ethnic territory. In the area of socio-economic organization, it rejects privilege based on the principle of ownership (landlords, capitalists) or party membership (exemplified by the party elites in the USSR and in Nazi Germany). In a free Ukraine, large industries, banks, trade and commercial enterprises are to remain nationalized, while enterprises of medium size are to be in private hands. Similar plans are made for agriculture, although peasants are to be guaranteed a free choice of individual or co-operative ventures.

Other provisions of this declaration guarantee workers' rights (the free choice of workplace, appropriate conditions and wages, social security, free trade unions, the right to strike, etc.), proclaim the equality of women, offer freedom to the professions and guarantee care for the young, the elderly and the disadvantaged. Additional provisions guarantee equal rights to all citizens, including freedom of speech, the press, freedom of ideas and beliefs, freedom of conscience and the right of minorities freely to develop their cultures. The programme also rejects official status for any doctrine. It does not discuss the structure of the future government, but aims generally at the radical democratization of existing legal and social structures in the Ukrainian SSR and emphasizes those principles which guarantee individual freedoms and a just socio-economic system.

The document "What is the Ukrainian Insurgent Army Fighting For?" is a shorter version of the programmatic resolutions described above. There existed an earlier version of this declaration, signed by the OUN leadership, under the title "What is the Revolutionary-Liberationist UPA Fighting For?" There are interesting differences in emphasis between the two versions. The provision for the free return of land to private ownership in the earlier version was modified to read that "the Ukrainian national regime will not impose on farmers any one method of working the land."[53] Also, in the second version, provision was made for compulsory secondary education and the separation of church and state. In addition, the original ending was excised.

The remaining materials are the principal statutory documents of the Supreme Ukrainian Liberation Council, the "Provisional Organization," "Platform" and "General Proclamation."

The first document establishes the organizational structure of the Supreme Ukrainian Liberation Council and sets out the rights, obligations and duties of its individual bodies, such as the Grand Assembly, the Presidium, the General Secretariat, the General Court and the Board of Control. The council is designated "the highest governing body of the Ukrainian people" during the period of struggle for sovereignty.[54] The membership of the council numbers twenty-five persons who may belong to any political party as long as they "support Ukrainian sovereignty, accept the political platform adopted by the Assembly of the Supreme Ukrainian Liberation Council and are ready at all times to put its programme into practice."[55] It is important to point out that this provision cancelled the previous claim of the OUN to monolithic control of the underground forces. The composition of the council substantiates this ideological shift at least partially.[56] The emphasis on the fact that the council was established at the initiative of the UPA and not the OUN is also important in this connection.[57]

The document suffers from poor drafting. The best example of this is the repeated confusion in reference to the "Supreme Ukrainian Liberation Council" and the "Grand Assembly of the Supreme Ukrainian Liberation Council." As Armstrong has written, "these obscurities . . . appear to have resulted from insufficient training in law and logic and from lack of real interest in constitutional questions."[58]

The "Platform" sets forth the council's political programme. It stresses that the council was established on the principle of Ukraine's political independence of foreign powers, that it will wage its struggle in co-operation with other subject peoples, and that its aim is to achieve peaceful co-existence with Ukraine's neighbours "on the basis of mutual recognition of the right of every people to its own state on its ethnic territory."[59]

In the exposition of the council's political and social programme, the following points are made: the Ukrainian state is to have a democratic form of government which will guarantee freedom of thought, world-view and belief, the rule of law and the legal equality of all citizens, full rights for national minorities, equal educational opportunity, freedom in the choice of occupation and the protection of workers by social legislation. In the economic sphere only the basic national wealth of the country (including land), heavy industry and national transport are to remain nationalized. Other sectors of the economy are to be left to co-operatives and private individuals. On the one hand, emphasis is placed on the exercise of free initiative in the economy (i.e., "free trade"), while on the other, the right is reserved for the state to guarantee a just social order, "free of class exploitation and oppression."[60]

The "General Proclamation" or "Universal" corresponds in its content to the "Platform," but is written in a more popular and emotional style, with many a patriotic turn of phrase, in an obvious attempt to mobilize the patriotism of the masses. This aim of the "General Proclamation" was probably misunderstood by Armstrong, who criticized it for containing too much "romanticized history and emotional appeals for action" instead of giving a proposal of clearly defined steps to be taken.[61]

The articles selected for this volume are presented in their entirety (with the exception of those by I.M. Kovalenko and D. Shakhai, which are much too long to reproduce completely) as documents of a particular historical period, even though they contain repetitious material, several inaccuracies and many vague formulations. The reader should keep in mind that these essays were written under conditions of difficult struggle, without access to libraries or works of reference, by individuals who in most cases were not professional journalists. In view of this it is remarkable how clearly the articles are written and how convincingly and passionately they argue their case.

In order to make the material more understandable to Western students, the editors have attempted to present as much explanatory information as possible in the notes and have provided brief biographical sketches of the authors whose works comprise this volume.

To the extent possible, sources of quotations have been identified and references provided to standard editions of the works from which they are taken. Renderings of quotations, however, are those of the translator.

Peter J. Potichnyj
McMaster University

Yevhen Shtendera
National Library
of Canada

NOTES

1. Myroslav Prokop, "UPA z perspektyvy 40-richchia," *Svoboda*, 24 September 1982, 2.
2. *OUN v svitli postanov Velykykh Zboriv, Konferentsii ta inshykh dokumentiv z borotby 1929–1955 r.* (n.p. 1955): 3–6. See also Petro Mirchuk, *Narys istorii Orhanizatsii Ukrainskykh Natsionalistiv* (Munich 1968), 1: 126.
3. Volodymyr Martynets, "My i ukrainski politychni partii," *Rozbudova natsii* 1, no. 5 (1928): 235–41.
4. Ievhen Onatsky, "Lysty z Italii," *Rozbudova natsii* 1, no. 3 (1928): 93–6; idem, "Italiiska Korporatyvna Derzhava," *Rozbudova natsii* 2, no. 3–4 (1929): 78–84.
5. Mykola Stsiborsky, *Natsiokratiia* (Paris 1935), 111–17.
6. *OUN v svitli postanov*, 7–8.
7. Mykola Stsiborsky, *OUN i selianstvo* (n.p. 1933); idem, *Zemelne pytannia* (Paris 1939).
8. *OUN v svitli postanov*, 14–15.
9. Ievhen Onatsky, "Ideologichni i taktychni rozkhodzhennia mizh fashyzmom i natsional-sotsiializmom," *Rozbudova natsii* 7, no. 5–6 (1934): 142–9; idem, "Kult uspikhu," *Rozbudova natsii* 7, no. 7–8 (1934): 162–9.
10. Stsiborsky, *Natsiokratiia*, 49–60.
11. Ryszard Torzecki, *Kwestia ukraińska w polityce III Rzeszy (1933–1945)* (Warsaw 1972), 128–9; Hans Roos, *Polen und Europa*, 2d ed. (Tübingen 1965), 147–55.
12. See, e.g., the editorial note to Oleksander Mytsiuk, "Fashyzm," *Rozbudova natsii* 2, no. 8–9 (1929): 262.
13. Mykhailo Sosnovsky, *Dmytro Dontsov: politychnyi portret* (New York 1974), 288–98.
14. Lev Rebet, *Svitla i tini OUN* (Munich 1964), 47.
15. Mirchuk, 539–41, 573–7; compare Zynovii Knysh, ed., *Nepohasnyi ohon viry* (Paris 1974), 182–5.
16. *Politychna Prohrama i Ustrii Orhanizatsii Ukrainskykh Natsionalistiv* (n.p. 1940), 55–64.
17. For eyewitness accounts of the Soviet occupation, see Milena Rudnytska, ed., *Zakhidnia Ukraina pid bolshevykamy* (New York 1958).
18. John A. Armstrong, *Ukrainian Nationalism*, 2d ed. (New York 1963), 73–4.
19. "Stalosia... velyka hodyna," *Nastup*, 23 June 1941, 1; "Ukrainskyi narode!" *Nastup*, 12 July 1941, 1; S. V. Savchuk, "'Akt proholoshennia Ukrainskoi Derzhavy' 30-ho chervnia 1941 roku," *Novyi litopys* 1, no. 1 (1961): 3–25.

20. Rebet, 98.

21. Armstrong, 104–17.

22. Alexander Dallin, *German Rule in Russia 1941–1945: A Study of Occupation Policies*, 2d ed. (Boulder, Colo. 1981), 320–75, 428–53.

23. On the expeditionary groups and the process of ideological revision, see Lev Shankovsky, *Pokhidni hrupy OUN* (Munich 1958).

24. See: "Resolutions of the Third Extraordinary Grand Assembly of the OUN," pp. 333–53 of this volume.

25. See: "What is the Ukrainian Insurgent Army Fighting For?" pp. 377–81 of this volume.

26. See: "Platform of the Supreme Ukrainian Liberation Council" and "Provisional Organization of the Supreme Ukrainian Liberation Council," pp. 359–63 and 365–76 of this volume.

27. On the debates which led to the split, see Roman Krychevsky (pseud. of Roman Ilnytzkyj), *Orhanizatsiia ukrainskykh natsionalistiv v Ukraini, Orhanizatsiia ukrainskykh natsionalistiv zakordonom i ZCh OUN* (New York 1962).

28. Armstrong, 163.

29. Ia.V. Borovych, "Ukraine and Poland," p. 66 of this volume.

30. P. Duma, "The Bolshevik Democratization of Europe," p. 100 of this volume.

31. O. Hornovy, "Idealism or Materialism: Which Philosophy are Members of the OUN Obliged to Follow?" p. 120 of this volume.

32. Ibid.

33. Ibid., 122.

34. Ibid., 123.

35. Ibid., 126.

36. U. Kuzhil, "The Scientific Validity of Dialectical Materialism," p. 140 of this volume.

37. Ibid., 140–41.

38. Iarlan, "The Spectre of Fascism," pp. 164–5 of this volume.

39. Carl J. Friedrich and Zbigniew K. Brzezinski, *Totalitarian Dictatorship and Autocracy* (Cambridge, Mass. 1956).

40. P. Poltava, "Our Teachings About the National State," p. 169 of this volume.

41. Ibid., 170.

42. Ibid., 171.

43. Ibid.

44. Ibid.

45. Ibid., 172.

46. For an interesting survey see Bogdan D. Denitch, *The Legitimation of a Revolution: The Yugoslav Case* (New Haven 1976), especially 149–206.

47. P. Poltava, "The Concept of an Independent Ukraine and Current Politi-

cal Trends in the World,'' p. 202 of this volume.

48. Ibid., 222.

49. Iu. M. Khersonets, ''At the Turning Point,'' p. 238 of this volume.

50. P. Poltava, ''Preparatory Steps Toward the Third World War and the Tasks of the Ukrainian People,'' p. 278 of this volume.

51. For a complete document, see *Litopys UPA* (Toronto 1980), 8: 203–56.

52. O. Hornovy, ''Our Attitude Toward the Russian People,'' p. 320 of this volume.

53. Both versions are reprinted in *Litopys UPA* (*Volyn i Polissia*) (Toronto 1978): 121–30. See ''What is the Ukrainian Insurgent Army Fighting For?'' p. 378 of this volume.

54. ''Provisional Organization of the Supreme Ukrainian Liberation Council,'' p. 365 of this volume.

55. Ibid.

56. See list of members of the Supreme Ukrainian Liberation Council elected at the First Grand Assembly in July 1944, pp. 372–6 of this volume.

57. ''Platform of the Supreme Ukrainian Liberation Council,'' pp. 359–63 of this volume.

58. Armstrong, 164.

59. ''Platform,'' pp. 362–3 of this volume. See also: M. K., ''Ukrainska Holovna Vyzvolna Rada,'' *Litopys UPA* (Toronto 1980), 8: 153–60.

60. ''Platform,'' p. 362.

61. Armstrong, 164.

I
UKRAINE IN IMPERIALIST PLANS

ON THE GENESIS OF THE UKRAINIAN—GERMAN WAR OF 1941–4

O. Brodovy

Unsuccessful Enemy Slander

Because of her geopolitical situation and her material wealth, Ukraine has become, in modern times, the point of intersection of the political tendencies of neighbouring countries and more distant states. They have attempted, at times acting in unison, to maintain or, more precisely, to impose their dominion over territories populated by Ukrainians. Despite the obvious insincerity of the stances taken by these countries toward the Ukrainian population's aspirations for liberation, these have been in accord with their own imperialist plans and endeavours. Thus, in 1918, Germany concluded a treaty with Ukraine at Brest,[1] near the River Buh, and recognized her as an independent state. But only a few months later the Germans dissolved the Ukrainian government, which refused to follow their dictates, and accused the Ukrainian people of having become Bolshevized.[2] Poland marched on Kiev, crying "independence for our ally, Ukraine,"[3] after having broken the Ukrainian Galician Army[4] with the help of General Haller's[5] army, which had been organized abroad and sent to western Ukraine to fight the Bolsheviks (!). Meanwhile, to the Allies, Poland represented the creation of the Western Provinces of the Ukrainian People's Republic as a German intrigue.[6] The Bolsheviks took up the slogan of national self-determination and went to war against a Ukraine "of capitalists and landowners, propped up by foreign interventionists,'' with the purpose of turning her into a ''Soviet'' Ukraine. When the Ukrainian people realized that this Soviet ''self-determination'' meant enslavement, they set into motion an underground revolutionary struggle for true liberation. Bolshevik Russia attempted to compromise these Ukrainian aspirations by slanderously attributing to them a Germanophile character. Thus the Ukrainian liberation and independence movement, whose policy was strictly autonomous, was denounced in various ways by the enemies of Ukraine, depending upon which label was, at any given moment, considered more odious in the world and internally, and against whom, in a given region of Ukraine, the Ukrainian liberation movement was directed.

The conflagration of the First World War was touched off by the Germanic states of central Europe. Because they caused the wartime devastation, it was only natural that they were held responsible for the horrors that resulted from the war and were hated by all those who fought against them. The nations of the victorious Entente and their satellites were extremely hostile to anything German or linked to Germany.

The outbreak of the March Revolution in 1917 brought the hope of freedom to the nations subjugated by tsarist Russia, including Ukraine, but by April of that year Polish propaganda had already begun to sound the alarm in Western Europe about the ''Ukrainian-German danger'' in the East. At this time, the Ukrainian state, well aware of the true danger posed by its northern and western neighbours to its efforts at establishing its independence, attempted to take advantage of the remaining potential of the Central Powers, which were then enemies of Russian imperialism. As a result, from that time on, Polish propaganda and, subsequently, Polish diplomacy worked for the benefit of Russian Bolshevik imperialism and against the independent Ukrainian state—a state which the most Germanophobic of all nations, France, was prepared to recognize, as is evident from the telegram sent from Paris by Maklakov,[7] the ambassador of Russia's Provisional Government, to Wrangel.[8]

During the period of peace negotiations, Polish diplomacy aimed at destroying Germany in the West and Ukraine in the East. Whatever Poland undertook in relation to the East, she did with a view to the effect it would have upon the Ukrainian problem. Her activity was based on the erroneous premise that Ukraine was bound, under any circumstances, to be hostile to Poland and favourably disposed toward Germany, and therefore it was essential for Poland's interests that Ukraine be carved up between Poland and Russia. This approach, conceived by Dmowski,[9] was clearly and openly formulated by the Polish ''National

Committee"[10] in Paris on 8 February 1918 and put forward by Dmowski in his memorandum to Wilson[11] on 8 October 1918. Subsequently, these ideas formed the basis of the arguments voiced in all Polish memoranda to the Entente and in all the propaganda written by Poles against Ukraine.

Bolshevik propaganda attempted to tar the national governments of Ukraine with a "pro-German" brush, but this proved unsuccessful, for the people could see that Petliura was driving out the German army of occupation.[12] In any case, from 1922, that is, from the time the German-Soviet pact was signed at Rapallo[13] to the time of Hitler's accession to power, Bolshevik Russia herself was allied to Germany; she confided her state secrets to Germany and maintained friendly relations with her. Attempts to impute a pro-German character to the activities of Shumsky,[14] Volobuev,[15] the Union for the Liberation of Ukraine[16] and Khvylovy[17]—activities which opposed Soviet totalitarianism—were not believed even by the most naive. Efforts directed toward national independence, military action and revolutionary activity were developing and gaining strength throughout Ukraine long before Germany was in any position to demand a revision of Versailles[18] and other related treaties. But it was in the imperialist interest of Bolshevik Russia somehow to discredit the movement which rose in opposition to her domination of central and eastern Ukraine and undermined her efforts to gain influence in western Ukraine. There, in addition to struggle against Polish rule, a major propaganda campaign, marked from time to time by manifestations against individual Soviet officials and institutions, was being waged to demonstrate solidarity and support for the liberation struggle in eastern Ukraine. Consequently all kinds of slanders were circulated against the "yellow and blues,"[19] the "sycophants of capitalists and landowners" and the "anti-popular" followers of Petliura, just as today all sorts of calumnies are propagated against the "German-Ukrainian nationalists," the "Banderites,"[20] etc. During the difficult postwar years, when the Soviet Union was isolated from the rest of the world, the Bolsheviks blamed the surrounding capitalist countries, to which they linked the Ukrainian liberation struggle, although in Europe the capitalist world was under the patronage of France, the country least envious of Soviet territory and wealth. Only with the accession of National Socialism to power in Germany did dormant German imperialism awaken. Because of Germany's rapid growth as a power, it became an ever greater threat to Europe and the world. This re-emergence of German imperialism reminded the world of the sufferings it had caused in the past, during the First World War and the postwar depression; nations bordering on Germany were put on a state of alert and German imperialism was regarded with revulsion and hatred throughout most of the world. From then on, world opinion again became suspicious of Germany and condemned anything that carried a German or Germanophile stamp. In order to set general opinion against any word or deed, all that was required was to point to its German origin. Thus, it again became fashionable for the enemies of Ukraine to ascribe a German origin to our liberation policy.

In the meantime, National-Socialist Germany was striving for a revision of the post-war treaties, which had shattered her internally, amputated her territorially and undermined the foundations of her imperialist tendencies. Taking up the slogan of revisionism, she launched abroad a lively propaganda campaign designed to channel the aspirations of nations dissatisfied with the state of post-Versailles Europe. In addition, the shadow of the Bolshevik colossus, which until this time had remained modest because of its internal weakness, began to appear on the European horizon. The Soviet Union had utilized this time to improve its industrial position, thanks to forced collectivization and the help of foreign technicians. It had also stifled, at least temporarily, the separatist national-liberation movements by means of military force, executions, exile and famine.[21] It had dealt with the faction that advocated world revolution and embarked resolutely on the path of Russian imperialism. These developments aroused ever greater fear in the post-Versailles buffer states bordering on the Soviet Union, for the fallacies that stood in the service of Russian-Bolshevik imperialism—the world-wide family of socialism and Pan-Slavism[22]—found countless adherents, disheartened by national persecution and widespread social and economic distress, in many European countries. Before Hitler's accession to power, Germany herself had had five million communist voters. Her anti-Bolshevik propaganda, which was understandable in view of Germany's internal situation, won over a number of small states which linked hopes for improvement in their situations to a reorganization of Europe. In no time at all, German imperialist policy drew some of them completely into the net of its own interests and held them there until the very end of the war.

The Ukrainian people were also in danger of being taken in by German interests. For them, this danger was all the greater, as their efforts to attain liberation and sovereignty were constantly subject to all the disadvantages that characterize the life of a stateless nation. And it should be stated that throughout this difficult period, during the struggle for liberation, Ukrainian policy succeeded in maintaining its complete independence of all external and foreign factors—a rare exception indeed in international affairs. Attempts of foreign interventionists—and there were many—to divert the liberation policy from its straight and narrow path were unsuccessful; threats and calumnies intended to discourage the popular masses from supporting the cause of liberation and to compromise it in the eyes of the outside world had no effect. All these enemy efforts were categorically rejected, as they deserved to be. Ukrainian liberation policy never wavered from its principle of independence, but this does not mean that it did not attempt to make use, for its own purposes, of such international developments as, for example, the revisionist movement. Germany was the only power in Europe or, for that matter, in the world that was striving to weaken the imperialist thrust of Ukraine's historic enemies and, to that extent, her aspirations coincided with the interests of Ukrainian policy. Britain had supported Germany in the interest of blocking French hegemony in Europe in the postwar period. At Munich in 1938, Britain and France sanctioned Hitler's destruction of Czechoslovakia and his inclusion of the Czech provinces in the German state as a protectorate. Bonnet[23] made it clear to Ribbentrop, during the latter's visit to Paris in December 1938, that France was disposed to give the Germans a free hand in the East—as has been shown by the French *Yellow Book*. Therefore, when Bolshevik Russia concluded a pact with Germany[24] on 23 August 1939, was it appropriate for Ukraine to come out against Germany at such a critical moment, when she was striving to destroy her age-old enemy? By her acts, Ukraine would later refute the slanderous accusation that she pursued a Germanophile policy. This would happen not at the moment desired by her enemies, but when it suited the purpose of her own liberation policy. And, compared to some world powers, she did so promptly, for on 30 June 1941[25] she stood openly in the anti-German front, while the United States, for example, was drawn into the war against Germany only on 11 December 1941, and that by Germany herself.

From the moment the German-Soviet war broke out, on 22 June 1941, the Soviets launched an attack, unparalleled in its vehemence, against the Ukrainian independence movement for its "Germanophile" tendencies, as though Ukrainians were duty-bound to defend the tyranny and coercion that the Kremlin had imposed upon them during its twenty-year rule. The Ukrainian people were acting to fulfill their own political goals and rose against Germany when these goals encountered opposition from the Germans. Then German propaganda gave voice, as though echoing the well-worn calumnies of Ukraine's historical enemies, to the charge that the Ukrainian liberation movement was . . . a Bolshevik intrigue. The events of June 1941 gave the Ukrainian liberation movement an opportunity to lay its cards on the table: it would fight anyone who dared to grasp at Ukrainian territory and to enslave the Ukrainian people. When the Poles and Bolsheviks did this, the struggle was taken up against them; when the Germans began to do the same, the struggle was directed against them as well. In those epoch-making times, the expansionist tendencies of the German and Russian nations, which made them imperialist powers equally hostile to Ukraine, became evident to the masses in Ukraine and the outside world. These were two imperialist powers which, in their apocalyptic gravitation toward each other, hovered as an eternal threat, ready to sweep from the face of the earth anything that stood on the path between them.

Illusion and Reality

Within the nations subjugated or threatened by the Soviet Union, certain groups cut off from the mainstream found it difficult to resist the suggestive influence of German propaganda. Fear of Hitler's categorical demands for "living space" in *Mein Kampf*[26] receded into the background, and these demands were regarded as a problem that would not have to be dealt with until some time in the future. The primary and most important concern was to bring about the fall of Russia. And the difficulties entailed in gaining dominion over the vast spaces of the East would probably compel the Germans to limit their planned demands in practice, at least to the extent that they had been forced to do so in 1917. Thanks to Germany's clever insinuations, it came to be believed that the Germans had sufficient political and military power to destroy Russia. While the central European states, frightened and confounded by hysterical threats and skillfully arranged demonstrations of military might, stepped into the gaping mouth of the Nazi Moloch, those Ukrainian circles that were cut off from the masses were already diligently counting out the time required to disperse the leaderless Red Army and overthrow the Soviet regime. At this time, these circles were issuing statements about the weakness of the Soviet Union based on the Bolsheviks' customary self-criticism and their cleverly devised propaganda. These assertions gained currency in official Nazi circles, for they were in keeping with the Nazis' ravings about "living space." The craftily conceived view that National Socialism would lead an anti-Bolshevik crusade found acceptance among people beset by nostalgia for their motherland or by a desire to obtain or regain within their country positions they had once held or to which they felt entitled. On the other hand, claims were made about the danger of world fascism and the need to protect the labouring proletariat from this danger. This only served to increase the apparent credibility of the pseudo-universal goals of the Soviet and Nazi doctrines. The conviction arose that two contradictory and mutually exclusive world-views were face to face with each other and heading toward an inevitable collision, and that this conflict, arising from the opposition of world-views, would give rise to fundamental transformations on the battlefield and bring to light all universal, social, economic, moral, religious, political and national problems.

A fatal illusion.

Did National Socialism really endeavour to destroy Bolshevism as a system and did the Bolsheviks strive to bring down National Socialism? In neither case was this so. Germany conquered Soviet territory in order to gain living space for her people; the Soviets were following in the footsteps of the Russian despots, who endeavoured to implement their own "truly Christian" order in Europe and the world and to expand the limits of their empire. *Drang nach Osten* (Drive to the East) and a campaign against "decadent Europe." Nazism was acting under the cover of destroying the enemy of culture and civilization—Bolshevism; Bolshevism was voicing rhetoric about the social liberation of the world proletariat and the destruction of its enemies—fascism and capitalism. These systems were not imposed from the outside, but were both products of their environment. Nazism was a form of degenerate Teutonicism, while Bolshevism was the heir of Orthodoxy, Pan-Slavism and populism (*narodnichestvo*), now taken out of their previous context, which were the former masks of Muscovite imperialism. Germany and the USSR are the only imperialist powers in human history whose development has led to interpenetration; according to the French historian Michelet,[27] this has been a fatal marriage whose mutual relations have been marked by an alternation of rapprochement and bloody collision. These two partners have been to each other, over the course of centuries, a source of stimulus as well as a hindrance, the closest of friends and bitterest of foes: each has manifested to the other prospects for copious increase and brought the darkness of the grave. Each of these powers has been to the other the cause of the highest flights and the most painful of descents in the social and spiritual realms, of brilliant victories and dismal failures, of great prosperity and woeful misery. Germany and the Soviet Union—they are the thesis and the antithesis.

It was not for the sake of flattering Emil Ludwig[28] that Stalin told him, during their meeting in 1931, that the Soviet people felt the greatest sympathy for Germany and the German people. He made his statement in the awareness of that historical process which over centuries had formed the complex of characteristics of the Germanic and Russian worlds, of which Nazism and Bolshevism are the current manifestations, the natural offspring. Germany has always gravitated toward the East, to those limitless spaces which lured her with their inexhaustible

sources of raw materials and whose enormous masses of population—
future slaves—fascinated her creative instincts. Entranced by the utopian prospect of feeding off those territories, she turned the creativity
of her mind and spirit in the same direction. Her philosophy and
science, her moral and ethical principles, her social, economic and military doctrines, her political formulae and her technical constructs—all
of these were created with Eastern Europe in mind. It was there that
she sent her ideas and her machines. Her politicians joined the courts of
Peter I and Catherine II; her technicians and capital were sent eastward
during the years after Rapallo; her colonists went to settle the Ukrainian plains, the Volga and the Urals;[29] and her strategists and military
instructors staffed Russian military institutes and barracks. No sooner
would the cannons grow silent and the wounds inflicted on Teutonicism
in a military offensive begin to heal than the peaceful offensive of ideas
and materials would begin again, following the age-old paths of *Drang
nach Osten*.

Just as Russia has always resisted Germany's military conquests, so
after the conclusion of peace treaties has she opened her doors to peaceful expansion. The tsars' court was Germanized: the tsars' families, the
ruling circles and influential classes were raised on German scholarship
and German culture. Whoever wanted to "rise in the world" behaved
according to "German ways." The minds of the Russian ruling class
were equally enthralled by German philosophers and military leaders,
scholars and poets, social theorists, engineers and builders. They were
captivated by Kant[30] and Hegel,[31] Clausewitz[32] and Schlieffen,[33]
Goethe[34] and Schiller,[35] Marx[36] and Engels.[37] Russia read them,
learned from them, imitated them, tried out their ideas in her own country, applied them to her own circumstances and amended them. In a
word, Germany produced the idea; the student, Russia, made it her
own, tried it out in practice and, because of her limitless possibilities,
provided the teacher with the impulse to form new conceptions.

Germany created on an Eastern scale. Her thought and the creativity of
her spirit could not find fulfillment in limited spaces with limited resources. Her discovery of the "Superman" (how it appealed to the adherents of "universal humanity"!), Prussian dogmatism and univer-
salism, Pan-German centralism, social and economic doctrines and political systems, including Nazism—none of these could find fulfillment
at home. They required new spaces: only expansion could save them.
So they took the age-old path eastward.

But the pupil had no intention of sacrificing herself for the sake of
scholarship. In any case, is it within a nation's power, in the span of
one generation, to turn away from its historical path, to renounce its
conscious and subconscious goals? And if one could not regard as sin-

cere the German National-Socialist propaganda concerning its aim of destroying Bolshevism, or Bolshevik propaganda regarding its desire to protect the world from fascism and capitalism, then in the same measure one ought to have remained wary of the tactical approaches of the Germans and Russians at Rapallo and, on 23 August 1939, in Moscow. For, as has been stated, both Nazism and Bolshevism were the products of their respective environments: the first, a purely Germanic phenomenon, the second, purely Russian. And the differences between nations cannot be levelled, for these differences are more than merely political or material; their roots go deeper. These differences exist in the world-views, ideas and morals of nations. The elements that make up these differences are the result of the opposition, even the contradictions, between the interests of individual nations; they are the result of the particular nature of each nation's historical development, of age-old stratifications of historical, spiritual and material characteristics. These differences represent the sum of the spiritual, moral and material potentialities of individual nations, and a compromise could not be reached among them even if these nations were headed by ideal democratic governments that took such a task upon themselves. To go backward in time or in history is impossible. Thus both Germany and Russia took well-trodden paths with respect to their aspirations, unquenched ambitions and unrealized expectations that had been handed down over generations. One looked to the East, the other to the West; both carried on an eternal expansion, an eternal offensive, attended either by words or capital, the sword of the conqueror or the plough of the colonist.

The periods of war between Germany and Russia, which followed periods of peaceful relations between them, have been among the most dreadful and bloody convulsions in human history. And this testifies to the character of the slogans that were carried on the bayonets of the warring armies. Had Hitler truly been bringing Eastern Europe liberation from Bolshevik tyranny and social serfdom, he could easily have spared himself the brutality and violence, the plundering of countries and physical extermination of peoples which began at the Soviet border itself, far from the boundaries of the true Soviet "nation," the Russian nation. The same can be said of the Bolshevik side, beginning with the first steps it took in 1917. Both one side and the other were guided exclusively by political motives, striving only to conquer and acquire new territory. In Germany and Russia we see an eternal, mutual gravitation of two energies, divided by fathomless hatred, aspiring to come into contact with each other and to flow into one; a mutual attraction of spirit and matter, in a fatal course toward a symbiosis whose consequences would be incalculable. The first sought space in the other's land, "living space" in which to unburden herself; the second wished

to shield herself behind the other from the unfamiliar West. Russia im-
bibed the German spirit and German thought. To Russia, a nation in-
toxicated with abstract imperialist theories which it could not itself
carry out posed no threat. But Germany could easily make common
cause with the West; united with the West, she would be a danger to
Russia. For this reason, willy-nilly, Russia had to win her favour; she
could successfully proceed westward only with the Germans. According to Marx, it was not Russia but Germany that was to become the
promised land of socialism. The German people were the most progressive in the world and the German working class constituted the leading
proletariat, the readiest to accept Marxist doctrine and spread it
throughout the world. Marx's ideas derived from matters related to
German interests and destined for the German masses, which, in turn,
would ease access to the French and North American proletariats,
which in their development of class consciousness and vitality followed
immediately behind the German. Moscow was only a temporary vault
in which the teachings of the bearded "prophet" were deposited and
kept safe until the eagerly awaited era of world revolution. And in the
meantime Bolshevik Russia was an experiment with revolution in one
country.[38]

No barrier was able to withstand the pressure of those two powers.
Everything was scattered, smashed, obliterated, conquered and enslaved. Ukraine and Sweden, Poland and Prussia, the Balkans and the
Baltic states, Turkey and Finland: all were submitted to the old political tactics of extermination, subjugation, conquest, denationalization,
assimilation, Russification and Germanization, Sovietization and Nazi-
fication. If persuasion did not work, threats followed; if deceit was in-
effective, force was applied; what was begun by propaganda was completed by violence. This was also the fate of the buffer states of post-
Versailles Europe.

And Ukraine?

The end of the First World War brought defeat to Germany. She
searched for a way to draw back; it was difficult to hold out on two
fronts. She could not find a common language with the West: here lay
the same abyss as later, in 1940. It was necessary to bring about the
capitulation of the East. How? By the age-old route of German-Russian
exchange. In a sealed car of a train, Lenin headed for Petrograd bearing
the German doctrine of Marxism.[39] The weak and unstable Provisional
Government was powerless to take command of the agitated masses,
whose undoctrinal anarchism, revolutionism and messianism, which are
natural to the Russian soul, constituted a formidable potential force. In
order to arm these masses, only a thought was required. Ideas and slo-

gans were needed in order to discharge this pent-up energy. And for this reason, Lenin appeared.

But the "leader of the proletariat" quickly perceived that the Russian proletariat still had more than one phase of the "capitalist process" to go through before it could step "onto the path of socialist construction." So he wrote amendments to classical Marxism, thus forming the basis of the general Leninist-Stalinist line. World revolution was put aside until a further ripening of the capitalist states and, for tactical reasons, efforts were concentrated on the realization of socialism in one country, which was proclaimed the basis of world revolution. The teachings of Marx were thus deposited in Moscow to serve as a lure to those whom it was necessary to win over (confound), while massive repression and levelling were applied to the conquered peoples. Included in the latter group were the Ukrainians. The state was a means of demonstrating to the masses the "real achievements of the revolution"; state policy served to reinforce "capitalist contradictions" in other countries and to sharpen and evoke conflicts and clashes. In the USSR, the old principle of "Russia one and indivisible" found its embodiment. Bolshevism is the synthesis of the historical stratifications of the Russian people's political inclinations and ambitions to rule within ever wider boundaries, to rule ever more distant lands, combined with Marx's doctrine of historical materialism, made more shallow, with its social tendencies removed and political, imperialist tendencies added. Both Lenin and Stalin were favourably disposed toward the German people as the nation destined to begin the "true" Marxist revolution and achieve "true" socialism.

On the basis of this analysis, it is clear that Ukraine stood as an obstacle to the imperialist aims of these two powers. Having found herself between the hammer and the anvil, between two mighty powers which were the destroyers of her sovereignty and the chief sources of the misfortune and devastation suffered by her people, Ukraine hated both enemies equally. Abroad, Ukrainian aspirations were generally met with misunderstanding and indifference. This was Ukraine's tragedy.

Just as one cannot separate Bolshevism from the Russian nation, one cannot separate Nazism from the German nation. But whereas the final synthesis of Russia—Bolshevik primitivism—is a phenomenon adapted to the actual level of the masses there, Nazism, the synthesis of Teutonicism, is a thoroughly abstract phenomenon. The ideas that provided the basis for Nazism were born out of German enthrallment with the prospects offered by the Russian environment. These ideas were lulled in their cradle by the symphony of the "unencompassed Russian land," with its limitless riches and incalculable possibilities. The political doctrine of German imperialism, the works of Frederick the Great[40] and Hitler, Clausewitz and Schlieffen—these were not created for Germany, as their creators were not using their own standards, but foreign, Russian ones. For this reason, Nazism was doomed to failure from the start. Thrown onto the limitless spaces of Eastern Europe, it soon saw the catastrophic error of its "living-space" fiction, which had been concocted from a mixture of bestial emotions and personal ambitions.

This matter would be of no concern to us were it not for the fact that a part of Ukrainian society, one which was rash and in a hurry to find new solutions, was pulled into the whirlpool of the Nazi catastrophe by incompetent politicians. At a time when the majority of Ukrainians took a stand dictated by history, these detached elements became the dung of Teutonicism. The results cannot be justified by any Wallenrodian[41] machinations.

For most of Ukrainian society, the memory of the German "liberation" of 1918 was still fresh. However, as has been said, in certain insignificant fragments of our society these memories had been effaced and, in these circles, the attractions of Nazism, which were conditioned by critical circumstances, lulled their watchfulness. When Hitler came to power, he launched a very harsh campaign against communism designed to entrance the foreign masses by pulling the wool over their eyes with cheap slogans and feeding them lies voiced by noisy demagogues, thus uniting for his purposes the agitated petty bourgeoisie and potential fascists. On the other hand, he diverted the attention of his own countrymen from the shallowness and primitivism of his doctrine's social theses which, incidentally, he took from the materialistic writings of his philosophical "opponents." Hitler's *ersatz* doctrine showed itself to be far from equal in rank with that of the Marxists, which flowed out of German philosophy. The anti-communist campaign was very useful to the author of *Mein Kampf*, for whom the essential matter was not the liberation of the East from communism but the acquisition of territory for his nation. Hitler's pilfered "socialism" served to attract the seven million German communists, who even tolerated the anti-Bolshevik campaign, for they had not yet completed their passage through the process of nationalism. Their qualms of conscience with regard to the "betrayal of socialism" were stilled by Hitler's social theses. These might have evoked suspicion among the German nationalists, but they were soothed by the nationalistic slogans of Nazi totalitarianism. This was the National-Socialist amalgam which, on the cheap fodder of a thoroughly abstract doctrine and under the cover of cunning twists of Nazi policy and propaganda, was preparing to retrace the steps of the ancient Varangians.[42] For the Germans, *Mein Kampf* stood as a steadfast guide; for Ukrainians, it was a terrible warning.

We hoped for a change in the postwar organization of Europe, but never at the price of surrendering our goal of sovereignty. Ukraine fought against Sovietization; her western borderlands, which had been incorporated into the territories of the buffer states created by the Treaty of Versailles, held the lateral front. In general, the attitude toward Germany was reserved and distrustful. The harsh reality of life under the Soviets taught the people not to delude themselves with hopes of foreign assistance, but to place their confidence solely in their own capacities. The various forms of liberation struggle on Ukrainian territory can be explained in terms of a realistic assessment of those capacities and serious thinking about sovereignty. No one can accuse Ukraine of going along with any political, social or ideological current. The suggestions of the *Reichswehr*[43] and the noisy Nazi rhetoric found a hearing only among emigrants cut off from their homeland and, because of the critical circumstances, among certain members of western Ukrainian party circles. All these people together represented such a small percentage of Ukrainian society that it was difficult to take the pro-German current seriously, although its adherents were recruited principally from the ranks of the western Ukrainian intelligentsia. In any case, this political tendency must be considered not so much a pro-German current in Ukrainian society as, rather, a faction of the Ukrainian revisionist front, which took the view that the leading role in altering the status of Eastern Europe would fall to Germany, while most people remained mistrustful of any engagement of foreign powers in the liberation of Ukraine.

The liberation struggle of the peoples subjugated by the Soviet Union aimed at the internal breakdown of the empire, although it also took into account the fact that such a breakdown could and should be assisted by the external conflict. On the other hand, the process of dissolution within the USSR began to meet with ever more ruthless measures from the destructive political centralization implemented by the Bolsheviks. The truly Russian character of this doctrine became a source of attraction for Russians who were not party members. By means of extermination, resettlement and deportation to Asian territories, attempts were made to create a uniform Soviet people. In that totalitarian, centralized and despotic regime, the people became an object in the hands of the purged party, which was, bone of the bone and flesh of the flesh, the leading body of the Russian people. Thus was the principle of "one leader, one people, one state"[44] callously put into practice.

Under such circumstances, what was the proper course for a people straining all its resources to defend itself against one beast of prey while the other was already aiming its claws in its direction? The

German-Soviet war would place Ukraine, for the first time in her history, between only two determining factors: Moscow and Berlin. Each side would try, with greater or lesser adroitness, to gain her for itself. At the same time, Sovietization, a new disguised version of Russification and of the principle of "Russia, one and indivisible,"[45] was proceeding at an ever increasing pace. And in some émigré Ukrainian hideaways, there flourished memories that had been invalidated irrevocably by a quarter-century of uncompromising, brutal transformations. The Nazi experiment with Carpatho—Ukraine did not bring these people to their senses. The masses, habitually cautious but attuned to change, awaited the emergence of an idea that would help them confront ensuing developments. Epochs usually give rise to individuals capable of keeping pace with events. Such people took the helm of the Ukrainian liberation movement and, on 30 June 1941, the day that Ukrainian sovereignty was proclaimed, the Ukrainian people went to war against Germany.

Sowing the Wind and Reaping the Whirlwind

"Because the newly conquered territories must be gained *permanently* for Germany and Europe, your bearing will play a decisive role. You must be conscious of the fact that you are representatives of Greater Germany and standard-bearers of the National Socialist revolution and the new Europe for centuries to come. For this reason you must carry out with dignity even the most severe and ruthless acts if they are dictated by reasons of state. Character deficiencies in individuals will lead to their being recalled. Whoever is recalled for such reasons will also be barred from holding responsible positions in the *Reich*." This is the text of one of the *Führer's* "twelve commandments" with which the Germans marched eastward in 1941. Is there anything surprising about the way history avenges itself on those who wish to create it thoughtlessly, in contradiction to the natural course and order of things, and about the way the most abstract slogans, products of utopian ravings, perish miserably, covering their trail with blood, ashes, ruin, hunger and misery?

Ukraine, the most important point in the internal political life of the Soviet Union, was designated the centre of German colonizing activity in Eastern Europe. It was to become the base of German imperialism, which was directed toward the Near East and India, where it was to meet the Japanese empire. In a few months, Field Marshal von Rundstedt[46] conquered an enormous amount of territory by means of masterful, lightning-quick encirclements of which the bloody conqueror of

Cannae would have been proud. The Teutonic panzer wave rolled ever further to the east at a demonic tempo. Gestapo[47] terror followed in its wake, and the unfortunate masses were left without a roof over their heads, without hope for the future. Ukraine, which under the terror of the previous regime had striven for political independence and national unity, found herself in a new situation that scarcely differed from the previous one. She was a conquered—seemingly conquered—prize of war.

An individual will bear poverty and misery, even the most painful blows and the harshest tyranny, if these privations are imposed on him in the name of ideas and slogans, regardless of the fact that these ideas may be abstract and incapable of realization except in the very distant future. For an individual is enticed by romance; he is exalted and moved to the greatest self-denial by hard but sound ethical and moral demands and postulates; he is captivated even by utopia. But never will he bear exploitation for foreign benefit, regardless of what cunning or morbid "theory" or "historical sanction" may be used to justify such exploitation, whether it be the theory of the "leading nation of the revolution," the "master race" or any other doctrine of a "chosen people."[48]

The vast expanse between the San and the Volga soon ceased to be a battlefield and loomed as a difficult political problem for the Germans. Their conquest of Ukraine had to be given appropriate significance. And here the deception of Nazi propaganda became immediately obvious. The occupation revealed itself as only a strategic, not a political operation. The land was to remain a jumping-off point for the Germans. The Nazis were enthralled by the prospects and possibilities offered by these thousands of newly conquered square kilometres at a time when the first priority should have been to face squarely the thousands of new problems and questions which had arisen. They did nothing with this enormous space, for surely the reactionary and primitively absurd "reforms" of Rosenberg[49] and Erich Koch[50] offered less than nothing to Ukraine. It turned out in practice that Hitler had neither an Eastern policy nor any solutions for the occupied territories of Eastern Europe. These territories were simply destined to be German booty, administered as a large battlefield. Ukraine, torn from under the Russian yoke, was to be placed under the German yoke. Under such conditions, there was not the slightest possibility that Hitler could attain a compromise with the conquered peoples. If the Germans could not deal with the Ukrainian problem, considering that Ukraine was the first territory on which their experiments were conducted, they could hardly expect any lasting success in the East. Brilliant strategy turned to nothing because of senseless policy. Ukrainian territory, whose loss the

USSR felt so keenly, became the site on which German strategy, en-
amoured of brilliant, quick manoeuvres, was forced to begin its retreat
from the East. Hitler's great expedition of conquest ended as a mere
adventure.

It might be noted that only a single step separates the conqueror from
the adventurer. For the greater the successes, the greater the dangers
and risks. But the heart of the matter is this: to what extent do actual requirements and circumstances justify increased risk? The important
point is the "political value" of the stategy. Bolshevism put strategy at
the service of policy (this was the reason for the fall of Tukhachevsky);[51] in Germany, there was briefly a tendency to make strategy independent of policy, and from 1941 there was no policy at all in the East.
Strategy alone was burdened with the overly heavy task of destroying
the base of Russian Bolshevism. The Communist party paved the way
for Soviet imperialism by various means. The Comintern[52] carried on
subversive activities in many nations, the state apparatus of the
"homeland of socialism" deepened the conflicts among states, and the
Red Army occupied new territories. After Rapallo, the Germans organized Soviet industry and, after the pact of August 1939, the Bolsheviks
drove all German colonists out of the occupied lands of the Baltic
region, Romania, Bessarabia and Bukovyna. Until the Nazis' accession
to power, Germany was making only strategic preparations for the
Eastern campaign. After 1933, these preparations were fortified only
by general propagandistic rhetoric about the destruction of communism,
which in the final armed phase was termed the destruction of the
USSR, the Bolshevik threat to the world. That was all. It did not suffice even for a few months; this "policy" did not even manage to stag-
ger along as far as Stalingrad or Moscow. "Do not bother trying to
sniff out communists. Russian youth has been raised in the communist
spirit for two decades. It has never had any other kind of education.
For this reason, there is no sense in digging up the past. We do not
want to convert the Russians to National Socialism, but only to make
them our tools. You must win over the young people, assigning tasks to
them and attacking them sharply and punishing them mercilessly whenever they sabotage these tasks or fail to carry them out." This is another of the "twelve commandments" that we mentioned earlier. Here
we see what was to take the place of the Bolshevism that was to be destroyed. How can we speak here about the equal value, let alone the superiority of this new "diet"? It was simply the fist against the idea
(whatever it might be), matter against spirit, strategy against policy.

From the start it was characteristic of National Socialism to trivialize
concepts and phenomena. It was thought that the Bolshevik doctrine
and regime had taken only shallow root on Soviet territory; that it

would suffice to give the state a good shake and destroy the Moscow centre in order to turn the people back to their natural state of undoctrinal anarchism and messianism, in which they would be prone to accept any new, stronger idea and to turn their territory into an opening for German experimentation with the "new order." The Germans were mistaken. Twenty-five years of Sovietization had left their mark. It is true that, for the most part, the newly reared society had had a one-sided, Bolshevik upbringing. In the event of the destruction of Bolshevism and the fall of its idols, this society would truly have found itself in a vacuum. But it was not in the power of Nazism to vanquish Bolshevism. In Ukraine, nationalism could rise to this task. In Russia, Marxist doctrine, applied in the manner peculiar to the Russian spirit, became the source not of abstract slogans but of slogans with age-old traditions behind them, which were an inseparable part of the rise and development of Russian statehood.[53] This doctrine had already managed to create new forces, to establish a new decision-making centre—the party—and to give a totally new face to Soviet-dominated territories. For the Russian people, the war with the German occupying forces became a "sacred war for the fatherland."[54]

In the conquered eastern territories, the Germans created a wasteland. They came with the one-sided idea that elements of weakness and strength were to be sought only in material values. They underestimated the obvious truth that, ultimately, it is not matter but spirit that stands over all; that this spirit conquers or dies depending whether it begins in falsehood or truth, whether it is directed onto a true or a false path by matter. This conquered mass of people, sixty million strong, had to think something. Whoever still hesitated or hoped for anything underwent a deep spiritual transformation. He became aware of the shameful bankruptcy of the Germans' shoddy "ideas" and "thoughts." From out of the chaos and cemeteries, the ruins and ashes, an elemental spirit arose; a generation armed with a newer, stronger wisdom grew up in the underground. While the Wallenrods were unmasked by the enemy, the conjuncturists laid down their lives for nothing or, more often, sent others to do so, while still others signed "memoranda" to . . . Hitler. At the same time they brought massive, bloody repressions upon the innocent population by falling prey to covert enemy provocations, which led them to square old, petty accounts on the sidelines of the liberation struggle. For the sake of historical truth, it must be said that these fine young fighters for Ukrainian liberation, who grew up in the tumult caused by the collision of spiritual and material world powers, sucked ten times, one hundred times fewer bloody juices out of the Ukrainian organism than the "chiefs," "leaders" and other speculators, acting "with the grace of God and in the name of the people,'' who attempted to profit from the nation's misery and thereby add ''weight'' to their signatures on ''memoranda'' to Hitler or to rise in the ranks of the occupying power's bureaucracy.

Never before had Ukraine's tragic situation reached such depths. To the waiting masses, disillusioned and deceived in their expectations, threatened by total extermination, some kind of protection had to be given. They had to be given faith in their cause and their future. They had to be given an idea. It was necessary to prove that this idea was truly viable and that it alone would give them the strength to achieve their salvation. They had to be shown that it was not an unattainable dream or utopia, but could be achieved immediately, the next day, even this very day; that it was not something meant for special occasions, but could cure the pains suffered every day and answer every need. It was necessary to show them how to die so that the nation might live. In Ukraine, the first to die were always the revolutionaries; the mass of the people followed their example. The masses had to be taught that the idea was given to them not in order to create a new prison or raise new tyrants to the heights, but in order that they might defend themselves. Under the conditions created by the German occupation, statements about ''constructive work'' and ''sparing the nation's strength and attainments'' became a mere fiction. To assert the contrary might be possible in distant émigré hideaways, but not amid the ruins of Ukrainian towns and villages and among the corpses of innocent, defenceless people. There were only two choices: either a spiritual crippling and physical extermination of the peaceable population, which would be carried out under any pretext or provocation, along with penal labour in Germany, concentration camps, gas chambers, injections and crematoria; or an active struggle to the death that would save the nation's soul. In order to live, the people had to choose either the liberation struggle or Bolshevism.

Let no one delude himself that it was possible to play cunning games with Nazi occupation policies aimed at preparing Ukraine for German colonization. We give here a few excerpts from the occupying administration's secret instructions, published for internal use in November 1942:

''Schools to be of only four grades. To be closed next year (1943).

Cultural and educational institutions, theatres and cinemas to be done away with.

As few scientific institutions of the laboratory type as possible. Only those to remain which are indispensable for the army.

No effort to be made to combat tuberculosis and typhoid fever. Hospitals for the population to be closed. Training of local doctors to be suspended.

Courts to be German only. All judges to be German.

Hooliganism to be punished only when it harms Germans.

Amorality to be spread among the population, abortion not be punished.

Everything that has a backbone must be broken. We want to produce a slave population.

Informers in factories, syndicates, churches, businesses, offices and so on. Enemies of Germany to be watched. Priests to be put into service.'' And so on and so forth.

In January 1943, the National-Socialist party passed several resolutions in Kiev. Their content was generally similar to that of the above instructions and, in some cases, was expanded and clarified in greater detail. Here are some of these resolutions:

To subject the church to the *Gebietskommissäre*[55] and to turn it into an instrument of the police.

To refrain from preventing criminal offences if they harm only the local population.

To refrain from punishment for abortion, to spread alcoholism and debauchery.

To stop the growth of the population by making it difficult to obtain permission for marriage from civil authorities.

To forbid communication completely for the local population.

To refrain from combating epidemic illnesses as long as they do not threaten Germans.

To take away "racially pure" children and have them brought up in German institutions.

To take girls by force to military brothels.

This suffices to illustrate one side of the coin.

And from the economic point of view? In July 1943, the *Reichskommissar* of Ukraine, Erich Koch, issued instructions to the general *Gebietskommissäre* concerning the imposition of quotas. Let us read from the beginning: "If we wish to carry out the duty assigned us by the *Führer*[56] of ensuring that there will be sufficient food for the front, we must take appropriate care as to the results of our work. In applying the necessary measures to fulfill our assigned task, there can be no place for any false sentimentality in our relations with the local population . . .

"The idea that the imposition of quotas on the local population obliges us to ensure that there will also be food for them is mistaken and shows a total misunderstanding of the political, economic and military situation. German soldiers sacrificed their blood to liberate this country from Bolshevism. All that the local population can do in return for this liberation is to render to Germany, by means of work and the fulfillment of quotas, that which she lost through the sacrifice of her finest sons. The death of German soldiers on Ukrainian soil and our military victory oblige us to state clearly that if there is a deficiency of food which is vitally needed to feed Europe and if the population somewhere has to go hungry, in no case must it be the German population that goes hungry. And if we find ourselves faced with the dilemma who is to go hungry, Germans or Ukrainians, then there should be no doubt about our decision. And to carry out this decision is the duty of the *Gebietskommissäre* and leaders in the economic sector.

"For our work in Ukraine, there is only one point of view: whatever fills the requirements mentioned above is correct; everything else is wrong. Better to bring cheap ornaments, used goods and necklaces into Ukraine than political discussions . . . "

What did the Germans actually have in mind? Let us listen further to the *Reichskommissar*, who aspired "to increase food allotments in the autumn on the basis of Ukrainian production. To do away with the bread-ticket is my greatest desire, my highest goal and a wonderful counter-measure against aerial bombardment." For the duration of the war, Ukrainians were to work only for the nourishment of Germany, to surrender everything "for victory"; it did not matter if they themselves swelled with hunger. And in this hopeless slavery they would have to find their purpose. They would possess no other rights. "Ukrainians do not have the right to institutions of higher learning," we read further. "We would be complete fools if we did anything to increase Ukrainian education or to raise the level of the Ukrainian intelligentsia." For "the *Führer* has directed that for the time being schools of four grades must suffice. There the Ukrainian will learn to read, write and count." And after the war? "Ten hours of work: eight for the *Führer* and two hours for the worker himself. Thus the worker will not be able to make any claims on the basis of his eight hours of work, but only on the basis of the results of the last two hours, which will also be worked for the *Führer*, but which will bring benefit to the worker himself." Even this would be preferable to what was likely to happen, for in fact, Ukraine was to be colonized by Germans and there would be no room for the local population, even in the role of slaves. For "it is necessary to consider the prospects for our soldiers after the war and the question of resettlement from West to East. A German resettlement policy must be put into effect on these territories. What will happen to the Ukrainians? When, for example, the residents of the destroyed city of Karlsruhe[57] come to live in Ukraine, obviously Ukrainians will have to move the same distance to the east." "A great space for German colonization must be created in Ukraine. Territories which never belonged to Europe should not be considered part of Europe. The claim that

Ukraine was ever a European factor is a historical lie.''

"The main task with which the *Führer* has charged us in Ukraine is to mobilize the maximum number of people for work in the Reich and to extract as much food as possible. We gave a million workers to the Reich. Our achievements on the food front are far better and greater than those of the Soviets in peacetime. Obviously our achievements were made at the Ukrainians' expense.'' "The thesis that the Ukrainians must be given something, so that they will have something to defend, is false. Millions of Germans are losing their wealth in the West; should we be expected to hand it out here?''

"The Ukrainians are co-operating with us. They are happy that they have work and bread and that they do not have to rehash political problems.''

There was no one from whom Ukraine could expect assistance. Some Ukrainians were beginning to turn their eyes northward. Soviet partisan bands organized there were bringing familiar misery to Ukraine. The population was obliged to protect itself from them in the same way as from the Germans. The country grew desolate while the people flocked to the forests, driven there by German destruction. Those who were to be taken to Germany fled with their families, for the principle of collective responsibility was applied; women and girls hid to escape the military brothels; shelter was sought by farmers, who could not surrender more produce than they possessed, and by priests, whose consciences did not allow them to enter into the service of the enemy police and to turn in their faithful. Those in the forests were exposed either to massacre or to being killed as bandits. The "forest problem" was part of the tragedy of the Ukrainian people at this time. This problem arose on its own; it was not artifically created. The new reality of the German occupation convinced the people that without self-rule there was no prospect of life on Ukrainian territory. Only through concern for one's own salvation while millions were dying could one refuse to recognize that this was the position of the Ukrainian masses. The first requirement was to protect these masses of "forest dwellers" from enemy massacres and attempts to smoke them out as bandits; then to prevent this useless migration from villages and towns; to save the people from starvation by providing them with protection while they worked the land and shielding them from the endless imposition of quotas; to protect human life and property, which had become a plaything in the plundering, colonizing plans of the occupying power; to guard and hand down to future generations what remained of the spiritual, moral and ideological values of the Ukrainian people; to neutralize the acts of provocation, inspired by the enemy and carried out by confused Ukrainians, which resulted in massive, bloody slaughter of innocent people wherever and whenever events were left to run their own course and to the will of the Germans and Bolsheviks. The Ukrainian Insurgent Army (UPA) arose; it channelled the nation's elemental force into the cadres of a disciplined military organization, gave this force the purposeful and rational form of struggle against the German and, subsequently, the Bolshevik occupation, and prevented a spontaneous revolutionary upheaval whose tragic and bloody results would have been difficult to imagine.

We believe in the nation's vitality and the strength of its spirit. The tragedy of long generations did not become its tragedy. We further believe that the tragedy of these few years will not be the death of the whole epoch. We say that today our land is in ruins. But current events become far more meaningful if we put them into historical perspective and take account of their genesis. Ukraine erected a barrier on the path leading to the destructive symbiosis of two dynamic powers: Germanism and Asiatic Russianism. The UPA devoted itself to Ukraine. From the longer perspective of centuries, a fair judgment will be passed on our endeavours. And this historic cataclysm, which today is cursed by the faint-hearted, but which may prove a blessing for future generations, will become more comprehensible.

The Last Island and the First Bastion

In the East, the battle for the freedom of peoples and individuals has intensified: there can be no return to previous conditions. The breakdown of Soviet political and military power on the territories of foreign empires in 1941 proved that for the enslaved member republics of the Soviet Union both Nazi and Bolshevik totalitarianism were equally foreign and hateful. The war unleashed the energy to fight with more than just Finnish knives and hand grenades. It awakened new passions, new ambitions, new yearnings. It freed the individual from a variety of fetters and chains. Its wholesale levelling eased the initiation of a struggle demanding even greater sacrifices for a better future.

The war has ended, but has failed to resolve many old problems, not to mention the new ones that developed during its course. Humanity aspires to absolute victory, a victory of spirit and thought. Mankind's enemy has not yet been vanquished. One materialistic world has been replaced by another; German totalitarianism has been replaced by Russian totalitarianism. For centuries they gravitated toward each other. They were united by co-operation or divided by hatred. Both strove to rule over Europe and the world. Never did one of them stand genuinely against the other on the side of Europe. Now Russia has reached the

German source from which she always drew the stimulus for her boundless prospects: territories, raw materials and masses of people. Europe is in mortal danger.

The military power of the West, even with its atomic bomb, is too weak to make a stand against the Eurasian masses inspired by messianic frenzy. Only nations inspired by high ideals will be capable of opposing them. A war from the outside would only serve to solidify further the "homeland of socialism." For this reason, the cessation of warfare can disarm only those living on illusions. The semblance of peace does not prevent the continuation of humanity's war to realize the ideas and exhortations which, over the ages, have stirred its conscience. The sounds of war are fading. Revolutionary upheavals are imminent, from which new fires of war will be lit.

Throughout the last world confrontation, Ukraine stood in the avant-garde of the march of universal human ideals. On Ukrainian lands, doctrinally conceived attempts to create a "new" German order met their death. A new reality has emerged. And now the blood chills in our veins as we consider how the liberation movement would have appeared and what dangers of physical extermination the Ukrainian people would have faced if Ukraine had accepted the insane suggestions of the "Wallenrods" and entered into the "political game" with the Germans. Today, our flags are unstained and the enemy does not have the pretext he needs to exterminate Ukrainians on the grounds of collaboration.

At the moment, the great expanses of Central and Eastern Europe are as silent as the grave. But from the very centre of that quiet sea, an island is rising from which echoes the unstifled conscience of the world. This is the UPA, which clove the Teutonic shields; the UPA, which is defending the last island from the inundation of the East and is the first bastion in the advance of the West. An analogy from the past comes to mind: Batu Khan[58] traversed Ukraine, but the hordes of Tamerlane[59] mortally bloodied themselves amid the ruins of Kiev and Lviv.

Source: Reprinted from the *Visnyk* (Bulletin) of the Supreme Ukrainian Liberation Council, no. 2 (October 1945). Original: Archive of the Foreign Representation of the Supreme Ukrainian Liberation Council. Photocopy: Archive, *Litopys UPA*.

NOTES

1. Reference is to the Treaty of Brest-Litovsk between the Central Powers and Ukraine, signed on 9 February 1918.
2. Reference is to the coup d'état of 29 April 1918 whereby General Pavlo Skoropadsky was proclaimed Hetman of Ukraine under German sponsorship.
3. The Polish-Ukrainian campaign against the Bolsheviks began on 25 April 1920 and resulted in the capture of Kiev on 7 May 1920 by combined Polish-Ukrainian forces.
4. The Ukrainian Galician Army comprised the armed forces of the Western Ukrainian People's Republic, which was proclaimed on 1 November 1918 in Lviv.
5. Józef Haller (1873–1960): Polish general in charge of the Polish Corps organized in Western Europe, equipped by France and sent to Galicia to fight the Bolsheviks. It was used primarily against the Ukrainian Galician Army.
6. The Western Ukrainian People's Republic united with the Ukrainian People's Republic on 22 January 1919 in Kiev. Subsequently, the name "Western Provinces of the Ukrainian People's Republic" was applied to the Western Ukrainian People's Republic.
7. V.A. Maklakov (1869–1957): Ambassador of the Russian Provisional Government to Paris. Active in his post until 1924, when France established diplomatic relations with the USSR.
8. P.N. Wrangel (1878–1928): Russian general, the last commander of the White Army.
9. Roman Dmowski (1864–1939): Polish politician who became minister of foreign affairs in interwar Poland. He was a strong opponent of Ukrainian independence.
10. The Polish National Committee was established in 1917 in Lausanne. The committee, headed by Dmowski, was recognized by the Entente as the official representation of the Polish people from November 1917 until its dissolution in August 1919.
11. Woodrow Wilson (1856–1924): President of the United States and author (8 January 1918) of the Fourteen Points that he believed essential to the peace settlement.
12. Reference is to the establishment of the Directory of the Ukrainian People's Republic (14 November 1918), which led a successful uprising against the regime of Hetman Skoropadsky and the German forces supporting him. Symon Petliura (1879–1926), a Ukrainian political activist and journalist, became Supreme Commander of the Army of the Ukrainian People's Republic in 1918 and Head of the Directory in 1919. When the Directory succumbed to the Bolsheviks, Petliura went into exile in Paris,

where he was assassinated by an alleged Soviet agent.

13. The Treaty of Rapallo, signed by Germany and the USSR in 1922, saw Germany accord the USSR *de jure* recognition. The treaty enabled the German army, through secret agreements, to produce and test in the USSR weapons forbidden by the Treaty of Versailles.

14. Oleksander Shumsky (1890– ?): Ukrainian political activist, member of the Socialist-Revolutionary and Communist parties. Member of the Central Rada, later minister of education of the Ukrainian SSR. Removed from office in 1926 for "bourgeois nationalist deviation." Died in GULAG camps.

15. Mykhailo Volobuev (1900– ?): Soviet Ukrainian economist of Russian origin who argued in 1928 that the Ukrainian SSR continued to be a colony of Russia as it had been before the revolution. He was supported by V. Dobrohaev and M. Shafir. Accused of "bourgeois nationalism." Died in internal exile in the 1930s.

16. *Spilka Vyzvolennia Ukrainy* (Union for the Liberation of Ukraine): according to a Soviet indictment, a secret Ukrainian nationalist organization created in April 1926 with the aim of liberating Ukraine from Russian control. The trial of 45 alleged members took place in Kharkiv in 1930.

17. Mykola (Fitilov) Khvylovy (1893–1933): Ukrainian writer. Khvylovy founded the Free Academy of Proletarian Literature (VAPLITE), which was liquidated in 1927. He called on Ukrainian writers to cultivate European literary traditions and to move "away from Moscow." Accused of nationalism, he committed suicide. See M. Khvylovy, *The Cultural Renaissance in Ukraine: Polemical Pamphlets 1925-1926*, ed. and trans. M. Shkandrij (Edmonton: Canadian Institute of Ukrainian Studies, 1986).

18. Treaty of Versailles: chief among the five peace treaties that ended the First World War, signed on 28 June 1919 by Germany and all the Allies except Russia.

19. Yellow and blue are the Ukrainian national colours.

20. Followers of Stepan Bandera (1909–59), leader of the Organization of Ukrainian Nationalists (OUN). He was arrested by the Germans and held in a concentration camp until September 1944. Assassinated in Munich by the KGB agent Bohdan Stashynsky.

21. Reference is to the famine of 1932–3 in Soviet Ukraine, which was caused by Stalin for political reasons. According to some observers, approximately 15 per cent (4–5 million) of the population of Ukraine died of hunger.

22. Pan-Slavism: theory and movement intended to promote the political or cultural unity of all Slavs. After the Crimean War, it was transformed into a militant and nationalistic Russian movement. During the Second World War, the Soviet government revived Pan-Slavic slogans to facilitate the domination of East European states.

23. Georges Bonnet (1889–1973): French politician and foreign minister (1938–9) who helped draft the Munich Pact. As a member of the Vichy National Council (1941), he supported collaboration with Germany.

24. Reference is to the Soviet-German non-aggression pact, known as the Molotov-Ribbentrop pact.

25. The Act of 30 June 1941 in Lviv by the OUN under Bandera's leadership proclaimed the independence of Ukraine and established a Provisional Government with Iaroslav Stetsko as its head. It brought on immediate repression by the Germans.

26. *Mein Kampf*: work of Adolf Hitler (1889–1945) in which he demanded more "living space" for the Germans. Hitler planned to turn Ukraine into a German colony and to incorporate Galicia and the Crimea into the German Reich.

27. Jules Michelet (1798–1874): French writer, the greatest historian of the Romantic school.

28. Emil Ludwig (1881–1948): German biographer known for his portraits of great men.

29. German agricultural colonization of Ukrainian lands and the Volga and Ural regions was initiated by the Manifestoes of Catherine II (1763) and Alexander I (1804).

30. Immanuel Kant (1724–1804): German metaphysician, and one of the greatest philosophers.

31. Georg Wilhelm Friedrich Hegel (1770–1831): German philosopher.

32. Karl von Clausewitz (1780–1831): Prussian general and writer on military strategy, of Polish descent.

33. Alfred von Schlieffen (1833–1913): German field marshal and strategist.

34. Johann Wolfgang Goethe (1749–1832): German poet, dramatist, novelist and scientist.

35. Johann Christoph Friedrich Schiller (1759–1805): German dramatist, poet and historian.

36. Karl Marx (1818–83): German social philosopher and radical leader, chief theorist of modern socialism.

37. Friedrich Engels (1820–95): German socialist.

38. Reference here is probably to Stalin's slogan of "Socialism in One Country."

39. After the outbreak of the Russian revolution of February 1917, the German government allowed Lenin to travel from Switzerland to Sweden in a sealed railway car.

40. Frederick II (the Great) (1712–86): King of Prussia.

41. Reference is to Adam Mickiewicz's poem *Konrad Wallenrod* (1828), in which the hero, a pagan Lithuanian raised as a German Christian, becomes aware of his true origins and brings about the destruction of a Teutonic army.

42. Varangians: name given by Slavs and Byzantine Greeks to Scandinavians who penetrated Eastern Europe by the ninth century.

43. *Reichswehr*: German armed forces permitted on a limited scale by the Treaty of Versailles. In 1935 all the limitations of the treaty were denounced.

44. Hitler's slogan.

45. Tsarist slogan.

46. Karl Rudolf Gerd von Rundstedt (1875–1953): German field marshal.

47. Gestapo: German secret police.

48. The reference is to the Russians as the ''leading nation,'' the Germans as the ''master race'' and the Jews as the ''chosen people.''

49. Alfred Rosenberg (1893–1946): Nazi leader. In 1933 he was made foreign affairs secretary of the party and in 1941 was appointed minister for the occupied Eastern territories. Executed as a war criminal.

50. Erich Koch (1896–): Nazi leader and *Reichskommissar* of Ukraine (1941–4). Charged with responsibility for the killing of 400,000 Poles, Koch was sentenced to death in 1959 by a Warsaw district court. The sentence was commuted to life imprisonment, and Koch remains incarcerated in Barczewo, Poland. He has never been indicted for his crimes in Ukraine.

51. M.N. Tukhachevsky (1893–1937): Marshal of the Soviet Union. Executed by Stalin in 1937 and rehabilitated by Khrushchev in 1958.

52. Communist International: name given to the Third International founded at Moscow in 1919. In order to allay the misgivings of its allies in the Second World War, the Soviet government dissolved the Comintern in 1943, only to replace it with the Cominform in 1947.

53. See Nikolai Berdiaev, *The Origin of Russian Communism* (London 1937), for a similar viewpoint.

54. The official Soviet name for the Second World War is the Great Fatherland War of the Soviet Union, 1941–5.

55. *Gebietskommissar*: territorial commissar.

56. *Führer*: leader. Reference to Hitler.

57. Karlsruhe: German city in Baden-Württemberg that was largely destroyed in the Second World War.

58. Batu Khan (died 1255): Mongol leader, a grandson of Genghis Khan.

59. Tamerlane or Timur (c. 1336–1405): Mongol conqueror.

THE AIMS AND METHODS OF GERMAN IMPERIALIST POLICY ON OCCUPIED TERRITORY

I.M. Kovalenko

VI. Unmasking the Aims and Methods of German Policy on Occupied Ukrainian Territory

The most complex problem confronting the Germans in the current phase of the imperialist war is how to deal with the question of Eastern Europe, including the ethnic territory of Ukraine. The theoretical principles for the solution of this problem have been clearly delineated by German National Socialism: Hitler's *Mein Kampf* sets forth the guidelines of German policy. The main points can be characterized briefly as follows: all of Eastern Europe is regarded as territory for German expansion; it is the German nation's "land of milk and honey," a source of strength that will guarantee Germany's leading position in the world. Because Germany's plan to become an imperialist power by acquiring new territory in countries outside Europe—a policy generally attributed to Bismarck[1]—met with failure in the last war, Hitler has shifted Germany's political orientation onto a new track and is now fanatically pounding his new concepts into the heads of those who share his views. This new approach is best described in the words of the German leader himself: *"Nicht Ostorientierung aber Ostpolitik"*—"not an orientation toward the East, but an Eastern policy." This means that current German policy excludes the concept of co-operating with present or future East European states and that Hitler rejects the idea of relying on the East as an organized political force, which had been the main thrust of Bismarck's approach. Hitler maintains that the collapse of Jewish-Bolshevik domination of Eastern Europe will signify the collapse of Russia as a state. Naturally, he has no intention of establishing new national states on the ruins of Moscow's empire and does not include in his political calculations the struggles for independence now being waged by the peoples subjugated by Moscow. But Hitler's calculations with regard to these territories are being made without consulting the owners, that is, without taking into account the wishes of the subject peoples of Eastern Europe. The Germans no longer conceal the fact that National Socialism's *Ostpolitik* is a thoroughly colonial policy: since no colonies are to be had in Africa, they must be created in Europe. This is the point of departure for Germany's present policy in Eastern Europe, especially in Ukraine. But when German policy confronted reality, that is, when the Germans occupied Ukrainian territory and began to put their theories into practice, it became apparent that the slogans of imperial conquest and exploitation with which the Germans came to Ukraine were not finding fertile ground; they have been unable to penetrate the hard wall of the Ukrainian people's struggle for independence. The insane folly of the Germans and the implementation of an unprecedented campaign of terror have not solved the problems; on the contrary, they have only added to the confusion. As a result, there is such chaos in the thought and behaviour of German officials that one can hardly comprehend them. In short, all the signs indicate that like Napoleon's plans for rebuilding Europe without consideration for Ukrainian sovereignty,[2] Hitler's plans to establish a "New Europe" without taking into account the Ukrainian struggle for independence will also be dashed on Ukrainian territory. The Germans' refusal to recognize the right of East European nations to independent statehood, their coercive repression of all independence movements on the occupied territories of the East, will bring about an inevitable collapse of their "Eastern policy" and of their imperialist plans in general.

(1) *The Basis of German Aspirations in Eastern Europe*

In order to obtain a clearer understanding of the aims and methods of German policy in Eastern Europe, we must examine the slogans that are being used as vehicles for the implementation of this policy. The purpose of these slogans is to justify German policy and to create an ideological foundation for the achievement of its goals. At the same time, these slogans are meant to weaken the resistance of the subject peoples, Ukrainians in particular, during the period when Germany's political goals are being achieved.

The first slogan is that of the struggle against Bolshevism, since the latter presents a threat to European peoples and culture. Just as in the Middle Ages the call to battle against the infidels for the recovery of the Holy Sepulchre roused all the nations of the West to march in the Crusades to the Holy Land, so today the call to battle against Bolshevism in order to defend the cultural achievements of Europe is supposed to mobilize all European peoples under the leadership of Germany.

The Ukrainians know the Soviets better than anyone, for they have been constantly at war with them for some twenty years; they were fighting against Moscow's Bolshevik imperialists at a time when other European peoples were sitting down at the same table with them; they were also fighting against them when Germany was signing a friendship pact with the Bolsheviks in 1939,[3] allowing them to occupy Western Ukraine. Even now the Ukrainian people have not ceased their struggle against Bolshevik imperialism. They will continue to fight until it is eradicated, but the Ukrainians, like all other subject peoples of the East, will continue to fight not for the sake of German imperialism and a new form of slavery, but only for the sake of national and individual liberty.

Further, German propaganda asserts that Eastern Europe is *a territory appointed by destiny to the Germans*. For this reason, the Germans have been called upon to protect it and to impose a new order upon it. This appointment by destiny, they claim, manifested itself throughout the ages in the efforts made by German colonists, who strengthened the hold of German culture and left countless monuments in their wake: castles, religious buildings, towns and ancient states, which are the traces of the creative work of the Germans. What could be more natural than to renew ancient traditions—to turn back the wheel of history and to relive the time when caravans of German colonists rolled eastward? The Goths, the Varangians, the Teutonic Knights[4] and the Hanseatic League[5] are, according to propaganda, illustrious examples of the close links that have existed between the East European peoples and Germany. For this reason, the Germans come to Ukraine and other eastern lands not as plunderers, but as rightful owners. They have only forgotten to add one thing: apparently Ukrainians did not prove very hospitable to the Germans, since the Goths and other "vanguards" disappeared so quickly from Ukrainian territory.

The most forceful slogan for the implementation of Germany's imperialist policy is that of a "New Europe." Germany is fighting for the restructuring of present-day Europe; for this reason all nations should aid her in her efforts, or at least refrain from placing obstacles in her way. But the German politicians remain silent about the actual organization of this "New Europe." It is still too early and too dangerous for them to betray themselves. All that is said is that in this Europe everybody will have "the right to work." Surely this is very niggardly! We already possess this right and the Germans are providing us with plenty of opportunities to exercise it, if only in various factories in Germany. They do not deny anyone this right; on the contrary, they are using all possible methods, including seizing people, deporting them to Germany, imprisoning them, and so on in order to enable them to exercise this right! But the question is whether the people of the captive nations will be exercising this right to work in a concentration camp established for all the peoples of Europe, under the command of German overseers and henchmen, or in their own homes, in their native lands, as free citizens of their own national states! For the "New Europe" of German imperialism is to be nothing other than a new prison of nations!

The German slogan of defending Christianity appears paradoxical and even comical. The Germans claim to have come to the occupied territories in order to defend Christian culture, faith and churches from godless Bolshevism. But when one looks at the religious policy of National Socialism in Germany and its position on existing faiths, when one considers that party members are advised or even ordered to abandon church organizations, when one recalls the attempts to revive the pagan cult of Woden,[6] then the Germans' claim to be defenders of Christianity appears odd and unnatural indeed! Evidently they need to say these things in order to win over religious believers to their cause.

To gain a better understanding of the methods used to implement German policy on occupied Ukrainian territory, we will examine some characteristic passages from material used in the party's political training conferences, which are held for the so-called political directors. The Ministry of the East sends these directors to Ukraine to work with students undergoing military training and, in particular, with the SS[7] and their guard units, including, during periods of inactivity, those who are at the front. (We covered this topic earlier in *Ideia i Chyn*, no. 3. Ed.)[8] Of these ravings, the passages that relate specifically to Ukraine are as follows: "The road to German rule over all Europe leads through the conquest of Eastern Europe. Here in Eastern Europe there are enormous spaces, land, raw materials and bread. Here is Ukraine, the fatherland of the Germans, the former state of the Goths and the Varangians. And here, in Eastern Europe, in fertile, limitless Ukraine, lies our future. This is the *heiliges Zukunftsland des deutschen Volkes*, the future holy ground of the German people! Here we will live in prosperity and abundance and will soon increase our numbers. We now number one hundred million. When we take the fruitful lands of Ukraine and Eastern Europe, we will grow to four hundred or even five hundred million within a century and will populate the whole of Europe. A great danger in this regard is the enormous reproductive power of the Slavic nations. But after the war, the Slavs and all other non-Germanic peoples will be deported from Europe immediately. All Europe will become the fatherland of the Germanic race. . . . '' Surely this is all too clear—any commentary would be superfluous!

And let us not forget that the present generation of Germans is being nurtured on these ideas, that these insane thoughts are constantly being pounded into their heads!

(2) The Dismemberment of Ukraine

Let us look now at the methods used to implement German policy on the occupied lands of Ukraine. If we clearly realize the aims of German policy in the present war on all the territory of Europe and especially in Ukraine, these methods will not appear so strange. It did not take long for the Germans to reveal their policy toward Ukraine. During the first months of their war with Moscow, the Germans laid the foundations of their policy, working toward the goal of the complete enslavement of the Ukrainian people and total control over Ukrainian territory. The rebirth of Ukrainian sovereignty, which the Ukrainian people achieved under the leadership of the members of the Ukrainian independence movement by means of the Act of 30 June 1941, was quickly suppressed, and on 1 August Western Ukraine was joined to the *Generalgouvernement*,[9] although there were no grounds for such an action. This decision was based solely on the desire of German political circles to weaken and shatter the Ukrainian national organism. It was a blow to Ukrainian aspirations for reunification. Just as the abolition, after 30 June 1941, of the short-lived sovereign Ukrainian state struck a blow to the idea of Ukrainian independence, so too the unification of Western Ukraine with the *Generalgouvernement* quashed the idea of reunifying Ukraine. The Germans believed that they would find it easier to digest Ukraine's enormous spaces if they cut them into little pieces! Other Ukrainian territories were turned into a *Reichskommissariat*,[10] in other words, a German colony. In order to satisfy the appetite of their Romanian ally, the Germans parcelled off Bukovyna, Bessarabia and the Odessa province (known as Transnistria)[11] and threw them to the Romanians to keep them happy, knowing full well that once the little lackey had played with these territories for a while, they would take them back for themselves. As we see, the Germans are generous in rewarding their "allies" with foreign territories. In this case, they are doing to the Romanians what they did to the Hungarians in 1939, when they gave Hungary Carpatho-Ukraine.[12] The Germans give with a light heart, for they know that what is theirs will not be lost. If only they can win the war!

The new occupying power has established new borders in Ukraine, dividing the land into small pieces. But the Germans do not have the power to create borders in the souls of the Ukrainian people, for a living idea cannot be torn asunder.

(3) Masters and Slaves

The Germans occupying Ukraine are assuming the role of masters, relegating the Ukrainian people to the position of slaves. Not only is this shown by events, which testify clearly to the Germans' behaviour, but also by a document of shame for the whole German nation—the instructions given to Germans setting out for occupied territories in the East. These instructions are entitled *12 Gebote für das Verhalten der Deutschen im Osten und die Behandlung der Russen* (Twelve commandments for the conduct of Germans in the East and for the treatment of Russians). The term "Russians" encompasses all peoples conquered by Moscow. Here are some excerpts from these "commandments." Commandment 4: " . . . make decisions quickly; it is better to make the wrong decision than not to decide . . . Do not explain or argue. The Russians want to see our people as leaders . . . Do not show your anger toward a German in the presence of Russians . . . Maintain your solidarity with regard to the Russians. Even an error made by a German must be defended in front of Russians." Commandment 5: "Stubbornness with regard to aims, the greatest flexibility with regard to methods . . . " Commandment 6: "Because the newly opened territories must be gained once and for all for Germany and Europe, your bearing plays a decisive role. You must be conscious that you are a representative of Greater Germany . . . For this reason, you must also carry out with dignity the most severe and ruthless acts if they are dictated by reasons of state . . . " Commandment 7: "Do not ask, does this benefit the peasantry? Ask only: is this useful to Germany? . . . Be self-assured and rigorous in relation to your subordinates . . . " Commandment 8: "Do not speak, but act. You will never outtalk a Russian or convince him by discussion. He is more articulate than you are, for he is a born dialectician and has inherited a 'philosophical nature.' In conversations and discussions, you will be the loser. You must act. Russians are impressed only by action, because they are 'feminine and sentimental.' 'Our land is large and beautiful, but there is no order in it. Come and rule over us.'[13] This was the main cry of the Russians at the inception of their state, when they invited the Norsemen to come, and it has continued throughout the periods of rule by Mongols, Poles, Lithuanians, tsars, Germans, right up to Lenin and Stalin. The Russians always want to be a mass ruled from above. This is how they will react to the arrival of the Germans, for it will again fulfill their wish: 'Come and rule over us.' For this reason, no Russian must ever sense that you are hesitant. Do not be soft and sentimental... Your will alone must be supreme... Keep your distance from the Russians; they are not Germans, but Slavs... From age-old experience, the Russian regards the German as a superior being... Guard against Russian intellectuals... they are incapable of doing anything, but have a particular facility and skill in influencing the spirits of Germans. This is true of Russian men, and even more of Russian women." Commandment 9: "Stay clear of the communists' scentings (*Kommunistenriecherei*)... We do not want to convert the Russians to National Socialism, but to *turn them into our tools*. You must win over the young people, assigning tasks to them, firmly holding them to these tasks and punishing them mercilessly whenever they sabotage them or fail to carry them out. Investigating past events and dealing with requests will take up time needed to carry out your German duties. You are not investigating judges or wailing walls (*Klagemauer*)." Commandment 11: "The Russian has been accustomed for long ages to bearing misery, hunger and foul weather. His stomach is elastic, requiring no sympathy on your part. Do not try to introduce the German standard of living as the norm or to alter the Russian way of life."

The limited format of this brochure does not allow us to pursue a more detailed analysis of these "brilliant commandments." But they speak for themselves. They stand as proof of the inferiority complex of the occupying German troops, as a revelation of their fear of confronting a foreign world. These commandments are no more than the instructions one would give a despised, dull-witted lackey to prepare him for the role of master in someone else's home. Stay away from foreigners, avoid discussions because you are unable to express any sort of view; instead, take the typically German approach: act, even if badly, but stubbornly; shout orders and punish mercilessly, regardless of whether the victim is innocent or guilty. And how, in light of all this, can the Germans assure themselves that we regard them as "superior beings"?

*(4) Material and Social Oppression—The Total
Exploitation of Ukraine*

German policy in Ukraine is a policy of exploitation of peasants, workers and intellectuals of a type unparallelled in the world. Recently, this exploitation has been most obvious on the agricultural front, where we have seen quotas, disproportionate to the ability of the villages to fulfill them, imposed in western and north-western Ukraine, where individual farm holdings still exist; the seizure and removal of all grain, even that intended for seed; the destruction of the cattle that still remained in Ukraine; total indifference to the needs of the village and the confiscation of goods and liquidation of farm properties.

The exploitation of the Ukrainian peasant has become very severe. Collective farms are not disbanded; here and there, they are turned into so-called "community farms," but the Ukrainian peasant does not see the difference between the one and the other, for, in fact, there is none. There is only a change in the sign that is hung up, from "collective farm" to "community farm."

Ukrainian workers are exploited even more. Many factories are not operating. The only ones in operation are those necessary for the war industry—for example, leather works. All the key positions are held by Germans, who control the destiny of every worker.

Beatings of workers in factories are an everyday occurrence. The Germans plunder everything and take it to Germany. The Ukrainian cannot make use of products made in Ukraine by Ukrainian workers, just as he cannot consume his own wheat, since the wheat goes to the Germans, while Ukrainians eat bread made from millet and chaff. Thus, Ukrainian workers barely manage to subsist; they exchange their last pieces of clothing in the villages for food and grain, which are confiscated by the Germans they meet on their way home. Given these circumstances, many workers in the Donbas[14] are abandoning their slave labour and fleeing from the towns to the villages, where, together with their families, they are somehow attempting to survive these times of plunderous invasion. For the Ukrainian worker, there are neither shoes nor clothing; meanwhile, the Germans are sending their plunder back to their families in Germany. There is no social security for workers. The Germans have taken cattle from the workers in the Donbas. Children as young as thirteen, fourteen and fifteen years of age are forced to do hard labour in factories.

As a result of the closure of schools, the dismantling of various institutions and allotment of senior positions to Germans, the Ukrainian intelligentsia is in a precarious position. Thus, highly qualified persons often take any kind of manual work in order simply to subsist and save themselves from deportation to Germany.

It is difficult to describe the material and social suffering into which the Ukrainian people have been plunged by foreign occupiers, first by the Bolsheviks during their twenty or so years of exploitation, and now by the Germans, with their unparallelled oppression and exploitation. We see here the policy of the pillager who takes all he can because he fears the not-too-distant storm of the Ukrainian people's wrath!

In conclusion, we shall cite a few more passages from the secret instructions given to the German police in Ukraine that were published in *Ideia i Chyn*, no. 2, under the title "Document of Shame." This document speaks of the following: that the Germans should not bother to combat tuberculosis and typhoid fever, closing down hospitals for the population and ceasing to train local doctors. Courts are to be German only. One passage worthy of particular attention discusses spreading amorality among the Ukrainian population.

(5) Ukrainian Cultural Achievements under the German Boot

Every war brings its share of upheavals and destruction. The Ukrainian people are conscious of this and accept, albeit painfully, news about the destruction of one or another cultural monument or museum treasure which has fallen victim to unavoidable events of the war. But their hearts grow angry and are fired with holy rage when they see how, before their very eyes, creations of the Ukrainian soul, its age-old achievements, are pillaged and destroyed for the sole purpose of turning Ukraine into a desert and a terrible ruin. And this is the intention of the occupying power. Almost all schools—secondary, professional, and institutions of higher learning—are being closed or dismantled. The teaching personnel is being deported to work in Germany. On the other hand, wherever a few Germans or *Volksdeutsche*[15] appear, German schools are immediately established for their use.

Religious life in Ukraine is under persecution. Conflicts between autocephalous and autonomist groups are provoked and a variety of sects are brought in, especially the Baptists, because they adhere to the principle of "no resistance to evil." Within the churches, Russians are given support and incited against Ukrainians. Finally, all church life in Ukraine is placed under the authority of German officials, so that the church can be totally enslaved and turned into a blind tool of the state, as it had been during the tsarist regime and, in the case of the Russian Orthodox Church, under Bolshevik rule. Here is the text of a characteristic letter received by all the bishops of the Orthodox Church in Ukraine from their general commissariats: "I designate you bishop in my general commissariat. You will no longer be subordinate to your religious superiors. You are subordinate only to me. Priests are also subordinate to me. The episcopate will be notified of any dismissals or appointments of priests.'' This letter from the general commissars is a unique document; nothing like it has been known in the history of the church in its nearly two thousand years of existence. But it would seem that all the current policies of Germany's barbaric imperialism are also unique in the history of mankind!

The suppression of the youth organization Sich[16] and of the ''Women's Service to Ukraine,''[17] the disbanding of cultural and educational associations, the Teachers' Associations, Prosvita[18] and others (in Kiev, Kharkiv and Poltava), the measures taken to place all national life in Western Ukraine under German control in the guise of the Ukrainian Central Commitee[19] and the ban on teaching Ukrainian history in schools have only one goal: to destroy Ukrainian cultural life completely, to pillage all objects of value (the pillage of museums in Kiev, Kharkiv and other cities), to erase all traces of age-old Ukrainian tradition and ancient culture; in a word, to turn the Ukrainian people into poor and ignorant slaves.

We must also add that nowhere, in all Ukraine, is there freedom of the Ukrainian press. True, a press intended for Ukrainians does exist, but it is a German press published in the Ukrainian language whose purpose is to indoctrinate the Ukrainians into accepting their role of slaves in the ''New'' Europe and to turn the Ukrainian people into a herd of meek lambs who will allow themselves to be led without protest—on the contrary, with joy—under the knife of the German butcher. The editors of these newspapers are common hirelings who were trained in their craft by the Bolsheviks while still in the Soviet Union, where they played the same role in relation to the Ukrainian people[20] (cf. *Nove Ukrainske Slovo*, Kiev, ed. Shtepa). Again we will conclude by citing the aforementioned ''Document of Shame'' of November 1942.

''Schools to be of only four grades. To be closed in 1943. The Prosvitas to be watched. Members of the Ukrainian independence movement are active there. Cultural and educational institutions, theatres and cinemas to be taken over. As few scientific institutes and laboratories as possible. Only that which is necessary for the army to be left for the moment.''

(6) *Foreigners in Ukraine Harnessed to the German Cart*

The Germans are too weak to fulfill their plans for the enslavement and extermination of the Ukrainian masses on their own. They are therefore skillfully exploiting the current political chaos in Europe, particularly in the occupied territories, and are harnessing to their imperialist wagon the ignorant, base and unscrupulous rabble of foreigners that has been brought into Ukraine and artificially propped up by the Germans in order to be used as a blind tool for their purposes. In this way, the Germans hope not only to weaken the resistance of the Ukrainian people, but also to weaken and destroy the common front of struggle of the peoples subjugated by Bolshevik and German imperialism. Thus we see, for example, that administrative posts are given to Poles in Western Ukraine and to Russians in Eastern Ukraine. Disregarding the situation in their own enslaved lands, these foreigners fraternize with the Germans and do all they can to harm and combat Ukrainians. Thus, they take on the role of hirelings of the foreign occupying power. The Germans gladly accept as collaborators informers, former communists, and agents of the Polish police and the NKVD,[21] all with one goal in mind: to destroy the Ukrainian independence movement and to enslave the Ukrainian people. Thus, for example, the network of informers that the Germans are trying to build up in Western Ukraine is comprised of Poles, whose task it is to denounce Ukrainians. In eastern regions, Russians are taking on the role of collaborators. They occupy the responsible administrative posts, pushing Ukrainians out of these positions, disregard the Ukrainian language and denounce nationally conscious Ukrainians. In the Crimea, they play the same role with regard to the Tatars.

Uzbek and Cossack legions are employed in terrorist campaigns against the peaceable population of north-western Ukraine; squads of Latvians and Estonians are hunting down people designated for deportation to Germany.

Particular services are rendered to the Germans by those aspirants to German nationality, the *Volksdeutsche*. They act not out of any desire to aid Germany, since they view Germany as foreign and hateful, but from an animal greed for gain, plunder and a comfortable existence. There is no end to the crimes of these newly converted Germans; thus, in Ukraine, the term *Volksdeutsche* has become synonymous with thief, swindler, plunderer and scoundrel.

(7) Cliques of Agents and the Attempt to Bring About a Moral Collapse of the Ukrainian Nation

A particularly painful aspect of the current situation is the attempt by the Germans, with the help of various cliques of agents who expect to gain the right of citizenship in Ukraine, to lull Ukrainian society into a state of moral defeatism. We state immediately that all these designs still remain in the realm of pleasant German dreams, for the Ukrainian people, sound in its collectivity, is well aware of their true worth. But we will discuss them because they are characteristic of our time and of the methods used to implement German policy on occupied Ukrainian territory. To incite one brother against another is characteristic of the German intruders. Their basic tactic is to court a few Ukrainians or a few cliques, while at the same time striking against the whole Ukrainian nation.

In Western Ukraine in particular, German dignitaries even resort to feigning friendship for the Ukrainian people whenever a difficult political situation requires it. Immediately afterward they deflect possible accusations of deviation from the general party line by declaring that this is only a "manoeuvre in the political game."

First, in accordance with the slogan "priests to be put into service," they draw Orthodox church dignitaries into their service; of these, some sigh for "beloved" Moscow and others jump to the Gestapo's commands. Here are some characteristic passages from a pastoral letter written in January 1943 by the Bishop of Volodymyr-Volynskyi which reveal the servile mentality that reigns in those circles: " . . . and when God heard our pleas and sent us Liberation (!) in the person of the Leader of the German People, we quickly forgot this, and instead . . . of working with our own hands we brought enmity into our home. . . ." But the Ukrainian people have not forgotten this "liberation," which is nothing more than a change of prison guards. As for the "knightly character" of the Germans, whole books could be written about it. Let His Grace remember the words of the Gospel, "Beware of the wolf in sheep's clothing," and "The thief comes only to break and to destroy." Let His Grace read the letter from the *Generalkommissar* that we quoted earlier and realize that the biblical thief has already come and is destroying everything, without sparing even the Orthodox church.

Similar appeals are made in letters from the so-called Ukrainian National Council, which tells us to "help the Germans to gain victory; then the whole world will be forced to recognize us"(!) One wonders who will force the world to do this—perhaps the "Ukrainian National Council"?[22]

Similar statements can be found in a letter from Mr. Kubijovyč's[23] Ukrainian Central Committee, which states: "The Ukrainian people have staked *everything* on the European card . . . " (cf. "Let us not heed evil rumours," 1 March 1943, published by the Ukrainian Central Comittee's Cultural Department). The Central Committee, with Mr. Kubijovyč at its head, has the right to stake *"everything"* on the *"European* card," but every conscious and faithful son of Ukraine stakes "everything," as well, on the *Ukrainian* card! Here lies the great difference.

Yet another means of oppression is the search for agents among the

Ukrainian people. In many regions, heads of villages are charged with the duty to provide lists of those who are politically suspect. The Gestapo is trying to employ the cultural and educational associations for this purpose, wherever they still exist.

To give another example: on 20 February 1943, at a gathering in Dnipropetrovsk, the head of the city administration uttered these exact words: " . . . the members of the Ukrainian independence movement are making co-operation with the Germans impossible. They are dangerous saboteurs and enemies and must be exterminated!"

And this extermination is being carried out, in many cases, by Ukrainians, agents of Moscow and Berlin. We must note in particular the activity of the so-called Ukrainian police,[24] into whose ranks the Germans have accepted many hirelings as well as common bandits. As a result, the police force now simply carries out German orders. There are in its ranks some decent people who are attempting to aid their countrymen, but they are few. Still, this system, which today has the agents dancing for joy, will not last forever! Let the hirelings remember that the cry of their brothers' blood resounds through the Ukrainian nation and that it will yet demand a terrible revenge!

(8) *To the Front for Foreign Imperialism!*

At the beginning of the war, the Germans did not allow foreigners to carry arms in battle for their imperialist goals. They wanted to prove to history that they alone had built the "New Europe," so that afterward they alone would rule it. But as the war dragged on, they took a leaf from the English book and decided that it would prove useful, and even necessary, to spill foreign blood for the sake of their own interests. As a result, they began to organize all kinds of "volunteer" units[25] made up of various national groups, including Ukrainians, for a variety of purposes. Just as foreign legions defended French interests in Africa, so these "volunteer" units are to protect the interests of the new "Germanic fatherland" on the territories of Europe.

In forming these units, the Germans are achieving yet another goal — physically weakening the Ukrainian nation by forcing Ukrainians to spill their blood in battle against partisans and various bands, as well as on the front.

Some Ukrainians are starved in prisoner-of-war camps; others are dying in the Red Army; still others in German and Bolshevik prisons, while the rest are recruited to military units so that they, too, may die for the sole purpose of enabling the Germans to pull the noose even more tightly around the neck of the Ukrainian people.

The methods used to recruit ''volunteers'' are well known. The ''volunteers'' are forced to report. If they do not, they are hunted down, assigned to German units, and all traces of them disappear. And an enormous variety of units is being created: the *Schutzmannschaft*, the *Werkschutz*, the militia, the Ukrainian People's Army, the ''Liberation Army,'' the *SS*—there is no end to them. These groups are all small, not linked to one another, commanded by German officers and non-commissioned officers and organizationally subordinate to the police authorities (Himmler).

On all the territory of Ukraine, this operation has been particularly notable for the recruitment of ''volunteers'' to the so-called *Schutzmannschaft* battalions in various centres—Kobryn, Dorohychyn, Kostopil, Ovruch, Kremianets, Proskuriv, Lutsk, Kovno, Mariupil, Stalino. After Kharkiv was taken, the so-called ''Ukrainian Liberation Committee'' was established there to organize the ''Ukrainian Liberation Army,'' based on the example of the Russians who, under the leadership of General Vlasov,[26] have been organizing Russian volunteers for some time. Some units of ''volunteers'' have already been dispatched to the front, but usually they are sent into battle against partisans. Recently many have been fleeing because of poor food, lack of clothing, the behaviour of the German authorities toward them and, above all, the lack of an idea worth dying for.

In May, the announcement concerning recruitment to the *SS Division Galizien* caused a great stir in Western Ukraine. The recruitment of these ''volunteers'' is being carried out in such a way that whoever does not want to join the army is taken away to work.

And these are the *neue Verbündete*—the new allies, about whom *Reich*, the leading organ of the German minister of propaganda, Goebbels,[27] has written so much.

(9) *Deportation for Work in Germany*

The German war machine has to keep operating. Meanwhile, the god of war is devouring thousands and millions of victims; as a result enormous gaps are opening up in the machine and new people are needed to fill them. What could be easier than to throw millions of people from the occupied territories of Europe into these gaps? And so they go from every land to the ''heart'' of Europe in order to save German agriculture and the German war industry. This is convenient for the Germans: first of all, it frees their own labour force to go to the front; second, it clears the occupied lands of undesirable youths who might, under the right circumstances, become a threat; and third, Germany gains a supply of cheap labour, people who can be worked for all they can give and whose stomachs are very "tractable," requiring little food. These workers from the East can be driven and deceived and their know-how and strength exploited; one need not be concerned about their clothing, salaries or social security.

In any case, these Slavs breed too quickly; it would be handy to reduce their numbers by exterminating some at the front, others in prisoner-of-war camps, and still others in camps for workers from the East.

This is the thinking that lies behind the recruitment of workers to Germany. At first people even volunteered for this work, particularly those who had lost all their possessions in regions that had been devasted by the war. They were lured by the promise of mountains of gold, or were simply curious to see the Germany about which they had heard so much!

But within a short time, the Ukrainian masses began to grow alarmed at the frightening warnings sent to Ukraine by relatives and friends. "We were deceived" is the phrase repeated in all letters from Germany. "We are placed in camps behind barbed wire and treated worse than prisoners of war." "We are forced to sew badges on our chests, with "East" (*Ost*) written on them; this badge means that you are not a person but a barbarian, a bandit." "The boss beats you and there is no one to complain to." "Here they do not recognize that we are Ukrainians; there are only Russians. But they recognize that there is a rich and fertile Ukrainian land that can be robbed without any concern that the people are dying." "But the time will come when they will not call us *Sowjetrussisch* (Soviet Russian). Then we and all Ukrainians will start living a better life." These are the thoughts that flow from the angry heart of the Ukrainian worker, thoughts which accurately portray the new environment in which he finds himself. Because of these conditions, many Ukrainian workers and peasants prefer to suffer the miseries of war as long as they can remain with their brothers on their native Ukrainian soil. They do not volunteer for work. But this brings on German repression. People are hunted down—anyone, anywhere. Whole families, including small children and young girls, are taken away. People are grabbed in markets, squares, crossroads, cinemas, theatres, at their places of work, even in private homes. Every day one sees these people, driven on by the Germans, enclosed in cattle wagons, behind bars, so that they cannot even see the world, and suffering from cold and hunger. We are reminded of past ages, when attacking Mongols, Tatars and Turks took people into captivity. Many Cossack epics have recounted these events. But will a singer be found to tell of this new German captivity, which forces Ukraine to give her children in sacrifice?

A few facts: in the Krynychansky district, two thousand workers have been designated for deportation to Germany. Lists of people are prepared, then those who have been chosen are hunted down. If someone runs away, his whole family is punished. For help in tracking people down, the Germans use Latvians and Estonians.

On 1 January, about three thousand people were taken from Voroshylovhrad. On 1 January 1943, a hunt was organized in cinemas and again about three hundred people were taken. The village of Bila, near Mariupil, was ordered to provide one hundred workers. No one presented himself. On 7 February of this year, the recruiting commission fled because the front was drawing nearer. Since the containment of the front, the forced recruitment and capture of workers has continued throughout the Mariupil region. In the villages of Bolshivets and Iunashkiv, a hunt was organized on the feast of the Epiphany during the blessing of the water.

We note that this seizing of people in trains, stations, and so on has been taking place all over Ukraine throughout the autumn and winter up to the present. In conjunction with this, a propaganda campaign for voluntary enlistment is being run by German hirelings in Western Ukraine.

The Germans are in a hurry to recruit workers, and are using a variety of methods: pleas, deceit, threats and coercion. As the old saying goes, a drowning man will clutch at a straw!

(10) *The Deportation of Ukrainians from their Ancestral Lands*

In conversations with Germans, one hears various views about what they intend to do with the Ukrainian population on Ukrainian ethnic territory after they win the war. Some say that Germany's ethnic boundary will be moved to the Zbruch;[28] others, to the Dnieper; still others, that Ukrainians, along with all other non-Germanic peoples, will be deported from Europe. We regard all these statements as the ravings of megalomaniacs and dismiss them totally, without discussion. The Germans can carry out their crazy plans only if the following preconditions are met: first, they must win the war and second—perhaps even more important—they must break the resistance of the subject peoples and turn them into flocks of sheep that will passively and mindlessly allow themselves to be led to the slaughter.

Although these preconditions have not yet been met, we shall speak of the German plans, for they have already begun to deport native populations from other foreign territories—Alsace, Lorraine, the Czech provinces and Poland—and are beginning to carry out experiments on

Ukrainian ethnic territory. For example, in some western Ukrainian provinces, lists have been drawn up of farm properties with detailed descriptions of the state of the buildings, the amount of land in each holding, the number of family members living there, the length of time people have lived on a given farm, and the like. People are frightened and are beginning to speculate that preparations are being made to deport Ukrainians in order to make room for Germans. Certain events that have taken place in Ukraine appear to support such speculation. We shall disregard earlier instances of deportation of Ukrainians (in the Lublin and Brest regions), but will cite instead a few more recent cases.

From three villages* in Stanyslaviv county, one hundred two persons were deported in a single month. In north-western Ukraine, on 6 November 1942, the following villages were deported: Sylno, Horodyshche (two hundred forty-two families), Holyshka Ruda.†

Deportations are taking place in the Zhytomyr district and elsewhere. Those deported are being settled on collective farms in the southern part of the Soloniany district (Pismycheve, Bezborotko, Kotliarivka, Oleksandropil and others). Thirty, forty or even one hundred families have been thrown into each village.

The method of deportation is as follows: the Germans arrive, inspect the houses and farms and note the best-kept ones. They promise to assign better lands. . . . The next day, the people are ordered to leave their farms immediately and to travel in a certain direction. They are not allowed to take anything with them; all their belongings are left behind for some German intruder.

We mention these facts about deportation in order to demonstrate the care and ingenuity of the Germans in designing all kinds of outlandish methods for implementing their plans.

(11) *The Teutonic Terror. Arrests, Shootings, Gallows. The Physical Extermination of Ukrainians*

Ancient Rome was shaken when it encountered the savage terror of the Teutons, the ancestors of today's invader of Ukraine. Even today, Ukrainian children still chant, "the Avars, the Avars, hide well,"[29] recalling in their game the attacks on Ukrainian settlements by the

---

*In the original text: provinces.

†The meaning of this sentence is not clear; something was omitted from the original text.

dreadful hordes of Avars. In the past, Ukrainians also endured the attacks of other hordes which turned the southern region of Ukraine into
a desert and forced the inhabitants to flee to the forests in order to save
their lives. Although the Ukrainian people have not yet recovered from
the wounds inflicted upon them by Moscow; although their memories
still retain vividly the horror, cruelty and ferocious terror of the Bolsheviks, the famine in Ukraine and the activities of the GPU and the
NKVD, under the present occupation they are undergoing a period of
unparallelled terror set into motion by the Germans, who want to exterminate Ukrainians by means of arrests, shootings and the gallows,
while heartily shaking the hand of Bolshevik Moscow.

*The two imperialists have joined forces in order to eradicate the
Ukrainian people from the face of the earth.* For twenty years the
hated red star bathed in a sea of Ukrainian blood, and now the German
swastika gnaws and lacerates the body of the Ukrainian people, tearing
it to pieces. It is hardly possible to write about these things; before the
fresh graves that have covered Ukraine in the recent years of German
occupation, one can only bow one's head, for these are the graves of
Ukraine's finest sons, who, by the sacrifice of their lives, have given
witness to the undying idea of an independent, united Ukrainian state.

*Under these circumstances, one can speak only of a merciless struggle
against the bloodthirsty invader to avenge the blood of our brothers!*

We shall mention here a series of events that have occurred in the most
recent period of the Ukrainian people's struggle against the plundering
German assailant.

On 27 February 1943, an order was proclaimed in Dnipropetrovsk
concerning the surrender of arms. Searches of homes were carried out.
On 1–2 March, 50 people were hanged at markets, squares and crossroads. The hangings were planned in advance as a means of frightening
the population. Since they had found no arms, the Germans decided to
hang some prisoners. The identity of the victims was evident, since
they had been starved and were ragged and covered with lice. Before
they were hanged, the prisoners' hands and feet were bound and their
faces covered. Signs were attached to their feet with the following in-
scription in Ukrainian and German: "I did not surrender my arms and
resisted arrest." Many Germans, among them women, come to look at
the hanged people and take photographs of them.

When retreating to territories conquered earlier, the Germans generally
destroy, pillage and burn whole villages. They shoot not only men, but
also women and young children. Here is one of countless similar occurrences: in the town of Znamenivka, Novomoskovsk district, the Germans threw grenades into cellars where people had hidden during a
battle. And here is yet another: a German arrives, shoots a man and,

with a knife, slits the man's wife's throat and disfigures his daughter's face. About two hundred people are murdered. Not far from Novomoskovsk, people hid from gunfire in the cellars of the Cossack monastery on the Samara.[30] The *SS* arrived, threw grenades at the people, then disposed of those who were still alive.

In western Ukraine, the wave of arrests began in November and December 1942 and continues in various places to the present day.

A particular campaign of terror is being waged in north-western Ukraine. Here are some events of the first months of 1943; we present here hard objective facts free of any tendentious colouring. The guard unit composed of Galicians was arrested. Ukrainian officials were also arrested: in Kostopil[31]—one hundred twenty persons, the whole city administration, including the bailiff; in Horokhiv[32]—thirty; in Berestia[33]—ten. Some of these people were shot, others deported as *Ostarbeiter*. At the beginning of March, forty people were shot in Kremianets,[34] among them the fifty-two-year-old Dr. Roshchynsky and his wife; Cherkavsky, thirty-nine; Hariachy, fifty-three; and a woman, Lebedivska, sixty. The prisoners are ordered to strip; they are then bound and shot.

On 7 March 1943, one hundred eighty people were arrested in Rivne.[35] Not wishing to take part in terrorist actions against the population, two hundred Cossacks and forty militiamen fled to join the pro-independence partisans. On 12–13 March 1943, policemen were brought in from surrounding territories to Rivne, where they were disarmed and placed in a camp. Three hundred of them fled into the forest to join the Ukrainian partisans; the rest were transported to Germany.

To end this far from complete survey of the German terror, we would like to draw attention to the methods used by the Germans to achieve their political aims. For example, the shooting of entire families, including young children, is becoming the basis of German rule. This shooting is done not only by policemen, but by high German dignitaries. And this is happening at a time when Stalin is threatening to exterminate all Western Ukrainians for collaborating with the Germans; when in Kovel an anti-Bolshevik demonstration by ten to twenty thousand Ukrainians is taking place; when Bolsheviks returning to Ukrainian territories are exterminating all nationally conscious Ukrainians and shooting on the spot all those who worked in the occupying administration; at a time when the Ukrainian masses neither desire a return of the Bolsheviks nor support German actions. Nationally conscious Ukrainians fear for their lives, as the spectre of the Bolshevik-German terror looms over them. *The Germans and the Bolsheviks have become friends with regard to one goal: the extermination of the Ukrainian people!* We are witnessing the concrete realization of the words of one

German dignitary who, at the news that Erich Koch had been appointed *Reichskommissar* of Ukraine, said openly, "Koch will rule Ukraine with the aid of the gallows."

But as the terror increases, the anger of the Ukrainian people against the German and Russian-Bolshevik imperialists is also growing. At the appropriate moment, this anger will transform itself into revenge!

VII. The Subject Peoples of the East

Germany's policy toward the subject peoples of the East has certain features in common with her policy on the occupied territories of Ukraine. It is possible that in the former case German policy is not yet as clear-cut in Ukraine, for at present these lands are still beyond the sphere of German influence and the Germans realize that it will be easier to deal with these peoples after they have completed their deliberate destruction of Ukraine, the most dangerous opponent of their imperialist plans. Nevertheless, the fate of Ukraine under German occupation should stand as a stern warning to all the subject peoples of the East. These peoples should become aware that Germany is bringing the same sort of "liberation" to them as she has brought to Ukraine. Thus, the peoples of the East are faced with two options: either to renounce their aspirations for independence and thereby fall victim to one of the two warring imperialist powers or to join the struggle against both forms of imperialism — Moscow's and Berlin's. There is no third option. Promises made by either of the imperialist cliques are nothing more than cunning manoeuvres designed to make the subject peoples serve the interests of Moscow or Berlin in the imperialist war and neutralize their independent forces. The Germans promised many of these peoples that they would renew or, more precisely, establish national states for them, just as they had promised the Ukrainians before the war with the Bolsheviks. But we know that while they were promising the Georgians that they would recognize an independent Georgian state within Georgia's ethnic boundaries and were organizing the Georgian legion to fight the Bolsheviks, the Ministry of the East was also organizing the so-called *Einsatzstab K* (Caucasus) department, which was preparing a complete takeover of all civilian rule in the Caucasus region. Here, a new *Reichskommissariat* patterned on Ukraine or, rather, on Latvia, Lithuania and Estonia was to be established.[36] These plans had been worked out in detail, even down to the designation of the people — Germans, of course — who were to begin their work in the Caucasus immediately after the occupation of the area by German troops. There was never the slightest intention of establishing even a fictional form of independent statehood.

A similar fate befell the Cossack state, known as *Kozakiia*,[37] which the Don Cossacks wanted to create. The Germans avoided making any clear commitment and would not allow dissemination of propaganda that specified any concrete goal. They organized the Don Cossacks to some extent in order to use them either at the front or in battle against partisans.[38] These examples demonstrate that national hopes for political support from the Germans for the establishment of sovereign states will remain forever in the sphere of illusion!

It is true that the Germans have organized a number of military or paramilitary units of Latvians, Estonians, Lithuanians, Belorussians, Georgians, Don Cossacks, Tatars, Kuban Cossacks, Uzbeks and others. Their intention, however, is not to create nuclei of national armies, but rather to exploit these military units for their own needs and purposes. Most important, the Germans are attempting to use these units to shatter the common front of struggle for free national states. And they do this skilfully; they send these units to foreign territories and use them to oppress and persecute other subject peoples. In this way, they sow the seeds of discord and suspicion, causing each subject people to distrust the others, and thereby weakening the front of struggle against the hated foreign imperialists. In Ukraine, for example, this situation already exists; foreign units are being used to massacre Ukrainians and to wage campaigns of terror against the population. Nevertheless, we know that the idea of common struggle against the common threat of enemy imperialism will be victorious; we even have proof of this. We know that in certain cases Cossack units have refused to take part in the campaign of terror. Kuban and Don Cossacks will yet have an opportunity to sacrifice their lives, not for the sake of foreign imperialist interests, but for the cause of restructuring Eastern Europe on the basis of independent national states!

Those peoples of subject Eastern Europe which, in spite of all, have staked everything on the German card would be wise to take warning from the German policy toward the Crimean Tatars. The Crimea is about 31 per cent Tatar; in the southern zone, Tatars form the majority. The cities, as is usual in lands formerly ruled by Moscow, are Russified. The Tatars tied their hopes to the Germans, who created a legion and promised them national and political freedom, even independence. But in reality this policy has led to a situation completely different from that which the Tatars desired. All power is in the hands of the German administrative command and the Crimea is divided into forty-seven administrative districts, also controlled by the Germans. The character of the administration clearly indicates what the Germans have in mind: the economic exploitation of the country. All agriculture, industry and trade have passed into German hands, while any initiative on the part of the local population is discouraged. The Germans have permitted the establishment of national committees—Russian, Tatar, Ukrainian and Armenian—but these committees are deprived of any influence. In addition, the Germans encourage and inflame any ill-feeling that exists among the national groups. The Tatars are incited against the Russians: at the same time, the Russians are granted important concessions and are set against the Ukrainians. Everything is done in accordance with a single guiding principle: crush the East, making use of the Eastern peoples themselves in the process, and thereby strengthen the position of German imperialism.

But the Tatar people is now experiencing yet another national tragedy: while one segment of Tatar youth is dying in the legion in battle against partisans, Tatar activists are being arrested and are filling up German prisons.

Our short description of current events and the situation created by the war can lead the subject peoples of the East to only one conclusion: *the only salvation lies in a common front of struggle against the two warring forms of imperialism—Russian and German—for the establishment of independent national states in the East.*

The Ukrainian people call on the subject peoples to join in this struggle!

Conclusions

It would appear that there is little to add to our reflections. The facts we have presented clearly illustrate the situation that now exists on all the occupied territories of Europe and, in particular, on the Ukrainian front. Ideologically and by their methods of operation on occupied territories, the Germans are throwing off their guise of defenders of a "new" order and culture and a "New" Europe. German National Socialism is Berlin's version of Bolshevism; it is a form of imperialism that is waging war against all of humanity's progressive ideas in order to attain the irrevocable ascendancy of the German race. And for this reason, all the youthful forces of freedom-loving peoples must mobilize in the name of liberty for all the nations of Europe and for all individuals, to build out of the ruins left by the present imperialist war a truly new and just order in a reborn Europe, free from all forms of imperialism!

In a Europe of free, independent, national states!

Source: Reprint of a brochure published by the editors of *Ideia i Chyn*, 1943. 48 pp. Original: Archive of the Foreign Representation of the Supreme Ukrainian Liberation Council. Photocopy: Archive, *Litopys UPA*. Partial text.

NOTES

1. Otto von Bismarck (1815–98): Prussian statesman who brought about the unification of Germany.
2. Napoleon I (1769–1821): Emperor of the French. In fact, Napoleon had several plans regarding Ukrainian territory, among them the creation of two separate states, one in Chernihiv and Poltava and one in the south to be called "Napoleonida."
3. The Molotov–Ribbentrop Pact.
4. Teutonic Knights or Teutonic Order: German military religious order founded (1190–91) during the Third Crusade. In 1226, the order undertook a crusade against the Prussians, whom they virtually exterminated and replaced with Germans.
5. Hanseatic League or Hanse towns: mercantile league of medieval German towns that controlled the Slavic lands of the Baltic.
6. In the pagan German religion, Woden was the supreme god.
7. *SS (Schutzstaffel)*: Nazi elite units and police, originally Hitler's bodyguard.
8. *Ideia i Chyn* (Idea and Action): official organ of the OUN, Bandera faction.
9. *Generalgouvernement*: central part of Poland (with Cracow as capital) occupied by Germany but not incorporated into the Reich. Established by Hitler's declaration of 10 December 1939. The Ukrainian territories of Lemkivshchyna, Kholmshchyna, and part of Posiannia were incorporated into the *Generalgouvernement* from the very beginning; Galicia was incorporated on 1 August 1941.
10. The *Reichskommissariat Ukraine* included Polissia, Volhynia, Right-Bank Ukraine, part of Poltava province and, from September 1942, the Zaporizhzhia province and some territory on the Sea of Azov. The rest of Left-Bank Ukraine remained under German military administration.
11. Transnistria included Bessarabia, Bukovyna, and the part of Right-Bank Ukraine between the Dniester and the Boh rivers. Odessa was its capital.
12. Carpatho-Ukraine was the name of the autonomous Ukrainian state within Czechoslovakia (1938–9) and of the independent republic from 15 March 1939 until its forcible incorporation into Hungary in the same month.
13. Reference is to the alleged invitation issued by Rus' to the Varangians.

14. The Donets Basin, abbreviated as Donbas, is one of the main coal-producing and industrial areas of Ukraine.
15. *Volksdeutsche*: ethnic or racial German.
16. Sich: Ukrainian gymnastic association.
17. A women's organization established in Lviv in 1941 with the aim of helping political prisoners, prisoners of war and children in regions suffering from famine. The Germans ordered the liquidation of this organization.
18. Prosvita: Society for Enlightenment.
19. A co-ordinating agency first organized in Cracow in November 1939 and definitively constituted on 15 April 1940 at the first congress of representatives. Professor Volodymyr Kubijovyč was chosen as its head. The Ukrainian Central Committee functioned only in the *Generalgouvernement*.
20. After the arrest and execution of the editors Ivan Rohach, Olena Teliha and Ivan Irliavsky in February 1942, the strongly nationalist Kiev daily *Ukrainske Slovo* (Ukrainian Word) was renamed *Nove Ukrainske Slovo* (New Ukrainian Word) and turned into a pro-German organ under the editorship of Konstantyn Shtepa, a Russophile.
21. The People's Commissariat of Internal Affairs.
22. Reference is probably to the Ukrainian National Rada (Council) organized at Rivne (Volhynia) in July 1941.
23. Volodymyr Kubijovyč (1900–85): a well-known geographer. Professor at the University of Cracow and the Ukrainian Free University. Editor-in-chief of *Ukraine: A Concise Encyclopaedia* and *Encyclopedia of Ukraine*. During the Second World War he headed the Ukrainian Central Committee in the *Generalgouvernement*.
24. A Ukrainian auxiliary police subordinate to the German police was established in the *Generalgouvernement* and in the *Reichskommissariat*.
25. The "volunteer units" were known by different names, such as *Hilfswillige* or *Hiwis*, *Schutzmannschaften*, and *Werkschutz*; their function was to guard industrial and communication centres. Among the larger units were the Sumy Division, 16 mobile units of the German Sixth Army, the *Division Galizien* of the *Waffen SS*, and the Vlasov Russian Liberation Army.
26. Andrei Vlasov (1900–46): Soviet Russian general captured by the Germans in 1942. Became head of the Committee for the Liberation of the Peoples of Russia and Commander-in-Chief of the Russian Liberation Army, both organized under German auspices. After the capitulation of Germany, he was forcibly returned to the Soviet Union, where he was executed.
27. Joseph P. Goebbels (1897–1945): Nazi propaganda minister (1933–45).
28. From 1772 to 1917, the Zbruch River served as the border between the

Austrian and Russian empires and, from 1921 to 1939, between Poland and the USSR.

29. Avars: Turkic nomadic tribe that invaded the territory of Ukraine in the middle of the sixth century A.D.

30. Samara River: left tributary of the Dnieper.

31. Kostopil: town in northern Volhynia.

32. Horokhiv: town in Volhynia.

33. Berestia: town in Volhynia.

34. Kremianets: one of the oldest Ukrainian towns in Volhynia.

35. Rivne: city in central Volhynia.

36. Latvia, Lithuania and Estonia were incorporated into the *Reichskommissariat Ostland*.

37. Kozakiia: federal state of the Cossacks, incorporating Don and Kuban Cossack lands and northern approaches to the Caucasus. The idea of Kozakiia arose in 1920.

38. During the Second World War, Cossack troops fought the Soviets either in German units or as part of the Russian Liberation Army. The British and American authorities forcibly repatriated them to the USSR, where most of them perished.

UKRAINE AND POLAND

Ia.V. Borovych

Polish-Ukrainian relations have existed almost as long as the history of the Ukrainian and Polish peoples. From the most distant past to the present day, these relations have been extremely complex and suffused with tragedy. They have never been able to proceed in an "ideal" fashion, for the simple reason that in antiquity, Ukraine and Poland were two separate *neighbouring* states and, in recent times, two *neighbouring* nations.

Conflicts between neighbouring states or nations have been common throughout the entire world. Although the reasons for these conflicts have not always been the same, they have always existed. If we consider border disputes between such neighbouring states as Germany and France, or France and England, or Spain and England, we will recognize that the external Polish-Ukrainian territorial, religious and political conflicts have not been unique in human history. These conflicts have existed in the past, exist at present and will continue to do so in the future. And no treaty, no neighbourly peace accord can bring them to an end at a single stroke.

Nevertheless, under the right circumstances and with the good will of both neighbours, these conflicts could, for a certain time, be moderated, suspended, or at least diminished. In order to achieve such harmony, a great deal of culture, political wisdom and mutual respect on the part of both neighbours are required. Unfortunately, these qualities have not been very evident in Polish-Ukrainian relations, either in the past or in the modern era. And they have been least evident—in fact, hardly perceptible at all—among the Poles.

In order to avoid delving too deeply into the recesses of history, we will restrict ourselves to noting, for the sake of example, a few dates from the past. In 1349, a critical year in the history of western Ukraine, Polish policy with regard to Galicia was born. So classically was this policy laid down at the time that for centuries it remained unchanged in principle. Having conquered Galicia, King Casimir[1] immediately set out to destroy the governing class in Ukrainian society, the nobility. He quickly destroyed it, not only by means of fire and sword, but also through his policy of depriving the nobles of rights and privileges. Full rights were reserved for the Polish Catholic aristocracy; it was granted access to offices, privileges and wealth seized from the Orthodox nobility. Those Ukrainian noblemen who were not immediately exterminated salvaged their livelihood by converting to Catholicism and becoming Polonized; thus, at the price of apostasy, they paved their way to offices, influence, honours and a comfortable existence on their ancestral lands. But did this mean that Galicia became Polish? No! However, the methods employed to bring about political "assimilation" in the fourteenth century retained their currency in the twentieth century. Let us recall the coercive methods used to draw large numbers of Ukrainians, who were dependent upon the Polish state apparatus for their livelihood, first to the Roman Catholic faith and then to the Polish nation during the time of the Austrian Empire. Even greater coercive measures were exercised during the period of the restored Polish state, from 1920 to 1939. Suprisingly, even after this most recent implementation of the Polish policy of assimilation and denationalization, the Ukrainian character of Galicia and, to an even greater extent, of Volhynia remained unchanged. Thus, the effects of Polish policies in both the fourteenth and twentieth centuries yielded the same results with regard to the general character of the region; they were not the same, however, with regard to the atmosphere surrounding Ukrainian-Polish relations, which became saturated with mutual distrust, prejudice and hostility.

Let us examine a second historical date, 1569, which brought the famous Union of Lublin.[2] What was the nature of this union? According to the Poles, it was based on the principle of a federation of "equals with equals." But in fact it marked the end of any equality for Ukrainians, because all Ukrainian lands were annexed directly to the Polish crown. Many Ukrainian principalities were abolished, princes were replaced by provincial administrators, and the princely and noble lands were distributed to the insatiable Polish aristocracy. Lithuania was ostensibly granted autonomy, along with a part of Belorussia which was included in Lithuania, but this autonomy did not last long. The result of this "union" was that Poland was unable to cope with the uprisings of Lithuanian and Ukrainian princes and became ever less stable internally, particularly after the institution of the election of Polish kings. With every new election came an unhealthy extension and consolidation of the privileges of the magnates and aristocrats, extorted before each election from the aspirant to the throne.

In 1596 Poland tried to rescue herself with yet another "union," a church union concluded in Brest.[3] This new "union" brought even greater internal disorder and, finally, the total disintegration of the Polish state, giving Ukrainians a powerful Cossack state.[4]

The treaties which Poland concluded with the Cossacks were never honoured. The prime reason for this was the belief, current among Polish aristocrats and magnates, that breaking treaties with the Cossacks was morally justified because they were unworthy partners, inferior to the Polish aristocracy. In the view of the Poles, treaties were to be made and honoured only when the other partner was in every respect equal to themselves. Thus, the aristocracy could conclude treaties with its own kings (*pacta conventa*) or with foreign rulers, but not with "peasants" such as the Cossacks. In time, Cossack-Polish relations degenerated into a state of such terrible strain and such tragic frenzy of hatred that the Polish magnate Czarnecki[5] did not hesitate to desecrate the grave of Bohdan Khmelnytsky and to destroy his mortal remains. Similarly, Hetman Ivan Vyhovsky,[6] author of the Treaty of Hadiach[7] with Poland, who broke with Moscow and smashed its army at Konotop,[8] received no better thanks from the Poles for his actions than to be tortured to death by the Polish military. Why did this happen? Simply because the Polish magnates and aristocrats of that era regarded every influential Ukrainian political activist, particularly one with whom the Poles were compelled to come to terms, as an ordinary "rebel" who was to be tolerated only as long as he was powerful and as long as they feared him.

Despite the fact that the Union of Lublin was based on the motto "equals with equals" (that is, magnates with magnates), the Poles did not honour the terms of the Union, particularly with regard to the Ukrainians. Ukrainian magnates and princes were considered by the Poles to be less worthy than themselves because they were Orthodox. Thus, the Polish aristocracy always found "moral" justification for its breaches of faith with the Ukrainians. And because of this Polish faithlessness, an enormous hatred developed over the centuries between the two nations. After the Union of Brest, the Uniate campaign which the Poles waged with fire and sword among the Ukrainian population caused this hatred to assume the dimensions of an apocalyptic monstrosity.

In spite of this, there were always Ukrainians who strove for political co-operation with the Poles. They regarded this as essential in view of the Russian threat to Ukrainian identity. Yet not once did any of these venturesome Ukrainians find, in Polish politicians, a reliable and faithful contracting party. All their initiatives ended in disappointment and bitter experiences as a result of Polish faithlessness, double-dealing and ruthlessness.

*   *   *

At critical moments in Polish history, when the whole structure of the Polish state was tottering, Polish politicians became great champions of "freedom" for Ukrainians because they hoped to win them over by means of such slogans as "equals with equals" and "for your freedom and ours" to a common struggle for the salvation of Poland. When Poland ceased to exist as a state, they attempted to incite Ukrainians to insurrections and revolutions by means of similar slogans.

But as soon as the situation turned in their favour, they mercilessly oppressed the Ukrainians, bound by no feelings of obligation toward them. Only those Ukrainians who became Polish were considered reliable and acceptable. There was among the Poles a certain breed of citizens who called themselves *gente Rutheni, natione Poloni*; they were great Polish patriots who admitted their Ukrainian origins only at such times as it was necessary to show the world that Ukrainians supported the Poles and their demands.

After the total collapse of Poland, when the Austrian constitution was undergoing its birth pangs, such eminent renegades as Count Dzieduszycki,[9] Prince Sapiha[10] and others represented themselves as "Ruthenians" at the Slavic Congress in Prague[11] in order to undermine the influence and significance of the true Ukrainian delegation at the congress.

After the adoption of the Austrian constitution, all attempts to patch up Polish-Ukrainian relations in Galicia proved fruitless. Again, Polish faithlessness and dishonesty were to blame. The initiatives of Lavrivsky[12] and Sembratovych,[13] as well as Romanchuk's[14] so-called new era in Polish-Ukrainian politics, yielded no positive results. Even the persistent and determined efforts of Oleksander Barvinsky[15] somehow to improve the Ukrainian-Polish *modus vivendi* within the Austrian Empire ended in such total failure that, in his later years, Barvinsky was the most implacable opponent of any kind of negotiation with the Poles on political matters. How can one explain this failure? The reasons remained unchanged since the time of the Unions of Lublin and Brest, since the days of Zboriv,[16] Bila Tserkva[17] and Hadiach. In Austria, Poles enjoyed greater influence than Ukrainians; for this reason, they attempted to make use of Ukrainians for their own purposes by making temporary agreements. They made no lasting pacts with Ukrainians, for they believed, just as they had for hundreds of years, that Ukrainians were not worthy partners. Polish policy was shaped by the legacy of their chronic megalomania, the Polish aristocratic tradition of breach of faith, the ancient Polish principle, "not what is honourable, but what is useful" and the Jesuit "arch-Catholic" political and religious doctrine that "the end justifies the means." The new Polish political elite, that is, the modern Polish democrats, not only failed to rid themselves of the political flaws of the past but, on the contrary, perfected them, adapting them to a new era and the new spirit of the age.

The Polish state of 1919–39 "made agreements" with Ukrainians in the same way as the aristocrats and, under Austrian rule, the Polish-Austrian ruling class had done in the past. The most notable attempt to improve relations between Poles and Ukrainians in the new Poland was the so-called normalization of Polish-Ukrainian relations, which was begun in the spring of 1935.[18] Within two years, Poland had so completely returned to her normal routine with regard to the points contained in the normalization policy that nothing remained of them. The normalization was carried out by Ukrainians, along with the Warsaw government. Even in the first year of the policy, Poles in Eastern Galicia, particularly in Lviv, began to undermine it; in the third year, what remained of it was given the death blow by the all-powerful Polish generals and colonels, representatives of the Polish army, which was rife with political intrigue.

If one brings to mind only the most important events in the history of Polish dealings with Ukrainians during the twenty-year life of the so-called reborn Poland, then one will reach the same conclusions about the nature of Polish policy as were drawn before the existence of the new Poland by such Ukrainian historians and writers as the great Shevchenko in "Haidamaky"[19] and Gogol in *Taras Bulba*.[20] But these authors based their conclusions on the history of the old, aristocratic Poland. It is in the new Poland that we must search for the basis of our own political conclusions.

Poland became as large as she had been in the past thanks to an exceptional political conjuncture at Versailles and to the weakness of the Bolshevik government in Russia. In the east she had a neighbour—the U.S.S.R.—whose potential was enormous and which was, for that reason, threatening to Poland. In the west, Germany was disarmed, it is true, but also to be feared because of her potential. What political conclusions did Poland draw from her dangerous position? None at all!

Under the leadership of the so-called National Democrats (essentially a Jesuit-trained, aristocratic, chauvinistic and imperialist Polish party which preached the extermination of the Ukrainian people), she oriented herself toward France, which was satiated with victory and thus demoralized. Moreover, Poland had not freed herself from the phantom of her former orientation on Russia—now Bolshevik Russia. Internally, she pursued a sweeping policy of denationalization of the non-Polish peoples, applying it by means of colonization, expropriation, terror and forced assimilation. Piłsudski's coup of 1926 seemed, at first glance, to put an end to the National Democrats' internal and external policies,[21] but only for a short time. In terms of external policy, the new government ostensibly began to change direction. With regard to internal policy, however, there was no other change than that of the individuals holding responsible positions; the political climate in relation to non-Poles, particularly Ukrainians, remained essentially the same. There were even some changes for the worse, for the government began to apply a double standard to Ukrainians, one to those in Galicia and another to those in Volhynia. Moreover, it totally abrogated the right of Ukrainians to live in the Kholm region, Polissia and Podlachia. Volhynia became an experimental zone separated by a boundary from Galicia.

Just as the clique consisting of the National Democrats, Chieno (Christian Democrats) and Piast[22] (a petty-bourgeois party which sought support from the Polish peasant masses and exhibited chauvinistic and imperialist characteristics in its attitude toward other peoples) had not intended to discharge its international obligations toward Eastern Galicia,[23] neither did the new Piłsudski government. Some of the members of the ''Piłsudski group,'' which formed the government in Poland from 1926 to 1939, were long-time associates of Piłsudski. The rest were deserters from various political camps and the sort of apolitical individuals, ideologically unaffiliated and even totally devoid of principles, who in every state orient themselves on those who hold power at any given moment. While the National Democratic-Piast clique had not even respected its own laws regarding administrative autonomy for three provincial administrative regions in Galicia and the establishment of a Ukrainian university,[24] under Piłsudski there was a change for the worse; Poland unilaterally denounced the treaty regarding protection of the rights of national minorities in the League of Nations.

The Piłsudski era in Poland brought the infamous pacification of 1930,[25] that is, punitive actions of units of the Polish occupation forces, which made a name for themselves by waging a campaign of terror and mass destruction against the Ukrainian population and Ukrainian culture. It brought the closure and demolition of Orthodox churches in the Kholm region and even in Volhynia. It brought a campaign against Ukrainian offices of vital statistics; systematic colonization, even more extensive than under National Democratic-Piast rule; a campaign against Ukrainian cultural and co-operative institutions; and the Corps of Border Defence [KOP] (the Polish border guard).[26] It also brought the forced conversion of whole villages in Volhynia from Orthodoxy to Catholicism and a two-pronged policy of expropriation on all Ukrainian ethnic territory: one policy carried out by the civil administration and a brutal pogrom policy implemented by military officials who were not part of the civil administration. Thus, in Piłsudski's Poland, and particularly in the Poland governed by the Piłsudski group after his death, all the methods by which Polish policy had been applied in centuries past by Polish aristocrats, magnates and Jesuits were manifestly revived. Obviously such an internal policy could not serve to consolidate Poland. On the contrary, it led inevitably to rapid disintegration, destabilization and a state of complete internal decay. The war of 1939 brought an end to this process, as well as to the existence of Poland. Given her boundaries, internal relations and position between two such neighbours as Germany and the USSR, Poland was unable to maintain her existence over the long term.

*   *   *

The twenty-year existence of the reborn Polish state manifestly proved that the experience of history was not valued when it came to setting Polish policy; instead, what was highly esteemed was the governing tradition of the former aristocratic Poland. Now that Poland is on her knees, groups have again appeared which are attempting to approach Ukrainians with a variety of slogans and so-called Jagiellonian ideas about common tasks and goals in the cause of a common "liberation." "Equals with equals" and "for your freedom and ours" are slogans as old as Poland itself and have been compromised for centuries by Polish politicians. Nevertheless, the Poles still use them, seeking assistance for their own salvation. There is no doubt that Poland alone will never be strong enough to withstand pressure from both east and west, particularly if she is compressed into her own ethnic boundaries. But she never thinks in terms of these boundaries when it comes to rebuilding her state. She is always entranced by her historical, Jagiellonian boundaries. Thus, in enticing Ukrainians to help rebuild the state they have lost, the Poles are in fact enticing them to take on a new Polish yoke. It would be different if the Polish politicians wished us to join forces with them to rebuild Poland and Ukraine as separate states on their own ethnic territories! Then it would be possible to speak seriously with them about this matter. But the fact is that no such Polish politicians exist.

Nor do they recognize the right of Belorussians or Lithuanians to independence. The Jagiellonian combination, "Poland, Lithuania and Ukraine" as a "triune trinity," is the ideal of every Polish politician. Megalomania in life and in politics: this is the terrible worm that gnaws at the Polish psyche and soul!

For purely humanitarian reasons one would be inclined to sympathize with the Polish people in their present sufferings, but when one reads in *Kresy wschodnie* ("Eastern Territories," a Polish underground newspaper) such a political slogan, intended for the Poles, as the following pseudo-Ukrainian proverb from Volhynia—"when we heard *da! da!* ("yes" in Russian) things were bad; now that it's *gut! gut!* ("good" in German) everyone is soundly beaten; but life will be good when we hear *dzień dobry!* ("good day" in Polish)"—then one cannot but wonder, not only at the political naiveté displayed in the revolutionary author's essay, but also at the narrowness of the whole Polish environment that he represents. How can one sympathize with these people if they prove incorrigible even when so badly buffeted by fate? What reason do they have to interpret the situation in such a naive fashion and to lead others to believe in this primitive "aphorism," obviously cooked up by some Polish politician and peddled to others as a true original? Wishful thinking is the source of this shallow and naive description of the state of mind of the Ukrainian population of Volhynia. The Poles would wish the situation to be as they describe it, but in fact the current situation in Volhynia shows that, in spite of the terrible conditions that exist there at present, hatred for the Poles remains boundless. The reason that such a proverb is hawked among the Poles can again be found in a single thesis which derives from the megalomania that has characterized Polish policy toward Ukrainians throughout history. This thesis is based on the following reasoning: the Ukrainian people are basically good, submissive, loyal and even necessary as long as nobody incites them to rebellion. In the past, they were stirred up first by the Orthodox Ukrainian nobility and later by Cossack activists; in recent years, it has been the Ukrainian intelligentsia that aroused them. This proverb, however stupid it may be, is highly significant for evaluating the political mentality and psychology of the present-day Polish politician. He is very much inclined to believe that in Volhynia every peasant thinks in the way expressed in the proverb and "eagerly" awaits the arrival of the *dzień dobry*, but he certainly does not believe that the intellectual there thinks this way. For that Ukrainian intellectual has always stood in the way and continues to obstruct the contemporary Polish politician. With the intellectual he would like to discuss political topics, convince him to take his side and accept his ideas, and offer him the idyllic prospect of harmonious, peaceful, even "fraternal"

Polish-Ukrainian coexistence in the future. But such coexistence must necessarily be circumscribed by the boundaries of Poland, that is, a Poland which includes Volhynia, Galicia and perhaps even the right bank of the Dnieper.

* * *

As one ponders more deeply the history of Polish-Ukrainian relations and analyzes the past and present Polish political mentality, one gains the profound conviction that it will never be possible to arrive at any useful and lasting agreement with the Poles as long as one holds to the idea of political independence and sovereignty for Ukraine. Objective conditions would direct Ukrainians to maintain friendly relations with Poland because of the great common enemy, Moscow. Similarly, objective conditions would direct the Poles to maintain friendly relations with a Ukrainian state because of the additional threat to Poland posed by her western neighbour, Germany. Nevertheless, these two theses are mutually exclusive because, in their megalomania, Polish politicians will always disregard one or the other danger. And they will do this because they believe in their own "strength," a strength attained at the price of subjugating Ukrainians, Belorussians and Lithuanians. They do not agree to the unqualified recognition of Ukrainian sovereignty within Ukraine's ethnic boundaries, even at a time when, politically speaking, Poland lies in a state of semi-consciousness, broken on the wheel of history.

What is the way out of this situation with Poland, our eternal neighbour? The way out is simple! We must make treaties of peaceful coexistence with Poland only when we hold at least as much power as the Poles. Only then will they respect our right to exist and only then will they honour, at least for a time, the treaties they conclude with us. They will always make use of any momentary weakening of our power for their own purposes, something *we* have never in history attempted to do. The Poles can be compelled to be loyal partners only by force, and manifest force at that.

Today the Ukrainian people, who since their most recent liberation struggle of 1917–20 have not for a moment ceased to fight for their own state, have at their disposal an organized political force which forms the basis of Ukrainian liberation policy. This strength allows us to speak openly about the necessity of solving the problem of our struggle on the Polish front. We are aware that, in the face of the dangers posed to all the subject peoples of the East by German and Russian imperialists, the formation of a common front of subject peoples against imperialism and the cessation of internal strife are the only correct responses of the subject peoples to the warring imperialists. This should also apply to mutual relations between the two nations, Ukrainian and Polish. For this reason, we are opposed to a struggle on this front at the present time and favour a search for peaceful ways of solving the problems that exist between the two nations. If the Polish ruling class wishes to impose a struggle on us, it will be an implacable struggle waged by the whole Ukrainian people against hostile imperialist designs.

We are conscious of the problems that block the way to an understanding. We are particularly conscious of the fact that the psychology of the Polish ruling class, its whole way of thinking, its unwavering chauvinist attitude and its imperialist dreams constitute a serious obstacle on the road to understanding. The entire history of our mutual relations and all the experience garnered over centuries teach us that even when its own people is undergoing the greatest tragedies and sufferings, the Polish ruling class is unwilling to renounce its plans to subjugate other peoples, particularly Ukrainians, Belorussians and Lithuanians. And for this reason, while desiring to find a peaceful solution to this problem, we are organizing our own forces, for only this can convince the Polish imperialists of the hopelessness of their designs for plunder and of the necessity of reaching an understanding with the Ukrainian people, who do not want anything from the Polish people and do not covet Polish territory, but who have sufficient strength to defend, at all times, their right to their own state.

And this must become the fundamental principle of our policy with regard to the Poles. Otherwise, there are no grounds for making agreements with them, for these agreements will come to nothing. Centuries of history tell us so. And something must be learned from history.

Source: Ideia i Chyn 2, no. 4 (1943): 10–15. Original: Archive of the Foreign Representation of the Supreme Ukrainian Liberation Council. Photocopy: Archive, *Litopys UPA*.

NOTES

1. Casimir III (the Great) (1310–70): King of Poland (1333–70). In 1349, he conquered Galicia, the Kholm and Belz lands and western Podillia.
2. Lublin was the scene of the diet which united Poland with Lithuania in 1569. This allowed the further expansion of Poland into Ukrainian territories which were part of the Grand Duchy of Lithuania.
3. In the Union of Brest (1596), the Ukrainian-Belorussian Orthodox Church accepted union with Rome.

4. The Cossack state came into being as result of the 1648 revolution against the Polish kingdom under the leadership of Bohdan Khmelnytsky.
5. Stefan Czarnecki (1599–1665).
6. Ivan Vyhovsky (died 1664): Hetman of Ukraine (1657–9).
7. The Treaty of Hadiach (16 September 1658) provided that the *voevodstva* of Kiev, Chernihiv and Bratslav were to form the Grand Principality of Rus' and enter into a federal union with Poland and Lithuania as an equal partner.
8. The Battle of Konotop (July 1659), during which Hetman Vyhovsky destroyed the Muscovite army of Prince Trubetskoi.
9. Włodzimierz Dzieduszycki (1825–99).
10. Lev Sapiha (1803–78).
11. The Slavic Congress held in Prague, June 1848.
12. Iuliian Lavrivsky (1821–73): judge, cultural and political activist.
13. Roman Sembratovych (1875–1905): Ukrainian journalist.
14. Iuliian Romanchuk (1842–1932): prominent politician, writer, educator and journalist in Galicia.
15. Oleksander Barvinsky (1847–1927): prominent educator, historian and political activist.
16. The Treaty of Zboriv of August 1649 between Khmelnytsky and the Poles, although ratified by the Polish Sejm, was never implemented.
17. The Treaty of Bila Tserkva of September 1651 was concluded between Khmelnytsky and Mikołaj Potocki (1594–1651) as a result of the Polish victory over the Cossacks at Berestechko.
18. Normalization: an attempt to improve Ukrainian-Polish relations, undertaken in 1935 by several leaders of the Ukrainian National-Democratic Union (UNDO) and the Polish minister Marian Kościałkowski. It was declared invalid by the UNDO leadership in 1938.
19. ''Haidamaky'': poem by Taras Shevchenko (1814–61), the greatest Ukrainian Romantic poet.
20. *Taras Bulba*: historical novel by Nikolai Gogol (Mykola Hohol) (1809–52), a Ukrainian-Russian writer.
21. Józef Piłsudski (1867–1935) overthrew the government by a coup d'état in 1926 and governed as virtual dictator until his death.
22. Reference is to the alliance of National Democrats, Christian Democrats and the centrist wing of the Peasants, ''Piast,'' led by Wincenty Witos (1874–1945).
23. Reference is to the decision of the Council of Ambassadors of the Entente, announced on 14 March 1923, to guarantee the autonomous status of Eastern Galicia within Poland.
24. By a law of 26 September 1922 on provincial self-government, the Polish regime was obliged to establish a Ukrainian university by 1924 at the latest. This legal obligation was never carried out. The Ukrainians main-

tained an underground university from 1921 to 1925.

25. Reference is to the so-called "pacification" carried out by the Polish government (J. Piłsudski and General Felicjan Sławoj-Składkowski) against the Ukrainian population in 1930.

26. In the autumn of 1938 special commandos of the Corps of Border Defence carried out a second pacification along the Soviet border.

THE PATHS OF RUSSIAN IMPERIALISM

U. Kuzhil

Ever since Stalin offered his memorable toast in honour of the Russian people during the Kremlin reception celebrating the victory over Germany, the Bolsheviks have been speaking out unabashedly about the primacy of Russians in the Soviet Union. Designating the Russian people as the creator and leader of the USSR, they have stressed the leading role it has played in the entire history of Eastern Europe as a founder of states on those vast territories. Gradually, Russian history has become the history of all the peoples of the USSR. The traditions of the Russian people have come to be the traditions of the whole of the Soviet Union; renowned Russian military leaders and statesmen have become the prime examples for all Soviet citizens to follow. But in one matter the Bolsheviks still retain their disguise: they strenuously disavow the title of successors to the imperialist colonial policies of Russian tsarism. To admit that they are the successors of the tsars would be to contradict their own propaganda, which they hope to use to dominate the world; thus, they have donned the guise of the world's foremost pacifists and opponents of the Russian Empire. Throughout Russia's history, her foreign policy has been expansionist in character, determined in its direction by her geographical position and her insatiable pillaging spirit, which moved her rulers to strive for ever greater territorial gains. The Bolsheviks, faithful sons of Russia, have not freed themselves of these tendencies. With regard to both the objectives and methods of aggression, one can trace an unbroken line from Ivan III to Peter the Great to the "great" Stalin.

The age of Ivan III (1462–1505) saw the definitive organization of the national Muscovite state. At that time, Muscovite tsars began to appear as players on the international stage and to become involved in international relations. They revealed themselves as politicians who, having been vassals of the Golden Horde,[1] had learned elasticity and cunning: "while they hate, they feign friendship and hide their insidious intentions behind flattering smiles."[2]

As the unifier of all ethnic Muscovite lands, Tsar Ivan III[3] marked out the directions of Russia's future conquests. Prime importance was attached to the question of "unifying" Ukrainian lands, then part of the Polish-Lithuanian state, with Muscovy. Having united the Muscovite principalities, Moscow proclaimed all Ukrainian lands that had once belonged to the Kievan state to be hereditary possessions (otchina) of the Grand Prince of Muscovy. For this reason, Moscow refused to grant legal recognition of the existing state of affairs and concluded only temporary treaties with Lithuania. All the international policies of Ivan III and his successor Vasilii III[4] were coloured by the basic objective of appropriating Ukrainian lands. For this reason, Moscow sought peaceful relations with the Ottoman Porte[5] and favoured every alliance that served to weaken Lithuania.

Ivan III also marked out Muscovy's line of expansion toward the Baltic Sea. Cut off by Lithuania and the Livonian Order[6] from a sea route to Western Europe, Muscovy was forced to pass through neighbouring countries. Her external trade and her cultural and political relations with the West suffered as a result. It was at this time that Russia began to direct herself to the sea, to a "window on Europe." Russia's search for access to the sea was a historical process which, from the time of Peter the Great, took on a very clear form. Although at times it appeared to be an aimless search, it was always consistent and conscious of its goal. Russia's seemingly aimless wanderings in the course of two centuries were nothing less than a consistent advance toward several objectives which, in fact, can be seen as one and the same: access at any price to the open sea. Every time one of the shores toward which Russia advanced proved unattainable, she headed toward a second, a third, a fifth. Whenever an opportunity arose, she again returned to the first, and so it continued. During the period of the early Muscovite tsars, Russia had already gained an enormously long coast along the Arctic Ocean, but this was not sufficient to traverse the maritime network of the later empire. At that time, the Arctic coast fulfilled only one of the functions of a border—defence. Only in the 1870s was it shown that this coastline was not without value, and it was not until the beginning of the twentieth century that Russia started to make use of the ice-free harbour on the Murmansk[7] coast. In recent times, after being more fully explored and tested, the Arctic Ocean took on special significance as the shortest northern sea route. These two basic objectives of Russian imperialism—the subjugation of Ukraine and access to the open sea—have retained their importance throughout the whole of Russian history, including that of the Soviet Union.

At the end of the sixteenth century, during the reign of Ivan IV (the Terrible),[8] Russia's expansionist policy embarked in two new directions. In 1556 the Muscovites conquered the Kazan khanate. This conquest gave them a trade route along the Volga and Kama Rivers and brought them into contact with states in Central Asia and along the Caspian Sea. The conquest of the Astrakhan khanate in 1556 led to the establishment of similar relations with the peoples of the northern Caucasus. These new commercial and diplomatic relations provided Muscovy with a base for further political penetration and extension of its sphere of dominance. The conquest of these two lands was not a chance occurrence: it was fully in line with the fundamental objectives of Russian aggression. As early as the beginning of the sixteenth century, Muscovite politicians stressed the "necessity" of subjugating Kazan, for along the Kama they could pass beyond the Urals and begin their conquest of Siberia and, by way of Tiumen, reach Bukhara and Khiva. In addition, the Muscovite tsars were eager to end the threat of attack from Kazan, so that they could be free to advance toward the Baltic. Even after the fall of Kazan, however, the Volga route was not free; penetration into Azerbaidzhan and Iran was barred by Astrakhan, so Moscow overran it without hesitation.

To the north and east, the direction of least resistance from the standpoint of physical geography and anthropo-geographical factors, the Russian state grew very quickly. Much slower, however, was its growth to the west and south. Although its movement in this direction was not hindered by any significant physical barriers, the anthropo-geographical factor in these regions posed greater problems. As far back as the first half of the seventeenth century, the Muscovites had reached the Pacific Ocean and thus gained for themselves the best possible natural boundary—the sea. In the north, they had done this even earlier. But their attempts at expansion to the south and west had met only limited success in the sixteenth century. Muscovy was not yet in a position to take on Sweden, Turkey or Poland. On the contrary, at the beginning of the seventeenth century Poland came close to destroying Muscovy. The subjugation of the Central Volga region and Astrakhan, in the second half of the sixteenth century, began the process whereby the Tsardom of Muscovy was transformed into a multi-national Russian state, a process which assumed even clearer form with the conquest of Ukraine and the eastern part of Belorussia in 1654[9] and 1661.[10] Bolshevik historians attempt to explain this process with artificial, deceptive arguments, consciously taking up the defence of Russian imperialism. They characterize Russia as a creative, organizing force in Eastern Europe and the vast spaces of northern and central Asia. According to the Bolsheviks, the factor contributing to the rise of the Russian Empire was, above all, the desire of these nations to create a strong state which would provide protection against the onslaught of the Turks and Mongols. Lenin wrote: " . . . the actual amalgamation of all such regions, lands and principalities into one whole was brought about by the increasing exchange among regions, the gradually growing circulation of commodities and the concentration of the small local markets into a single, all-Russian market."[11] According to Stalin, "In eastern Europe . . . the creation of centralized states, which was hastened by the need for self-defence, preceded the abolition of feudalism as well as the rise of nations. For this reason, nations could not develop into national states, but created instead several mixed, multinational, bourgeois states, which generally consisted of *one strong, ruling nation and a few weak, subordinate nations.*"[12] He added: "In Russia, the function of unifying different nationalities was taken on by the Great Russians."[13] This explanation of the origins of the Russian Empire assumes the voluntary participation and the conscious gravitation of the annexed nations toward the centre, whereas the recent history of Russia entirely contradicts this interpretation. The concentration of markets was determined by the economic interests of the ruling nation, Russia, while the annexation of more and more new territories was undertaken to enlarge her economic base as well as for strategic reasons, to protect the ever-expanding borders of her empire.

After the destruction of Kazan, the tsarist government settled accounts with the native population in the savage manner that has typified Russian imperialism. The male population was slaughtered, while the women and children were turned into serfs. For a long time the peoples of the Central Volga region staged a tenacious resistance, but Russia had already begun to apply her policy of domination over subject lands: persecuting all those who strove for independence; awarding portions of land taken from the local population to Russians; buying the support of part of the Kazan nobility; and, above all, spreading Christianity in order to use the resources of Muscovite Orthodoxy, that instrument of Russian imperialism, to increase her influence over the population. Basing herself in fortresses built in the lands of the Kazan khanate, Muscovy made her way beyond the Urals. These fortresses and military garrisons, which were established to lend support and protection to the Russian administration on conquered territory, were a clear illustration of the people's "voluntary" desire to create a single state united with Moscow. With the penetration of private capital, backed up by military divisions, the population was forced pay a tribute—the *iasak*—and the way was paved for the complete political takeover of these regions. Amid battles and rebellions, the Russian administration advanced into the depths of Siberia. The representative of the Russian government lured the Siberian khan, Seid Akhmat, into meeting with him for negotiations, then threw him into prison (no doubt the Bolsheviks followed this example when they invited Okulicki[14] and his comrades to take part in negotiations). Subsequently, the Russian armies occupied Kashlyk,[15] the centre of western Siberia. By the middle of the seventeenth century, they had consolidated themselves along the rivers Ishim, Irtysh and Ob.

The first half of the seventeenth century saw the conquest of western Siberia in its entirety. The first stage of Russia's advance was the conquest of the passage from the Ob to the Yenisei Rivers; this was followed by an advance to Lake Baikal and to the "great river" Lena. From that time forward, the acquisition of new lands proceeded more energetically, as the Russians advanced in four directions: to the northeast—to the shores of the Arctic Ocean; to the east—to the shores of the Sea of Okhotsk; to the south—to Lake Baikal; and to the southeast—to the Amur River. Russia's advance from the Yenisei to the Sea of Okhotsk took a mere twenty years, for this was a conquest of lands populated by nomadic and, in part, even primitive peoples. On the Amur, however, Russia encountered similar penetration on the part of a civilized nation—China. The Treaty of Nerchinsk,[16] signed in 1689, established trade relations between Russia and China, but it also marked the first collision of the opposing interests of these two states, an issue of contention to this very day.

The seventeenth century found Russia far beyond the bounds of her ethnic territories. In the east, her aggression advanced relatively easily, but other important and unresolved questions still faced the Russian government:

1. The "unification" with Russia of Ukrainian and Belorussian lands which had been under Polish rule.
2. Penetration into the Baltic region.
3. At the end of the century, the necessity for war with Turkey and her vassal, the Crimea.

Ukraine's war of liberation against Poland and the Treaty of Pereiaslav

[1654] brought a complete shift of power in Eastern Europe. At the same time, this treaty forever marked the Russian ruling class (whether "White" or "Red") as a faithless partner in international agreements. Taking advantage of the weakening of her ally, Ukraine, Moscow chose to ignore the actual contents of the treaty, which set forth terms of mutual assistance and co-operation between two equal, sovereign states, and gradually turned Ukraine into a colony. In 1667, by the Treaty of Andrusovo,[17] Russia obtained a base from which to proceed toward the shores of the Black Sea and the Caucasus. Two ideal natural boundaries thereby came within reach of the Russian Empire with the annexation of only one part of Ukraine. The first result of the annexation of Ukraine was Russia's involvement in the Eastern Question.[18] Before occupying Ukraine, Muscovy had not engaged in any major wars with Turkey, but immediately after the signing of the Treaty of Andrusovo, military preparations were made by these two states (1674–81) and Russian diplomats bustled about Europe in search of allies. Muscovy joined the Christian coalition against Turkey, marched on the Crimea and took Azov in 1698.

The second question, that of access to the Baltic Sea, could not be resolved because of an unfavourable distribution of power on the international front and because of Russia's preoccupation with her activities in the south. But Russia's rulers remained unperturbed, for they were certain that the work they had begun would be continued by their successors. Russian diplomacy had already laid the foundations and established proven methods of interference in the internal affairs of enemy states. In her struggle with Turkey, Russia took advantage of the natural enmity between the Turks and their subject Christian population; she made her first appearance on the international scene as the protector of Orthodox Christians. Through their participation in international affairs, Russian diplomats acquired a reputation among foreigners that is valid even to this day: "They bring together all the subtleties of cunning hypocrisy in order to deceive; they either present lies as truth or fail to state what should be said, weakening the binding power of every decision by means of a thousand artful turns that totally alter its original meaning."

The beginning of the eighteenth century bears the stamp of Tsar Peter I, a figure in Russian history whose political activities have been accorded full recognition and approval by the Bolsheviks; he is highly esteemed in the so-called classics of Marxism and in official Bolshevik histories. "With Peter I, a Russian empire was established whose dominion extended from the Baltic to the Pacific Ocean. Russia became not a colony or a semi-colony of any of her economically more powerful Western European neighbours, but rather one of the strongest states in Europe. In the bosom of that empire developed the proletariat which carried out the Great October Socialist Revolution.''[19] Peter's judgement regarding Russia's position in the international sphere and the paths she should pursue in her expansionist policy in order to assure herself a permanent place as a world empire have remained authoritative even for the Bolsheviks. His plans with regard to the Black Sea were partially realized by Catherine II, while his watchword, "Toward India," and his Persian policy, put into action during the war of 1722–9, still await their fulfillment by the Soviet government.

As a legacy of the seventeenth century, Peter I inherited two complex problems: the Turkish and the Swedish. Both were linked to one and the same question, that is, access to the open sea.

"From the very outset," writes Marx, "Peter I broke through all the traditions of the Slavonic race. 'It is water that Russia wants.' These words are inscribed on the title-page of his life. The conquest of the Sea of Azov was aimed at in his first war with Turkey, the conquest of the Baltic in his war against Sweden, the conquest of the Black Sea in his second war against the Porte, and the conquest of the Caspian Sea in his fraudulent intervention in Persia. For a system of local encroachment, land was sufficient; for a system of universal aggression, water had become indispensable.''[20] In a word, Marx perceives in Peter a typical imperialist conqueror, while the Bolsheviks regard him as an illustrious figure in the history of all the peoples of the Russian Empire, a ruler who carried out a civilizing mission by organizing a multi-national state in Eastern Europe. "The wise activity of Peter I significantly increased the might of the Russian state," wrote the editors of *Bolshevik* in 1945.[21] In other words, in the eyes of the Bolsheviks, a "wise policy" is one which leads a state to wage wars and subjugate peoples for the sake of its own imperialist expansion.

Russia's desire to rule over the shores of the Black Sea necessitated a prolonged war with Turkey, which had regarded the Black Sea as her internal sea and barred foreign vessels from plying its waters. After Russia's acquisition of Azov, her defeat on the Prut River in 1711[22] brought only a short pause in her aggression in that direction. The international situation was more favourable to the resolution of the Swedish question: it fell to Peter the Great to end the century and a half of struggle for the Baltic region with the annexation of Livland, Estland, Ingria and Vyborg in 1721.[23] "We emerged from darkness into light," said Peter, "and those who were unknown in the world are now respected." It did not perturb the Muscovite tsar that, concurrently, his conquest thrust the Baltic nations from light into darkness as they exchanged independence for life in the "prison of nations." Moscow needed a "window," so the subjugation of the far more cultured Finns

as part of the process of carving out the window was numbered among
the achievements of the predecessors of the Bolshevik overlords. The
importance ascribed to this outlet to the Baltic Sea is shown by the fact
that in 1703 St. Petersburg was founded on the first piece of coastline
to be conquered, only a cannonball's flight away from enemy borders.
The removal of the capital from Moscow to this coastal city required
the further conquest of the whole coastline from Liepaja[24] to Tornio[25]
in order to safeguard St. Petersburg's strategic position. This task was
completed only by Peter's successors with the conquest of Finland in
1809. And Peter's wishes were not forgotten by the Bolsheviks: they
did not rest until, in their war with Finland in 1940, they had regained
those territories lost in the First World War which flank modern-day
Leningrad.

Control of even this small stretch of Baltic coastline definitely provided Russia with a "window on Europe." In time, this window
proved to be too small, for at any moment it could be curtained off by
foreign hands. As long as world politics embraced Europe only, the
Baltic shore might have satisfied Russia. Already a great power, she
was pained by the fact that the keys to the Baltic were in the hands of
Denmark, Sweden, and especially Germany. But as soon as the world
ceased to consist only of Europe, Russia was forced to direct herself to
a free ocean, to gain access to international routes, rather than limit herself to closed lateral seas. Thus, after the conquest of Courland in 1795
and Finland in 1809, the main focus of Russian policy shifted south-
ward. The Ukrainian shore of the Black Sea, along with the wealthy
and populous lands adjacent to it, became a firm base from which the
Russian Empire could begin its expansion toward the temperate seas.

Immediately after the successful conclusion of his northern war, Peter
turned his attention to the south. The Russian envoy in Iran reported a
propitious situation in Persia and advised that Russia meddle in Iran's
internal affairs under the pretext of combating rebellious vassals. Russia assumed her tried and true mask of "protector of Christians," concluded agreements with the Christian vassals of the Persian shah and
began a war that was to bring her nearer to the temperate seas, perhaps
even to India. After the successful conclusion of these military activities, Peter paved the way for Russia's first incursion into the Caucasus
(Baku, Derbent) and along the western and southern shores of the
Caspian Sea. Peter's successes led to conflicts with Turkey; this time,
Russian diplomacy made use of its second weapon, which had already
been tested in the seventeenth centry: agitation among the Christians
who were subject to the sultan and the conclusion of pacts with
Turkey's Orthodox vassals, the Moldavian and Wallachian *hospodars*.

Having carved out a window on Europe, Peter attempted to consolidate his position in the East, believing that Russia should serve as the intermediary in trade between Europe and Asia. With this purpose in mind, he sent out numerous expeditions aimed at gaining possession of Siberia and finding suitable trade routes. In the eighteenth century, Kamchatka became a convenient base for further Russian penetration into the Far East. The Russian government attempted to establish trade with Japan and even turned its thoughts to America. Having gained possession of the islands in the Sea of Okhotsk, Russian industrialists and Cossacks carried on further exploration of the Kurile Islands. Siberia was becoming an ever more exploited colony. The military requirement for metal necessitated the exploitation of Siberia's underground wealth, which was mined by the forced labour of serfs and exiles. Constant uprisings by the indigenous population forced the government to establish a series of fortified lines from which the Russian garrisons kept the population in check. In this enormous, far-off expanse, Russia expended vast amounts of energy, wealth and blood in order to assure her gigantic complex of lands an outlet to the ice-free lateral seas of the Pacific Ocean. Her efforts foundered because of a lack of population and development in the hinterland. Only much later did the Amur and the coastal regions become more developed.

At the end of the eighteenth century, under Catherine II, Russian diplomacy picked up the threads of the foreign policy of the seventeenth century and Peter I. This period saw the realization of the following plans:

1. The "unification" of the remainder of Polish-ruled Ukrainian and Belorussian lands.
2. Consolidation in the Baltic region.
3. A further thrust to the Black Sea.

Russian diplomacy reached the peak of its skillfullness in forming coalitions, taking advantage of the internal problems of enemy states and cunningly instigating international intrigues. Catherine II took care to conceal her empire's policy of plunder with the phraseology that was fashionable in that age of enlightenment. With every new annexation and international manoeuvre that served the interests of Russian imperialism, the diplomats came forth with the appropriate set phrases that justified their activities and made them appear to be defenders of peace and justice.

In order to carry out the first task, that is, to gain possession of all Ukrainian and Belorussian ethnic territories, Russia had to bring about the downfall of Poland. In the second half of the eighteenth century, the Polish state showed signs of total collapse, but Austria and Prussia also had designs on Polish territory, and Russia brought her plans into accord with theirs. Thus ensued the three partitions of Poland, which brought an end to the Polish state. While undermining Poland's sovereignty and preparing its partition, Russia dressed her deed in the guise of defending the "freedom" of the Polish people. Together with Prussia, she demanded that the Polish parliament grant the non-Catholic population of Poland rights equal to those of the Catholics. At the same time, Russia did all she could to impede developments that would improve relations within the country (the abolition of the *liberum veto*). The corruption of part of the Polish nobility and the entry of military divisions into Poland made relations even more anarchic. The Russian envoy organized a confederation of the corrupt, anti-social elements of Polish society and, under the pretext of protecting this confederation, brought Russian troops into Warsaw. These were the circumstances under which the first partition of Poland took place, giving Russia a significant part of Belorussia. The approbation granted to this act of coercion by a Soviet—not a tsarist—historian is both interesting and extremely significant: "Part of Belorussia—ancient Russian territory— was also absorbed into the empire. The unification of Belorussian lands with the empire saved the Belorussian people from denationalization and from the persecution of their faith. Unification with Russia was beneficial to Belorussia's economical development."[26] The pretext for the second partition was very simple. A confederation composed of a sector of the Polish nobility, under the protection of Catherine II, rose in opposition to the Constitution of 3 May;[27] in order to aid the confederation, Russia occupied Poland. But the fact that a confederation of Poles had invited her armies into their country did not satisfy Russia. She demanded that the Polish parliament in Grodno ratify the second partition of Poland. Russian armies surrounded the parliament building, preventing the members from leaving. The members remained silent; finally, under pressure, the chairman proposed that silence be taken as a sign of assent, and thus, with the "assent" of the Polish parliament, Russia, the "liberator," remained in Poland. By 1795, after the third partition of Poland and the annexation of Courland, all of Belorussia, Lithuania and Ukraine, apart from Galicia, were within the borders of Russia. In the south, the empire reached to the shores of the Black Sea and could expand only toward the Balkan Peninsula and the Caucasus. As can be seen, Moscow's appetite grew with every new conquest, and each generation of the ruling class set itself ever greater imperialist goals.

At the same time as Poland was being partitioned, Russian imperialism was active on the Black Sea. Here one can list as first among the achievements of Russia's ruling class the consistent eradication of all centres of the Ukrainian independence movement. With the liquidation of the Hetmanate and the destruction of the Zaporozhian Sich,[28] Russia again emerged from darkness into light, from a boarded-up continent to the sea, to world-wide ocean routes; but this meant that Ukraine was deprived of sovereignty and slipped from independence into Russian slavery. In 1791, after two wars with Turkey, Russia finally gained the lands between the Buh and Dniester Rivers, as well as the Crimea, to which a Russian politician of the day referred as ''a wart on the nose of Russia.'' These new territories placed the northern coastline in the hands of the Russian Empire and thus strengthened its position on the Black Sea. But these achievements hardly began to satisfy Russia's appetite. It manifested itself clearly in Catherine II's "Greek project," which, as it turned out, remained no more than a dream. The objective of this project was no longer simply to make territorial gains at Turkey's expense, but to drive the Turks entirely out of Europe and to create a Greek empire out of the eastern part of the Balkan Peninsula and the Aegean coast. The crown of this empire was to go to Catherine's grandson. Moldavia and Wallachia were to be formed into a buffer state, Dacia, while the western part of the Balkan Peninsula was to be given to Austria. "Constantinople as the third Russian capital," writes Engels, "would have meant for Russia not only moral dominance over the eastern Christian world, but also a decisive step toward rule over Europe. This would have meant the transformation of the Black Sea into a harbour for Russian warships. It would have meant rule by a single state over the Black Sea, Asia Minor and the Balkan Peninsula."[29] These precise objectives remain the goals of Russian-Bolshevik imperialism in that region.

The second half of the eighteenth century also saw diplomatic and military preparations for the takeover of Georgia. Russia represented herself as a protector of the Georgians against both Turkey and Persia, and Soviet historians perpetuate this view: "The only solution for Georgia was to strengthen ties with her strong northern neighbour, which, by the end of the century, had extended its rule to the northern foothills of the Caucasian Mountains. Ties with Russia would ensure Georgia's economic development and establish links with Western Europe and all its technical knowledge and culture, whereas subjection to Persia and Turkey brought her only primitive and brutal feudal oppression and discord. Georgia was also tied to Russia by religious and cultural links that were increasing in the eighteenth century."[30] Thus, according to the Bolshevik interpretation, all of tsarist Russia's imperialist pillage can be explained as a desire on the part of various peoples to take refuge under Russia's protective wing in order to escape the prospect of destruction under the rule of any other imperialist state.

In the era of Catherine II, Russian diplomacy succeeded in completing the tasks left to it by its predecessors: Peter's gains in the Baltic region, in Courland, were consolidated, while Ukrainian and Belorussian lands were "united" with Russia. Russia gained a firm foothold on the Black Sea. And finally, the Russian Empire acquired a decisive voice in the general affairs of Europe. In international affairs, Russia's basic objectives were to further her own intrinsic interests and to move from a position of dependence upon foreign governments to one from which she could force others to work with her for the attainment of her own goals. The new directions of her foreign policy awaited their fulfillment in the nineteenth century: first, penetration into the Balkans, and second, the weakening of Britain's maritime supremacy.

Russia's earliest conquests did not bring her into the diplomatic game that was being played out by the states of Europe. But as she advanced ever further along her imperialist path, she eventually came into collision with other imperialist states and was forced to play a part in the international game of diplomacy. In the nineteenth century her advances were directed toward the Baltic region, the Far East, the Slavic nations of the Balkans, and Central Asia. In the last three regions in particular, Russia's interests conflicted with those of other great European states, so her resources were strained to the limit. This was no longer a matter of subjugating Oirots or Kamchatkans; it was a conflict with the military and political powers of the world.

The Eastern Question remained current throughout the whole of the nineteenth century. Turkey was falling into a state of decay; her socio-economic order was antiquated and her state organization unsuited to the demands of the contemporary world. The European empires kept a watchful eye on developments in Turkish territories and in particular on Constantinople, a convenient economic and political base located in a first-rate strategic position. Seizure of Constantinople meant control over the Black Sea, the Aegean and the eastern basin of the Mediterranean. Greatest interest in the Eastern Question was shown by Russia, Britain, Austria and France. Austria was gradually increasing her trade traffic along the Danube and her economic penetration into the north-western regions of the Balkan Peninsula. At the end of the eighteenth century, Egypt and the Near East became the targets of France's efforts at expansion. Nevertheless, Russia's major adversary on this front was Britain. The economic and political objectives of the British Empire required that Greece be freed from Turkish rule. Therefore, from the British perspective, the best way to resolve the Eastern Question was to push Russia into a war with Turkey, which would liberate Greece but, at the same time, not weaken Turkey excessively, so that Constantinople would remain in Turkish hands. To defend Turkey and Persia by all possible diplomatic and military means was the first duty and the basic task of British policy. Were Britain to allow Russia into Constantinople, she would see Russia enter India within a few years; to lose India would mean a decline to the status of Holland or Belgium. The prevention of Russian military moves in Turkey was regarded by British politicians as essential to the continued existence of Britain as a great power. By opposing Russia in the Crimean War (1853–6),[31] Britain intended to check Russian aggression to the south. According to the British plan, the Crimea, as far as the Isthmus of Perekop, was to go to Turkey, while Georgia and the south-eastern Caucasus were to become a vassal state, a British-Turkish protectorate. Circassia, as that state was to be called, was to block Russian penetration into Persia. Because of Britain's inability to obtain the agreement of France, this plan was never realized, but Turkey, the Caucasus and Persia remained the most sensitive spots in Britain's relations with Russia.

In the general European scramble for new markets and trade routes, Russia held a strong trump card: the support of the Balkan Slavs, who hoped, with her assistance, to achieve independent statehood. Russia played this political manoeuvre in a masterly way, turning the question of ''protecting'' nations of her own faith into a point of departure for her diplomatic and military aggression. Her goal was to establish bases on the Balkan Peninsula and the Caucasian isthmus from which to begin her advance upon Constantinople and ultimately to establish her undivided dominion over the shores of the Black Sea. Whenever her military potential was reduced, she concentrated her efforts all the more strongly on carrying out acts of sabotage among the Turkish population. Her usual manoeuvre was to raise in international forums the question of the plight of Christians in Turkey. Russia wanted the Christian population to be granted legal recognition of their rights and hoped to acquire the supervision of these rights for herself; this would give her many opportunities to interfere in Turkey's internal affairs. After her defeat in the Crimean War, Russia set into motion the policy of ''peaceful penetration'' of the Balkans. She extended her influence in Serbia and, with the latter's aid, organized a union of Balkan Slavs under Serbian leadership which became an instrument of Russian imperialism in the Balkans. She also provided assistance to Greek insurgents, but only as long as their insurrection proved useful to her on the international front.

As international conflicts increased, the Eastern Question was complicated by new problems. In her advance on Turkey, Russia established a base in the Caucasus and attempted to gain control of the Black Sea-Caspian basin. This led to a long struggle between Russia and Iran, which brought Moscow into conflict with Britain in the Middle East.

At the same time, the struggle for the Caspian shore was inextricably tied to an advance into Central Asia, toward Kazakhstan and the Central Asian khanates. The Near and Middle East became the main centres of international conflict among the great European states.

Through her conquest of Ukraine, Russia gained access to the Caucasian isthmus. Although straddled by the mighty ridge of the Caucasus, which prevented easy passage, this territory provided enormous opportunities for expansion into the lands of the Near East lying immediately beyond the Caucasus. These lands, which form a transitional region between Asia Minor in the west, Iran and the Persian Gulf in the east, Eastern Europe in the north and Egypt and Arabia in the south, include Transcaucasia, Armenia, western Iran, Mesopotamia, Syria and Palestine. The conquest of the Caucasus began with the campaign of Peter I; the peace of 1774 gave Russia a boundary along the Kuban and Terek Rivers, while a series of further wars, which continued until 1864, gave her full possession of the natural fortress of the Caucasus and of large territories in the Near East, including the eastern shore of the Black Sea, Batum and Baku. The conquest of the Caucasus is a typical example of Russia's double-dealing and deception. Threatened by Turkey and Iran, Georgia's King Giorgi XII turned to Russia, proposing that Georgia be brought under her protection. No mention was made of a total dismantling of the Georgian state. Giorgi was to remain on the throne. But at the moment that Russian troops entered Georgian territory, in 1801, Tsar Alexander I[32] issued a proclamation announcing the annexation of Georgia as an integral part of the Russian Empire and the transformation of her lands into another administrative unit. Thus the "Treaty of Pereiaslav" was repeated. This act gave rise to a protracted struggle and a series of uprisings against Russia. The main features of Russian colonial policy in Transcaucasia were forced Russification and the spread of Orthodoxy. To achieve even greater centralization, the Russian government decided to place the clergy and all church properties under the authority of the synod and the exarch, the head of the Georgian Orthodox Church, who was appointed by the Russian government. The coercive implementation of Russian Orthodoxy was met with bitter opposition, renunciation of the Orthodox faith and expulsion of Orthodox priests. In its coercive imposition of Orthodoxy on the western regions of Ukraine, it is evident that the Soviet Russian government took its lesson from Russian tsarism's activities in Georgia. Russia made ever greater use of her Transcaucasian lands in order to further her southern aggression, which advanced in three main directions: through Asia Minor to Constantinople; south-west to the Iskenderun Inlet, Syria and the Red Sea; and south-east to the Persian Gulf. The main objective of the western advance through Asia Minor was to transform the Black Sea into a Russian *mare clausum*. The creation of the Balkan states of Romania and Bulgaria in the nineteenth century prevented Russia from surrounding the Black Sea from the west, but in Asia Minor no serious obstacle lay between Moscow and the capital of the crumbling Ottoman state. On the contrary: the Armenian question always provided opportunities for interference.

While consolidating herself in Transcaucasia, Russia continued the Persian policy begun by Peter I. The war of 1826–8 was concluded with a peace advantageous to Russia; Persia renounced the right to a Caspian fleet and withdrew from Erevan and Nakhichevan. Subsequently, Russia preferred to rely upon peaceful penetration rather than military action. Taking advantage of Persia's disintegration, Russia increased her influence in that region by peaceful means, preparing to make her move at the decisive moment. The Persian Gulf and the port of Bandar Abbas played the major role in these machinations. While increasing her influence in Persia from the north-west, Russia advanced further along the eastern shore of the Caspian Sea, finally reaching and even crossing Iran's northern frontier. Here we see another direction of Russia's past and present expansion in Asia: toward the Arabian Sea and India. Russia became Iran's sole northern neighbour. This circumstance led to an enormous growth of Russian influence in Persia from the end of the 1880s. Road and telegraph lines were built deep into Persian territory; in every large city, consulates were established, as well as branches of banks and commercial houses. The Persian government received loans from Russia, which it guaranteed with proceeds from customs receipts; the Persians even agreed to borrow only from Russia and to refuse railroad concessions to any other country. By the first decade of the twentieth century, Russia's trade with Persia had already outstripped that of Britain. Subsidized Russian steamships were plying the Persian Gulf; the Transcaucasian[33] and Transcaspian[34] railroads were capable of flooding Persia's northern frontier with Russian armies at a moment's notice.

By the middle of the nineteenth century, Russia's borders met those of the states of Central Asia. At the same time, British dominions in north-western India met Central Asia from the south-east. Thus, Central Asia became the site of a struggle between Russia and Britain. Russia looked upon Bukhara, Khiva and Tashkent not only as cotton centres for supplying Russian industry, but also as important markets for her industrial products. In the West, Russia presented herself as an agricultural country; in the east, she played the role of an industrial state, searching out raw materials and markets for her products. By conquering Central Asia, Russia also hoped to gain a trump card for her foreign policy. When the Crimean War shattered her plans for

Constantinople, Russia was forced to search out ways of putting pressure on Britain. The Russian government considered it imperative to reach the borders of India in order to force Britain to be more compliant with regard to the straits—the Bosphorus and the Dardanelles. In any case, it is well known that since the time of Peter I, India had been one of the goals of Russian imperialism. This fact was plainly voiced by Russian public opinion as expressed in the press, in books and in the writings of publicists. The gravity of Russia's threat to India is indicated by the fact that for a full century it was the main source of tension in British foreign policy. In 1885, when Russian advance troops encountered the Afghans, whose land was a British protectorate, the danger arose of a Russo-British war.

In the middle of the nineteenth century, Russia established herself permanently in Kazakhstan. The official pretext most commonly given by Russia for further aggression into the depths of Central Asia was the necessity of responding to attacks by non-Russian military units of independent countries that had not yet been occupied. (In the same way, the official reason for the war with Finland in 1940 was little Finland's supposed aggressive intentions toward the Soviet empire). Step by step, Russia acquired Tashkent (1865), Samarkand and Bukhara (1868), Khiva and the Transcaspian territories (1873). In 1891–5, Russian armies occupied most of Pamir; thus, only a very small outcropping of Afghan territory separated the monolithic Russian Empire from the Anglo-Indian colonial state.

Russia was also stabilizing her borders in the Far East. Although she had reached the shores of the Pacific Ocean back in the seventeenth century, she was not at that time in a position to make use of her acquisitions. The enormous spaces, the distance from the centre and, above all, the constant insurrections by dissatisfied and brutally exploited peoples often reduced Russian administration in these territories to a mere fiction. It was not until the middle of the nineteenth century that the government organized an expedition along the River Amur and the first peasant settlers arrived to build the town of Nikolaevsk[35] at the mouth of the river. Only then could one begin to speak of Russian dominion over the Far East. Russia took advantage of the conquest of China by the Western Europeans and, in 1860, by means of the Treaty of Peking, gained for herself the same trading rights as the other states, the right to consular jurisdiction over her citizens, and so on. In addition, she confirmed her control over lands along the left bank of the Amur, the Ussuri territory and Sakhalin. The lands flanking the Amur, now populated and developed, provided Russia with extensive opportunities for further expansion into western China, eastern Turkestan and Mongolia. At the same time, a division of Russian sailors occupied the

Bay of Golden Horn in 1860, where they founded Vladivostok, an extremely important economic and political base for the Russian state in the Far East.

The end of the nineteenth century saw the definitive stabilization—with the exception of a few minor shifts—of the borders of the Russian Empire. Conflicts of interest arose between Russia and other world powers, and the main points of international conflict, which would ultimately lead to the outbreak of the First World War, made themselves apparent. The main points of contention were, in fact, the same as before, but the rivals had changed. In the Far East, Japan became Russia's new rival and, in the victorious war of 1904–5, wrested from Russia the southern part of Sakhalin, the Southern Manchurian Railroad[36] and de facto control over southern Manchuria and the Liaotung Peninsula, including Port Arthur. In addition, Japan forced the Russian government to recognize Korea as a Japanese sphere of influence. After this defeat, Russia again turned her attention to the Near East and the Eastern Question. Here she found a totally changed situation. It was no longer Britain who was her closest rival with regard to the straits, but Austria and Germany. Austria was attempting to pave the way to control of Salonika and widening her economic contacts throughout the Balkans. German influence in Turkey had increased markedly and Germany was preparing to make use of her concession to build the Baghdad Railway. Once more the Balkan nations had become a sword in the hands of rival empires, and the two Balkan Wars of 1912–13 inflamed the situation to such an extent that the war of 1914 became inevitable. Russia entered this war on the side of Britain, her former rival. The improvement in Anglo-Russian relations served the interests not only of Russian, but also of British imperialism. Until the time of the Russo-Japanese War, Britain had regarded Russia as her most dangerous rival in Asia. But now this point of view had become antiquated. Russia's defeat in the Russo-Japanese War resulted in a further decline of her international prestige, which had begun to crumble with the Crimean War. British politicians were growing convinced that the chief threat to Britain was no longer Russia but Germany.

In order to determine whether Soviet Russia picked up the threads of tsarist Russia's imperialist foreign policy, we must discover what tasks were left unfinished after the last stage of tsarism, the First World War. Thus, we must determine the following:

1. The imperialist goals that tsarism intended to pursue after winning the war.
2. Russia's borders and her position in international affairs after the conclusion of all post-war peace treaties.

According to plans laid immediately after the outbreak of the war for the division of territorial spoils, Russia was to be given the lower reaches of the River Niemen, Poznań, Silesia and Galicia, as well as a guarantee of free transit through the straits. At this time, Russia was not yet making any direct demands for Turkish territory. With the widening of the war, the members of the Entente extended their discussion of the straits question, for once Turkey allied herself to Germany, questions were raised about the "Turkish legacy" and the division of Turkish lands among the Allies. At the beginning of 1915, an agreement was reached ceding Constantinople, the straits and the Sea of Marmara to Russia. This agreement signified the renunciation by Britain and France of their opposition to Russia's ambition to become a Mediterranean state. The successes of Russian armies on the Caucasian and Persian fronts obliged the allies to go still further. They concluded a new treaty in 1916 concerning the division of Asiatic Turkey which added to Russia's promised territories Greater Armenia, including Erzurum, Trabzon, Van, Bitlis, Urmia and Kurdistan. Russia was also promised a significant tract of the Black Sea coast west of Trabzon, a region inhabited by a purely Turkish population, whose boundaries the tsarist government did not yet dare to mark out exactly. Further, Russia intended to take advantage of the weakening of China and to strengthen her hold on the Far East. At this time, China was dominated to an ever greater extent by Japan, which was in the comfortable position of seeing her rivals' forces tied up by the war in Europe. Thus, after Japan presented her Twenty-One Demands to China, Russia planned to obtain an extension, to ninety-nine years, of the term of the lease on the right of way of the Chinese Eastern Railroad in Manchuria and to broaden her rights in northern China on the pattern of the Twenty-One Demands.

Such were Russia's imperialist goals in the First World War. However, after all the peace negotiations, what was now Bolshevik Russia found her holdings reduced, even in comparison with pre-war tsarist Russia. Most of her territorial losses were lands that had become independent states: Finland, Estonia, Latvia and Lithuania. Thus, all the gains that had been made toward ruling the Baltic region were suddenly dissipated: Petersburg—now Leningrad—was once more merely one cannonball's flight away from enemy boundaries. A part of Poland fell away, as well as a portion of Ukrainian and Belorussian lands, and the "gatherer of Russian lands" was left with only an incomplete array of the lands that composed her "national" heritage. Romania took Bessarabia. Most importantly, the Balkan states, which had once served as a base for Russia's advance on the straits, fell under the economic and political influence of France and Britain. In the Far East, China was weakened, but a reborn, strengthened Japan arose in her place and barred the way to Russian imperialism in Manchuria, Korea, northern China and other areas of former Russian expansion. After the First World War, Russia, as a great power, disappeared from the international scene.

The revolution of 1917 toppled tsarism, but failed to destroy either centralism or imperialism, which since time immemorial have appeared to be determining factors in the psychology and political thought of the Russian ruling class. Russia's first revolutionary government was already strictly centralist and appropriated all the imperialist slogans of tsarist Russia. The later Bolshevik government was even more centralist. It fought against Ukrainian independence for many years and its imperialist advances, although dressed in new guises and reformulated, faithfully followed the old, well-worn paths. After the victorious October Revolution, the Bolsheviks uttered a single cry: "peace," peace at all costs. It was essential for them to suspend all external military operations in order to bring an end to internal chaos and to deal with all the independence movements that were creating national states on the ruins of the Russian empire. Moscow was ruled by a revolutionary government which proclaimed the right of all peoples to self-determination; yet, strangely enough, it continued to regard all the lands of tsarist Russia as its own "national" heritage (*otchina*) and assumed responsibility for preventing, above all else, the separation of Ukraine, Kuban, Georgia, Armenia, Kazakhstan and other lands from the RSFSR. By refusing to recognize the Treaty of Versailles, the Bolsheviks included themselves among the ranks of the so-called revisionist states (that is, states which had been wronged territorially), for, after all, they had been deprived of some of the possessions of the Russian tsars!

Compared to the other Entente states, the Soviets had been seriously weakened by the time peace was finally achieved, and this fact determined their tactics with regard to foreign policy. In their relations with the West European states that fell under the economic and political influence of the Entente, they took the position of a principled, revolutionary workers' government which was conscious of being encircled by capitalist states and which, if it agreed to sit at the same table with representatives of such states, would do so only to discuss peace and general disarmament; it would not speak of territorial claims or division of spheres of influence. Lacking strong military and economic support, Bolshevik diplomacy remained silent on these issues. Its sole achievements were the initiation, in 1922, of a series of trade agreements with European states and, as of 1924, a *de jure* recognition of the Soviet government.[37]

However, in relation to the semi-colonial nations of Asia—Turkey, Persia, Afghanistan, the Mongolian People's Republic—the Soviets played a different role. Here Russia appeared as a defender of peoples harmed by tsarist colonial policies and modern-day capitalist imperialism. Immediately upon taking power in 1917, the Soviets published proclamations addressed to "all the labouring Muslims of Russia and the East."[38] By means of these propagandistic, demagogic appeals, they sought to strengthen their position in the Asian states in order to counter the financial and political influence of Britain and France. The Bolsheviks represented themselves as champions of independence for colonial peoples and as opponents of secret diplomatic agreements. They annulled all the writs of privilege granted by those states to tsarist Russia, claiming that these were coercive and advantageous only to Russia, and concluded new agreements in which both partners supposedly stood on an equal footing. The 1924 treaty with China[39] spoke of "equality, mutuality and justice"; the Soviets renounced all special rights and privileges and the right to consular jurisdiction but, at the same time, strengthened the communist movement in China and took advantage of the spread of the communist revolution in order to interfere in Chinese internal affairs.

In the West, in Europe, official Soviet diplomacy trimmed its imperialist claws; however, the unofficial foreign office—the Comintern—set to work throughout Europe all the more briskly. This tactic had often been used before in Russian history. After the Crimean War, when Russia lacked the power to speak out strongly about the straits, her Pan-Slavic slogans rang out all the more clearly in the Balkans. The Comintern[40] followed the line of adhering strictly to principle, maintaining communist purity and distinguishing communist parties from all "opportunistic" forms of socialism. Having formed well-trained party cadres by these means, it came out of its isolation and, in accordance with the resolutions passed at the seventh Comintern congress in 1935,[41] began to organize a "single labour front" and a "popular front" composed of all "progressive democrats" and headed by a communist core. At the same time, after the implementation of the Five-Year Plans, official Soviet diplomacy also came out of isolation. In 1934, the USSR entered the League of Nations,[42] concluded a series of agreements regarding non-aggression and mutual assistance and became active in international diplomatic affairs. Great changes were also taking place in the internal life of the Soviet Union. The October Revolution was not a mere palace revolt which simply changed the person of the ruler; it was a deep transformation that rocked the foundations of society and brought in a wholesale rethinking of values. But in the Russian Revolution, as in the French, this "Jacobinism"[43] could not last forever; soon, in spite of changes in world-view and in the composition of the ruling classes, the face of old Russia began to peer through. As a result, at the outbreak of the Second World War in 1939, Soviet Russia was a purely imperialist state which had picked up all the threads of tsarist Russia's foreign policy and renewed its aggression in preparation for completing the work left to it by the tsars. Whatever changes may have occurred within the Russian ruling class, its first duty has always been to carry out the imperialist tasks left to it by its predecessors.

Let us begin with the Baltic region. After the First World War, Soviet Russia was left with only a small piece of the Baltic coast; Leningrad found itself without any ultimate strategic protection. But the Bolsheviks remembered Peter I's contention that Petersburg must be safeguarded from Liepaja to Tornio; the result was the Russo-Finnish War of 1940.[44] The "peace-loving socialist state" attacked Finland in order to gain the territory flanking Russia's outlet to the Baltic Sea. What difference did it make that the Bolsheviks officially proclaimed that Lilliputian Finland had aggressive designs on the gigantic USSR? Set phrases had to be found to justify Russian aggression. Next came the annexation of Lithuania, Latvia and Estonia as union republics ("ancient" Russian lands acquired long ago by the tsars).[45] Soviet Russian diplomacy failed to obtain the agreement of the great world powers to the annexation of Finland in 1945, but she was given to Russia as a sphere of influence; in other words, Russia was granted the freedom to meddle in Finland's internal affairs.[46] Thus, the Bolsheviks succeeded in ensuring that Leningrad would be flanked by Russian-controlled land from Liepaja to Tornio.

The second matter facing the Soviets was Tsar Ivan III's plan for the "gathering of Russian lands." In 1939 Hitler rewarded the Bolsheviks for their neutrality in the war between Germany and the West by allowing them to occupy all Ukrainian and Belorussian lands.[47] "When the Polish state collapsed, Poland became a convenient location for all kinds of contingencies and surprise developments that could threaten the USSR. In order to prevent the possibility of such occurrences and to take under its protection consanguineous Ukrainians and Belorussians, whom the bankrupt Polish government had thrown to the four winds, the Red Army, on orders of the Soviet government, crossed the Polish border on 17 September 1939 and liberated western Ukraine and western Belorussia."[48] These again are set phrases! History shows us that Muscovite tsars have liberated consanguineous Ukrainians and Belorussians more than once. Catherine II "managed" the affairs of a shaky Polish state to the point of partitioning it among neighbouring imperialists, always taking care to protect the dissidents and the endangered Confederation of Targowica. We see the same thing with the Polish government of Osóbka-Morawski,[49] which was brought in from Moscow. For her assistance in combating Germany, Russia demanded, among other territories, western Belorussia, the western Ukrainian lands, Transcarpathia, Bukovyna and Bessarabia. And thus, for the first time in Russia's history, Moscow's rulers have fulfilled the plans of Ivan III: the whole "national" heritage (*otchina*) of the Grand Princes of Muscovy is gathered around the Muscovite throne. Extremely significant in this regard is the fact that in 1945, in Bessarabia, there was a celebration honouring the 155th anniversary of the conquest of Izmail Fortress by the tsarist general Suvorov.[50] Can it be that all the territorial plunder of tsarist Russia is recognized and celebrated by Soviet Russia?

Ever since Russia reached the shores of the Black Sea, a major concern of Russian foreign policy has been the straits, and thus Turkey and the Balkan question. Today the Soviets have installed themselves for good in the Balkans (Romania, Bulgaria, Yugoslavia and Albania), and they hold sway over these pseudo-independent states, aided by occupation troops that have not yet been withdrawn. The first violin is played by Yugoslavia, as it had been by Serbia under Nicholas I;[51] today, Yugoslavia is organizing unions of Slavic peoples to serve as instruments of Moscow's policies, just like the union of Balkan Slavs in the 1860s. To the old tsarist slogans of Pan-Slavism and Orthodox unity, the Bolsheviks have added democracy. But in exactly the same way as the tsars, they are establishing a base for an advance to the straits from the west. Of the Balkan states, only Greece is not playing in unison with Moscow's Balkan orchestra; this is the reason for Moscow's sharp diplomatic struggle with Britain for the establishment of a friendly government in Greece. But for centuries, the greatest obstacle to Russia's advance toward the Mediterranean Sea has been Turkey, so it is on this country that the greatest efforts of Russia's foreign policy are focused. First, the Soviet press branded Turkey a fascist state and directed a harsh campaign against her. Then, Soviet diplomacy began its secret machinations, and a world-wide movement dedicated to the "liberation of Turkish Armenia" sprang up. In November 1945, a committee of "progressive" Armenians was established to support the demand of the Armenian people that part of the Turkish-ruled Armenian lands be united with Soviet Armenia. "The fate of the Armenian people is inextricably bound to the Soviet Union," proclaimed a statement issued by this committee.[52] In December 1945, the "Armenian National Council of America" sent memoranda containing the same statement to Truman, Attlee and Stalin, and similar national Armenian councils in Egypt and Lebanon demanded of the UN General Assembly the "unification of the Armenian people," naturally under the auspices of the Soviet Union. But the most interesting document of this campaign was a letter written by two Georgian professors "Concerning Our Legitimate Demands to Turkey" in *Radianska Ukraina*,[53] in which these two characters demand for the Soviet Union (officially, for Soviet Georgia) exactly the same territories as those promised by Britain and France to Tsar Nicholas II in the agreement concerning the division of the legacy of a defeated Turkey after the First World War. At that time, the Entente agreed to allow tsarist Russia to become a Mediterranean state, and today Soviet Russia consistently demands the same thing, that is, the partition of Turkey. What is more, she goes even further than tsarist Russia, for she already wants a colony on the Mediterranean Sea, in Tripolitania.[54]

The activity along Peter I's Persian route to India is no less lively. Tsarism's achievements on that front were already significant. In 1907, an Anglo-Russian treaty concluded in Petersburg divided Persia into three zones: the northern zone, the largest, was to become Russia's sphere of influence; the south-eastern was to be a British sphere of influence, while the rest of Persia was to become a neutral zone. It is true that this treaty placed theoretical limits upon Russia's expansion but, in fact, it significantly aided her expansionist efforts. All the wealthier Persian provinces fell under Russia's direct influence; Russian troops were able to move directly to the Persian border and even into the heart of Persia, there to establish garrisons. By 1908–9, Russia's trade with Persia was already double that of Britain. The First World War and the Russian Revolution brought an end to these developments, but the Second World War provided Bolshevik Russia with the opportunity to undertake a new offensive. Taking advantage of the fact that the course of the war necessitated sending Russian troops to northern Iran, the former tsarist sphere of influence, the Soviets refused to withdraw their divisions at the end of the war. Basing their action on the fact that conflicts were occurring in northern Iran between the Azerbaidzhanis and Teheran, the Soviets began, with the help of the Azerbaidzhani Democratic Party, to organize opposition to Teheran. In November 1945, a General Popular Assembly was called, elections held and a national government of Azerbaidzhan created.[55] Official Soviet diplomacy claimed strict neutrality throughout. This Soviet-Persian policy aroused uneasiness in Britain and the United States, which led to the well-known events in the Security Council. Ultimately, the truth came out: on 4 April 1946, a Soviet-Iranian treaty was signed creating a Soviet-Iranian petroleum partnership in northern Iran, more or less on the same territory that had been the Russian sphere of influence in 1907.

In the Far East, after the capitulation of Japan, the Bolsheviks took pains to ensure that their interests did not suffer. In the first place, they appropriated the southern part of Sakhalin Island[56] under the pretext that it had once belonged to tsarist Russia. In Korea, together with the Americans, the Soviets are ''helping'' to establish a democratic government (read: a government favourable to themselves), for Russia once fought Japan for possession of Korea and regards it as territory for future expansion.[57] In northern China and Manchuria, the Soviets are engaged in fierce competition with the Americans, for on those territories the tsars paved the way for Russian imperialism back in the nineteenth century. It does not matter that the Chinese themselves have asked the Russian armies to remain; we know very well that throughout the entire history of Russian imperialism, from the time of Ivan III to that of Stalin, the Russians have always managed to find someone to invite them to ''come,'' ''assist,'' ''remain,'' ''take them under their protection,'' and so on.

One might think that the world's first socialist workers' and peasants' state would follow new paths, organizing blocs of the most progressive, democratic, ideologically affiliated states, or blocs of small states that are targets of capitalist imperialism. In fact, we see the exact opposite: the USSR acting in unison with the two strongest capitalist world powers, Britain and the United States. Thus, we see a union based on power and on the common interests of great states rather than one based on the interests of workers or on ideology. Even after the Bolshevik revolution, Russia has been unable and has consciously refused to stop treading the well-worn paths of Russian imperialism, paths that were marked out by Russia's geographical position and her age-old political traditions. In the same tradition as the tsars, the Bolshevik overlords are forcing the Russian people to enslave other peoples which, at their expense, will help turn Russia into a world power.

The foreign policy adopted by the Union of Soviet Socialist Republics is not internationalist, worker-oriented or peace-loving; it is the policy of an imperialist Russian great power.

May 1946

Source: Typescript copy: Archive of the Foreign Representation of the Supreme Ukrainian Liberation Council, Folio U4–2. Photocopy: Archive, *Litopys UPA*.

NOTES

1. Golden Horde: the Mongol host. Its empire was founded in the mid-thirteenth century and comprised most of Russia and Ukraine, with its capital at Sarai. The increasing power of the Grand Dukes of Muscovy after 1380 brought about its decline.
2. V.P. Potemkin, ed., *Istoriia diplomatii* (Moscow 1941), 1: 130.
3. Ivan III (the Great) (1440–1505): Grand Duke of Muscovy, which he freed from allegiance to the Golden Horde.
4. Vasilii III (1479–1533): Grand Duke of Muscovy. Annexed Pskov, Riazan and Smolensk.
5. The Ottoman Empire.
6. A German military-religious order (1202–1561) founded by the bishop of Riga to christianize the Baltic lands.
7. Murmansk: city on the Kola Peninsula, strategically important in both world wars as a port to which supplies intended for Russia and the U.S.S.R. were sent by the Western Allies.
8. Ivan IV (the Terrible) (1530–84): Grand Duke of Muscovy; adopted the title of tsar.
9. In 1654, the Treaty of Pereiaslav was concluded between Hetman Bohdan Khmelnytsky and Tsar Alexei Mikhailovich. It established a military-political union between Ukraine and Muscovy which subsequently led to the complete annexation of Ukraine by Russia.
10. The significance of the year 1661 is not clear. It may be that the author had in mind the Treaty of Andrusovo of 1667.
11. Lenin, "What the 'Friends of the People' Are and How They Fight the Social-Democrats" (1894), *Collected Works* (Moscow 1960–70), 1: 155.
12. Stalin, *Marksyzm i natsionalno-koloniialne pytannia* (Kiev 1935), 62; English ed.: "The Immediate Tasks of the Party in the National Question: Theses for the Tenth Congress of the R.C.P.(B.) Endorsed by the Central Committee of the Party" (1921), *Works* (Moscow 1952–5), 5: 16–17.
13. Stalin, *Marksyzm i natsionalno-koloniialne pytannia*, 12; English ed.: "Marxism and the National Question," *Works*, 2: 314.
14. Leopold Okulicki (1893–1946): Polish general and last commander of the Polish Home Army. Arrested by the Soviets and sentenced to ten years' imprisonment, he died in a Soviet jail.
15. Kashlyk: capital of the Siberian Khanate (at the end of fifteenth century). Taken by Iermak in 1582.
16. By the Treaty of Nerchinsk (1689), Russia conceded Far Eastern Siberia to China.
17. As a result of this treaty between Russia and Poland, Smolensk and Ukraine east of the Dnieper, including Kiev, were ceded to Russia.
18. Eastern Question: European problem presented by the decline and dis-

integration of the Ottoman Empire after 1700 and attempts by Russia to profit from this state of affairs.

19. *Istoriia SSSR* (Moscow 1939), 1: 645.
20. Karl Marx, *Secret Diplomatic History of the Eighteenth Century*, ed. Eleanor Marx Aveling (London 1899), 87.
21. Editorial, "Russkii narod—rukovodiashschaia sila sredi narodov nashei strany" (The Russian People—The Guiding Force Among the Peoples of Our Country), *Bolshevik*, no. 10 (May 1945): 4.
22. By the Treaty of Prut (1711), Peter I restored Azov to the Turks and agreed to remove Russian troops from Right-Bank Ukraine.
23. As result of the Northern War (1700—21) and the Treaty of Nystad (1721), Sweden ceded Livonia, Ingermanland, and part of Karelia to Russia.
24. Liepaja: city in Latvia. Along with Courland, it was ceded to Russia in 1795.
25. Tornio: town on Finland's border with Sweden.
26. *Istoriia SSSR*, 1: 695.
27. The Polish constitution of 3 May 1791.
28. The Hetmanate was abolished in 1764, but did not actually cease to exist until 1782, when the Cossack administrative structure was finally liquidated. The Zaporozhian Sich, a fortress on the Dnieper River which served as the military and administrative centre of the Zaporozhian Cossacks, was destroyed by Catherine II in 1775.
29. Friedrich Engels, "Die auswärtige Politik des russischen Zarentums" (1890), in K. Marx and F. Engels, *Werke*, ([East] Berlin 1963), 22: 17.
30. *Istoriia SSSR*, 1: 719.
31. Crimean War (1853—6): conflict between the Russian Empire and a coalition of West European nations.
32. Alexander I (1777—1825): Russian tsar (1801—25). During his rule Russia annexed Georgia (1801—10), Finland (1809), Bessarabia (1812), and Azerbaidzhan (1813).
33. The Transcaucasian Railroad extended from Baku via Tbilisi and Kutaisi to Tuapse on the Black Sea. In 1958, it became part of the Teheran-Moscow line.
34. The Transcaspian Railroad, built 1880—1905.
35. Also called Nikolaevsk-on-Amur.
36. The Southern Manchurian Railroad was a trunk line between Changchun and Dairen. Originally it was part of the Russian-built Chinese Eastern Railroad.
37. The first *de jure* recognition of the Soviet government came from Germany at Rapallo in 1922.
38. Reference is to the proclamation of the Council of People's Commissars of 3 December (20 November) 1917.

39. Reference is to the Agreement on General Principles for the Settlement of the Questions between the Republic of China and the USSR of 31 May 1924.
40. Comintern: abbreviation used to designate the Third (Communist) International established in March 1919 and disbanded in May 1943.
41. The seventh congress of the Comintern (July-August 1935) gave official blessing to the concept of the Popular Front. This new policy contributed a great deal to the spread of Soviet influence in the trade union-movement and among intellectuals and radical youth in many countries.
42. The League of Nations was a product of the First World War and aimed at the maintenance of peace, the arbitration of international disputes and the promotion of international co-operation. It was founded at the Paris Peace Conference in 1919. The League dissolved in April 1946 and transferred its services and real estate to the United Nations, which had been established at the San Francisco Conference (25 April–26 June 1945).
43. Jacobinism: the egalitarianism and terrorism of the Jacobins in the French Revolution.
44. The war actually began on 30 November 1939, when the USSR attacked Finland. In the peace treaty signed on 12 March 1940, Finland ceded part of the Karelian Isthmus, Vyborg and several border territories to the USSR.
45. The Baltic republics were incorporated into the USSR in 1940.
46. According to the terms of the peace treaty signed in Paris in 1947, Finland was obliged to pay the USSR $300 million in reparations and did so by 1952. Since that time Finland has pursued a policy of neutrality and co-operation with the USSR.
47. Reference is to the Molotov-Ribbentrop Pact of 1939.
48. "Zovnishnia polityka SRSR," *Politychnyi slovnyk* (Kiev 1940), 222.
49. Osóbka-Morawski, Edward (1909–): head of the Lublin Committee and Premier of the Polish Government, 1945–7.
50. Izmail: city in south-western Ukraine. It was a strong Turkish fortress captured twice by the Russians in 1770 and 1790. The second assault was directed by the Russian general A.V. Suvorov (1729–1800).
51. Nicholas I (1841–1921): prince (1860–1910) and king (1910–1918) of Montenegro, not Serbia.
52. Cf. J. V. Stalin, "Turkish Armenia," *Works* (Moscow 1952–5), 4: 26–7.
53. *Radianska Ukraina*, 21 December 1945.
54. Tripolitania: region in West Libya along the Mediterranean coast.
55. Under foreign pressure, however, the Soviets withdrew their troops in 1946, and the two governments set up by them were abolished in 1947.
56. Sakhalin: island off the coast of Siberia. Under joint Russo-Japanese control until 1905, when the Treaty of Portsmouth gave Japan the southern

half of the island. After World War II, the Japanese territory was given to the USSR in accordance with the Yalta agreement.

57. At war's end (1945), Korea was divided into occupation zones—the Soviets north and the Americans south of the 38th parallel. This led to the Korean War in 1950.

THE BOLSHEVIK DEMOCRATIZATION OF EUROPE

P. Duma

Events on the international arena do not always unfold in the way that a nation might desire. Currently, we see our enemy, Bolshevik Moscow, marching victoriously into Europe and strengthening its position in the world. But it need not necessarily be so in the future. In any case, in a subject people's struggle for its own state and its own existence, all international developments are simply more or less convenient backdrops; in no way do they free the nation's activists from the obligation to struggle relentlessly for the attainment of their ideal. Today, as Bolshevik armies storm Berlin, we are reminded of the years 1918–20, when the small Ukrainian army blocked the path of the Red hordes led by Muravev[1] and Budenny,[2] which were heading through Ukraine to conquer the West. At that time, the world was deaf and blind to our unequal struggle. It is true that we did not succeed in holding back the invasion. But nobody can say that we were broken, that we meekly placed our necks into the foreign yoke. It took no time at all for our people to see through the "wolf in sheep's clothing" and to respond to the violence and occupation with weapons and blood. Perhaps Colonel Ievhen Konovalets[3] was correct when he advised that we allow the Bolsheviks into Europe. Why should the Ukrainian people have been saddled with the burden of protecting and defending Europe against the new approach of Genghis Khan? Why, as in the twelfth and thirteenth centuries, should we again have spent a century engaged in unequal struggles with the hordes of the East, while Central and Western European cultures flourished? Were we again to serve only as the "outpost" of the European stronghold? And perhaps it is true that had it not been for the battles at the Rivers Kaiala[4] and Kalka,[5] Ukrainian history would have recorded a shorter period of subjugation and statelessness.

As we watch the Red Army "liberate" various European countries, we cannot help but make some comparisons. When we observe what is happening to the "powers," countries, states, republics and kingdoms which recently displayed such arrogance, we feel . . . consoled. This is not because we are spiteful, or because we take pleasure in the misfortunes of our neighbours. No, we are incapable of rejoicing at another's suffering, for we have known much ourselves. But we cannot help recalling the attitude of those "neighbours" to the tragedy that was occurring in Ukraine when the Ukrainian people were struggling against an enemy common to us all. We had occasion to hear many acid remarks concerning our nation's maturity, political astuteness and even honour. Now events are unfolding in such a way as to reveal these very qualities in our western and southern neighbours. We see nations, long since established and possessed of their own states, capitulating without firing a single shot and falling like drunkards into the arms of the enemy. And we are reminded of the words of the Polish writer who states that "even a great nation can fall, but only an abject one can be broken." At present, those words serve as our measure of the worth of the national societies now faced with a great threat. And in this regard, we can point with pride to our own revolutionary armed struggle for liberation against the Soviet invader, not because we seek praise or recognition, but because our assessment is objective. We feel morally strengthened and joyfully conscious of our national self-worth.

But events are unfolding very quickly and we cannot waste precious time. We see how assiduously Moscow is capitalizing on the collapse of the German empire for its own purposes. We have no reason to mourn the fact that hostile imperialist forces are collapsing, but at the same time it makes no sense to aid Russian imperialism. At present, when the Russian imperialists are seizing a number of European countries under the guise of "liberating" them, our task is to decipher Moscow's objectives and the methods it uses to attain them in order to reveal the Bolsheviks' true face to the peoples subjugated or threatened by her and to outline their prospects in their struggle for freedom. This duty falls to us because we Ukrainians have lived for decades under Bolshevik occupation and have experienced Bolshevik reality not from a distance or on film, but in the most direct way.

We might add here that what is now going on in such countries as Poland, Romania, Hungary, Bulgaria, Yugoslavia and elsewhere in terms of building the state, social reconstruction and philosophical reassessment is not accidental, nor is it in any way organic to national existence or related to progress. These processes have long since been set down in the works of communist theoreticians and practitioners, and Bolshevik practice over several decades has served to confirm them. Of course, this does not mean that the leaders of the proletariat are putting into effect the Marxist-Leninist concept of reordering the world. They have simply harnessed the revolutionary theories of communist utopians to the building of a new world empire which, for the sake of camouflage, is now called the USSR. And they have made use of the strategy and tactics of the proletarian revolution in order to establish a new world centre—Moscow. The point is not whether and to what extent all the social changes that are being implemented today in the above-mentioned countries are beneficial, for this is a separate, purely national, internal matter for each nation to decide; the point is that all this is being done under the obvious direction of Moscow, whose goal is not to improve social conditions for peasants or workers, but to draw them and their entire nations into a new political system in which these same peasants and workers will be nothing but slaves of the Stalinist overlords. Thus, as we examine the current "liberation," "democratization" and "nationalization" of European countries, we shall not stop to analyze all the measures that the "provisional governments" are so hurriedly putting into place. Instead, we will point directly to the ways in which the enemy is imperceptibly undermining these societies even as he readies the slippery slope along which they will slide into the abyss unless preventive measures are taken.

For the most part, Western Europeans do not realize how much the Bolsheviks have changed since the October Revolution. They still maintain their old views about "the land of victorious socialism," "the dictatorship of the proletariat," "democracy," "equality of nations," and so on. Meanwhile, the present-day USSR has clearly become a new Russian empire and displays all the characteristics of an imperialist power. To continue to see it through the eyes of nineteenth-century socialist leaders and to gaze devoutly into its messianic face is as naive as to believe the wolf in the fairy tale who dons a red cap and pretends to be the grandmother... [6]

We shall not discuss why events have unfolded in this way, for that is less important to the threatened nations. We will only state that the discrepancy between theory and practice was so great, and disillusionment so painful, that the Bolsheviks were compelled to make numerous tactical zigzags before finally coming upon Russian ultranationalism. There were laws at work here that were born in the period of building socialism in one country. The Bolsheviks were forced to confront two mutually exclusive ideas: "uncompromising Marxism," which recognizes not nations, but only classes, and "uncompromising nationalism," the gravitation of individual nations toward independence. The Bolsheviks capitulated and chose to side with the Russian nation, basing themselves on the principle that it was preferable to have at least one nation, and the most populous one at that, behind them than to have all nations against them. This led to the rise of Stalinism, the new Russian imperialism, which donned a red shirt and set out to conquer the world.[7] And precisely because this form of imperialism hides behind deceptive slogans of socialism and democracy and follows the path and methods of revolutionary Marxist doctrine, it is all the more formidable and dangerous an enemy of all subject and threatened peoples, particularly those in close proximity to the state of "workers and peasants."

What is the basis for our claim that the USSR is not "the bastion of the world proletarian revolution," but a *Russian imperialist state* which uses the slogans of socialism to implement its imperialist concept? We base our claim on the following points.

First of all, pride of place in the state leadership is given to the imperialist element of the Russian nation. Regardless of whether qualified political workers can be found within the individual union republics, the Kremlin fills all higher positions with "true" Russians or people whose sense of national identity has been reduced to mere tokenism, for in every way they have become "Russians." Ukraine stands as an example of this practice: throughout the period of Soviet rule, all the secretaries of the Communist Party, that is, all the actual dictators of the country, have been foreigners—Russians.[8] This is also true of other union republics. And we see the same practice at work in the Red Army, where Russians are assigned to armoured and motorized units, where they enjoy greater comforts and run a smaller risk of being killed than members of other peoples, who are assigned to infantry units. The fact that at the moment a Georgian, Dzhugashvili, occupies the Kremlin throne is not significant, for history has known many such cases: they only prove that no one is as capable of brutality in his dealings with other peoples as a ruler who has betrayed his own. Now as never before, feelings of national pride, chauvinism, inflexibility and dominance are being awakened in the Russian population. The proletarian anthem has been exchanged for one that is patriotically Russian, and every Soviet child now repeats in song that the USSR was "forged forever by great Russia."[9] These feelings are being aroused in the Russians by the disinterment of the history of their infamous tsars, Ivan the Terrible[10] and Peter,[11] the tsarist generals Suvorov,[12] Brusilov[13] and Kutuzov,[14] tsarist officials such as Griboedov[15] and others. The Red

Army is completely and indissolubly bound to the traditions of the tsarist army, and already it is impossible to tell where tsarism ends and socialism begins. Proletarian marshals and generals proudly display golden epaulettes on their shoulders and the Kremlin court is ablaze with brilliant medals and orders. From every word and every line printed in the Soviet press ring out the messianic words of Andrei Bely:[16] "Russia, Russia, Russia—Messiah of the future." At the same time, anything that even hints at the national feelings of any other, non-Russian people is stifled and destroyed by executions, deportations and terror.

Second, within the USSR, and particularly on the territories of non-Russian republics, provinces and regions, plans are being implemented to weld together the entire Soviet population on the basis of a single language, a single fatherland, a single patriotism, a single state, a single social order, a single culture, scholarship and art, a single ruling authority and party, a single capital and, at the top, a single "genius"—"a man for the whole world." This is, in practice, the creation of a single nation, even if one takes nationhood to be as Stalin defined it, that is, a community of "language, territory, economic life and psychological makeup which manifests itself in a community of culture." There is no need even to speak of the position occupied at present by the Russian language. It is the language of Lenin, the language of the "older brother," the language of the land of "victorious socialism." Community of territory is guaranteed by the constitution, for every citizen of the USSR is simultaneously a citizen of all the republics. Furthermore, the concept of the "fatherland" is not synonymous with that of the national fatherland, but only with the USSR as a whole. Community of economic life exists too, for Stalin's pseudo-socialism extends over all Soviet territory, and the exploitative system of state capitalism makes itself felt by all workers. As for the community of "psychological makeup which manifests itself in a community of culture," its existence is proved a million times over in every newspaper, every poem, every school textbook, every scholarly work. It does not matter that, according to official terminology, this culture is "socialist in content and national in form," for in the Soviet Union the concept of socialism has long since been bound inseparably to that of Russia. The process of creating a single Soviet nation, which is nothing less than a coercive assimilation of non-Russian nations, goes even beyond the Stalinist definition of nationhood. It also includes the attempt to inject all peoples of the USSR with such features as racism ("consanguineous fraternal peoples"), militarism (the cult of the Red Army), expansionism (the "liberation" of other peoples), traditionalism (the disinterment of past history), autarchy (complete isolation of economy and trade) and messianism, all of which add up to attaining one's goals by force—in short, imperialism. Stalin's so-called "nationality policy" is nothing less than the creation of a single Russian imperialist nation.

Third, old tsarist imperialist ideas, which had been concocted for export and which the international proletariat once rooted out with such passion, are now being disinterred in the USSR. Slavophilism and Orthodoxy are two such ideas, linked in every nerve to the reactionary regime of old imperial Russia. And it must be pointed out that in these matters, as in all the social novelties propagated by the Bolsheviks, the essence lies not in Orthodoxy as a faith or in Slavophilism as a form of international cultural symbiosis, but in the fact that these ideas are harnessed to the imperialist concept of the present Kremlin rulers, who use them to deceive and assimilate other peoples. There is surely no need to remind the reader of how much money the tsarist government used to spend to disseminate Slavophilism in the regions of the former Austro-Hungarian empire in order to build up sympathy for Moscow as the capital of all Slavs and induce these peoples to look to Russia as the "protector" of all subjugated Slavs, the older brother who would "turn all Slavic rivers to the single Russian sea."[17] Since Moscow always dreamed of hegemony in Europe, she had to search for ideas which would appeal, if not to all European peoples, then at least to Slavs. And in practice, Slavophilism is nothing more than patent Russophilism. The tsarist regime proved this by its treatment of those "Slavophiles" who hoped to build a Slavic capital, but... in Kiev. Needless to say, these people, among them Kostomarov,[18] Shevchenko and others, paid heavily for their anti-Russian ideas. And what can one say of Orthodoxy in the tsarist era? Ever since Khmelnytsky's Treaty of Pereiaslav, through all the ruin and destruction of the eighteenth and nineteenth centuries, the Orthodox clergy in Ukraine, its leaders in particular, have served as agents of the occupying power. Thus it is not surprising that when the October revolutionaries were overturning the old tsarist order in Russia, they had to deal mercilessly with the Orthodox clergy, the most visible and loyal representatives of that order. Nor is it surprising that under Soviet rule, that is, during the official campaign of atheism, the Orthodox clergy has fallen so hopelessly into the moral abyss. Under such harsh conditions, only honest and morally steadfast individuals could survive with dignity: obviously, such people are not to be found among agents of the state. Now the Bolsheviks have changed their tactics and channelled the surviving remnants of the Orthodox clergy into the imperialist mainstream. And those clerics who only yesterday were undergoing persecution today sing "Hail to Comrade Stalin," in harmony with the secret police which so recently was putting them away. By the grace of the Bolshevik dictator, a Russian has assumed the patriarch's throne, where he glories in the imperial tsarist title of "Patriarch of Moscow and all Rus',"[19] shamelessly forgetting that it is not Rus' but, as it is officially termed, a union of republics which today forms the backbone of the state. But, of course, all this has its reasons and its purposes.

Fourth, the entire Soviet economy is built on the pattern of imperialist colonial states. In conquered countries, such as Ukraine and others, industries based on extraction and raw materials are being built on a large scale, while all manufacturing industries and factories are located at the centre. The subject countries are thus placed in a subordinate economic position. For Russia, the union republics are simply bases of supply and raw materials. Is it not significant that of all the heavy industries in Ukraine, that is, industries related to fuel (coal, oil, peat), electrical energy, mineral ore, iron, steel, cast-iron, non-ferrous metals, chemical products, machinery and so on (in other words, all those things on which the industrialization of a country and a nation's economy are based), none has its own commissariat in Kiev, but all fall under the direct jurisdiction of the government in Moscow, which is, in fact, also the government of Russia? The same is true of all forms of transportation, including rail, water and air transport. And even those People's Commissariats of industry that do exist in Kiev—for example, those related to such industries as food, fish, meat, light industry, textiles, timber and building materials—are not independent, but are under the jurisdiction of similar commissariats in Moscow and are, in practice, only branch offices. Only two industrial commissariats are "republican" in nature, those relating to local industry and local fuel industry; these the Moscow centre has magnanimously ceded to the union republics. The exploitative nature of Muscovite centralism can best be understood if one compares state budgets. But this is not the place for a detailed discussion of such matters. The result of all this is that the "concentration of production and capital" has fallen into the hands of a small group of Kremlin capitalist dictators (as has the deciding role in the whole economy); there has been a fusion of all the capital of state and society, creating "finance capital" and thus financial oligarchy. Lenin set out the place of non-Russian peoples within the Russian socialist empire in his explication of "national self-determination up to and including separation."[20] He wrote, "We have no reason to believe that, in a socialist society, the nation will exist as an economic and political unit. In all probability, it will only assume the character of a cultural and linguistic unit, because the territorial division of a socialist cultural zone, if practised at all, can be made only according to the needs of production and, furthermore, the question of such a division will naturally not be decided by individual nations alone and in possession of full sovereignty, but will be determined jointly by all the citizens concerned."[21] Here we find, among other things, the justification for the annexation of the Crimea,[22] Kuban[23] and other Ukrainian territories directly to the Russian Republic. But Lenin, when he wrote these words, was still thinking of building socialism, while Stalin has long since reduced everything to building the Russian empire, and nothing more.

Fifth, the Bolsheviks are inexorably pursuing the old tsarist policy of building Russia by annexing a number of other countries and states. Here we must mention their seizure of Finnish territory in 1940, as well as western Belorussia and Ukraine, Bessarabia and, finally, the Baltic states of Lithuania, Latvia and Estonia. All these lands were annexed by force to the USSR, not for the sake of liberating the proletariat, but on the basis of the historical and strategic reasoning of Russian imperialism. There is no need even to mention the other nations conquered and subjugated earlier—Ukraine, Georgia, Azerbaidzhan, Turkmenistan, Mongolia and others—for these conquests took place during the period of so-called "war communism." Under the pretext of defending the proletariat in other countries, the current Russian leadership does not hesitate to enter into partnership with the most powerful enemies of mankind in order to further Russian interests (as it did, for example, with Hitler in 1939) and to assist them in the conquest of other nations.[24] How can this be explained if not by the imperialist nature of present-day Russian policy? What would Marx and Engels say today if they were to rise from the grave and see how their theory of the building of communism is being carried into effect? Without a doubt, they would relegate Stalin to his proper place, to the ranks of tsars and capitalists. And we must bear in mind that the Bolsheviks do not stop at annexation. Immediately afterward comes every type of misery, brought on by a form of occupation unparallelled in human history. From the very first day an enormous administrative and police apparatus, composed mainly of Russians, is planted on the annexed territory; then come arrests, deportations, executions, plunder and the reassessment of all national values; the people undergo re-education and the younger generation is reared in the spirit of slavish devotion to Moscow. Socialism and democracy are merely smokescreens behind which a brutal process of denationalization and assimilation is carried out.

Sixth, under the guise of "liberating" nations from German subjugation, the Bolsheviks are inciting so-called "bourgeois-democratic revolutions" in the Central European countries occupied by the Red Army with the eventual aim of annexing these countries to their empire centred in Moscow. They are thus preparing the ground for complete Russian hegemony in Europe. For the purpose of world conquest, the

Muscovite Bolsheviks have their "domestic" concept of proletarian revolution, but during the struggle with Nazi Germany and whenever they have had to ally themselves with Western capitalist imperialist powers, they have been unable to make use of this concept. For this reason, the German fascist and fascism in general, rather than Marx's bourgeois, have now been declared public enemy number one, and it is on the fascist that they have trained their weapons, monopolizing and exploiting the liberation struggles of European peoples subjugated by the Germans. Of course, this has nothing in common with building socialism, but that fact does not prevent the Bolsheviks from beginning to effect the socialist revolution within the "liberated" countries and thereby sowing confusion in the adjacent states, over which they hope to gain control all the more easily later on. With their revived militarism, the Russians are following the well-trodden path taken by every victorious army, from which they will not stray. Those nations which fail to realize this fact, which are now assisting the Russians and helping to strengthen their position in the world, will very soon learn where all this is leading. To Poland, Bulgaria, Czechoslovakia and Yugoslavia, the Slavophile bait—and, in some cases, the Orthodox one as well—is still alluring. As a result, their way into the embraces of the Kremlin octopus will be eased, not only by external force, but by their own psychological predisposition.

Seventh, by means of the Comintern or, as we see at present, the international trade union organization,[25] the Bolsheviks are conducting subversion in all countries of the world, particularly in the capitalist states currently allied with the Soviet Union. The major goal of this activity is not to fight for any improvement in the lot of the proletariat, but to undermine the strength of the imperialist states in competition with the Bolsheviks and to extend their own fifth column, military intelligence and everything else that may prove useful for the establishment of the "Union of Soviet Socialist Republics of the World." A state that is not imperialist does not meddle in the internal affairs of foreign countries. By all their Comintern and trade union activity throughout the world, the Bolsheviks prove that they are imperialists, and of the first rank at that.

Eighth, the USSR has joined the other imperialist powers in dividing up the world and is now proceeding to safeguard that division by means of an international organization which is to serve as a protector of its interests. Notwithstanding all their slogans about equality and democracy, at the conference in Dumbarton Oaks[26] the Bolsheviks pushed through a thoroughly undemocratic voting scheme and in this shameless manner guaranteed themselves a permanent place on the so-called "Security Council," thus buying a period of tranquility in which they can complete the process of forced Russification in their own country and proceed to add successive satellites to the Kremlin orbit.

These are the main imperialist features of present-day Russia, an empire which, for the sake of deception, has assumed the guise of a "union of republics." Anyone who points the tip of the Bolshevik imperialist sword at another and fails to recognize these features is clearly either suffering from political "night blindness" and incapable of perceiving the truth or has become, by force of circumstance, a physical slave and spiritual eunuch and thus does not want to perceive it.

It has been our misfortune, in part, that until now Bolshevik imperialism has generally subjugated peoples that hardly remembered their previous independence and whose consciousness of national and social freedom was as limited as that of all the Leninist socialist and communist theories. This made it possible for Moscow to focus all its attention on Ukraine and the other nations that opposed it. Thus it is not surprising that all attempts on the part of Ukrainian and other anti-Bolshevik forces in the USSR to bring down the Bolshevik prison of nations by various actions, uprisings and revolutions have not yet proved successful. But today the situation has changed. The Bolsheviks have trained their weapons on the states of such European nationalities as the Finns, Poles, Hungarians, Romanians, Bulgarians, Serbs, Croats, Slovaks and Czechs. This, in turn, poses a threat to the Swedes, Norwegians, Greeks, Turks and others. It is worth recalling, for the sake of comparison, that the weakest point in Hitler's imperialist strategy was the dispersion of German forces throughout Europe. Now the Russian bear has also crawled out of his lair and is lumbering menacingly around the capitals of Europe. Although only the future can tell what results this will bring him, we do not doubt for a moment that his end will be similar to that of the Germans.

It makes no difference that, in contrast to the Germans' overt policy of occupation, the Bolshevik imperialist strategy and tactics are carried out by covert, deceptive and cunning means and implemented by stages. Although this will impede the full consolidation of anti-Bolshevik forces, it simply means that there is no time to lose in deciphering all the Stalinist measures now being applied "according to plan" in the "liberated" nations. Hitler was of enormous assistance to the Bolsheviks in the fulfillment of their grasping plans. Had it not been for him, they would have had to take the difficult route of preparing and effecting social revolutions in various European states. Let us recall all the activities of the Comintern prior to the outbreak of the Second World War. At that time, its activity devolved upon those who initiated and conducted acts of sabotage and strike actions and worked to legitimize its agent, the Communist Party. When this produced no results, the Comintern worked to establish the so-called "popular front," which made repeated demands for such things as the six-hour work day, the reorganization of trade unions, constant changes of government, complete freedom of speech, of the press and of association (which was synonymous with open Bolshevik agitation), and the admission into various countries of the Soviet press, literature, film and the like. While in the USSR the Soviet worker was undergoing unparalleled exploitation, while he was being bound like a serf to his workplace and perishing from hunger and excessive Stakhanovism in an atmosphere of brutal police terror, Bolshevik agents were inciting other European countries to anarchy and sowing the seeds of confusion, thereby facilitating the seizure of their prey. The result was increased unemployment, popular dissatisfaction and general economic crisis, accompanied by a spiritual crisis. Although at home, in the USSR, the Soviets had built an immense war machine and were armed to the teeth, in Europe the Comintern apostles were praying ecstatically to the idols of pacifism, humanism, socialism and other such demobilizing ideas. Through their mouthpieces—persons devoid of national consciousness, including certain "professors," the déclassé elements and the dregs of society, as well as a certain number of foreigners—the Comintern agents attempted to demobilize the armies, or even completely disarm them, and to do away with police forces, prisons and political trials; in a word, they were fighting for what was generally termed "people's democracy."[27] Of course, this "democracy" was quickly unmasked and the Comintern agents had to yield one position after another on the world stage to the new, growing national movements which arose as an antidote to the Bolshevik attempts to destroy national identity.

Today things are different. As a result of their insane occupation policies, the frenzied German imperialists have put the Bolsheviks back on their feet, giving them a new ideological weapon: the struggle for the liberation of the European peoples. And the Bolsheviks have understood that under present conditions the Comintern as such is no longer needed, for it is not by establishing "popular fronts" but by means of "national liberation" that they will implement their imperialist concept. Had it not been for Hitler, what pretext could the Red Army have found to enter nine European states? Under what other circumstances would the populations of these states have greeted the Red Army as they do today, after the terrible period of German subjugation? Every prisoner rejoices when he is released from prison and smiles happily not only at those who free him, but also at the people he meets, at the sun, the trees and his own home. The Bolsheviks are rushing to capitalize on this reaction and, during this period when enthusiasm runs high, they are consolidating their position by drawing up formal acts of state, such as those creating "provisional governments" composed of their puppets. Thus the Bolsheviks have made use of the liberation movements of peoples subjugated by Nazi Germany in order to build their own empire. Their policy is fully in accord with Leninist thought: "Leninism instructs us to regard the liberation struggles of oppressed nations primarily from the point of view of class, or social revolution. It considers how best to make use of the great revolutionary forces potentially inherent in the struggles of oppressed nations for their liberation" (Second Congress of the Comintern).

Their tactics are as follows:

First,

a) along with the democratic bourgeoisie, to give full support to the liberation movement of any oppressed people that is directed against an imperialist power in competition with the USSR;

then,

b) having helped the oppressed people to liberate itself with the aid of the Red Army, to side with that people's proletariat, peasantry and poorer classes against the bourgeoisie and landowners;

further,

c) to side with the proletariat, poor peasantry and somewhat more prosperous peasants against wealthy farmers and the remnants of the petty bourgeoisie;

and, finally,

d) to side with those most devoid of national consciousness against the nationally conscious proletariat and thus to liquidate the nation.

Lenin had something to say about this: "Combat all national oppression? Yes, of course! Fight *for* any kind of national development, *for* national culture in general? Of course not."[28] Depending on the strategic significance of a given country, its formal inclusion into the "family of nations of the USSR" may take place at any one of the above-mentioned stages.

In the countries of Central Europe "liberated" by the Red Army, the second stage in the implementation of the Bolshevik imperialist concept is now taking place. This entails conducting so-called Leninist "bourgeois-democratic revolutions," the tactics of which Lenin delineated as far back as 1905 in his book *The Two Tactics of Social Democracy in the Democratic Revolution*. Stalin has learned his lesson well from Lenin and is applying his teacher's sociological and political ideas. Although at present he is "liberating" nations from German occupation, as soon as this "liberation" is completed he begins to implement Lenin's plans by forcing the initiation of "bourgeois-democratic revolutions" in the "liberated" states. He is proving successful, for the Red Army now has free access to every one of these "independent" states, and agents of the NKGB[29] have guaranteed freedom of movement. Here is what Lenin wrote on this matter: "We should not forget that at present there is not and cannot be any other method of hastening the approach of socialism than complete political freedom, a democratic republic."[30] It is clear that the Bolsheviks will consciously encourage the state of confusion that comes with "bourgeois-democratic revolutions" in "liberated" countries in order to foment the greatest possible dissension and internal strife between "bourgeois democrats" and "bourgeois reactionaries" or, as they are now conveniently called, "fascists." By this means, the Soviets will widen the rifts in these societies and finally force the so-called "reactionaries" to form an illegal underground and armed defence force and push the so-called "democrats" under the protective wing of the USSR.

In order to ensure themselves complete success in the "democratic revolutions," the Bolshevik imperialists are following a well-trodden path and applying the same tactics in all the "liberated" countries. Basically this consists of the Bolsheviks, or rather, their local puppets, excluding the so-called "reactionary" elements from the country's leadership. At present, this is still being done under the guise of struggle against German hirelings. This process can be seen clearly in Poland, where the *Armia Krajowa*[31] has not only been removed from power but also subjected to terror. The same has happened in Finland, where even social democrats have fallen into discredit. Furthermore, arrests, trials and public denunciations of former allies from non-democratic and even democratic circles occur whenever they refuse to swallow Moscow's bait blindly, as in the case of certain Polish émigré circles in London. In the "liberated" countries, Moscow is elevating all the scum of society and the antisocial elements, giving them unlimited power to abuse former allies; in this way it consciously pushes these societies toward bloody internal struggles.

But the basic feature of this exercise, which sets its whole tone, is the so-called "land reform." Lenin stated that "only the proletariat can be a consistent fighter for democracy. It can become a victorious fighter for democracy only if the peasant masses join its revolutionary struggle."[32] At the particular stage that Lenin describes here, the Bolsheviks need the peasantry. Later, when socialism is being built, the peasantry will be shunted aside and state power taken over by the proletarian dictatorship. But in the meantime, the Bolsheviks are feverishly ordering the immediate distribution of land in the "liberated" countries. Odd though it may seem, just at the time when bloody battles are raging at the front, Moscow is engaged in handing out the landowners' estates. She is doing so not by means of sensible, logical state land reforms, but by passing a coercive, seditious act with the aim of inflaming the social passions of the population and deepening internal strife and dissension. By these means, the Bolsheviks are finding faithful adherents among the peasant masses, for by granting the peasants "ownership" of the landowners' estates, they make them dependent upon the "government" that protects their "ownership" rights by law. The Bolsheviks are very clearly conscious of the role of the peasantry at this stage. Lenin has written as follows: " . . . at present, the peasants are interested not so much in a categorical defence of private ownership as in the confiscation of the landowners' estates, one of the chief manifestations of this type of ownership. Although they do not become socialists or cease to be petty bourgeois, the peasants are capable of becoming the most radical adherents of the 'democratic revolution'."[33] How shameless and dishonest all this appears when the Bolsheviks know full well that very soon they will deprive the peasants not only of the estates taken from the landowners, but also of all their ancestral land except for tiny private plots, and harness them into the yoke of a new serfdom on collective and state farms. Lenin clearly promises this: "From the democratic revolution we shall at once . . . begin to pass to the socialist revolution. We stand for uninterrupted revolution. We shall not stop half-way."[34]

Let all those who now rejoice at Stalin's benevolent "liberation," "democracy" and "distribution of land" well remember Lenin's words. The time will come when all this benevolence will turn into slavery, for Stalin will build his "socialism."

It is odd how the nations of Europe, which give the appearance of being politically well-educated, fail to perceive Moscow's evil intentions. Moscow pulls the wool over their eyes by allowing all sorts of symbols from the past to remain—flags, coats of arms, anthems and other symbols of national values—in order to create the impression that she is not opposed to patriotism and independence. Meanwhile, she elevates to the ranks of national heroes and geniuses new historical personages, particularly those who at some time proved their devotion to Russia or to socialism (for Moscow has claimed a monopoly on all socialist and social matters). At the same time, all those historical forces which opposed the interests of the old Russia or the present-day USSR are vilified. By means of formal peace treaties, the Bolsheviks have gained control over all forms of propaganda, art and literature and thus have totally limited freedom of speech and of the press. Is it necessary to point out what fatal consequences this will have for the cultures of the subject peoples, for the education of their younger generations? Only organizations favourable to Moscow are allowed to exist; all others are immediately branded counter-revolutionary, their members portrayed as fascists and agents of the Germans. Only state-controlled organizations are permitted to exist, such as the "Association of Friendship with the USSR." Artists and scholars, often the most spineless elements in any society, are recruited for special excursions to Moscow and Leningrad to be shown the "fraternal" Russian culture and impressed by the blood-and-tear-stained power and beauty of the Russian centre. A great deal of activity is generated with regard to theatre, cinema, schools, mass political education, trade unions, councils and so on, in order to confuse the people, to divert their interest from the vital problems of the nation to secondary matters, and thus to ease their way into the [Soviet] yoke. Finally, state treaties of friendship, assistance and post-war co-operation with the USSR are concluded which, on the one hand, give the Bolsheviks unlimited access to the "independent" states and, on the other, prepare the psychological ground for their future an-nexation to the USSR.

This, then, is the present face of the "bourgeois-democratic revolu-tions" taking place in countries "liberated" by the Red Army.

To round out the picture and, in particular, to explain the prospects which these countries now face, we must mention the methods [the Soviets] use to annex individual nations. The peoples of the Baltic region (Lithuanians, Latvians, Estonians), as well as western Ukrain-ians and Belorussians, have already gone through this experience and thus can share their impressions and observations. Very often for-eigners, particularly those from Western democratic regimes, are skep-tical when told that all elections in the USSR take place under NKVD[35] terror. These foreigners judge every regime by its constitution; natu-rally, the constitution of the USSR is among the "most democratic" in the world. When Western Europeans learn from newspapers that, in elections to the higher Soviet bodies, 99.9% of the citizens vote for the state candidates, they naturally become deeply convinced that the USSR is "the happiest country in the world." But the point is that for-eigners do not understand the word "terror." Bolshevik terror is not the same as European or American; it is, above all, Siberian terror. Were it not for Siberia, with all the horrors of its concentration camps, and were it not for the inhuman mentality of the regime in power, per-haps Soviet terror could become more European. But as it is, every citizen of the USSR suffers constantly from a psychosis of fear, which stems not from some sort of nervous oversensitivity, but from a practi-cal assessment of the existing brutal reality. NKVD agents find their way to every individual; they place the barrels of their guns to his breast and smile maliciously at the person who will be their next victim if only he dares to disobey. This is how the "nation-wide voting" pro-ceeds, how the selection of candidates and the casting of votes are car-ried out. Who would dare vote against the candidates? And even less likely, who would have the courage to run as a candidate against the wishes of the Communist Party? Those elected are totally incapable of dealing with complex problems of state; they come together and, with loud applause, pass every resolution on annexation, reunion and the like.

The prospects before the peoples of Europe, should they become citizens of the Soviet Union, are not at all rosy. Apart from the compulsory purge from their societies of all nationally conscious individuals and the economic ruin and complete improverishment of all workers that will follow enforced collectivization and exploitation, the "allied nations" will also have to undergo a profound reassessment of their cultural values and dispense with all that is their own in favour of the common, "great" Russian culture. The citizens of these nations will have to learn to live in a police state, in which loyalty alone does not suffice; one must actively profess the Bolshevik faith and be an ever smiling, happy, joyful participant in the "new life." It does not matter that a person's heart overflows with sorrow and his stomach cries out for a piece of black bread; he must rejoice, for he is a "free" citizen of a "free and happy" country. Denunciation and co-operation with the secret police are the sacred duties of every citizen. As a result, after a certain time people grow silent, distrustful and submissive; they gaze hopelessly into a terrible future. We do not exaggerate in this depiction of the future prospects for the European peoples currently rejoicing at their "liberation." Citizens of the USSR, especially soldiers of the Red Army, can now be found on those peoples' territories. Let whoever still harbours doubts about the way in which the Bolsheviks manage their affairs at home ask a private Red Army soldier, but only when he is alone, at a time when he can be momentarily honest.

The European nations are thus faced with the problem of organizing an armed defence against the new, brutal and menacing imperialist force of occupation. This is not the time for petty disputes among nations, nor "the time to mourn for the rose, when the whole forest is burning." All past quarrels about boundaries or historical wrongs must be laid aside, for the European peoples face the great problem of preserving their age-old national cultures and defending millions of their countrymen, who at any time now may become slaves and victims of the great prison of nations. May the consciousness of success in the destruction of Nazi Germany, which so recently seemed invincible, strengthen these nations' awareness of their power and self-worth. At present, Europe and the whole world are beginning to realize that humanity is headed not for peace, but for new wars, which may prove even more bloody and brutal than those fought so far. And it must be so if truth, justice and freedom are to prevail. A particularly responsible role has fallen to the "liberated" Central and Southern European nations. By their organized popular revolutionary actions, they must be the first to bar the way to the loud-mouthed Bolshevik-Muscovite "trinity" and to take a firm stand.... Within the USSR a revolutionary liberation front of peoples subjugated by Moscow is maturing and consolidating itself by the heroic deeds of its revolutionaries; the Central European peoples must develop links and co-operate with it. It must be borne in mind that we can place our hopes only in ourselves. The prospects for victory are great, and it will not be long before the world is surprised by the emergence of a new force which, in the heart of the Bolshevik empire, has organized itself into a formidable avant-garde of fighters for a new, just order in the world. By the force of its revolutionary actions, it will hasten the day of the final collapse of Stalinist tyranny.

On its flags will be emblazoned these great words:

Death to Boshevik imperialism!

Long live freedom for nations and individuals!

Source: Ideia i Chyn 4, no. 9 (1945). Also published as a separate pamphlet. Original: Archive of the Foreign Representation of the Supreme Ukrainian Liberation Council, Folio B9.5–1. Photocopy: Archive, *Litopys UPA*.

NOTES

1. M.A. Muravev (1880–1918): Lieutenant-colonel in the Tsarist army. Military commander of the Boshevik forces during the early stages of the Russian Civil War. At the beginning of 1918 he commanded the invasion forces against the Ukrainian Central Rada.
2. S.M. Budenny (1883–1973): Founder and commander of the Soviet cavalry, became Marshal of the Soviet Union and a government official.
3. Ievhen Konovalets (1891–1938): Colonel, Army of the Ukrainian People's Republic. Head of the Ukrainian Military Organization and of the Organization of Ukrainian Nationalists. Assassinated in Rotterdam by a Soviet agent.
4. Kaiala: river mentioned in the "Song of Ihor's Campaign," where Ihor Sviatoslavych was defeated by the Polovtsians in 1185. Present-day Kalmius.
5. Kalka (Kalchyk, Kalets): tributary of the Kalmius, where in 1223 the

Ukrainian and Polovtsian princes were defeated by the Tataro-Mongolian forces of Genghis Khan.

6. Reference is to "Little Red Riding Hood."

7. This is an obvious comparison with the black- and brown-shirted imperialisms (i.e., Italian fascism and German Nazism).

8. O.I. Kyrychenko (1908—75): First Secretary, Central Committee, Communist Party of Ukraine (1953–7), first Ukrainian to hold that position. He was succeeded by M.V. Pidhorny (Podgorny) (1903–), who held the post from 1957–63; by P.Iu. Shelest (1908–), who was First Secretary from 1963 to 1972 and by V.V. Shcherbytsky (1918–), who has held the position since 1972—all of them Ukrainians.

9. Reference is to the replacement of the "Internationale" by the "Anthem of the USSR," which was performed for the first time on 1 January 1944.

10. Ivan IV (1530–84).

11. Peter I (1672–1725).

12. A.V. Suvorov (1729–1800).

13. A.A. Brusilov (1853–1926).

14. M.I. Kutuzov (1745–1813): Russian field marshal.

15. A.S. Griboedov (1794–1829): Russian diplomat and writer.

16. Andrei Bely: pseudonym of Boris Bugaev (1880–1934), Russian poet and writer, one of the main theoreticians of Russian symbolism.

17. An allusion to Aleksandr Pushkin's poem "Klevetnikam Rossii" (To the Slanderers of Russia), 1831.

18. Mykola Kostomarov (1817–85): Ukrainian historian, ethnographer and writer. One of the founders of the Society of SS. Cyril and Methodius. Taras Shevchenko was also a member of the society, and both men were arrested for belonging to it. The Cyrillo-Methodians advocated the destruction of the Russian Empire, which was to be replaced by a federal republic of Slavic nations.

19. Reference is to Aleksei (S. V. Simansky, 1877–1970), who was elected Patriarch in 1945.

20. Reference is to Lenin's "The Discussion on Self-Determination Summed Up" (1916), *Collected Works* (Moscow, 1960–70), 22: 320–60. The phrase in question appears on p. 325: "the delineation of state frontiers in accordance with the 'sympathies' of the population, including complete freedom to secede."

21. Ibid., 322. This passage does not represent Lenin's views, but those of the editorial board of the Polish social-democratic newspaper, *Gazeta Robotnicza*. Lenin quotes the passage in order to attack it.

22. The Crimean peninsula on the north shore of the Black Sea was annexed to Russia in 1783. During the Second World War the Tatar population, charged with aiding the Germans, was forcibly deported and the Autonomous Tatar Republic (created in 1921) abolished. In 1954 the Crimea was

transferred from the Russian SFSR to the Ukrainian SSR.

23. The Kuban steppe, a major grain region on the lower course of the Kuban River (North Caucasus), was settled by Ukrainian Cossacks in 1792.

24. Reference is to the Molotov-Ribbentrop Pact of 1939.

25. The World Federation of Trade Unions, organized in October 1945.

26. Dumbarton Oaks: estate, now in Washington, D.C., scene of a conference (1944) at which the USA, Great Britain, the USSR, and China reached an agreement to create the United Nations.

27. People's democracy, according to Soviet ideology, is that form of political organization of society which leads to socialism, or one of the forms of the dictatorship of the proletariat.

28. Lenin, "Critical Remarks on the National Question" (1913), *Collected Works*, 20: 35.

29. NKGB: People's Commissariat of State Security.

30. "The Two Tactics of Social Democracy in the Democratic Revolution" (1905), ibid., 9: 12.

31. *Armia Krajowa* (Home Army): Polish nationalist underground during the Second World War. Dissolved by the communists in 1945. The remnants organized themselves into *Wolność i Niezawisłość* (Freedom and Independence).

32. *Collected Works*, 9: 60.

33. Ibid., 9: 98.

34. "Social-Democracy's Attitude toward the Peasant Movement" (1905), ibid., 9: 236–7.

35. NKVD: People's Commissariat of Internal Affairs.

II
IDEOLOGICAL QUESTIONS

IDEALISM OR MATERIALISM: WHICH PHILOSOPHY ARE MEMBERS OF THE OUN OBLIGED TO FOLLOW?

O. Hornovy

The Third Extraordinary Grand Assembly of the Organization of Ukrainian Nationalists[1] clearly resolved that the OUN will not bind itself to any philosophy and *its members are thus free to subscribe either to philosophical idealism or to materialism*. This clear resolution, coupled with the fact that adherents of both philosophies are fighting side by side in our ranks, should provide an unequivocal answer to the question posed in the title of this article. On this point there should be no doubt. Nevertheless, since the question is still raised, a fuller explanation of this matter is required.

Two fundamental tendencies exist within philosophy: *Idealism* affirms that mind, or spirit, preceded nature and forms the basis of the world; matter is regarded as following from spirit. *Materialism* maintains that matter is the basis of all things, for it is primary and objectively existing, while spirit, or consciousness, is derivative. Each of these two basic philosophical tendencies is further subdivided into a number of separate schools.

The battle between philosophical idealism and materialism *has not yet been resolved by science*: neither of these tendencies has yet gained a final victory. Philosophy, which is a synthesis of all the natural and social sciences, develops in accordance with them. Thus, each new discovery in physics, chemistry and biology, every new theory in sociology, sheds new light on the fundamental philosophical question: the

primacy of spirit or of matter. These new developments in scholarship
add support at some times to idealism, at others to materialism, but
they have not yet proved one or the other correct. And the natural and
social sciences are steadily advancing, constantly furnishing new material for philosophy. The enormous advances, gains and discoveries
made by the natural sciences in recent years have not yet been fully
utilized by philosophy; they still await their full philosophical synthesis
and it is not yet known whether they will tip the balance in favour of
idealism or of materialism, or how far they will lead toward the solution of the fundamental philosophical question.

Given that the correctness of either idealism or materialism has not yet
been scientificially established, what would it mean for us, as members
of a political organization, to bind ourselves categorically to one or the
other philosophy?

A wholesale linkage of our organization with some particular school of
idealism or materialism would mean that we would have to ignore developments in science that contradicted our philosophy; that we would
have to close our eyes to all new scientific discoveries or advances
which failed to support the philosophy we had chosen to acknowledge.
And if, in the face of scientific discoveries which conflicted with our
philosophy, we continued to maintain our chosen position, then this, in
turn, would doom us *to a standstill, to ossification*, for only that political movement can remain vital which moves forward with science and
with life. If we wished to emerge from this state of ossification, we
would be forced to renounce our official philosophy, which had been
contradicted by new advances in science, and to embrace some different philosophy.

Would it not be better, under the circumstances, to leave the battle between philosophical idealism and materialism entirely to science? This
is precisely what we are doing. *We do not want to doom ourselves to a
standstill; we do not want to ignore developments in science and we do
not want to find ourselves exchanging one philosophy for a second or a
third. For these reasons, we leave it to science to resolve the question
of the correctness of idealism or materialism. For the same reasons,
our organization grants full freedom to its members to profess either
philosophical idealism or materialism.* Every one of its members can
subscribe to whichever philosophical school lies closest to his own convictions.

It might be argued that such a position deprives us of integrity, orderliness and completeness of world-view and thus weakens us on the ideological-political front. The first part of this argument we do not dispute;
the second is convincing only at first glance. Undoubtedly, orderliness
and completeness of world-view are factors which strengthen a political

movement, but only if its world-view accords in all respects with science. For of what value are orderliness and completeness in a theory if it is not affirmed by experts? Can it have any mobilizing power or be a source of strength? In any case, even if orderliness and completeness in themselves serve to strengthen a political movement, they do so only for a short time, only up to the moment when this orderliness—built on assumptions that have not been refuted by science, although perhaps not fully confirmed by it either—collapses in the face of new scientific achievements. When the orderliness of a political movement's world-view collapses in the face of scientific discoveries, a crisis is provoked within the movement, and the greater the original orderliness, the greater the crisis. Today, if a world-view really wishes to reckon with science, it cannot be orderly in all respects. As long as many questions still remain to be resolved by science, numerous changes of position may be necessary as science progresses.

To take an example: Marxism is a model of an integrated, orderly and complete theory. But do its orderliness and completeness endow it with mobilizing power? No. Today, this theory no longer retains even its original orderliness. From Marx's[2] day to the present time, it has undergone countless revisions, corrections and additions—"we will replace the old with the new," as Stalin put it. All those who consider themselves Marxists, from Western European socialists to Bolsheviks, have continually struck at the integrity and orderliness of Marxist theory. Why? Do they not wish to strengthen themselves on the ideological-political front? Indeed they do, and that is why they behave as they do, for it is the orderliness and completeness of the theory that have caused deep convulsions, schisms and rifts within Marxist ranks. In order to strengthen their movement, adherents of Marxism, whether in word or in deed, have been forced to make corrections to their theory and to reject one or another of its assertions. The example of Marxist theory demonstrates that orderliness alone is not sufficient to a world-view, that the success which comes from orderliness is short-lived and that when a theory's orderliness comes into conflict with science and with life, ideological revisions and ideological-political crises are inevitable.

We do not wish, for the sake of maintaining the integrity and orderliness of our world-view, constantly to be forced to change it, to reject each year those scientific assertions which the previous year we had declared unshakeable truths. Such yearly changes do not strengthen a political movement; they only compromise it and lead to serious ideological-political crises. For this reason, our organization does not bind itself either to philosophical idealism or to materialism, but leaves philosophical questions entirely to science.

The full, all-round development of the Ukrainian nation in an independent, united Ukrainian state, the creation of a *truly national regime and a classless society, the destruction of imperialism*, the establishment of international accord among *free and equal sovereign states of all peoples—these fundamental points of our ideology do not lose any of their mobilizing power by the fact that we do not recognize the primacy either of spirit or of matter*. Although it does not base itself on any philosophical school, our ideology provides a basis for the solution of national and social problems; it provides a clear vision both of the internal political order of the Ukrainian state for which we are fighting and of a just international order. *Our lack of completeness of world-view does not and will not weaken us on the ideological-political front. On the contrary, it strengthens us, for it spares us endless ideological vacillations, changes and additions; it saves us from compromising ourselves and from experiencing constant crises of world-view*.

Were we to recognize either idealism or materialism as uniquely correct, and yet, for the sake of preserving the strength that comes from orderliness and completeness of world-view, wish to avoid the revisions necessitated by the development of science, we would have to condemn science, prevent it from developing freely, make it partisan and subject to politics, as the Bolsheviks have done. But even this would not save us from yearly fluctuations in our world-view; it would only alter the character of the changes, which would now be dictated not by science but by politics. This is all too evident in the case of the Soviet Union.

The Bolshevik overlords consider their dialectical and historical materialism to be the only correct philosophy. They claim to use it as a scientific guide in setting their policies. But in fact, Stalinist policies are not determined by dialectical and historical materialism; they are not guided by it and are not based on any science. Instead, dialectical and historical materialism is subjected to Stalinist policies. It simply provides the party with a means of justifying its anti-national, imperialist policies; a means of claiming that it has built a socialist state that is leading to communism, rather than a colonial-exploitative regime; a means of ascribing to itself the ability to foresee future events scientifically and to discover the laws of social development.

Stalinist dialectical and historical materialism is completely unable to withstand scientific criticism. For this reason, Stalin, basing his policies on force, disallows any kind of scientific criticism, stifles even the smallest manifestation of free scholarship and subjects it entirely to official policies. As a result, Soviet science, and social science in particular, has fallen into great decline. One cannot even speak of any kind of philosophy existing in the Soviet Union.

Stalinist dialectical and historical materialism not only fails to correspond to science; it does not even correspond to what the party has built in real life. For this reason, the Stalinist overlords constantly revise and make additions to their ideology in order to suit it to their policies. In official language, these changes are termed "further development and enrichment of Marxist theory." With each such change in ideology, science is "corrected," for "scientific errors" have supposedly been allowed to creep in. In the end, Soviet ideology can maintain itself only by political force.

In regard to the above discussion, we note that one must differentiate between the dialectical materialism of *Marx and Engels*[3] and that of *Stalin*. The first we consider a separate philosophical school of materialism; criticism of it belongs to science. *But the dialectical and historical materialism of the Stalinist stamp we reject absolutely as deeply anti-scientific and totally hostile to science, as a tool used by the ruling party for the justification of its exploitative colonial policies.* By now, Stalinist dialectical and historical materialism bears very little resemblance to the dialectical materialism of Marx and Engels. In addition, it has ceased to be any kind of science. Stalinist philosophy is, in essence, a *modern scholasticism* which enables Stalin and his gang to justify anything they want. For example, to the accusation that national subjection and colonial oppression exist in the USSR, they reply, "This is impossible, because the national question has been settled fairly in the USSR for the first time in human history. The USSR is a country where true friendship flowers among nations." To the accusation that people are exploited in the Soviet Union, they answer, "That is impossible, because the USSR is the first country in the world to have built socialism and to have laid the foundations for the building of communism." To the accusation that a rule of terror exists in the Soviet Union, they reply, "Soviet punitive institutions are directed outward, not inward," and so on. Just as medieval scholasticism needed the support of the Inquisition,[4] so Stalinist scholasticism requires the support of MVD[5] and MGB[6] terror. Just as in the Middle Ages freethinkers were burnt at the stake, so today anyone in the USSR who has the courage to come out against the official Stalinist philosophy or to advocate free scholarship is destroyed. Furthermore, in spite of the official acceptance of materialism in the Soviet Union, the deification of a single individual—the ascription to Stalin of a truly godlike role—has reached such proportions as to surpass the position taken by even the most ardent adherents of that idealistic philosophy which affirms the individual as the motive force of history.

In order to avoid annual politically motivated ideological changes, in order to allow science to develop freely, we wish to avoid subjecting science, and thus philosophy, to politics. We are fighting for free scholarship and want to ensure it full freedom of development in a Ukrainian state. The correctness and scientific validity of different theories can only be decided by free debate and confrontation. Science can find its affirmation only in real experience, never by means of political force. We are fighting for true freedom of speech, of the press and of conviction. *For this reason, we do not give the right of monopoly to any philosophical current and do not oblige even our own members to recognize any one particular philosophical school.*

Were we to make adherence to philosophical idealism obligatory for members of our organization, we would be forced to exclude from our ranks all adherents of philosophical materialism. Were we, on the other hand, to make recognition of materialism obligatory, we would close our ranks to all those who subscribe to idealism. But our organization takes the position that the plight of the Ukrainian people is equally painful to adherents of both philosophies, that they feel the same hatred for Ukraine's oppressors and that they can fight with the same ardour for the full liberation of the Ukrainian people and for the establishment of an independent Ukrainian state. And the validity of our position is proved by our struggle itself. Within the ranks of our organization, adherents of idealism and materialism are fighting with equal devotion. All our members, regardless of their philosophy, are united by our organization's progressive socio-political ideology and programme. Our members are obliged to recognize not one or another philosophy, but the OUN's socio-political ideology and programme. *Every member of the OUN enjoys total liberty with regard to philosophical convictions, but he is obliged to adhere fully to the OUN's ideology and programme; he must propagate them and fight for their realization.* The OUN member embodies our great ideas of liberation and fights passionately for their realization. Our organization excludes not those who recognize one or another philosophy, but those who cannot accept our goals; who cannot develop enthusiasm for our ideology and programme and willingness to die for them; who cannot subject themselves to our hard organizational discipline. This must always be kept in mind, for herein lies our strength. *Without ideological-political unity and revolutionary discipline among our members*, our organization would be unable to sustain itself, much less carry on an active, prolonged struggle against so enormous an imperialist machine as the Soviet Union.

Those of our members who wish to make idealism our dominant philosophy would do so not primarily because they are convinced of the intellectual superiority of idealism over materialism, but because of their desire to foster in our cadres attitudes which, they feel, are likely to flow from philosophical idealism: a highly principled approach to life, the capacity to be enthralled by great ideas, an unbending strength of will.

The moral qualities of our cadres are *based on great idealism and high-mindedness*; these are the *strength* of our organization. To encourage and foster these qualities is the duty of every one of our members and the chief aim of our educational work. This we must never forget. But philosophical idealism in itself does not give anyone high ideals or strength of will, nor does materialism deprive anyone of these moral qualities. An individual may be an idealist by philosophical conviction, but in his personal life be shamelessly materialistic, selfish, spineless and indifferent to great ideas. On the other hand, an individual may be a materialist by philosophical conviction, but in his own life distinguish himself by his high idealism, his disdain for all things base, his indifference to personal gain and his iron character. The examples of philosophical materialists who have died for totally non-material ideals have been so numerous that we do not need to mention them here.

Of course it would be wrong to deny or to underestimate the influence, either harmful or beneficial, of philosophy upon the moral worth of individuals. It can be very strong. But education plays a more fundamental role, for it can increase or diminish this influence. Thus, we ensure high idealism within our cadres not by adhering to one or another philosophy, but by properly educating our members.

Our education is based not on philosophy, but on arousing in our members a fanatical love for Ukraine, as well as anger and hatred for her oppressors; it is grounded in our progressive ideology and our rejection of all discordant ideologies, in our history and in the heroism of our struggle. The OUN educates its members to be highly idealistic and strong-willed by stressing the example of those thousands of our comrades who have denied themselves everything personal, abandoned their homes and schools, given up careers and taken the path of revolutionary struggle for the sake of liberating the Ukrainian people. Our education is based on the example of those individuals who exchanged a peaceful existence for the hard life of the insurgent and for prisons, on the example of those who even under the most brutal tortures refused to betray secrets to the enemy, who stepped onto the gallows with their heads raised high and died with revolutionary slogans on their lips, who rejected with the greatest contempt the enemy's offers of pardon, who preferred to end their own lives rather than submit to the enemy. Our organization educates its members according to those hard principles of revolutionary discipline upon which it is built. The OUN tempers its cadres by direct revolutionary struggle and practical revolutionary work.

As we have demonstrated, there is no validity to the suggestion that the OUN should accept any particular philosophical school as obligatory, whether it be idealism or materialism. For this reason, the OUN permits its members to subscribe either to an idealist or a materialist philosophy. The members of the OUN are bound only by the ideology and program of our organization. Since it is fighting for a truly national regime that will guarantee all democratic rights and freedoms to the people, the OUN will not attempt, in a free and independent Ukrainian state, to make its own ideology supreme.

March 1948

Source: Typescript copy: Archive of the Foreign Representation of the Supreme Ukrainian Liberation Council, Folio U1–4. Photocopy: Archive, *Litopys UPA*.

NOTES

1. Third Extraordinary Grand Assembly of the OUN (21–5 August 1943), at which important changes were introduced into the organization's political programme and organizational structure.
2. Karl Marx (1818–83): German social philosopher, chief theorist of modern socialism.
3. Friedrich Engels (1820–95): German socialist, co-founder of Marxism.
4. The medieval Inquisition began c. 1233 when Pope Gregory IX commissioned Dominican friars to investigate the Albigensians, a religious group in southern France.
5. MVD: Ministry of Internal Affairs.
6. MGB: Ministry of State Security.

THE SCIENTIFIC VALIDITY OF DIALECTICAL MATERIALISM

U. Kuzhil

The tremendous advances made by science in the nineteenth and twentieth centuries have raised it to an unprecedented level of prestige. We have all witnessed its unprecedented ability to master and harness the powers of nature. Thus, it is not surprising that science has become the ultimate authority even for the dullest layman and that any theory, in whatever sphere, is considered indisputable if it is grounded in scientific arguments.

In the battle of ideas and world-views, reference to science is a means commonly used to strengthen a position. Science is a weapon: if well used it ensures a large measure of success. This fact is very well understood by the Bolsheviks. In promoting their world-view they have taken full advantage of the argument of "scientific validity" as a means of deceiving the average Soviet citizen, whose education is limited and uncritical. It is well known that no Soviet citizen has the opportunity to read scientific source books and come to know other ideologies. Although scientific books do exist in the Soviet Union, they are all seasoned with Marxism and do not transmit the original thoughts and arguments of world scholars and philosophers. Knowing full well that science is generally considered an indisputable authority and that a critical analysis of the "scientific" basis of dialectical materialism is beyond the intellectual capabilities of the average person, the Bolsheviks perform sleights of hand with the words "science" and "scientific validity.'' From the time of its birth, Marxism has fortified itself with the self-deception that it is the only scientifically possible world-view, firmly grounded in the indisputable findings of natural science. Paying no heed to logical difficulties and easily side-stepping them in their exposition, Marxist writers have presented materialism as following strictly from facts and doing away with all misunderstandings. From the beginning, Marxist socialism immodestly proclaimed itself ''scientific socialism,'' thereby differentiating itself from all other socialist tendencies and emphasizing its scientific foundations. It has professed to be a world-view based only on phenomena whose objective existence can be ascertained by the senses and by experience; that is, on positive knowledge. How can the Soviet citizen even attempt to counter so formidable an authority as scientific theory when he is deprived of the opportunity to read anything other than the latest expression of Soviet philosophical thought: Chapter 4, Section 6 of *Istoriia VKP(b)* on ''Dialectical and Historical Materialism''?[1] In the presence of science, the lay dullard has no choice but to bow his head. But considering the fact that for years the poor wretch has been barraged with such statements as ''in order to avoid political errors... etc., it is necessary to employ the scientific dialectical method, which enables us to reach the only correct conclusions,'' it is not surprising that he regards the political wisdom of the Bolshevik party as boundless. After all, it is guided strictly by science. Thus, every law becomes indisputable and the state, based upon scientific ideas, invincible.

Materialists rely solely upon sensory experience and positive knowledge. But do the experimental sciences tell us about origins and reasons for existence? Absolutely not! Scientists speak only of facts and phenomena that succeed one another in turn; they investigate these phenomena and establish the laws that govern them. The experimental sciences say nothing about the origins of prevailing causes, about the existence of predetermined plans for the development of phenomena. Yet, without the slightest hesitation, materialists call upon science to provide solutions to problems which are totally outside the scientific realm. We can say that materialism embodies a principle, but the proofs upon which this principle is based fail to demonstrate anything.

No scientist of the experimental school (i.e., no objective scientist) will disagree when we state that contemporary science has provided no positive data which permit conclusions of the sort made by materialism regarding matter and the origins of natural phenomena; that by its very nature experimental science is unable to deal with questions about matter and the origins of natural phenomena; that science tells us what exists, treating facts and present conditions, not the origins of things; that to answer the question ''how?'' and to point to the most immediate causes of things are all that science can do; that from the moment materialism becomes a clear, doctrinal negation of metaphysics (in the scientific sense of this term, meaning the enquiry into fundamental concepts—matter, existence, etc.), it becomes another form of metaphysics, for it attempts, on the basis of data taken from the experimental sciences, to make assertions about matters that lie outside the scientific realm.

To proceed further: can science make dogmatic assertions about the future and speculate about invariable results of causes? Materialism delights in basing itself upon positive knowledge, but it casts aside the sceptical caution characteristic of science, and thus degenerates into scientific dogmatism. In dealing with questions that have not been investigated by science, it relies solely upon faith and demands that everyone accept its dogmas. A brief look at the history of scientific world-views will clearly demonstrate the shakiness of this dogmatism.

To primitive man, nature appeared as capricious as himself, and he imagined it to be made in his own image. He mistakenly thought that nature was a state of chaotic disorder and ascribed this turmoil to the capricious acts and outbursts of gods and benevolent or malevolent spirits. Only through experimentation did man finally discover the great law of causality and learn that it governed all of inanimate nature. He determined that a cause, isolated in its action, always produced the same result. Thus, events were not determined by the caprices of supernatural beings, but issued from the existing state of things in accordance with immutable laws. And this existing state of things, in its turn, inevitably issued from some previously existing state, going back in this way to infinity. Thus, the whole course of events was predetermined by the state of the world in the first moment of its existence. From the moment this first state was established, nature was destined to follow its fixed path toward its appointed goal. In other words, the act of creation not only brought the universe to life, but also determined its whole future history. Of course, man did not cease to believe in his ability to influence the course of events by his own actions, but this belief was based on instinct rather than logic, science or experience. As of this time, events were ascribed to the law of causality rather than to the actions of supernatural beings. The final acceptance of causality as the governing principle in nature was the triumph of the seventeenth century, the great century of Galileo[2] and Newton.[3] It was confirmed that heavenly phenomena are governed by the general laws of mechanics and that comets, previously regarded as harbingers of the fall of empires and the death of kings, moved according to the formulae of the general law of gravity. As a result of these discoveries man began to perceive the whole material world as a machine. This tendency grew ever stronger, until it reached its apex in the second half of the nineteenth century. All that was needed, it seemed, was for man to extend his efforts to understand the world; all of inanimate nature would then be revealed as a faultlessly running machine.

As one might expect, this conception of the world significantly influenced enquiries into the meaning of human existence. With each widening of the realm governed by the law of causality, with each victory for the mechanistic interpretation of nature, belief in free will became more difficult. If all of nature was subject to the law of causality, why should life be an exception? Such thinking led to the birth of the mechanistic philosophical systems of the seventeenth and eighteenth centuries, as well as the idealist theories which sprang up as a natural reaction to this trend. Nevertheless, up to the beginning of the nineteenth century it was still possible to regard life as something distinct from inanimate nature. Then it was discovered that living cells are composed of the same atoms as inanimate matter and are thus undoubtedly governed by the same natural laws. The question arose: why should the atoms that make up our bodies and brains not be subject to the law of causality? It was supposed and even categorically affirmed that life itself is also a completely mechanical phenomenon. The minds of Bach, Newton and Michelangelo, it was said, differed only in their degree of complexity from printing presses, whistles or saw mills; their sole function was to respond precisely to external stimuli.

With the turn of the century came a kaleidoscopic transposition of scientific ideas. The nineteenth century gave science enough time to realize that certain phenomena, radioactivity and gravity in particular, could not be explained in mechanistic terms. Theoreticians did not cease to debate the possibility of building a machine capable of reproducing the emotions of Bach, the thoughts of Newton or the inspiration of Michelangelo, but all attempts in this direction proved fruitless.

In the final years of the last century, Professor Planck[4] attempted to explain those phenomena of radioactivity which until then had defied explanation. His first attempts eventually gave rise to modern quantum theory, which became one of the dominant principles of modern physics. The appearance of quantum theory marked the end of the mechanistic age in science and the beginning of a new epoch. Planck's original theory merely touched upon the supposition that nature proceeds by means of small leaps and fluctuations, rather like the hands of a clock. Nevertheless, in 1917, Einstein[5] demonstrated that the theory laid down by Planck led to a number of revolutionary conclusions. It became evident that this theory simply overthrew the law of causality, which had seemed to govern the course of natural phenomena. Earlier science had announced with certainty that nature could proceed only upon a single path, determined from the beginning to the end of time, by way of an unbroken chain of causes and results: state A was inevitably followed by state B. But the new science could say nothing more than that state A could be followed by B, but it could just as well be followed by state C, D or a countless number of others. It could state that it was more probable that states B, C and D would follow A, but because it dealt with probabilities it could not predict with total certainty which state would follow the preceding one.

As we can see from this brief overview, science is incapable of providing answers to questions regarding basic philosophical problems. The picture of the world drawn for us by science changes with every age, as new discoveries are made by the natural sciences. And we cannot say whether each of these successive pictures comes closer to being an objective view of the world or whether we are simply regarding the world from a constantly changing point of view. No scientist who has lived through the last thirty years takes a dogmatic approach to the future direction of science or to the discovery of objective truth. We cannot expect science to be a bearer of great news. On the contrary, science must not foresee or announce anything; it has changed its course too often heretofore.

Such is the state of science; such are its possibilities. Given these facts, the abuse of its authority by the Bolsheviks becomes clearly apparent. Having created the illusion that the Bolshevik world view is strictly scientific, they force the ordinary citizen, who is not conversant with the present state and possibilities of science, to accept without reservation policies that are supposedly based on precise scientific findings.

In order to determine which elements of the Bolshevik world-view are in accord with positive knowledge and which are mere hypotheses, or simply arbitrary assertions not based on any scientific data, we shall examine Chapter 4, Section 6 of *Istoriia VKP(b)* on "Dialectical and Historical Materialism." This work of Stalin's should be taken into account because of its particular significance in the Soviet sphere. The ruling powers have officially designated this book the source of Bolshevik philosophical wisdom for all, worker and university professor alike. It is regarded as the only correct interpretation and exposition of Marxist philosophical doctrine as a whole. In any case, since 1908, when Lenin produced his *Materialism and Empirio-criticism*, nothing new has appeared in this field. Contemporary Bolshevik philosophy consists of nothing more than repeating old saws and finding ways of twisting citations from Engels and the above-mentioned work by Lenin.

According to the dialectical method, everything in the world is changeable. Every category acquires a different meaning in a new age shaped by epochal scientific discoveries. But the verification of fundamental ideas that is supposed to take place, and their re-evaluation in relation to new scientific achievements, has never been made. On the contrary, all attempts in that direction have been condemned as deviations and their instigators branded enemies of the people. Thus Bolshevik philosophical thought has ossified and, although the Bolsheviks claim that new scientific discoveries support their theses, these assertions remain completely unsubstantiated.

In the first place, the above-mentioned work by Stalin, like all Bolshevik writings, is characterized by its use of a singular terminology which not only is not accepted anywhere in the scientific world, but stands in contradiction to the fundamental concepts of science. The whole of Stalin's exposition of the dialectical method bases itself upon the opposition of dialectics to metaphysics. Since the post-Aristotelian era, metaphysics has had a precisely defined meaning. It is the study of questions for which the natural sciences provide no answers, i.e., the fundamental questions of existence, matter and so on. The Bolsheviks have banished to the realm of metaphysics all theories and philosophical systems that are not in accord with Marxist dialectics. Furthermore, in their account of the opposition of Marxist dialectics to metaphysics, the Bolsheviks attempt to create the impression that all philosophical systems which preceded their own were totally absurd and unscientific and that they all regarded the world as a system of unrelated and independent phenomena. In this juxtaposition of Marxist theories with others, the whole of human philosophical thought is presented as having no link with science. The impression is created that the first scientific understanding and interpretation of the universe came with Marxism. But who among the philosophers of the modern age has disputed the fact that things are changeable, that natural phenomena are interdependent and so on?

By constantly repeating the phrase, "in opposition to metaphysics," the Bolsheviks are simply creating windmills with which to fight, like Don Quixote. They present all non-Marxist philosophy in caricature, thereby enabling themselves to point to their own genius in having determined the laws that govern nature.

In the second place, to claim that the dialectical method is the means to obtain the correct solution to any problem is totally unscientific and unscholarly. The Bolsheviks forget that method alone is not enough. It was by means of this same dialectical method that Hegel[6] arrived at his apotheosis of Prussian imperialism. Just what the doctrinaire application of method can lead to is wonderfully illustrated by what happened to Hegel himself. Employing his dialectical method, Hegel ascertained that it was impossible for a greater number of planets to exist than those that had already been discovered at that time. Nevertheless, another—Neptune—was later discovered. His embarrassed assistants timidly pointed out to the professor that his theory did not correspond to reality. The answer they received was significant: "So much the worse for reality." And so much the worse for reality today, for it does not fit neatly into a box and refuses to develop in conformity with Chapter 4, Section 6 of *Istoriia VKP(b)*. The attempt to force natural phenomena, particularly social and political events, to fit an a priori method of investigation is totally characteristic of the Bolshevik world-view.

The first two elements of the dialectical method were not discovered by Marxism. It cannot claim as its own the establishment of the two generally known and accepted natural laws concerning the interdependence of phenomena and their mutability in time and space. However, the Marxist claim that events occur suddenly, in leaps, is not so straightforward. For one thing, the concept of a leap is not precisely defined. What sort of rapidity is required for the transition from one state to another to be considered a leap? A leap, in the sense attributed to it by Marxism, is a relative concept. In the realm of natural phenomena, an absolute leap has not yet been discovered, for it would have to introduce a qualitative alteration in time. Stalin defines a leap-like transition as a process in which "changes occur not gradually but rapidly, suddenly." But what does this mean, "rapidly, suddenly"? This, too, is a subjective concept. For a human being who lives, on average, fifty to sixty years, a "rapid" passage would take, let us say, an hour, or a minute. But for a different being, one that lives seven years or, like the May bug, only one month, "rapid" would have to be 1/10 or 1/1000 of the human being's hour or minute. Under these circumstances, the concept of a leap is not an objective one; it is not inherent in nature but simply tailored to human thinking and to the human concept of time. Perhaps a certain number of phenomena will be discovered which pass very rapidly from one qualitative state to another, but at the same time, we can point to a million examples in which this transition occurs over a long period of time and in which qualitative changes are proportional to quantitative ones. Before doing so, however, let us examine the boiling of water as an example of a leap-like process. "Thus, for example," writes Engels, "the temperature of water has at first no bearing upon its physical state. But as the water's temperature increases or decreases, the moment comes when its state of agglomeration changes—in the first case, into steam; in the second, into ice."[7] The phenomenon is presented inaccurately. It is generally known that water is transformed into steam at any temperature. Water in an open container at normal room temperature is already evaporating. If the temperature of the water is increased, it evaporates more rapidly; that is, the amount of water transformed into steam in any given second increases according to the increase in temperature. At the boiling point, the rate of evaporation is greatest, but no leap ever takes place. Here is the more evident relationship: with a quantitative increase in the movement of water molecules, that is, with an increase in the temperature of the water, there is an accompanying increase in the rate of evaporation. Where do we find a rapid and sudden transition? It is true that certain natural phenomena occur rapidly or, in Marxist terms, "in leaps" (for example, certain qualitative changes in atoms), but the enormous majority of transformations in nature take place slowly and in proportion to quantitative changes. If the length of light waves increases slowly, then the quality, that is, the colour of the light, changes slowly in proportion. As we see, the Marxist concept of leaps is a mixture of naive observations and even more naive generalized conclusions.

In characterizing Marxist philosophical materialism, Stalin writes, "The world and the laws to which it conforms are fully knowable. Our knowledge regarding the laws of nature, when verified by experiment and practical experience, becomes a certainty that can be termed objective truth."[8] Following from this assertion is a "scientific" explanation of the basis of social behaviour and an affirmation of the infallibility of the party, which bases itself upon these "scientific" concepts. The criminal activity of the Bolshevik party and all the artificial, anti-natural social and political experiments that it has conducted make it necessary for us to scrutinize Stalin's statements more closely. We must point out that we shall not consider here whether matter is primary or derivative; whether materialism or idealism provides better responses to questions concerning fundamental matter and existence. These things are a matter of faith, as contemporary science is incapable of answering all these questions. The relevant problem is to ascertain whether the Bolsheviks are abusing science and taking advantage of its authority in order to give the stamp of approval to their own insane theories. The position of the Bolsheviks has already been characterized briefly in Stalin's words. In order to deal with the problem at hand, we must answer the following two questions:

1. Is it possible for human beings to attain objective knowledge of nature?

2. Is it possible, on the basis of what we have discovered about the world's conformity to established laws, to construct dogmatic theories concerning future states of nature and society, or are we limited to forming working hypotheses, which of necessity entail certain reservations?

Human beings identify and investigate natural phenomena by means of their senses. This fact alone makes objective knowledge impossible, for the structure of the sense organs determines in advance the degree and quality of the knowledge that will be attained. All external stimuli pass through the appropriate sense organs and through the nervous system; only then do they reach human consciousness. As impressions pass through this whole apparatus, they are appropriately transformed, giving the impression of colour, of a degree of hardness, of form, etc. Science has given us instruments more perfect than human sight, for example, which demonstrate its limitations. They enable us to observe the white light of the sun split up into a spectrum, but this spectrum, again, is nothing but a visual stimulus which enters our consciousness through the whole system of our sense organs. Thus, because human beings know the world through their senses, their impression of the world is subjective and dependent upon these senses. A blind person has a different impression of the world than one who can see, and a being who had some other sense, one that is unknown to us, would have a still different impression. So whose knowledge of the world shall we call objective? All attempts to investigate the nature of matter will be fruitless until such time as we have an external basis for comparison. Since human beings comprise only a minimal part of the world, they cannot regard it from a distant perspective or grasp the totality of the problem. Do we know whether distant heavenly bodies which we cannot see even through the largest telescopes are governed by other laws, different from those we have discovered in the world accessible to our telescopes? And let us look at science: has it given us any real basis for the knowledge of matter or has it simply described and investigated the laws which govern changes in matter and thus create phenomena in the external world? Let us consider, for example, what science has told us so far about the essence of light. At first, light was compared to and described as consisting of small particles, or corpuscles; later, it was described as consisting of waves. Finally, scientists concluded that they were coming no closer to discovering the nature of light; at one time they were simply comparing its behaviour to the movement of corpuscles and, at another, to the movement of waves. Today, science cannot predict which of these forms light will take in its activity. Does the statement that light behaves like waves on the surface of the water as they pass by cliffs tell us anything about the essence of light? Corpuscles and waves—these are only symbols to enable us to express our degree of recognition and understanding of light and to discuss it and explain its behaviour. The corpuscle theory preceded the wave theory. At first it seemed that the wave theory explained the behaviour of light more accurately and provided answers to questions that could not be answered by the corpuscle theory. But it soon became apparent that the two theories complement each other: in some instances, the corpuscle theory is more satisfactory, in others, the wave theory. One might have expected that since the wave theory is more recent, coming at a time when science was more advanced, it should have provided information about light that was closer to absolute truth. Instead, it was found that light behaves in a dual manner (we clearly emphasize that we are speaking of the behaviour of light, not its essence).

No one has ever seen an electron; only its motion has been observed. Scientists have observed the electron's behaviour and compared it to natural phenomena perceived through the senses. As science advances in its investigation of the electron, it will discover more precise formulae for determining its behaviour, but these formulae will not tell us about its essence. The further we advance, the more we grow convinced that matter is not what we have thought it to be. Splitting the atom shattered our previously held assumptions about matter and provided us with a new picture, but is this new picture any closer to objective truth?

In Marxist terms, the mechanistic concept of the universe is regarded as a relative truth, limited by the level that human knowledge had attained by the time of its formulation. Every successive relative truth represents progress and greater perfection, a further step toward absolute truth. But what happens in reality? Each successive theory, whether it be quantum theory or Einstein's system, provides a new picture of the universe, but this new picture is based not upon perfected mechanistic principles, but upon concepts totally different from those of the preceding age. Were not all of Newton's laws verified by experiment? Yet we see that Einstein also made use of experiments to reveal certain deviations from the laws of gravity and to establish new laws, based on the theory of relativity and the negation of the Newtonian force of gravity. Popular science has taken the symbols representing the behaviour of particular natural phenomena to be the forms of the phenomena, for the sake of explaining them more clearly. A similar popularization can be seen in the Marxist depiction of the universe. It is represented as a completed system in which there are no deviations, in which everything occurs as a result of known causes and with predictable results. This image of the world is transparent and understandable, but it is inaccurate.

Our conception of time was considered so intelligible and indisputable that no one doubted its objectivity or imagined that it would change. This Newtonian time was regarded as an absolute, independent of matter or space; time advanced regularly and incessantly. Such an understanding of time makes possible the acceptance of the law of causality, for if time goes forward, then cause can precede effect. All laws were verified experimentally, based upon the Newtonian understanding of time. But along comes Einstein and his theory of relativity, in which time becomes a relative concept, dependent upon space and matter and closely linked to them. Again, certain formulae in physics regarding the length of a body at rest and its length in motion have been confirmed by experiment. Many experiments conducted upon electrons in motion have also confirmed the relativity of time. Thus time, an absolute according to the naive Newtonian concept, has become, with Einstein, essentially mutable. But positive experimental results have been obtained using each of these concepts of time. So which is the more objective or the closer to absolute truth?

Let us consider another question: can science, on the basis of the data available to it today, foresee the future state of every phenomenon and make infallible predictions in every realm? Belief in the possibility of making predictions was based on the law of causality, which completely dominated science during the mechanistic age. The law of causality proclaimed: "If the state of a given system at a given moment is known, then all the states of that system, past and future, are thus determined." How did this principle arise? It was observed in the operation of every machine, every instrument of measure. Whether one observed an electric current or the swing of an ammeter needle, one could see that everything was linked by the chain of cause and effect. The same was observed in astronomy. By calculating the positions and velocities of planets at any given moment, the astronomer could calculate what their positions and velocities would be at any other time and thus determine when eclipses of the sun and the moon would occur. And in those realms, the principle of causality was indeed confirmed, proved by the laws of mechanics and verified by experiment. But one must clearly emphasize that this applies to *those realms*, the realms of the macroscopic world, i.e., the world of bodies much larger than atoms. However, on the basis of observations made in physics and astronomy regarding the supremacy of the principle of causality within the macroscopic realm, unfounded generalizations were made and the principle of causality was extended too hastily to embrace the whole universe, all of nature, organic and inorganic, and even human beings and societies. For we know that what is valid for one realm of natural phenomena is not necessarily so for others. Determinism found its way from classical physics into philosophy and became the basis for the materialistic world-views of the nineteenth century.

Today the basic concepts of determinism must be revised, for positive science, which takes a rigorous approach to the investigation of phenomena and the formulation of conclusions, has determined that the microscopic world, i.e., the world of atoms, electrons and quanta, is not governed by the principle of causality. The next state of a given system can be determined only in terms of greater or lesser probability and nothing more. Why is this so? Because in the microscopic world it is impossible to fulfill the basic prerequisite of the principle of causality, that is, it is impossible to determine the exact state of an electron at any arbitrary moment. The state of every body, including the atom and the electron, is determined by its position at any given moment and by its momentum (mass multiplied by velocity). But it is impossible to determine at any given time both the speed and the position of an atom or electron. This "uncertainty principle" was discovered and elaborated by the physicist Heisenberg.[9]

Classical physics always dealt with measurable objects; these were the things of which it spoke. Having discovered the electron, physicists were also able to gauge its velocity or position, but not both simultaneously. Thus, until 1927, the atom and the electron were regarded as physically measurable entities. Then Heisenberg proved that to determine the state of an electron at a given moment, i.e., to determine simultaneously its speed and position, is a scientific impossibility. For a detailed explanation of the experiment that Heisenberg conducted, we would have had to take a closer look at quantum theory. As it is, we can only describe it in essence. For experimentation in the macroscopic world we make use of our senses of sight, touch, hearing and so on. But for dealing with the microscopic world, we can employ only our sight, with the help of a kind of ultramiscroscope ("Heisenberg's microscope") which enables us to view the position of the electron. If we are to see the electron and determine its position, it must be illuminated. But a quantum of light, as it falls upon the electron, alters its velocity. For this reason, in order to determine the velocity of an electron, we use weaker light rays which do not significantly alter the electron's movement; however, illumination with these rays does not clearly show the electron's position. This gave rise to Heinseberg's famous postulate, the uncertainty principle. The extent of uncertainty is determined by Planck's constant, a very small number, which clearly demonstrates that the universe is not an exact machine, as the mechanistic school thought it to be, for among its smallest particles there are no absolute, precisely determined interrelationships. Experiments in physics have demonstrated that the act of observation itself affects the state of the observed system. Of course, if light falls upon a large object while it is being observed, no noticeable change takes place, but in the case of the electron, a change does occur. If one determines the position of the electron, one cannot determine its velocity and vice versa. This fact cannot be altered. Physics concerns itself only with phenomena that can be observed by human beings; it does not deal with that which could, perhaps, be observed by a superhuman being, one which was more perfect and had other means of knowing. Thus, the question of how things "really" are (in the metaphysical sense)—the question whether it is "really" the case that electrons do not travel along determined paths at determined velocities—is not a scientific one and has no specific meaning. For this reason, it is useless to make predictions concerning future states. What will follow a given, insufficiently determined, state is impossible to say. The principle of causality cannot be applied to the world of atoms, electrons and photons; it cannot account for what occurs in the microscopic world. The processes we have observed in the microscopic world are subject to Heisenberg's uncertainty principle; they are not deterministic. To predict the behaviour of a given atom or electron is beyond human capacity.

How is it that in the world, which is composed of atoms, there is such perfect order? How is it that the multitude of atoms is governed by laws from which there are no deviations? For it would be a mistake to think that the microscopic world exists in a state of chaos. It is true that the laws of quantum mechanics, which govern this realm, are not deterministic, but they determine very precisely the probability that a given process will occur. These laws of quantum mechanics are formulated with the help of differential equations. A particular, individual process such as, for example, the emission of light by an atom, may or may not occur at any given moment. Nature permits here a certain measure of freedom, as though it were allowing the atom a variety of possibilities. It is not known which of these possibilities will occur: all that is known is the probability of the occurrence. Thus groups of atoms are governed by a law which states only that the probability that one event or another will occur is extremely high. Global processes are subject to the law of causality; in them, we see the order of nature. When we deal with large masses of atoms and electrons, we see the mathematical law of averages imposing a determinism that could not be established by the laws of physics. This can be explained in terms of an analogous situation in the macroscopic world. When we flip a coin, we can never be certain which way up it will land. Nevertheless, if we flip a million tons of coins, we can say with great probability—a probability that is regarded as a certainty, not only in everyday life, but also in science—that 500,000 tons of coins will land "heads" and 500,000 tons "tails." We can repeat this experiment as many times as we wish and almost always achieve the same result. We say "almost always" rather than "always," as in the mechanistic age. We can consider this consistency a result of the law of causality, but in fact, it is simply the result of mathematical laws of chance. The number of coins in a million tons is nothing in comparison with the number of atoms in even the smallest bit of matter upon which physicists of the previous age conducted their experiments. Thus, we can now see how the illusion of determinism entered science.

In many other areas we can observe a certain measure of chance and find phenomena that are governed only by the laws of probability. For example, it is known that radium and other radioactive substances decay in time into atoms of lead and helium. The mass of radium decreases constantly as it turns into lead and helium. The law that governs the rate of decay is worth noting: the total number of radium atoms decreases in exactly the same way as the number of soldiers in a division exposed to random gun fire. From this example we see that for any individual atom of radium the law has no significance: the atom dies because, for some secret reason, destiny has called it.

In conclusion we can evaluate, on the basis of the present state of science, how dialectical materialism fares in its approach to the natural sciences. First of all, before exposing the total groundlessness and senselessness of the so-called dialectical method, we must point out the obvious fact that no scholar outside the Soviet Union is interested in this "theory." Scientists and philosophers subscribe to a variety of world-views. They support some theories and dispute others, but none of them wastes time discussing Marxism's naive philosophical absurdities. Analysis of Bolshevik philosophical writings shows them to be a chaotic conglomeration of unrelated aphorisms. Laws governing the development of particular natural phenomena are simply generalized, in a totally unjustified way, to embrace the whole of nature. Facts and scientific theses, long since discovered and well known for hundreds of years, are bombastically presented as though Marx and Engels were their discoverers. None of Marxism's nonsensical "concepts" in the realm of natural philosophy issues from contemporary science; on the contrary, Marxist "theory" stands in contradiction to the most recent, experimentally and theoretically grounded conclusions reached by physics. It is worth noting that philosophical Marxism categorically states that in the development of science there is no immutable dogma; yet, for some reason, its own theory is regarded as unchangeable. Marxists claim that as each scientific theory develops, contradictions inevitably arise to spell its doom. Why, then, should their own ideology be forever perfect and immutable? Marxists do not wish to see what every objective reader sees from the start as he reads their writings: that all of their theory is one great contradiction.

What is the significance of determining the true value of Marxist materialism as a scientifically based world-view? The significance is enormous. For if Marx's greatest achievement was to transfer the principles of dialectical materialism from natural phenomena to society in the form of historical materialism, then the teachings of historical materialism about society have as much value as the teachings of dialectical materialism about inorganic nature: that is, the value of fantasy. Marxists have developed an intellectualized image of the development of society as they would like to see it, not as it is. Dialectical and historical materialism is a set of abstractly created systems for which confirmation in nature and society can be found only at the cost of enormous effort. All the unfortunate and downright tragic results of attempting to confirm these theories in the social and political sphere can be seen to their full extent in the Soviet Union.

Source: Ideia i Chyn 5, no. 10 (1946): 27–34. Original: Typescript of 8 pages, Archive of the Foreign Representation of the Supreme Ukrainian Liberation Council, Folio U4–3. Photocopy: Archive, *Litopys UPA*.

NOTES

1. Reference is to the *Short Course of the History of the All-Union Communist Party (Bolshevik)*, first published as a collective work in October 1938, then reprinted in 1946 and attributed to Stalin alone. The essay "On Dialectical and Historical Materialism," which formed part of the *Short Course*, has been regarded as Stalin's work since its first appearance. See Robert H. McNeal, *Stalin's Works* (Stanford 1967), 166.
2. Galileo Galilei (1564–1642): Italian astronomer, mathematician and physicist.
3. Sir Isaac Newton (1642–1727): English physicist, mathematician and philosopher.
4. Max Planck (1858–1947): German physicist and Nobel laureate.
5. Albert Einstein (1879–1955): Jewish-American theoretical physicist and Nobel laureate.
6. Georg Wilhelm Friedrich Hegel (1770–1831): German philosopher, formulator of an idealistic philosophy.
7. Engels's statement is quoted by Stalin in the *Short Course*. See I.V. Stalin, "O dialekticheskom i istoricheskom materializme," *Sochineniia*, ed. Robert H. McNeal (Stanford 1967), 1: 284.
8. Ibid., 1: 294.
9. Werner Heisenberg (1901–76): German physicist and Nobel laureate.

THE SPECTRE OF FASCISM

Iarlan

There has been a fascist reaction everywhere! We are now witnessing an unusually interesting phenomenon around the world—the pitched battle raging over the so-called problem of fascism—despite the fact that this very fascism lost the war. Surely it would seem that after so total and overwhelming a defeat, not only military but ideological and political as well, which shattered both the regimes that embodied the concept of fascism in Europe and in the world and which resulted in the deaths of their leaders, there could no longer be a place in society for such a shameful phenomenon, at least for a long time.

And yet... this problem has never been so topical and prominent; it has never been fought over and written about so much and in such heated terms as today. Wherever we look, in every newspaper, in statements and publications, on every page, we come across one and the same thing: "the danger of fascism," "the battle against fascist reaction," etc. It exists and lives on. The danger is even growing and spreading throughout the world: in Ukraine and in Finland, in Poland, Yugoslavia, Greece and Turkey, in China and in Portugal, not even sparing America, where, as the newspapers put it, "a Congressional commission studying the question of anti-American activities" is also nothing but a typical reactionary fascist institution engaged in persecuting the best American patriots and democrats. Never before, not even in the heyday of Hitler[1] and Mussolini[2] (in 1939 and long afterward), has so much been written about this problem, and in such heated terms, as now, after their defeat and death . . .

The ghost of fascism continues to frighten the world and haunt it with its spectres . . .

We should acquaint ourselves more closely with the actual meaning of this term and with the problem that continues to stir up such a stubborn conflict.

Let us begin by examining the main issue of this whole matter and asking ourselves:

What is Fascism?

For more than twenty years, right up to the outbreak of the last war, we in the East were taught that fascism was the principal bastion of the capitalist system. This system, rotten to its core, can no longer survive and fulfill its normal functions because of internal weaknesses, growing contradictions, and incessant class struggle. And yet, in order to survive at all costs, it is grasping at the last straw—fascist dictatorship. Seen in this light, fascism is the last stage of dying capitalism.

This line of argument, however, did not withstand the test of real life. The first nations that fought against fascist Italy and Nazi Germany were precisely capitalist and democratic states—Great Britain, the United States and others. The first victims of fascist invasion and plunder were Czechoslovakia, Poland and other countries whose political systems were also more or less capitalist. It was not possible, even in the most roundabout way, to place these attacks under the rubric of class struggle in which fascism was the tool of the bourgeoisie against the workers. Entire nations came out solidly against the aggression and destructive terror of the fascist states.

Everywhere the resistance to fascist invasion clearly took on the character of a struggle for national liberation, for the restoration of independence to nations subjugated by force at the beginning of the war by the aggressive, rapacious imperialism of the fascist states. Thus, the struggle against the fascist bloc that spread like wildfire during the last war was not a struggle for this or that economic system, for capitalism, socialism or communism, but rather a struggle for *the people's freedom, for the rights of the individual and the rights of nations destroyed by fascist ideology and brutally crushed by the force of states established on this ideology.*

Only now, in the face of adversities brought on by foreign occupation and slavery imposed by terrorist regimes that many nations had never before experienced, has mankind realized the true and irreplaceable value of freedom, whose expression and guarantee are sovereign *nations established on the principles of a democratic system.*

Thus, in the course of the war, there emerged two completely distinct camps with opposing ideologies. A decisive struggle took place between the aggression, imperialism and terrorism of the fascist camp and the freedom of the democratic camp.

This division, however, was not always completely distinct. Some countries entered the war and took one side or the other voluntarily; others were obliged to do so because of prevailing circumstances or were motivated by the selfish prospect of victory. In this way, there were powers that found themselves compelled to join the anti-fascist bloc in order to repel their neighbours' aggression. They did not and do not have anything else in common with the democratic camp of liberation.

This unclear ideological division became even more obscure after the war. Political speculators have been attempting to exploit the victorious slogans of independence for their own purposes, even those who have completely different objectives and hold political views opposed to the concept of democracy. Quite a few political crooks, whether they operate on a small scale or on a larger world scale, are trying to hide their real objectives with democratic slogans and chants, readily branding their political enemies with the accursed stamp of fascism. Thus, we bandy about the concepts of democracy and fascism left and right today so widely and profusely that the average person is completely confused about what these concepts actually stand for.

It is, therefore, essential that we determine what the concepts of fascism and democracy actually mean, as we stated at the beginning, so that we can objectively determine who and what belongs to the camp of democracy and who belongs to the camp of fascism.

In this article, we shall attempt to explain the essential features of fascism.

The Beginnings of the Fascist Movement

In order to explain the essence of fascism, we must thoroughly analyze this problem. The fascist movement came into existence in Italy immediately after the First World War. At first, fascism had anticommunist and antianarchist characteristics and aimed at preserving unity and order in Italy; it did not, however, initially have a developed and fully formed ideology. In the course of time, when the party had come to power and governed the nation for many years, the fascist movement developed its own clearly defined ideology which found adequate support and acceptance through many years of practice. At the same time as the fascist movement was victorious and developing in Italy, more or less similar movements also arose in some other countries of Europe. Irrespective of their individual names, they were often called fascist movements after the example of their Italian prototype. Besides Italy, the most prominent representative of this political trend was the Nazi movement in Germany. Both movements left behind a very rich legacy because of their many years of rule, as well as an abundance of political writings that give us the means to define their principles and characteristics very clearly.

The Basic Principles of Fascism

Total Dictatorship

An objective description of fascism can briefly be given as follows: *fascism is a totalitarian system of government*. It is based primarily on the absolute dictatorship of the person who rules the nation—the *Duce*, the *Führer*, the leader, etc. He wields power by relying on the party that helped him attain his position. In practice, there are no constitutional and civil rights or freedoms under a fascist regime. It is solely the will or caprice of the dictator and his closest confidants that is binding in every matter. If the citizen is sometimes left with theoretical or practical rights, these are not based on any fundamental and constitutional legal guarantees. Nor are these rights lasting; depending on the will of the dictator, they can be withdrawn or changed at any moment. Among such limited civil rights in some totalitarian systems are certain remnants of democratic forms such as voting for parliamentary representatives. These remnants are usually vestigial. Changed, twisted and deformed, they are implemented in such a way that they completely lose their primary significance, becoming pliant instruments in the hands of the dictator to be employed according to his absolute will. Elections and representation in totalitarian systems have nothing in common with genuine national representation.

Complete Disregard for the Individual

In a totalitarian system, the state ceases to be a legal organization in relation to the citizen, becoming instead the representative of power and force. In the official ideology, this is described in various beautiful platitudes such as "the superior authority of the state over the individual," "the superiority of the interests of society represented by the state to the egotistical interests of the individual," etc. In reality, however, this kind of claptrap hides the loss of all the fundamental civil and, consequently, universal rights of the individual to the benefit of the all-powerful, dictatorial state apparatus. Man as an individual disappears more and more, whereas the importance and interference of the state increases in all areas of individual and collective life. Man is transformed into a servant and prisoner of the state, of a handful of people belonging to the state apparatus who consider themselves the sole representatives of the nation.

In this kind of system, the concept of the omnipotence of the totalitarian, dictatorial state often becomes so far-reaching as to push the very idea of the people into the background. The people come to be considered a secondary or "obsolete" factor. The doctrine of fascism has given the state and its power such tremendous and decisive significance in human life that it has completely eliminated not only the individual, but also the national collectivity. In this kind of system the state apparatus turns into an all-powerful totalitarian machine, while man becomes a mute little cog that can be turned in any direction from above.

All totalitarian regimes have developed more and more along these lines. It has long been well known that it is in the nature of every absolute power to seek expansion to the maximum limits of totalitarianism if it encounters no restraints.

A Centralist System

The logical result of this system was even greater state centralism. The entire life of huge national regions down to the smallest detail was ruled from state headquarters by an inflexible dictatorial hand. Such centralism was a source of power for totalitarian regimes with which they long impressed the rest of the world in certain respects. The centralized system produced a great deal of false grandeur which served to delight the dictators.

Police Terror

Totalitarian governments are often called police states, and justifiably so. Extensive police control and police terror are most often the mainstays of totalitarian regimes. The Nazi regime can serve as an eloquent example of this, not only in the occupied countries of Europe, but also in Germany itself. The ruthless and bloody system of political terror gives a dictatorial and totalitarian authority a feeling of omnipotence and power. It is, therefore, one of the main characteristics of any totalitarian system. Totalitarianism as a fascist form of government is, essentially, police terror.

Government Propaganda

A similar characteristic feature of totalitarian regimes is inflated, monopolistic state propaganda. Every citizen is silenced by police control and terror, whereas government propaganda has the unlimited resources of the state apparatus at its disposal. Under these conditions it not only serves to mobilize opinion for the benefit of the prevailing regime, but also, like a heavy stone or scourge, very effectively strengthens police terror and oppresses the individual who has been deprived of his rights and "made to conform to a pattern."

Glorifying the Person of the Dictator

The glorification of the *Duce, Führer* or chief who is the initial organizer and leader of a given political movement, becoming a dictator after his rise to power, goes beyond all reasonable bounds and is transformed into unlimited praise. The dictator is "great," "brilliant," a superman, almost God himself. This unlimited, slavish glorification of the person of the dictator is also a highly characteristic feature of all fascist-totalitarian regimes.

Megalomania

All totalitarian systems are also characterized by a very strong tendency toward megalomania. This is not so much a result of the centralized economy, which is conducive to such aspirations, as of psychological motives, namely the pride and conceit of individual leaders. This is already strikingly illustrated in earliest biblical history by the gigantic Tower of Babel [literally Tower of Babylon in the Polish text—Trans.]. It matters little whether the tower was imaginary or real, for it is nevertheless accurate in the light it sheds on the psychological basis of this phenomenon. All absolute leader-dictators, following the example of the ancient Egyptian pharaohs—the builders of the pyramids—try to build lasting monuments for themselves. They try to write their names into the history books by performing some exceptional feat, so they drain huge regions of swamp, dig new canals of unprecedented size, build huge factories and roads, construct enormous, gigantic, monumental buildings that are "the biggest in the world," and carry out many other similar undertakings that are "the biggest in the world"... Who among the living or, even more, among future generations, could deny that these are good works and undertakings, even great ones... And yet, it all looks competely different if we consider that these same works, often very useful in themselves, are built by dictators not for the general good, but for their own praise and glory, usually with the slave labour of subordinates organized by force. Just as in the splendid thousand-year-old pyramids of antiquity, or in the grand castles of medieval lords, but a thousand times more so, every stone and every metre of excavated soil in these giant edifices and other modern works of present-day satraps and tyrants are bathed in streams of tears and blood of millions of new slaves, wretched victims of dictator-tyrants.

What does it matter whether these huge edifices, factories and canals some day perhaps serve a good purpose, if they are constructed by means of slavery, misery, force, blood and tears, and if tyrants advertise the splendour and future usefulness of these works in order to buy recognition and fame for themselves and "oblivion" for their crimes? In the estimation of truly cultured people, even the greatest and most gigantic works do not justify, even in the slightest degree, the criminal methods of terror and slavery used in their creation. Instead of being enthralled by the enormous achievements trumpeted to the world again and again by the propaganda of totalitarian states, let us first ask by what means they were created, through whose work and at what cost. How many thousands of concentration-camp prisoners worked to build them under sentence of death? How many died or were shot? How many tears and how much blood was spilled before those canals, edifices, and industrial plants were built in praise of tyrants in the deserts, swamps or in the polar taiga?

If these same works were created by other methods in conditions of freedom, most of them would be useful and laudable. Built by force with the use of slave labour, however, at the cost of the suffering and lives of hundreds of thousands of people, and erected for the pride and glory of a dictator or to increase the size of his unbridled rapacious appetite, they bring no benefit or happiness to the mass of mankind, but constitute an even greater burden and yoke. Nor do they bring the fame that dictators desire, but eternal damnation.

Monopolistic Parties

Yet another highly characteristic feature of all totalitarian systems that allows us to distinguish them easily from other kinds of systems is the monopoly of a single governing party. Totalitarian states allow the activity of only one party—the tool of the dictator. All other parties, political groups, and even any political beliefs or independent thoughts that an individual might have are generally forbidden and persecuted.

Lately, this thoroughly reactionary, tyrannical, one-party form of politics, which stifles the development of the human spirit and denies nature and the very essence of humanity, has been masked in some countries by a facade of several official parties or a bloc of parties. This apparent multiparty system is a result of the pressure of world public opinion. In reality, however, this is only a piece of propagandist deceit calculated to "trick" naive people. Dictatorship and totalitarianism fear all truth and criticism; they fear human freedom, for they are in no position to withstand its scrutiny. That is why they clutch at the shadows of the dark and reactionary powers of force.

For wherever the free human spirit and the light of truth prevail, it is impossible for the corruption of a one-party dictatorship to survive.

A Return to the Middle Ages

All fascist-totalitarian movements readily relate their ideology to the history of the Middle Ages and even to remote periods of antiquity. They most often draw their inspiration from those early times, finding there the beloved figures of stern absolute rulers, kings, tsars, emperors and chieftains. Because of their autocracy, martial spirit and flashes of might, these personages inspire the admiration of today's imitators and candidates who want to emulate autocratic lords, rulers and tyrants, disregarding the intervening centuries and the progress made by mankind since that era. Disinterring and glorifying past historical events, they look to them first and foremost in order to justify and strengthen their own methods of absolutism, "supreme command," thirst for conquest, ruthless despotism, etc. This is a conscious turning away from human progress and development back to the barbarism of the Middle Ages.

Militarism

Fascist-totalitarian regimes strive to attain maximum military might. In order to reach this goal, they use all possible means at their disposal.

They militarize life in its entirety and greatly expand war industry, mobilizing the whole of public opinion for war. As a result, the nation is transformed into a military camp. Sooner or later, all this results in the outbreak of war. Once unleashed, the destructive elements of aggressive fury seek an outlet, driving those obsessed by such ideas into a military cataclysm. No one produces guns, tanks, ammunition, dynamite and bombs for fun or trains hundreds of thousands of military specialists for this purpose. Incessant war games always end in real war. The total militarization of the fascist states creates a permanent danger for other peoples and countries.

Imperialism

In their foreign policies, totalitarian systems are distinguished from others by their rapacious imperialism. It is precisely in this unrestrained, bloodthirsty, rapacious imperialism that the whole fascist ideology and all its most characteristic features find their best expression, their crowning glory and outlet. All the characteristics of a totalitarian system—tyrannical dictatorship, the centralized organization of every sphere of existence, the complete subordination of the individual and the sacrifice of his life and interests to the will and guidance of omnipotent gods, and rampant militarism—lead without fail to the constant growth of imperialist appetite, to the use of force and violence, and to a thirst for conquest. The American minister of foreign affairs, Byrnes,[3] recently reminded us—and rightly—that the Nazis began their march to world conquest with a policy of terror and tyranny in their own country. He also pointed out that we should not forget this instructive fact. For state authority, expanded to the farthest possible limits at the price of the freedom and rights of its citizens, accustomed to methods of terror and the ruthless squandering of the lives of its subordinates, and unchecked by any limitations, is very naturally also bound to seek greater and greater expansion outside its borders.

Racism

The ideologues and heads of fascist states try to "justify" their bloodthirsty, rapacious imperialism by putting forward the thesis of the alleged "superiority" of their people over other peoples and races. In other instances, they speak of their alleged cultural mission or of the more or less messianic mission of certain ideas. In actual fact, this is the simple violation and plunder of the weaker by the stronger. Armed from head to foot, brought up in a savage, aggressive, rapacious and militaristic spirit, the predator pounces on the weaker prey and tries to destroy it or subordinate it. This has nothing to do with the ideological principles that have been proclaimed, which only serve to cover up the real content. The ideology and practice of German Nazism was especially extreme and dangerous because of its racist madness. This ideology openly proclaimed and carried out the total destruction of all other peoples and races. Not all imperialist predators admit this so openly in their ideology, but all dream of their "superiority," "calling," and "destiny" to "liberate" and "bring happiness" to others, which really means to control them.

Ruling Out Moral Principles

The politics of fascist states do not recognize any binding obligations or moral principles. Politics have been known everywhere and in every age for their "elasticity," inconstancy and deceit (to put it mildly). As a result, politics have earned numerous unsavoury and scandalous labels. The entire history of diplomacy, however, pales in comparison with the deceitful methods of guile, duplicity, and the most refined Machiavellism employed by states of the fascist type. The politics of normal states, whatever "versatile" methods they employ, must nevertheless take the opinion of society into consideration; they are to some extent dependent and must take the principles and opinions held by society into account. Politics in fascist states, on the other hand, pay no heed to anyone or anything, employing (along with the method of total violence) methods of total falsehood and deceit. All commitments, treaties, assurances of eternal friendship, all the slogans and ideas that are advocated, the promises and oaths, all the principles upon which mankind can base its relations and collective life, lose any practical meaning when they come into contact with the total duplicity and violence of fascist-totalitarian states that we are currently witnessing.

*   *   *

This brief survey of the major characteristics of fascist-type systems provides us with a basis for identifying them even in cases where their identity is masked by deceptive slogans. In every doubtful case where we come across labels being bandied about blindly, we have only to establish immediately the actual state of affairs. The answer will be easy and clear: fascism exists wherever there is *dictatorship, a totalitarian system, violation of the rights of the individual, state centralism and concentration camps; wherever there is a one-party system and govern-*

ment propaganda; wherever there is official and obligatory exaltation and worship of the ruling dictator; wherever militarism and rapacious imperialism prevail; wherever there is no national or personal freedom and no freedom of conscience, thought, speech, press and association; wherever there are no authentic and completely free elections and parliamentary governments; and wherever there is no human dignity or humanism, but where there is hatred, terror and banditry.

This is a picture of that black phantom which has been terrifying mankind with its spectres. All nations and all peoples, and even more their children and descendants who want to protect themselves from the terrible consequences of slavery and genocide, must begin a resolute struggle to rid the world of this danger once and for all, thereby eliminating all systems of dictatorship and totalitarianism from the globe.

*   *   *

Red Antifascism

How different this clear picture becomes when we analyze the words and deeds of those who are making the most fuss today about the danger of fascism, who bandy this concept about the most and use it to slander others, crediting themselves with the label of antifascists but completely failing to explain what they mean by this widely used concept. In the first part of this article we explained the concept of fascism; in what follows, on the other hand, we shall attempt to determine the real meaning of the concepts of red and authentic antifascism and the actual positions taken by their opponents.

Falsehood and Falsification

Bolshevik propaganda today most often remains hidden behind the screen of antifascism, while branding all who oppose Bolshevism as fascists. Using such methods, Bolshevik propaganda very often finds this notorious danger of fascism not in the great imperialist, totalitarian powers where we would most likely expect it, but in ... Switzerland, Finland, Ukraine, Lithuania, etc. This is so surprising that we immediately want to find out what kind of fascism and danger they find in a small, highly developed country of four million people such as Switzerland—a democracy through and through, and at peace since the Middle Ages. Or in Finland, a country that is just as small. Or else in Ukraine, which itself has been downtrodden for centuries by great-power imperialism, has the greatest possible hatred for it and wants nothing more than its own liberation and freedom. It wants a system of free nations to prevail throughout the world, a system of freedom, equality and justice, humanism, culture, and true democratic conditions that would also help us Ukrainians obtain an ultimate guarantee of equal rights with other nations. After all, considering our current situation and the entire course of our history, as well as our natural, deeply rooted national characteristics, there can be nothing more alien and hateful to us than dictatorship or totalitarianism, systems of force, exploitation and imperialism, all of which have brought so much suffering and misery to our people. It is also for this reason that all the aspirations of the Ukrainian people are of the most progressive and liberty-loving kind.

Fascist-totalitarian, militaristic-imperialist systems are born, find suitable conditions, and come to power not in small or enslaved nations. *On the contrary, as a rule and a law of nature, they come to power in great ruling nations that seek to expand their power and dominance*. Fascist-totalitarian ideologies and systems, as we have shown in the preceding section, are an expression of a great power's imperialist aspirations. The liberation movement of the Ukrainian people, characterized by the most progressive and radical ideals in every sphere of existence and fighting to establish an independent Ukrainian state, as well as similar liberation movements branded fascist by Bolshevik propaganda, clearly have nothing in common with fascism. Nor can we attach the label of fascism to truly democratic but anti-Bolshevik political movements that predominate in Switzerland, Finland and other similar countries that threaten no one and observe democratic principles in their internal relations. If we come across such censure today, it is truly false and deceitful.

Where Should We Look for the Real Danger of Fascism?

The true danger of fascism—the threat of war, the danger of total dictatorship, total terror, militarism, rapacious and bloodthirsty imperialism, as well as the other calamities connected with fascism—still exists, but the threat comes from an entirely different source.

For a long time fascist Italy was a source of danger to several nations. To a greater extent, this danger existed for all of Europe and even for the whole world because of Nazi Germany. This fascist danger was most intense, however, and remains so to this very day, in none other than Bolshevik Russia—the same one that is making so much noise about so-called ''antifascism.''

For some Europeans who do not know Russian Bolshevism in practice but have only heard its loud propaganda, and who still judge Bolshevik Russia according to the theories of socialism, communism and even internationalism, our allegation about Russia's fascist aspect may come as a surprise, especially since the Soviet Union took such a great and active part in routing Nazi Germany in the last war.

The Ukrainian people, however, experienced all the atrocities of Hitlerite fascism in its most terrifying "Western" version during the recent three-year German occupation. It has also lived under Soviet rule for more than 25 years and has again been subject to this rule for two years since the crushing defeat of the Germans. For the Ukrainian people, who underwent the most basic training in both systems, it is clear that in practice both these regimes completely resemble one another and belong to one and the same fascist type.

A Comparison

As we have already mentioned, we base our assertion that Russian Bolshevism, in its basic characteristic features, conforms to the notion of pure, almost classical, fascism in its worst and most dangerous version on our personal observation of its reality over many years. A survey and comparison of the characteristic features of Russian Bolshevism and those of fascism as previously specified irrefutably confirms our assertion.

Russian Bolshevism, not in the theory of communism but in its practice, is above all a ruthless, tyrannical dictatorship carried to its uttermost limits. As always, in every totalitarian system, this is accompanied by total terror. The extent of Bolshevik terror is in no way inferior to the bloodiest practices of Nazism. In the practice of Bolshevism we also encounter the tyrannical rule of a dictator that we have seen in other fascist systems — a dictator who is an absolute ruler and a bloody tyrant recognizing no limits. We also come across the idolatrous worship of the person of the dictator, practised at his command and desire.

People do not worship or idolize their gods in any religion anywhere else in the world as they do in the Bolshevik paradise, where the inhabitants (who are also condemned men), degrading themselves, must bow down under duress to worship and loudly idolize the bloody Kremlin idol . . . Russian Bolshevism is also one huge system of concentration camps, Siberian penal colonies and forced slave labour, where masses of political prisoners numbering many millions have been sentenced to death. The camps of horror, ruin and human degradation, those famous death factories — Auschwitzes[4] and Majdaneks[5] — existed not only in the West in the land of the totalitarian barbarian. Just as many such camps also existed and exist to this day in the East in the country of his own younger brother, as it were. The only difference is that no one talks about the millions of wretched victims in these camps except, one supposes, in the case of Katyn.[6] There are certainly no fewer such Auschwitzes, Majdaneks, Vinnytsias[7] and Katyns in the East than there were in Nazi Germany . . . And yet, no one sees what is happening in these camps of death and human anguish on the Solovetsky Islands,[8] in the tundras and polar snows, on the distant banks of the Pechora[9] and Volodga,[10] and on the shore of the Arctic Ocean[11] . . . The Bolshevik butchers guard their terrible secrets and conceal themselves better than their butchering cannibalistic colleagues under the Nazi banner . . .

But for countless millions of victims of this terror it makes absolutely no difference who tortures and murders them. There is only one deep conviction, as well as the most irrefutable discovery, that these are identical terrorist methods, identical systems and identical criminals — perpetrators of genocide.

The Bolshevik system is one of collective responsibility. Such a system is rejected in the civilized world based on law. But here in the Bolshevik system a man is not the only one responsible for his own thoughts and actions. His wife, his children, parents, relatives, friends and those close to him, sometimes neighbours or even fellow townspeople are also responsible. For a repressive system demands of all citizens the strictest, most active co-operation with the police in the form of constant spying and informing on their neighbours. If someone is dilatory and not active enough, he is regarded as an enemy and an accomplice, an opponent of Bolshevism and therefore a candidate for one of the mass graves or a polar concentration camp.

The Boshevik system is that of one ruling monopolistic party. All other political parties, groups, and even the most innocent manifestations of one's own independent political thought have been condemned, denounced as "enemy counterrevolutionary activity," and destroyed in blood. Even in this very same ruling monopolistic Bolshevik party, the smallest signs of independent thought have been drowned in blood. Everything that is not a blind execution of orders, that does not begin and end with the slavish adoration of the tyrant, is condemned to persecution and destruction.

Dozens of scholars are sentenced to death not only because they hold different political views, but also, for example, because they have used a different word in a scholarly dictionary than the one desired by the ruling clique. Several editorial boards made up of the most outstanding professors of linguistics were shot to the last man solely because, as it was later announced officially, they had used the term *dvoie vider* instead of *dva vidra* (two pails)[12] in the Ukrainian-Russian dictionary, or still other similar expressions. The poor fellows did not suspect that the Kremlin butchers would not like this and would prepare a statement to the effect that this was "fascist sabotage intended to make a separation between Ukrainian and Russian . . . " And how many revisions of dictionaries and history textbooks, as well as other changes, have there been during the twenty-five-year period of Bolshevism, almost every one of them stained with blood! Under the Bolshevik regime terror and death also rule over human thought and learning. After all, the Soviet state has achieved "socialism" and eliminated illiteracy—we have enough schools now. Unlike other countries, we do not have to worry that we will ever lack scholars. After all, in order to replace one or two thousand scholars who were shot, we will produce twice as many new ones at an "accelerated" pace who will certainly be more obedient and docile. Taught by experience and suitably trained, they will immediately be able to guess the thoughts and wishes of their employer and will constantly glorify and praise him . . .

Just as in all the examples of fascist systems with which we are already familiar, but even more so in the Bolshevik system, the individual is completely denied his basic rights, "made to conform to a pattern," and reduced to the status of a mute cog in the huge state machine. He becomes inanimate building material in the hands of a small group of privileged foremen, all-powerful heads of the state apparatus. Such things as elections, a constitution, and representation are out of the question, at least in the sense in which these institutions are known in the rest of the civilized world. There are, however, certain "substitutes" and remnants of these institutions. There is much loud talk of elections and all available means are used to advertise the Stalinist constitution as "the most democratic in the world," but all this is one great and total lie, a hoax. In reality, these democratic institutions do not exist at all. There is only a total terrorist dictatorship, more or less skillfully covered up by propagandistic bluffing. It would be enough, for example, to look more closely at the official resolutions of this "most democratic constitution" alone and examine them in detail to document the enormity of the lie put forward in Bolshevik propaganda. For the official constitution is antidemocratic in its most fundamental contents, not only in practice but in its very essence, clearly establishing a government and political order contrary to the sovereign will of the people but congruent with the rule of the dictatorial clique—the supreme, monopolistic Communist party. In practice, though, the only real constitution is the terror of the Bolshevik police—the NKVD-NKGB. Under the Bolshevik system, all the achievements of the great French Revolution have been shattered. The Declaration of the Rights of Man and Citizen[13] has been cancelled, along with the achievements of enlightened periods in the development of human civilization and culture. Life has swerved from the road of progress to that of totalitarian barbarism. We can also find some grounds for this assertion if we look more closely at other characteristic features of all totalitarian-fascist systems, especially the megalomania that we have already mentioned, the regression to the ideology of the Middle Ages, monopolistic government propaganda, militarism, imperialism, racism, etc.

Soviet megalomania is so well known and advertised to the point of exaggeration by the Bolsheviks themselves that we do not even have to prove that this totalitarian disease exists in Russia. Let us only recall once again the psychological motives that are the underlying factor of this phenomenon, which is typical of all totalitarian systems: the immense pride and megalomania of dictators who want to "immortalize" themselves in this way instead of thinking of the welfare and happiness of society as a whole. We must also call to mind the unparallelled exploitation of the whole people and the use of slave labour in building monumental structures and huge industrial complexes. The observer who is unaware of the actual state of affairs and who looks at these Soviet colossi from a distance, in almost the same way that we look at the pyramids of the pharaohs today, can sometimes be dazzled by the proportions of these undertakings. This is what Bolshevik propaganda is counting on. Because of our own terrifying experiences, however, we know that as far away as the shores of the Arctic Ocean these splendid edifices and canals, these new railways, roads, mines and towns that grow like mushrooms after rain are built on slavery and exploitation unparallelled in all the history of mankind—built on blood and, literally, on human bones. These colossi are built by millions of workers who are flagrantly chained to their work under circumstances one would not encounter anywhere else, circumstances that are simply unbelievably difficult. Other, even larger, colossi in this huge polar state of NKVD concentration camps are being built by the hands of millions of political prisoners condemned to torture and extermination.

This centralist totalitarian economy has achieved a number of triumphs that have made themselves apparent, among other things, in several great undertakings. Of course, all tyrannies, absolute governments, and totalitarian systems have had and continue to have such triumphs, and these successes are very often no less grand than those of the Soviets. Nazi Germany and fascist Italy had them, as did other nations, both ancient and modern, that were governed by absolute and centralist systems.

Bolshevik propaganda persists in claiming that the most significant proof of their triumph and also of the justness of their policies lies in the fact that, under their rule, Soviet Russia has grown into a great world power during the past twenty-five years. Yes, this assertion is true. This truth, however, only confirms our basic argument about the similarity of totalitarian regimes. For it is also true that in only half that time the Nazi regime brought Germany—defeated, divided, impoverished and disarmed after the Treaty of Versailles—to an even greater height of power, so that six years after this regime came to power it was already reaching for world domination. This would only lead us to the conclusion that, using the methods of military mobilization, force and terror, etc., one can sometimes actually get more sweat and effort from people and bring more than one undertaking to completion. No one denies this fact. But these achievements should be evaluated differently, judging them not by their temporary success in the eyes of the outside world, but gauging their pertinence, justice and accordance with binding principles as a measure of their historical value. In the light of these facts, the staggering triumphs of Nazism certainly did not bring the German people happiness and a better existence. The triumphs of Russian Bolshevism will end in the same way. It is perfectly clear and natural that a great planned economy has its own undeniable merits. Perhaps others have different ideas about this matter, but we admit this openly and are always prepared to draw appropriate, positive conclusions from this fact.

But should we renounce our ideals of freedom for these so-called triumphs of Nazism, fascism and Bolshevism in the sphere of the centralized state economy? Should we therefore renounce this most precious treasure of human life, without which there can be no human dignity, but only the wretched bestial life of slavery? Can it be true that in order to regulate economic life it is necessary to renounce human freedom and introduce state totalitarianism?

No, a hundred times no! Therefore we never intend to renounce the treasure of freedom at any price. Neither do we believe, nor will we ever believe the false propaganda that tries to persuade us of the necessity of dictatorship and totalitarianism by arguing the advantages of a planned economy. On the other hand, we believe and know that all the world's economic affairs can be regulated quite well for the good and happiness of all humanity without any totalitarian dictatorship. We also believe that this can perhaps come about in a short time, not through the victory of totalitarianism, but precisely through its overthrow. But let us return to the beginning of our logical chain of reasoning and argumentation, whose next link is the statement that we have already made about the reversion of Bolshevik ideology to that of the barbaric Middle Ages.

At first glance this accusation, more than any other, may seem strange to all who have not experienced the profound ideological changes that have affected Soviet Russia in the last ten years and who remain unaware of them. Those changes were fundamental. By the use of ruthless methods of the utmost economic centralization and tyrannical, reckless totalitarianism, by the subordination of every sphere of existence to the requirements of military mobilization, by such ruthless and inhuman methods, Soviet Russia was able to wrest the maximum output of work and outlay of funds from about 170 million of its citizens—especially from Ukraine—and to become one of the world's great powers.

At the same time that these fascist-totalitarian methods were being applied in all areas of national life, parallel processes of ideological change inseparable from them were also in progress, owing to the natural laws of sociology. To begin with, as happened in other types of fascist systems, red-internationalist Bolshevik messianism became more and more coloured by elements of ordinary nationalism and imperialism (but of greater than normal proportions). Various forces and laws of group psychology—both general and associated with the particular nature and history of the Russian people—influenced this process. To a considerable extent, mimicry of the principles and methods of fascist movements also had an effect. The initial successes of their fascist competitors impressed the Bolshevik dictators. Therefore, in more than one respect, they sought to imitate fascist methods and make use of the forces on which the others had built their strength. As a result, therefore, we can observe greater and greater mutual imitation and actual similarity between these competing totalitarian systems...

One of the most striking indications of this process was the distinct, radical change in relations among nationalities and in the study of history.

When, in the first period of Bolshevism, the whole tsarist Russian past was studied thoroughly, both the reactionary foreign and internal policies of the tsars were judged and censured. In keeping with the growth of Bolshevik Russia's new power, a radical change has occurred in its historiography, which now tends to exactly the opposite extreme, namely to traditionalism and to whitewashing and idolizing all of Russian history. The reactionary imperialist policies of the tsars have suddenly been forgotten, along with their rapacious conquest and oppression of other nations. Everything that was taught until now as immutably sacred Marxist history has been forgotten; we have returned to everything that was cursed until recently and labelled as fascism and reaction.

Thus, in a manner quite similar to that of Nazi Germany and fascist

Italy (countries that looked for their inspiration, ideals and models to the history of medieval or ancient Germany or to the Roman emperors, rulers and legions), the Bolsheviks have reached out for models. They have, therefore, dug up and dragged in as "progressive" idols Tsar Peter I, the great imperialist and oppressor of other nations, the generals of Tsarina Catherine II, and a whole series of other historical and quasi-historical figures. They have been gilded and drawn into the ranks of almost saintly heroes. In this sudden patriotic, nationalist and imperialist zeal, all of early tsarist historiography has been transcended. Lately the Bolsheviks have also dug up the figure of Tsar Ivan the Terrible. Even more recent tsarist historiography was ashamed to idealize the figure of this almost insane barbarian of the Middle Ages, famous throughout the world for his obscurantism and ignorance, his mad notions and excesses. Today, however, Bolshevik history, cinema, the press and literature are loud in their praises and exalt this personage to the heavens as a model of the ideal ruler—the architect and founder of the Russian Empire who wanted to transform Moscow into the "third Rome." His insane imperialist plans and appetites please today's red tyrants in the Kremlin so much that they are justifying and whitewashing all his excesses and crimes, passing over his insanity in silence and drawing him into the ranks of their "saints."

Lately we have read in the press that Soviet-produced films about Ivan the Terrible will soon even appear on movie screens abroad. This is how Russian generals and tsars have suddenly crossed over from the reactionary, imperialist and fascist camp to join the ranks of the patrons of Soviet "progress" and "democracy." But since it is absolutely certain that after so many centuries they have remained the same reactionaries and enemies of freedom and human progress that they were during their lifetimes, it is clearly evident that not they but their newest devotees have made this devious jump from the summit of the high-sounding theories of socialism, communism and internationalism into the naked reality of fascism and imperialism. It appears that the same kind of totalitarian methods lead to the same end. Just some forty-odd years ago, several great Russian free-thinkers and revolutionaries wrote about this most aptly and almost prophetically. Already at that time they foresaw that if Lenin came to power with his group, he would become a new red tsar who would be even more of a despot than the white Russian tsars of their time. The centralist opinions Lenin voiced in the columns of the émigré Russian paper *Iskra* (The Spark), as well as the position taken by Lenin's group on various contemporary issues, especially on the question of the aspirations to independence of Ukraine, Poland, Finland and other nations enslaved by Russia, showed most clearly even then that they were on the road that surely had to lead to such results. For every power seeks to broaden its authority in the natural course of its development. If it does not encounter sufficiently great barriers in its path, however, and is already centralist and absolutist in its views, it must change in time into a despotic tyranny.

But this is by no means all. There are many more common features between the ideology and practice of red Bolshevik totalitarianism and the ideology and practice of black fascist totalitarianism. Among these are the unusually strong militarist tendencies that are the same in all fascist-totalitarian regimes. In the Soviet state these tendencies have taken on such huge proportions as to dominate all of economic life, the education of young people, and other spheres. The famous five-year plans of Soviet industry are nothing but a programme for the expansion of the war industry. The entire state apparatus works feverishly to further the militarization of life. All the forces that can be mobilized are thrown into this tremendous race of armaments and war preparation. Life and prosperity, the freedom and happiness of citizens, are sacrificed to the insatiable Moloch of imperialist militarism. Russian dictators dream about becoming the world's foremost military power in the same way as Hitler, the bloody god of German fascism, dreamed about this not long ago.

Just as in German Nazism and Italian fascism, the crown of all these features of the Bolshevik system is rapacious imperialism. The imperialism of Bolshevik Russia, however, is many times stronger than that of tsarist Russia. Following in the footsteps of its tsarist predecessors, Bolshevik Russia first defeated Ukraine, Belorussia and the Caucasus by armed invasion and force, and then the Baltic countries and Finland; now, following the same historical course, it has set out to take Poland and the Balkans. In its dreams, however, and not only in its dreams but in its plans and preparations, the next phase of the battle is world domination. This unrestrained greed for world domination, clothed in the propaganda of various ideas—Pan-Slavism, socialism and communism—is actually the main feature of Russian Bolshevism. The red imperialism of Russia is the most striking and dangerous imperialism of our time. Surely the imperialism of Nazi Germany alone could compare with it in its appetite and proportions.

Nor is the ideology of Russian Bolshevism devoid of strong emphasis on the insanity of racism. Bandying about the exceptionally alluring slogan of equality for all nations and peoples in their propaganda to the outside world, the Bolsheviks treat these principles solely as a propagandistic slogan. Within its own empire, the Soviet government adheres to entirely different principles. Some time ago official government circles and the press, as well as all internal propaganda, clearly broke with the principle of racial and national equality and began a strong campaign extolling the Russian people as the ''first'' among others and praising it as the most worthy, ''especially gifted,'' ''ruling'' people, etc., while all other peoples are supposed to listen to their ''older, ruling brother.'' For Russia, after all, has been appointed to rule, and others to listen and obey. Simply and clearly interpreted, ''ruling'' is always and everywhere equivalent to domination. The fairy tale about the Russian people's supposedly being ''chosen'' and ''appointed'' to dominate other peoples that need its care and guidance is a sign of the same racist insanity that we saw recently in Nazi Germany in a different guise.

The institution of monopolistic official propaganda also belongs to the series of common features that unite the Bolshevik system with other fascist systems. In the Bolshevik system it is a real curse and plague of all citizens. Untold and countless material resources have been placed at its disposal. Our entire literary and artistic output has been pulled down from the pedestal of the temple of the human spirit and harnessed in the service of propaganda, along with the press, cinema and radio. Even such an institution as the church, long oppressed and persecuted, has been partly revived and harnessed to the wagon of official propaganda, with its positions of leadership occupied by trusted members of the party and police. On the external front, propaganda is a prime offensive weapon clearing the path for Bolshevik imperialism. On the internal front, it supplements police terror and functions as a whip unceasingly flogging all citizens and forcing them to work beyond all norms—indeed, beyond human capacity—in order to augment further the resources of the red tyrants so that they can carry out their insane plans to conquer the world.

In much the same way, Soviet politicians and diplomats have been more than a match for all their fascist colleagues in the evasion and breaking of international treaties, commitments and promises. Soviet politics does not acknowledge any moral principles at all and cynically ridicules them as prejudices. Soviet politics is the art of lying and deceit, double-dealing and refined Machiavellism. Soviet politicians and diplomats proudly consider their greatest revolutionary method the artifice of cynically uttering lofty universal slogans and manipulating the noblest ideals that have hitherto been the dream and the sacred shrine of mankind, only to use them for their own imperialist ends with cold and treacherous calculation. There are no sacred ideas or words in human speech that they would not trample, bandying them about as propaganda devices without being at all concerned about putting these same lofty principles into practice. The loftiest propagandistic slogans do not prevent them from going on with their most cruel and inhuman daily dealings. It is the same in the sphere of international relations, treaties, pacts and alliances. As an eloquent example of this behaviour we have the six months of lengthy negotiations with England and other Western powers in 1939 over the alliance against Hitler. After these negotiations failed, there was a sudden and totally unexpected Soviet alliance with that same Hitler. According to Bolshevik propaganda, all those who oppose Bolshevism are now fascists and Nazis, even though they may have long years of fighting against fascism behind them, long years of prisons and concentration camps, and even though they may hold the most honest and sincere democratic beliefs. But in their own opinion only the Bolsheviks have the right to "antifascism" and a monopoly on it, despite the fact that they had a friendship pact with Hitler and sent him an inexhaustible supply of wheat, gasoline and iron, despite the fact that they torpedoed plans for the creation of an anti-Hitler bloc at the most critical moment in 1939 and helped Hitler directly by their treacherous policies and indirectly by their alliance. They helped Hitler declare war and conquer half of Europe. Hitler helped the Bolsheviks subjugate Lithuania, Latvia and Estonia, as well as to conquer Western Ukraine, Bessarabia and south-eastern Finland. Thus, everything was all right, for the Bolsheviks could do anything they wanted, even to the point of being friendly and co-operating with Hitler or the devil himself; it was all the same, as long as their imperialist interests benefited. What did they care that their actions were incompatible with all moral principles, that they were dishonest and despicable, that millions of people had to pay for them with their suffering and blood, and that these actions were actually totalitarian-fascist methods denounced by the whole world?

After all, that was the reason they developed their enormous apparatus of propaganda, which was supposed to whitewash all that was black and cover up whatever was white, to twist one thing and turn another around, to depict honest and noble people as fascists and to make notorious totalitarians and recent allies and helpmates of Hitler into "antifascists."

*   *   *

A survey of the main features that characterize Russian Bolshevism, which is attempting to play the role of a fundamentally anti-fascist movement in world opinion, reveals not only a great similarity *but an outright identity between the Bolshevik regime and typical fascist regimes.*

It is the same kind of totalitarian, dictatorial, militaristic and imperialist system, but one that is even more extreme.

Italian fascism, German Nazism, and Russian Bolshevism are identical totalitarian movements and systems that came into existence and developed in various European countries after the First World War. They are all typical totalitarian systems and are so very much alike that *we could call Bolshevism Russian fascism absolutely without hesitation, or, better still, Russian Nazism, whereas Nazism could equally well be called German Bolshevism.*

Undeniably, there are also some differences between them. Italian fascism had its own characteristics, as did German Nazism. Russian Bolshevism has them as well. The environment of a given nation, within which its new totalitarian and imperialist movement comes into being and grows, endows it with more than one original feature.

The universal scope of contemporary Russian imperialism, as interpreted and carried out by Bolshevism, differs in more than one way from Italian fascism, which represented the imperialism of an Italian state that was still young and relatively small. Among other differences, the greatest lies in the sphere of theoretical ideological doctrine.

As an expression of its unusually strong imperialist tendencies, Russian Bolshevism adopted the broad doctrine of internationalism. This gave it the widest possible universal scope and the capacity to employ special tactics and propaganda that cover up all the most blatant imperialist aspirations and achievements with so-called internationalism. This is precisely what makes Russia the most dangerous member of its gang of totalitarian-fascist companions, whose doctrines (of much narrower scope and less well camouflaged) do not give them such a wide reach or such versatile and dangerous tactics.

All the more so today, after the defeat of black Italian fascism and brown German Nazism, we should pay close attention to the fact that one member of this "worthy" family still remains—red fascism, or Russian Bolshevism, the last and worst enemy of human freedom, which hides its real imperialist aspect behind the screen of internationalism, and its totalitarianism behind false "democratism."

All civilized mankind should come forward in solidarity and take up the fight against this spectre of red fascism, which is a much greater danger than many people in Europe and abroad imagine. The heroic struggle carried on by the Ukrainian people for a great many years against Bolshevik imperialism and tyranny, whose goal is to cast off its yoke and secure its own national independence, should serve as a warning and an example to those peoples that have not yet come to know Bolshevism through their own direct experience.

As long as a system of imperialism and tyranny reigns over the enormous territories of east-central Europe and Asia, it will continue to be a source of mortal danger to other peoples. During the war,

Lithuania, Latvia, Estonia, Finland, Poland, Romania, Bulgaria, Hungary and other nations, in part, became convinced of this fact. Now Turkey, Persia and China are becoming convinced of this same danger as well. Soon other nations and the whole world will also be convinced. Only the abolition of Bolshevism and the break-up of this enormous prison of nations into its separate, integral, national parts built upon the principles of national self-determination, freedom, equality and justice can do away with the lasting source of this danger.

(Translated from a brochure printed in Ukrainian and published by Ukrainian revolutionary underground organizations.)

Source: Jarłan, *Upiór Faszyzmu*. Tłumaczenie z oryginału ukraińskiego. Mimeo 150 x 205 mm., 29 pp., 1946. Original: Archive of the Foreign Representation of the Supreme Ukrainian Liberation Council, Folio E4–1. Photocopy: Archive, *Litopys UPA*. The translation was prepared from the Polish text, as the Ukrainian original could not be located.

NOTES

1. Adolf Hitler (1889–1945): German dictator, founder and leader of National Socialism.
2. Benito Mussolini (1883–1945): Italian dictator, founder and leader of fascism.
3. James F. Byrnes (1879–1972): American political leader and Secretary of State (1945–7).
4. Auschwitz (Oświęcim): town in Poland where the Germans maintained a concentration camp and where some four million inmates, mostly Jews, were killed.
5. Majdanek concentration camp in Poland, where the Germans killed about 1.5 million people, mostly Jews.
6. Katyn: village near Smolensk where some 10,000 Polish officers were killed by Soviet security forces.
7. Vinnytsia: city in Ukrainian SSR. Location of nine mass graves of approximately 9,400 Ukrainians killed by the Russian communists in 1937. The graves were discovered in May 1943.
8. Solovetsky Islands: archipelago in the White Sea. A place of exile for political prisoners under tsarist and communist regimes.
9. Pechora: river in north European Russia. A place of exile and forced-labour camps.

10. Vologda: city in north European Russia. A place of exile and forced-labour camps.
11. The shore of the Arctic Ocean, a place of exile and forced-labour camps. For a detailed account of the forced-labour system, see Aleksandr I. Solzhenitsyn, *The GULAG Archipelago, 1918–1956: An Experiment in Literary Investigation*, 3 vols. (New York 1974–8).
12. In Ukrainian there is a system of collective numerals used primarily when referring to a company of persons of both sexes or to young animals and with personal pronouns, or, as in this case, by analogy. *Dva vidra* is closer to Russian usage.
13. The Declaration of the Rights of Man and Citizen was passed by the French National Assembly in 1789, during the revolutionary period.

OUR TEACHINGS ABOUT
THE NATIONAL STATE

P. Poltava

Just as in the case of our doctrine with regard to the nation, our doctrine with regard to the state has grown out of the ideological and political struggle that we have been waging on two fronts—against the imperialist views voiced by representatives of the great powers and against Marxist views of the state.

The views of the representatives of the dominant great powers have consisted in an overt, grossly imperialist denial of the right of small peoples to their own independent states. We have already discussed these views in our writings concerning the position taken by representatives of the dominant great powers on the national question in general.

The Marxists have taken a different approach to this issue. They attempt to ground their hostile attitude to the state in supposedly scientific arguments. According to their views, the state always has been and continues to be nothing more than a tool of oppression in the hands of the dominant, economically superior social classes. In the Marxist view, the state came into existence at the same time as, within tribes, classes of exploiters and oppressors were created. In order to safeguard their positions as exploiters, as well as their economic and political dominance, these classes also established a state organization which, with its enormous apparatus of coercion—prisons, the police, the army, the bureaucracy, a subservient judiciary—is nothing more than a machine of oppression. This whole machinery of oppression not only enabled the exploiters to keep the working masses in a state of slavery, but imposed a heavy economic burden on those masses. In order to maintain this state machine, workers have been compelled to pay huge taxes, undergo military service, sacrifice their lives in wars and fulfill all sorts of other obligations. From all these facts, the Marxists draw the following conclusion: the state must disappear, for it is unnecessary. Only when the state is destroyed will humanity live a truly free and happy life. This, in short, is the Marxist view of the state.

This view of the state, like the Marxist-Bolshevik view of the nation, is false and tendentious. In the first place, it is mistaken in its analysis of the rise of the state. In the second place, while the Marxists are correct in criticizing the shortcomings of the state in various historical periods, they have used this criticism to draw improper conclusions about the character of the state as a whole. Their view that nations will be able to manage without states in the future is utopian, fantastic and deprived of any basis in reality. In all Marxist theory about the state there is a clear effort to deny that the state has any significance for the people and for humanity in general, as well as an attempt to present history as nothing more than a class struggle, which, as we have already stated, is totally incorrect.

The state arose as a natural way of organizing first clans, then tribes, and finally nations. Clan and tribal organizations constitute a rudimentary form of the state, its prototype. Clan and tribal organizations had two main purposes: to organize and impose order upon life within the clan or tribe and to organize the defence of the clan or tribe against external enemies. All scholars who study the subject agree on this point. Clans and tribes had their own forms of government, their own laws, and their own means of enforcing these laws. And this was at a time when within the clans—or, in some cases, tribes—there was not yet any division of the population into classes of exploiters and exploited, when neither the one nor the other existed. Even the Marxists do not deny this. Thus, given these historical facts, it is clear that *the state arose not as a tool of oppression in the hands of the wealthy classes to be used against the economically weak classes, but in response to the natural need to bring order into the life of society and to defend that society against external enemies.*

With the passage of time, we know that the population came to be divided into classes of exploiters and exploited. *From this time onward the exploiting classes have in fact been attempting to transform the state organization into a tool of their economic and political rule. Their success in this regard has varied depending on time and place. Thus, one can speak of the state as a tool of class oppression only from the time when class society came into existence.* This is how it is at present, to a degree that varies from one country to another.

The ruling classes make use of the state organization for more than just oppressing their own working masses. To an even greater extent they use it to conquer foreign territories, to subjugate other nations. This is how, as a result of the grasping policy of imperialists, *multinational states have been established. A multinational state in which society is also divided into classes of exploiters and exploited is a double tool of oppression.* In the first place, it is a tool of *social* oppression of the working masses of the dominant nation. In the second place, the multinational state is a tool of *national* oppression and exploitation of the subjugated nations. *Obviously states of this type should not exist; they should be restructured as soon as possible.* Single-nation states which serve as tools of oppression and exploitation used by the ruling classes against their own working masses should also be restructured socioeconomically and politically.

But can mankind exist without any states?

It cannot. In order for the human race to exist and develop, it must be organized in some way. On this point there is no doubt.

Given that 1) the human race is divided into different nations, 2) nations, as we demonstrated in the preceding section, are *the highest* form of human society, and 3) the yearning for an independent state is a *natural* desire of *every* people, *only a system of free national states of all peoples of the world can be the organization that is required for human life and development.* Any system that fails to take these facts into account will always *stand on shaky ground.* For this reason, a system of free national states of all peoples represents not only the most *just* solution to the problem of international order, but also the most *viable,* the most *suited to reality.*

The establishment of a system of free national states *will destroy the multinational state and thus put an end to national oppression and exploitation.* That will be mankind's first major step forward. Furthermore, in order to take the state out of the hands of the ruling social classes, to prevent the state from being a tool of exploitation and oppression employed by the wealthy classes against their own working masses, *it is necessary to rebuild the present social order on the basis of a classless society.* When the national state ceases to be composed of exploiters and exploited, *it will cease to be a tool of oppression and will become, as it was at its very beginning, simply a form of organization of the internal economic and cultural life of the nation and a tool of defence against external enemies.* Furthermore, should the world reach a state of development in which there no longer existed any threat of attack by one nation against another, or in which any attack of this sort could be repelled by the forces of a capable international organization established on the principles of justice, then the national state would no longer need to be a form of defence against external enemies; it would only retain the function of organizing the internal economic and cultural life of the nation. *But the state can never disappear as a form of organization of the internal economic and cultural life of the nation. In that role the state is essential and cannot be replaced by anything else.* In that role, it is an institution of great social value. Were the state to function in this way, the apparatus of coercion would be limited to the minimum degree necessary for maintaining internal order; the maintenance of the state would no longer require any great material sacrifices from the people; all the nation's material and moral wealth would be geared to its economic and cultural development. However—and we stress this again—this would be possible only if the nation could be certain of not being threatened by any external danger. As we know, at present we are nowhere near such a state.

We nationalists believe in this eternal truth—*that an independent national state is the only form of political organization that guarantees a people the best conditions for all-round development of its spiritual and material resources.* Without its own national state, that is, without a state extending over all its ethnic territory, a people cannot fully develop. Furthermore, without its own national state, a people is doomed to extinction. A stateless people must always endure oppression and exploitation from invaders, who always strive for the political, cultural and even physical destruction of the people they subjugate, whatever slogans they may use to disguise their intentions. This is obvious from all of Ukrainian history and the histories of all other subject peoples. From the fourteenth to the eighteenth centuries we Ukrainians were oppressed by aristocratic Poland, which strove for our destruction; from the seventeenth to the twentieth centuries, tsarist Russia sought to destroy us; after 1920, we were oppressed by the Muscovite Bolsheviks, Poles, Romanians, Czechs, Hungarians and Germans. Now the Muscovite Bolsheviks are once again attempting to destroy us. We nationalists have taken into account the whole historical experience of the Ukrainian and other subject peoples. For this reason, we consider that the first and most essential condition of a people's existence and healthy development is its own independent national state. We must decisively reject and oppose states of the type of the Bolshevik Soviet Union, which serves only as a cover for Muscovite-Bolshevik imperialism. We also reject and oppose all other forms of multinational states built upon national oppression and exploitation.

The idea of having one's own independent national state springs from every people's deepest desires and national feelings. Peoples want to be their own masters on their own land; they want to be free and to rule over their own territory. Their sense of national honour, national pride and patriotism demands that it be so. Peoples despise subjugation; they always strive for liberty. And only an independent national state can give them true and complete liberty. This desire on the part of individual peoples, as we have already stated, springs from their very essence. Nobody can change this or stifle these feelings in a people.

But a system of independent national states would not only coincide with the interests and respond to the needs of individual peoples. It would also suit the interests of all peoples as a whole, of mankind in general.

We nationalists believe that the highest calling of all peoples of the world as a whole and every people in particular should be the greatest degree of development of spiritual and material human culture. Mankind's general progress is the sum of the achievements of individual peoples. If humanity today is legitimately proud of the high level of its culture, of that culture's *wealth and diversity*, it should bear in mind that human culture today is the result of a process in which *many different peoples* have taken part. Present-day culture would be even more advanced, even richer and more diverse if all those peoples that have been in a state of subjection and thus have not been able to make their contribution to this process of cultural development had been able to participate fully. For the greatest development of mankind's spiritual and material culture, for the greatest progress of humanity, all peoples of the world must participate fully in the cultural process. Were this the case, human culture in general would be incomparably richer and more diverse than it is today. For such participation by all peoples in the cultural process to be successful and yield the desired results, it is essential that all peoples of the world enjoy the possibility of maximum development of their own resources and capacities at home in their own countries. As has already been indicated, peoples are best able to develop their own resources when they live in their own independent national states. Thus a system of free national states is in the best interests of the development of humanity as a whole.

As we see, peoples and nations, which are the products of both the natural process of differentiation of the human race and of historical development, are something that mankind should strive to preserve and foster. The path of human progress lies not through an artificial or, even worse, coercive union of peoples, not through the policy of melting and recasting various peoples into a single whole, but only though granting each people full freedom to create and develop. This development can take place only in a system of independent national states. Any people that oppresses other peoples, prevents their development or destroys them undermines the foundations of human progress and is an enemy not only of the peoples it subjugates but of humanity as a whole. At present, the Bolshevik USSR is an implacable enemy of individual subject peoples and of humanity in general.

Taking into account, on the one hand, the natural desires and interests of each individual people and, on the other, the interests of humanity as a whole, we nationalists are struggling for a system of free national states of all the peoples of the world. The immediate goal of our struggle is the realization of the age-old dream of the Ukrainian people—the establishment of an independent united Ukrainian state on Ukrainian ethnic territory. We regard the struggle for the establishment of an independent Ukrainian state on Ukrainian territory as the major task facing the whole Ukrainian people today.

Source: This article appeared in the collection *Shliakh do voli* (Pathway to Liberty), published by the Centre of Propaganda and Information of the OUN, 1950. An excerpt from this article appeared in the newspaper *Suchasna Ukraina* (Munich), no. 9 (1951). It was published in full in P. Poltava, *Zbirnyk pidpilnykh pysan* (Munich: Ukrainskyi Samostiinyk, 1959), 71–7.

THE CONCEPT OF AN INDEPENDENT UKRAINE AND CURRENT POLITICAL TRENDS IN THE WORLD

P. Poltava

The concept of an independent Ukraine envisages an independent Ukrainian state established by the Ukrainian people on their own ethnic territory.

The historical experience of all mankind has demonstrated that a people's desire to live in its own independent state is *an inherent and natural desire*. All peoples have always striven to secure their existence and to create the best possible conditions for their development through their own state institutions. The national identity of any people is most fully expressed through its own state institutions.

The desire of the Ukrainian people for their own independent state is an inherent and natural desire, one that has always existed among them. It was this desire that impelled them in the tenth and eleventh centuries to establish the first state in their history—Kievan Rus'.[1] It also impelled them to establish the Cossack Republic in 1648[2] and the Ukrainian People's Republic in 1918.[3] Because of this desire, the Ukrainian people have never ceased to struggle for national and political liberation during their periods of statelessness. *Thus, the concept of an independent Ukraine, for which the Ukrainian people are now struggling, is above all the expression of the natural, historic desire of the Ukrainian people for an independent existence.*

The concept of an independent Ukraine is also a response to the bitter historical experience of the Ukrainian people.

In their struggle against nomadic hordes, imperialist Russian tsars and Polish nobles, the Ukrainian people were not always able to maintain a separate national state organization. Kievan Rus' collapsed under the blows of the Tatars. The Cossack Republic could not hold out against attacks on two fronts from tsarist Russia and aristocratic Poland. After the fall of Poland, the Russian and Austro-Hungarian Empires divided Ukrainian lands between themselves. The Ukrainian People's Republic fell in the struggle against Bolshevik Moscow and imperialist Warsaw. When their lands were annexed to foreign states, the Ukrainian people were subjected to savage oppression, exploitation and abuse. While other peoples were progressing on all fronts, the Ukrainian people fell yet further behind: they became increasingly more oppressed, disenfranchised and worse off economically; their language, culture and customs were trampled upon with ever greater brutality. Even when changes occurred in the empires in which the Ukrainian people lived, their lot did not substantially improve. All of the "democratic" reforms in Vienna and "socialist" revolutions in Moscow did nothing to liberate the Ukrainian people.

Given this situation, the Ukrainian people quickly realized that the sole reason for their difficulties was their lack of national independence, their lack of an independent state. The most manifest expression of this realization was the establishment by the Ukrainian people of the Ukrainian People's Republic in 1918, a state carved out of the ruins of the Russian and Austro-Hungarian Empires. Further expressions of this realization were shown in the heroic military and political struggle in defence of that state waged by the Ukrainian people during the years 1918–20 and in their underground revolutionary struggle for an independent state in the period between the two world wars. The revolutionary insurgent struggle undertaken by the Ukrainian people against the Nazi and Muscovite-Bolshevik occupations of Ukraine during the Second World War, and waged to this day against the Bolshevik forces of occupation, is the most recent expression of this desire for independence.

Because the concept of an independent Ukraine was born of the natural aspirations of the Ukrainian people for an independent existence and conceived in response to their own unfortunate historical experience, it represents for the Ukrainian people the highest ideal, one which cannot be tarnished or destroyed. Because the concept of an independent Ukraine coincides with the deepest, age-old aspirations of the Ukrainian people and because it came into being in response to centuries of oppression and exploitation, it is *the most logical, real and viable idea, and thus the only valid and possible political concept for the Ukrainian people.* For this reason, the Ukrainian people will never cease to struggle for the complete realization of this concept, even if it requires the most extreme sacrifices and even if it sets the whole world against them.

The concept of an independent Ukraine is also *the concept of a future social order in the Ukrainian state that will be free of any exploitation of one person by another*. This social order will be based upon state and co-operative ownership of industry, banking and trade, and upon state ownership of land with individual or collective management, depending upon the will of the population.

This concept of the social and economic order of the future Ukrainian state is in accord with *the actual situation in Ukraine at the present time*. At present there is no private ownership of industry, trade or banking and no private landownership in Ukraine. The present economic exploitation of the Ukrainian people is due to the colonial status, both political and economic, of Ukraine within the Bolshevik USSR. The Ukrainian labouring masses are enslaved by a class of Bolshevik overlords who enjoy both political and economic privileges. These two facts alone—Ukraine's colonial status within the Bolshevik Soviet system and the social enslavement of the Ukrainian toiling masses by the Bolshevik overlords—are the main reasons for the present economic misery of the Ukrainian people. When the Ukrainian people attain their full political independence and establish a just and democratic internal political and social order, these conditions will no longer apply. Then and only then will it be possible to put *the principle of public ownership* fully at the service of the Ukrainian people—the peasants, workers and intellectuals. Only then will the principle of public ownership become the basis of a truly happy, prosperous and civilized existence for the Ukrainian people and a powerful instrument for developing the productive forces of Ukraine. A return to capitalism in Ukraine would in every sense be a step backward, a regression. This is the conclusion drawn by the members of the Ukrainian revolutionary liberation movement after giving full consideration to *the historical experience of all mankind*, as well as *the historical experience of the Ukrainian people*, while also taking into account the views of the greatest authorities in the fields of science and practical politics.

The Ukrainian people are like all other peoples—they do not live in isolation. They live surrounded by many other peoples, by neighbours near and far. If one regards the Ukrainian liberation movement from a broader perspective, one sees that it too, does not exist in isolation. It is active at a time when dozens of peoples around the world are struggling, often with great determination, for the attainment of their political and social ideals. It is active at a time when certain types of ideas are inspiring tens of millions of people around the world, the spiritual elite of mankind and the world's best political leaders. For this reason, it is worth examining the links between the struggle waged by the Ukrainian people and other events currently taking place around the world in order to determine whether or not the aspirations of the Ukrainian people for an independent state are in accord with present tendencies. An affirmative answer will not only suggest that the struggle will be easier because the Ukrainian people will be able to count on sympathy, understanding and perhaps even support from their neighbours. *An affirmative answer will indicate above all that the Ukrainian people's struggle for liberation forms an integral part of the present tide of history and that from the perspective of modern history their struggle is completely normal and legitimate, as it is caused by powerful, invincible forces that are active throughout the world.* An affirmative response will indicate that far from running contrary to the mainstream of historical development, the Ukrainian people's liberation struggle is one of the streams that make up the main current of present-day history, a stream which strengthens that current and helps move it forward. A closer look at all these issues will help us see how the concept of an independent Ukraine is related to the major tendencies currently in existence throughout the world.

Although some time has passed since the world first began to undergo enormous political and social change, it is still far from having achieved stability. Most nations of the world, including the most advanced, are going through radical changes. Various states, including large and powerful ones, are disappearing, while others are appearing in their place. As great upheavals occur, various political ideas, systems and institutions are becoming outmoded and being destroyed while others rise up to take their place. Social and economic principles espoused at one time are no longer respected, while new views, often opposed to the old ones, are gaining currency. In this regard it is essential to determine to what extent the Ukrainian national-liberation movement *represents the new, objectively progressive current which is just in the process of emerging, albeit with tribulation, around the world, and which will be the wave of the future.* For it has always been so in history: in the midst of great upheavals, old worlds have been destroyed and new ones born. New political and social systems arose which, in comparison with those existing previously, were always more progressive. That is why they dominated the future. In the face of all the great changes currently taking place in the world, members of the Ukrainian national-liberation movement must clarify for themselves what that movement represents from the universal historical perspective and from the perspective of the Ukrainian nation. Is it the epilogue of a passing era or the prologue of a future which is just emerging and which cannot be checked in its forward progress to victory by any power?

Whether our struggle fits in with the tendencies currently gaining ground everywhere, and whether it represents a new force emerging in the world, a force of the future—the answers we give to these two questions will be significant not only because they will place our struggle into the context of current world events, but also because they will answer *the attacks made against the Ukrainian national-liberation movement by its most bitter foes—the Muscovite-Bolshevik imperialists and their agents.* The Soviets and their agents are making every possible effort to demonstrate that the Ukrainian revolutionary liberation movement is reactionary, that it is out of touch with current reality both in Ukraine and in the world. They argue that, being out of step with "objectively determined laws of social development," this movement cannot be successful. Here, for example, is what a certain Novychenko[4] has written on this issue:

> Reactionary ideologies (he has in mind the ideology of the Ukrainian nationalists—P.P.) are always devoid of even ostensibly convincing positive arguments drawn from current events. There is a good reason for this—reality itself and its basic developmental tendencies stand as the strongest proof against such ideologies.

Positive answers to the questions we posed above will demonstrate to what extent the views being disseminated among the Ukrainian people by the Muscovite-Bolshevik imperialists and their agents are false. If they want to find "convincing positive arguments," Novychenko and his ilk would do well to seek them in the underground literature of the Ukrainian revolutionary liberation movement, in the movement's program, in reality itself. There they would find them in an abundance to satisfy any unbiased person capable of independent thought.

I

The concept of an independent Ukraine and the revolutionary struggle of the Ukrainian people for national liberation form part of the larger issue generally referred to as the "national question." The national question arose as a consequence of the birth of the idea of the nation. We shall examine how the concept of the nation came into being and developed into one of the fundamental forces influencing the course of modern history, how it compares with other factors influencing that same course, how that concept has been dealt with over the last century, its relevance today and how it may develop in the future.

The idea of the nation, as it is currently understood, came into being during the French Revolution of 1789. That revolution marked the beginning of a great epoch of transformations in the history of Europe—one might even say the history of the world—which continues to this day. For this reason, we shall begin our discussion with the French Revolution.

In the French Revolution, the members of the so-called "third estate" (the new, primarily commercial, bourgeoisie, the new proletariat and the peasantry) rose up against the absolutist feudal regime that existed in France at that time. Taking up the slogan "Liberty, Equality, Fraternity," the third estate demanded the establishment of a constitutional parliamentary regime; it demanded the "sovereignty of the people." The idea of the sovereignty of the people was first advanced and given its classical definition by that forerunner of the French Revolution, Rousseau.[5] He maintained that the state's highest authority should be representative of the general will of the people. By "people" Rousseau understood all the citizens of the French state of the day, i.e., chiefly the third estate, which constituted 98 per cent of the population of France. Thus *it was during the French Revolution, in the struggle for the sovereignty of the people, that the concept of the nation was born, that is, the nation was recognized as a separate social and political entity.*

At the time of the French Revolution, the term "nation" was understood to refer to the totality of citizens of a given state, regardless of their ethnic derivation (earlier the word "nation" had had a different meaning). Very soon, however, in the first few decades of the nineteenth century, the term "nation" began to be applied to specific nationalities, that is, those social groups which correspond to our present definition of the word "nation." The concept of sovereignty was also applied to these groups. This process was accelerated by the Napoleonic Wars,[6] which greatly contributed not only to the spread of the concept of democracy, but also that of national consciousness. National consciousness is inseparable from the idea of the nation; on the one hand national consciousness has its origin in the nation and, on the other, the nation is the inevitable result of national consciousness.

Certain readers may well ask how it can be that the concept of the nation arose only in the first half of the nineteenth century when we all know that, objectively speaking, nations existed much earlier.

Separate peoples (at present, the concept of a people is identical with that of a nation), in the sense of separate social groups with a common origin, common language, commonly inhabited territory and commonly shared temperament, who struggle in common against foreign enemies, live in common under a particular regime and share a common culture, have existed since the dawn of human history. Egyptians and Persians, Greeks and Romans were each, in their day, separate peoples. From the earliest times individual peoples were naturally inclined to form their own states, fight battles for their independence and struggle for liberation. Nevertheless, there was *almost no consciousness of the idea that a people, as a separate social group, had the right to an independent existence*. The realization that such social groups as nations are entitled to political rights, that the will of that group is "sovereign," that "nature" herself has granted nations the right to lead a free existence, that this right is "legitimate"—none of these ideas gained currency until the end of the eighteenth and beginning of the nineteenth centuries. Since these ideas in themselves constitute the essence of the concept of the nation, we can say that this concept was born at the end of the eighteenth century and the beginning of the nineteenth.

The concrete political meaning of this concept for any given nation has depended on the political condition of that nation.

As stated earlier, in France the idea of the nation assumed the form of *a demand for the sovereignty of the people*, that is, of *all the citizens of the state*. Since France was an ethnically homogeneous state, the idea of the nation did not run counter to that of the state, but was identical with it. The term nation pertained to a people which had its own state.

Somewhat later, among the German and Italian peoples, the idea of the nation took the form of *a desire for national unity within an independent national state*. This particular interpretation of the idea resulted from the fact that the German and Italian nations were divided into different political entities. The so-called Holy Roman Empire of the German Nation,[7] formed in the Middle Ages, had broken up into 296 small states by the beginning of the nineteenth century. Similarly, a dozen or more states existed on the territory of present-day Italy. These divisions greatly impeded the political and economic development of those nations. Other nations, which had already been united into single national states, were making great progress and assuming world supremacy. Only by creating unified national states could the Germans and Italians escape political collapse and catch up to other nations.

In Italy the drive to unification was also closely tied to the drive to liberate part of the country from the foreign rule of Austria. The national struggle for unification took the form of an underground revolutionary struggle (Mazzini,[8] Garibaldi[9]) and often turned into a struggle waged by various Italian states against Austria.

The political formulation of the idea of the nation in regions where people were not living in their own national states, but in total subjection to foreign nations, took on a different form. These nations were subjected to national (political and cultural) oppression and economic exploitation. Here the idea of the nation evolved into *the aspiration of stateless peoples to found their own national states*. The concept of the nation manifested itself as a force directed *against the existing state, a force that strove to overthrow the existing state and replace it with a new, national state organization.*

This is the form in which the concept of the nation has manifested itself in the whole of Southeastern and Eastern Europe, Asia and all those parts of the world where we find societies that are, on the one hand, conscious of their identity as nations and, on the other, oppressed and exploited by states of foreign nationals. This process is developing with extraordinary force. More and more new nations are asserting their desire for liberation from foreign rule.

Some nations in Asia, Europe and South America that had already attained their independence have fallen into economic and thus political dependence upon large, economically powerful states. All these nations have recently begun to strive for true independence by working for a maximum degree of economic independence.

As we see, the concept of a nation is always closely allied to that of *a single, completely independent, national state organization*. This is confirmed by all of mankind's past and present experience. The concept of the nation as an entity with its own independent national state took root most quickly and fully in Western Europe. In other parts of Europe and the world it is still far from being realized. This is why in those regions the national question remains such a vital issue. *Henceforth, when we speak of the nation, we will refer to a nation's independent existence in its own national state.*

II

The nature of a given historical current, and the direction it takes, is invariably the result not of a single factor or force but of many factors and forces. Among the influential forces are nations and the goals they strive for, social classes and their different and often mutually exclusive interests, different social and political ideas and economic factors. These forces vary in their strength and move in different, often opposite directions. They often cross paths and collide with one another. It could be said that history is a constant collision and struggle among many different forces. Under the influence of different forces operating simultaneously, the course of history takes on a specific direction and tendency. Not unexpectedly, the nature and direction of a given historical current is most strongly affected by whichever force is dominant at that particular time. Thus, if we want to determine the developmental tendency of the contemporary world, we must take into account, in addition to the idea of the nation, all the other major forces that have had a decisive influence in shaping the course of history from the end of the eighteenth century to the present time. We must consider the development of the idea of the nation against the background of many other forces that have been at work and in collision with one another during that period.

As we have stated, at the beginning of the French Revolution, the entire third estate, i.e., the new bourgeoisie, the petty bourgeoisie, the new proletariat and the peasantry fought side by side under the slogan "Liberty, Equality and Fraternity." This slogan, especially its first two elements, had found its legal expression in that famous document of the French Revolution, the "Declaration of the Rights of Man and Citizen."[10] The slogan "Liberty, Equality and Fraternity" and the ideas set forth in the Declaration of the Rights of Man and Citizen were disseminated all over Europe as a result of the many wars that Napoleon I[11] waged throughout the continent.

The technical progress that characterized the eighteenth century was accompanied by the development of the capitalist mode of production. New types of industry were constantly being created, new plants and factories established. Capitalism developed with particular rapidity in Western Europe during the nineteenth century. The development of the capitalist mode of production brought into existence two new social classes—the bourgeoisie, which controlled the means of production, and the proletariat, which sold its labour to the capitalists. The economic interests of these new social classes were often diametrically opposed.

The bourgeoisie, which was the strongest social class in economic terms, appropriated the so-called rights of the citizen for itself exclusively, thereby securing political dominance in the state. This only served to deepen the antagonism between the bourgeoisie and the workers. The peasantry and, in particular, the proletariat were left politically powerless and economically exploited. This was the basis for the rise of socialist ideas in the mid-nineteenth century. In order to struggle for the realization of these ideas, the working class began to organize itself into its own political parties.

In the nineteenth century, the main forces affecting the course of history were: a) *the concept of the nation, which impelled various peoples to begin an active struggle for the fulfillment of their national ideas; b) the concept of a democratic, constitutional, parliamentary state, which impelled the entire third estate to rise up in struggle against a feudal, absolutist system; c) the new social classes, the bourgeoisie and the proletariat, which often acted in accord with their own class interests and failed to consider the needs of the entire nation. The proletariat generally adopted socialist ideas.* These forces—political concepts and social classes with their own particular economic interests—had a decisive influence on the historical development of the entire nineteenth and twentieth centuries. They still have a decisive influence on the course of history today.

When we consider these forces, which arose in connection with the development of the capitalist mode of production, it is not difficult to characterize all the historical events and phenomena—wars, revolutions, political movements, organizations, political and economic struggles—which occurred during the historical period under discussion. All those events and phenomena (we speak here primarily of European countries) can be fitted into the following categories: a) a struggle originally waged in common by the bourgeoisie, proletariat and peasantry of various nations against feudal, absolutist systems for the "natural rights" of man, for a parliamentary form of government, for democracy—i.e., a struggle to change the internal forms of government in the most highly civilized countries; b) struggles between, on the one hand, the bourgeoisie and the landed aristocracy and, on the other, the proletariat and peasantry, waged in each country in the name of individual class interests; c) struggles of individual civilized countries led, as a rule, by the bourgeoisie, often allied with the landed aristocracy, for the acquisition of colonies; d) struggles among these countries for the redistribution of colonies and spheres of influence; and e) intensified struggles for the implementation of the concept of the nation.

Let us attempt to make our general description of the historical trend of this period more concrete by citing some specific examples.

The Napoleonic Wars were a direct continuation of the wars that France was compelled to wage at the outset of the Revolution and which continued until 1815. They were, on the one hand, defensive wars waged against the advance of the forces of European feudal absolutist reaction and, on the other, attempts by the French bourgeoisie to secure economic and political influence and control of Europe for itself. The Russo-Turkish War of 1806–12, which Russia waged for the purpose of acquiring Bessarabia, was a war fought in the interests of the Russian nobility. The Russo-Iranian War of 1804–13, which was waged with a view to the acquisition of new colonial territory (Georgia) and commercial rights for the Russians in Iran and on the Caspian Sea, was a war waged in the interests of the Russian nobility and commercial bourgeoisie. The British struggle against the Mahratta principalities of India in the years 1817–18 was intended to strengthen the dominant position of the British bourgeoisie in India. The uprising of the Germans of Westphalia against Napoleon in 1809 was a struggle for national liberation and thus a struggle for the concept of the nation. The uprising of the Greeks against Turkey in 1821 was a struggle for nationhood. The uprising of the Serbs[12] against the Turks at the beginning of the nineteenth century was a struggle for nationhood. The July Revolution in France in 1830[13] was a struggle of workers, the petty bourgeoisie and the peasantry against the monarch in support of a democratic republic. The November uprising of the Poles against Russia in 1830 was a struggle for nationhood. The Chartist movement in Britain[14] (which had its beginnings in 1835–8) was a struggle of the British proletariat against the British bourgeoisie. The "Opium War" of Britain against China in 1839–42 was a struggle of the British bourgeoisie for the economic subjugation of China. The revolutions in France, Germany, Austria and Italy in 1848 were struggles of the third estate against the feudal absolutist systems in their countries, struggles for democracy and constitutionality. In many cases these struggles were also waged for nationhood—for national liberation (Hungary, Galicia, Bohemia) or for national unification (Italy and Germany). Because 1848 was a year in which many nations adopted the goal of independence, it has been called the "springtime of nations." Quite often the working class participated in these revolutionary movements in an organized manner and made its own separate demands (e.g. Louis Blanc[15] in Paris).

We could continue to list historical facts, but the major events of the 1848 period already mentioned are sufficient to confirm our characterization of the last one hundred fifty years. If we consider the course of history in Europe, we will find very few events that do not fit into our general outline.

As we see, the concept of the nation is only *one of several factors influencing and shaping the course of world history. We should therefore consider what role the idea of the nation plays in relation to many other factors operating concurrently and moving either in the same direction as the concept of the nation or in the opposite direction.*

Let us begin by considering the forces *moving in the same direction as the concept of the nation.*

One is the idea of a constitutional, parliamentary state, the idea of democracy. In fact, the concept of the nation owes its rise largely to democratic ideas. Without the concept of the legal equality of all citizens, that of the sovereignty of the people could not have arisen. And as we have stated, it was only with the concept of the sovereignty of the people, an idea advanced by the French Revolution, that there developed the concept of the national independence of peoples in their own independent states. The struggle for democratic reform which swept all the countries of Europe during the nineteenth century was never directed against the idea of the national independence of peoples. On the contrary, by encompassing the broad masses of the population, this struggle raised national consciousness, improved internal relations and thus served to strengthen the concept of the nation. It can be said that the concept of the nation can exist only along with the idea of political democracy.

Does a conflict exist between the concept of the nation and *the interests of the bourgeoisie?*

In the first three quarters of the nineteenth century, the bourgeoisie led the struggle for democratic reforms in various countries. As we have stated, the struggle for democracy only served to strengthen and complete the concept of the nation. Thus the interests of the bourgeoisie do not run counter to the concept of the nation in this respect. In many cases the bourgeoisie's struggle for democracy was tied to the struggle for national unification or for national liberation. Obviously, in such cases the interests of the bourgeoisie did not conflict with those of the nation as a whole; in fact, one cannot regard the bourgeoisie as a separate force in the course of history, but rather as part of that larger force which is the entire nation.

However, having secured dominant economic and political status for themselves, the bourgeois classes of the advanced nations *tended to abuse and vulgarize the idea of the nation as applied to their own people*. Thus, for example, the bourgeoisie tried to present its imperialist drive to conquer ever more new territory and subdue weaker nations *as being in the national interest*.

It is generally known, for instance, that the greatest interest in the conquest of French Equatorial Africa was among the French bourgeois elements; in the conquest of the Cameroon, among the German bourgeois elements; in the subjugation of the Boers, among the British bourgeoisie. The workers, peasants and the petty bourgeoisie—in other words, the overwhelming majority of the French, German and British people—were thrown only a few leftovers from the spoils that the bourgeois classes of those countries took for themselves from the conquered territories. But it was the peasants and workers who had to conquer and later defend those colonies. So, for the sake of the peasants and workers, the bourgeoisie invented myths about "national interests" and their nations' "civilizing missions." It is known that the conquest of Eastern and Southeastern Europe served the interests of the Nazi rulers. The conquest of the Balkans and Ethiopia served the interests of the fascist clique, the Italian bourgeoisie. In order to conceal from the masses the true reasons for the war, to arouse them to fight the war, the ruling classes had to put forward some higher aims than simply the narrow interests of the dominant cliques. Some sort of "patriotic" myths had to be created. One such myth in Nazi Germany was the theory that the German people were suffocating on their own territory; another was the theory that the German people were racially superior, that they were the world's most creative people and, as such, had the right to rule over others. The Italian fascists fabricated the myth that the supreme national calling of the Italian people was to restore the Roman Empire. Concealing its true intentions behind the slogan "Asia for the Asians," militarist Japan strove to gain dominion over many Asian nations. Clearly the bourgeoisie and ruling circles of these countries abused and vulgarized the concept of the nation by using it in this way. By its very essence, the concept of the nation cannot be linked to imperialism or used to justify it. It implies the sovereignty and equality of all nations. The concept of the nation refers to the right of every people to absolute sovereignty in its own state. And history itself frustrated all the plans of the German Kaisers, Nazis and Italian fascists, showing how badly these imperialists had corrupted the idea of the nation.

While in its dealings with its own people the bourgeoisie often corrupts the concept of the nation, *in its dealings with other nations the bourgeoisie of the ruling nation acts as a force opposing the concept of the nation.* The bourgeoisie and landed aristocracy of such countries as Russia, Germany and Austria-Hungary oppressed and exploited the Ukrainians, Poles, Czechs, Slovaks, Serbs, Croats, Romanians, the Baltic nations, the peoples of the Caucasus and those of Central Asia. During the nineteenth century, the bourgeoisie of the Western European countries built enormous colonial empires that took in dozens of nations in Asia, Africa and America. All these nations were oppressed and in many cases are still politically and culturally oppressed and economically exploited. By the end of the nineteenth century, the Western European bourgeoisie had managed to take for itself literally the entire world. All the West European states—Britain, France, Portugal, Spain, Belgium, Holland, Italy—became colonial powers. Because the bourgeoisie trampled on the right of many colonial and European nations to live independently, it became a force directed against the concept of the nation.

As for the *working class*, it began to emerge only in the first decades of the nineteenth century. At that time the workers were most numerous in Britain and France. Having found themselves in a most unenviable economic position, they began to struggle for the defence of their class interests in the early nineteenth century. At first this struggle was weak and disorganized. Its most notable manifestations included, in Britain, the destruction of machines by workers and the Chartist movement (the struggle of workers organized in labour associations for democratic reforms); in France, the formation of secret organizations, the uprising of workers in the silk industry in Lyons, the uprising of the Parisian proletariat in 1848; in Germany, the uprising of the Silesian weavers in 1844. Generally, these struggles were simply economic, but in some cases they were accompanied by slogans of democratic reform. *Thus the struggle of the working class at this time was not directed against the concept of the nation.*

The working class became a serious factor in the course of history only after the emergence of the socialist movement, i.e., only after workers had begun to organize themselves into political parties governed by socialist theories. We shall say no more about the working class or socialist ideas as separate entities, but will discuss the socialist movement as a force influencing the course of history.

The most carefully elaborated and widespread socialist theory was Marxism. *In its basic philosophy, Marxism is directed against the concept of the nation.* Its basic tenets are as follows:

1. The nation is a historical phenomenon that is not inherent in every society. The nation emerged and took shape during the period of capitalist development. During the capitalist era the process of the withering away of the nation begins; increasingly, alienation and conflicts among nations fade away and the elements of a new international society come to the fore.

2. The history of humanity is essentially a struggle among different social classes for their own economic interests. The national factor is a far less significant one.

3. The proletariat is by its nature international; it "has no fatherland." The proletariat must free itself from all "national superstitions," such as "all-national ideas," "the good of the nation," "the nation's honour," etc.

4. Humanity will attain happiness only when the united working class of several of the most highly developed countries attains victory. From the moment of the victory of the working class, the need for national states will disappear. The new, nationless society will create a single social and economic organization. The conditions for this are already developed during the period of capitalism, which increasingly brings nations together. The proletariat is the social class that is developing and to which the future will belong.

5. The proletariat can carry out the ideas of socialism only through world proletarian revolution and by establishing the dictatorship of the proletariat—i.e., through a violent overthrow of the existing political and social order.

This, more or less, is the theoretical position on the concept of the nation taken by Marxism when it made its appearance in the middle of the nineteenth century.

Naturally, from the moment the working class began to accept Marxist ideas and organize itself into political parties to struggle for the fulfillment of those ideas, *it began to turn into a force directed against the concept of the nation*.

Thus, as we have seen, the imperialist bourgeoisie of the more advanced nations and the socialist proletariat are historical forces existing simultaneously with the concept of the nation, but directed against it.

Have the forces directed against the idea of the nation succeeded in destroying it?

Has the imperialist bourgeoisie managed to destroy the concept of the nation among colonial and certain European nations?

The facts show the contrary to be true. At the beginning of the twentieth century, the largest colony in the world, India, began a struggle for liberation, a struggle under whose pressure the British bourgeoisie was compelled to yield. By 1919 India had a constitution which considerably increased its rights. After the Second World War, the cause of independence for India was greatly advanced. As a result of Egypt's struggle for national liberation, Britain was forced in 1922 to recognize that country as an independent and sovereign state.

While the imperialist bourgeoisie was completing its division of the world, the Philippines launched a national-liberation struggle against Spain. In 1898 the Philippine insurgents declared their country an independent state. The United States, which gained the Philippines as its possession and at first set limits on Philippine independence, was forced to increase the country's autonomy greatly during the First World War. After the Second World War, the Philippines were formally declared an independent state. These facts *indicate that the imperialist bourgeoisie, which at first succeeded in subjugating various nations, was forced to retreat under the pressure of the liberation struggles of colonial nations*.

All that we have said about colonized peoples is even more applicable to the enslaved nations of Europe. The Austrian bourgeoisie and aristocracy were unable to cope with the efforts of the peoples of Austria-Hungary to attain liberty. The Habsburg monarchy collapsed because of the desire of all the different peoples in the state to live independent lives in their own national states. The German bourgeoisie was equally unable to retain Polish lands under its control. So we see that the bourgeoisie *was unable to destroy the concept of the nation even among the European peoples which it had subjugated*.

Subject peoples struggle to realize the concept of the nation. The bourgeoisie, which in certain instances opposes the concept of the nation, *is finally compelled to accept it*. When it collides with the imperialist bourgeoisie, the concept of the nation emerges victorious. If one considers the general policy of the bourgeoisie, one can see that this is completely logical. By supporting the idea of the nation with regard to its own people, and denying it to those it has subjugated, the bourgeoisie puts itself into an untenable position—it deprives itself of any ideological basis for its colonial policy. And any policy devoid of a deeper ideological basis is bound to fail in the long run. A policy that denies an idea such as that of the nation is inevitably bound to fail.

Did the other historical force directed against the concept of the nation, the socialist movement, succeed in destroying it?

In response to this question, we indicate the following:

1. *All socialists have formally recognized the right of the nation to self-determination (Second International) and separation (the Bolsheviks, the Comintern).*[16] This is in open contradiction to their internationalist philosophy and their internationalist concept of the future. In spite of the fact that in most cases socialist recognition of the right of nations to self-determination was inspired exclusively by tactical considerations, this recognition nevertheless represents *an ideological and political triumph of the concept of the nation over the socialist movement.*

2. *The socialists united in the Second International decided not to incite a world-wide proletarian revolution and struggle for the dictatorship of the proletariat.* That is to say, they renounced those ideas of socialism which were most dangerous to the concept of the nation and *opted for a policy of peaceful struggle for the most necessary social reforms, to be carried out within individual national states in a manner dictated by the specific conditions in each country.* We can list as examples of this tendency the current policies of the Labour party in Britain, the socialists in France, and the former policy of the German Social Democrats, as well as the policies of the socialist parties in all other countries of the world. All abandoned the idea of world-wide proletarian revolution in order to concentrate on the struggle to attain a majority in parliament and to reform the existing social and economic order wherever it is most obviously outmoded. *Clearly, the socialists' peaceful struggle for social reforms is a progressive one and does not pose a threat to the concept of the nation.*

3. *The socialists have not freed themselves from "national superstitions" or "prejudices" and, like all other parties and social classes, are guided in their actions solely by the good of their own people.* This is shown by all the domestic and foreign policies of socialist governments and parties. What, if not the interests of the British people, does the present Labour government in Britain defend? What, if not the interests of France, have the French socialists always had in mind when they determined the policies of the French state? Were the socialist

parties free of "national superstititions" during the First World War when, despite all their earlier propaganda against war and all their anti-war resolutions, almost all of them voted in favour of military budgets and supported their governments? (We mention these things in a positive light only because we are here examining the problem from a theoretical, sociological point of view.) From the perspective of the political interests of a subject people, the support extended by socialists to governments that were essentially imperialist, i.e., governments hostile to subject peoples, must be regarded negatively. Similarly, the foreign policy of those socialists who pursue imperialist goals must be regarded negatively. Were the Polish socialists of the Polish Socialist Party (PPS) free of "national superstitions"? Up to 1918 their slogan was the establishment of an independent Poland; in 1920 they defended Warsaw against the Red Army.

4. *Socialism has in no way created a new nationless society or attained any success in developing an international consciousness among the proletariat.*

"The first socialist state in the world," the USSR, has already existed for almost thirty years. Have the Soviets been able to destroy the national sentiments—the source of all "national superstition"—of the peoples of the USSR? Have they managed, by applying socialist economics, to develop any elements of a new, nationless society? Thirty years should be sufficient time for national feelings at least to have diminished. But we observe that the exact opposite has taken place. The so-called "patriotic war"[17] was waged mainly under the slogan of defending the "national independence of the peoples of the USSR" (in fact, the national independence of the Russian people). The idea of defending "the first socialist country in the world" was relegated to second place. Anyone who is aware of what the USSR is today knows the strength of Russian chauvinism. It has been there from the very first days of the Soviet Union's existence. At present, having been stirred up to a higher pitch than ever before by the Bolshevik clique, it is making itself felt among all the non-Russian peoples of the USSR. And what conclusion can be drawn from the fact that the strongest desire of the non-Russian peoples of the USSR is to free themselves from the rule of Bolshevik Moscow and to create their own independent states? What conclusion can be drawn from the fact that for the last three years (if we count only their most recent campaign) the Ukrainian people have been waging an underground insurgent struggle for their national liberation, for their separation from the USSR and for the establishment of their own independent national state? Where are the beginnings of the new, nationless society that was supposed to come into being after the triumph of socialism? In the unprecedented patriotism displayed by many peoples during the Second World War in their struggle against Hitler's aggression? The attitude taken by all European peoples and all the world's peoples toward the issue of national independence during the Second World War compels us to draw just the opposite conclusion.

5. *All socialists, without exception, are turning increasingly away from Marxism*. At present, Marxism is not the "guide to action" the Bolsheviks try to claim it is, but at best a smokescreen to mask the often quite non-Marxist domestic and foreign policy of many socialists. *In some cases, socialists are even formally renouncing Marxism.*

Nearly a century's experience with socialism has shown that that philosophy has never succeeded in destroying, or in any way shaking, the concept of the nation. In its clash with socialism, the concept of the nation emerges victorious.

It should be emphasized that *the working class has always been very patriotic*. German workers were always in the vanguard of the struggle for the unification of Germany. Italian workers fought no less obstinately for the unification of Italy. Polish workers provided the shock troops for the pre-1918 Polish revolutionary liberation movement.

When the working class organized strikes, clashed with the police, the army and the laws of the land, or carried out anti-government propaganda, it was not opposing the state in its role as guardian of the nation's independence. It opposed the state only in its role as an instrument of class oppression in the hands of the ruling classes. The struggle waged by the working class was simply a struggle for its own just interests. National independence was regarded by the working class of every state as the most basic precondition, without which nothing else could proceed. There is nothing in the history of the labour movements of independent states to contradict this statement.

Things were rather different when it came to the subject peoples. The representatives of the working classes often opposed political separation from the states that opressed their nations. Such was the case, for example, of the Polish workers. Some of the Polish proletariat, those in the ranks of SDPiL (Social Democracy of Poland and Lithuania),[18] opposed the idea of Poland's separation from Russia. This can only be explained by the fact that long-term subjugation has a horrific effect on the psyche of oppressed nations. It may also be due to the lack of political acumen among the leaders of that segment of the Polish proletariat which was unable to see that the centralist views of the Russian Social Democrats concealed their desire to preserve the Russian Empire intact. It must also be remembered that, as we have already pointed out, most of the Polish proletariat was in the ranks of the PPS and supported the idea of Poland's independence and separation from Russia.

Groups such as the SDPiL, however, were to be found throughout the territory of the former tsarist empire. The Ukrainian socialists also opposed separation from Russia.[19] This can only be explained by the conditions in which the masses lived in tsarist Russia. Oppressed by the autocratic tsarist regime, they took no part in the political developments taking place throughout Europe. It must be borne in mind that while most European peoples enjoyed the benefits of democracy and constitutional rule, tsarist Russia remained an absolutist regime until 1917. Nevertheless, in spite of these terrible conditions, most of the peoples subjugated by the Russians strove for local autonomy and, later, complete independence and separation from Russia. Even where the greatest barriers stood in the way, the concept of the nation prevailed. The mass of the workers also opposed the imperialism of the bourgeoisie. It is generally known with what great enthusiasm and sympathy German workers greeted the Polish insurgents who took part in the uprising against Russia in 1831 and who, after the uprising was quelled, crossed over into German territory. During the Polish uprising against Russia in 1863, the workers of Britain and France staged mass protests against the suppression of the uprising by the tsarist army. This is what the British workers wrote in their appeal to the workers of France to join in a common struggle in support of the Polish uprising:

> People of great talent . . . , heroic people who are defending their nation's freedom and the rights of the masses, are condemned to permanent exile, if they succeed in escaping death, or are mercilessly driven to foreign lands. This state of affairs is the shame of our century.[20]

Even the founders of Marxism, Marx and Engels, were not bereft of patriotic feelings. Thus, for example, they supported the unification of Germany. And although they justified their position by economic arguments, claiming that it reflected the interests of the proletariat, we have only to read some of Marx's articles to realize to what a great extent these exponents of socialism were prone not only to national feelings, but even to the chauvinism cultivated by the ruling classes. Considering the issue of the Polish-German frontier in 1848 and asserting that this frontier had been pushed considerably eastward by German colonizing efforts, to the advantage of the Germans, Marx wrote:

> Can one be expected to give up regions inhabited mainly by Germans, and large cities that are wholly German, to a people which so far has given no evidence that it is capable of shedding its feudal character, which is based upon the enserfment of its peasantry?[21]

In the statement of his position on Pan-Slavism, Marx wrote in 1852:

> There are twenty-two million Poles, forty-five million Russians, eight
> million Serbs and Bulgarians; why not organize a strong confederation of
> eighty million Slavs in order to push out or destroy the conquerors of the
> holy Slavic lands—the Turks, Hungarians and, above all, the hated, but
> much-needed Germans. This is the reasoning by which this ludicrous
> anti-historical movement came about in the studies of some dilettante Sla-
> vic scholars. It aims at nothing less than the subjugation of the civilized
> West by the barbaric East; of the city by the village; of trade, industry
> and spiritual culture by the primitive agriculture of Slavic serfs.[22]

Marx's chauvinism is readily apparent in his discussion of these issues.

On the basis of what we have said so far about the socialist movement
and the working class, it becomes obvious that all the Marxist theories
with regard to the nation are either wrong (if they are drawn from an
"analysis" of past history) or utopian (if they fall into the category of
"scientific predictions" of the future). Historical experience shows
with absolute clarity that (a) the nation is not "disappearing"; (b) the
national factor plays not a subordinate, but a primary role in human history; (c) the proletariat is, by its nature, as national as all other social
classes and, like them, believes all the "national superstitions" and regards the struggle for these "superstitions" as its primary duty; (d) no
solidarity (in the Marxist sense) exists among the international proletariat; (e) national interests are of greater importance to socialists than
the world-wide proletarian revolution and the dictatorship of the proletariat.

Just how wrong Marx and Engels, who are regarded by socialists as
the supreme authorities in the realm of socialist theory, were in their
analysis of the national question is evident from the following two examples.

Discussing the Czech question in relation to the Austrian revolution of
1848, Marx wrote in the *New York Tribune* on 5 March 1852:

> ... as often happens, the Czech nationality, which, if we judge it by all
> the known historical facts of the last four hundred years, is dying away,
> made a final effort in 1848 to regain its former vitality. The failure of that
> effort should in itself, independently of all revolutionary considerations,
> demonstrate that Bohemia can really exist only as part of Germany, even
> if some of its inhabitants should continue to speak a non-German lan-
> guage for several centuries.[23]

Thus Marx regarded the Czechs of 1848 as a "dying nationality." The struggle of the Czechs against German domination in 1848 was, according to Marx, only the last-ditch effort of a "dying nation," an effort destined to "fail." And this was "proof" that "Bohemia can really exist only as part of Germany." Meanwhile, we find that in 1918, the people Marx had written off as a "dying nation" in 1848 established their own state and existed for twenty years, demonstrating that Bohemia could live very well apart from Germany. At present, the Czech people are fulfilling some socialist ideas within their own national state.

In a letter to Marx dated 23 May 1856, Engels wrote about the Irish as follows:

> ... notwithstanding the Irish national fanaticism that is so natural to these people, they no longer feel at home in their own land. Ireland for the Saxons! And this is what has come to pass. The Irishman knows that he cannot compete with the Englishman, whose ways far surpass those of the Irish. Emigration will continue until the predominant, or even exclusive, Celtic character of the population disappears entirely. How often have the Irish attempted to attain something and each time been politically and economically crushed.[24]

Thus Engels did not believe that the Irish struggle for national liberation would succeed. In 1856 he contended that "Ireland was meant for the Saxons." Meanwhile, after fifty more years of struggle, the Irish finally attained full independence in 1937.

On 18 August 1869, Marx wrote to Engels:

> In Poznań, the Polish workers carried out a successful strike, thanks to the help of their comrades from Berlin. This struggle against "lord capital," even in its lowest form, that of a strike, will do away with national prejudices more effectively than any speeches about peace from the bourgeoisie.[25]

It is a pity that Marx did not live to see 1918, when Polish workers in Poznaln disarmed and shot German soldiers, many of them "comrades from Berlin," members of the German army of occupation who opposed the national-liberation struggle of the Polish people. He would have seen for himself how badly he was mistaken in assuming that the struggle against "lord capital" would bring an end to "national superstitions." "National superstitions" proved to be a power from whose grip the working class could not free itself. Fifty years after Marx prophesied an early end to "national superstitions," the Polish proletariat stood ready to die for their sake.

Both Marx and Engels underestimated the significance of the national factor in the lives of peoples and failed to foresee the decisive role that the concept of the nation would play in the near future. They were misled by their one-sided, class-oriented approach to the analysis of history and by their lack of understanding of the aspirations of the subject peoples. In addition, they were blinkered by their chauvinism.

In our discussion of the socialist position on the concept of the nation, we cannot overlook the fact that in *the dominant nations, socialists, having gained power, have adopted imperialist positions*. Like the bourgeoisie, they deny many peoples the right to independent states. But by practising this policy, they, like the bourgeoisie, place themselves in a precarious position, for in depriving their policy of any ideological basis, they doom it in advance to failure.

The Russian Bolsheviks have adopted the most reactionary imperialist position. Immediately after seizing power, they set about suppressing the national-liberation movements of the peoples that had been subjugated by tsarist Russia. Having broken these peoples' resistance and destroyed their national states, the Bolsheviks began openly to restore the tsarist empire by establishing the USSR. Within the USSR all non-Russian peoples undergo brutal political and cultural oppression and unprecedented economic exploitation. The manner in which the Bolsheviks trample on the principle of self-determination, as well as their unprecedented oppression and exploitation, arouses the opposition of the subject peoples. The Ukrainian people are expressing their opposition in the form of an insurgent, underground struggle. The idea of destroying the Bolshevik prison of nations by revolutionary struggle and of rebuilding the USSR on the principle of self-determination for individual nations is gaining ever greater currency. At present, the Soviets are experiencing great difficulties in dealing with the national-liberation struggles of the Ukrainians and other subject peoples. When all the subject peoples of the USSR take up the struggle—and that will happen as an inevitable result of Bolshevik policy—the Bolshevik prison of nations will collapse.

From what we have said so far, it is clear that *the concept of the nation is the main factor influencing the course of history. It is the historical force which wins out in any clash with forces directed against it. It is, accordingly, the idea that determines the main tendency of current historical development.*

Let us look at a few more facts that support our thesis of the dominance of the concept of the nation.

Let us consider, for the sake of example, some critical events in the histories of individual nations. Among such events were, for France, the siege of Paris by the Germans in 1870; for Poland, the year 1920; for Britain, the years 1940–41; for the Ukrainian people, the period of renewed Bolshevik occupation after 1944.

In 1870 the Germans surrounded Paris. The French army had been routed. France and her national independence stood in mortal danger. French national pride was deeply wounded. Despite the Parisian workers' dislike of the regime in power, in a surge of patriotic fervour they moved *en masse* to join the ranks of the national guard and declared their readiness to defend the capital to the bitter end. The national guard quickly grew into an impressive force, 300,000 strong. All reports of military capitulation, negotiations with the Germans, or the government's intentions to yield even one fortress or one patch of ground were greeted with enormous dissatisfaction by the Parisian masses. The Paris revolution, which came to be known as the Paris Commune, was largely the result of the wounded national pride of the French proletariat. The proletariat did not wish to submit to a government that had signed a shameful treaty of capitulation with the Germans.

In 1920 the Bolshevik army reached Warsaw, the capital of the newly established Polish state. Recognizing the threat to Polish national freedom, in a surge of patriotic fervour, every man able to bear arms volunteered for the front. This patriotic fervour and the unity that was created among all social classes of Poles were the only factors that saved the young Polish state from collapse in 1920.

In 1940–41, after the fall of France, Britain remained alone in the struggle with Nazi Germany. German planes constantly bombarded London and all industrial centres. There was a sea blockade and talk of a German invasion of the British Isles. In spite of the attacks, industry had to be geared up for maximum production. London had to adapt itself to the conditions created by an aerial war. This could only be done if the mass of the British people fully understood the enormous danger threatening Britain. A great deal of patriotism was required from the population. It displayed this needed patriotism and, as a result, Britain ultimately won the war.

With the renewed occupation of Ukraine by the Bolsheviks in 1944, the Ukrainian people were faced with a choice: should they submit voluntarily to the occupying power, thereby sacrificing all the gains the Ukrainian liberation movement had made and renouncing the idea of an independent Ukraine, or resist to the last man and defend the cause of Ukrainian independence? Although the Ukrainian people had sustained terrible losses in their struggle against the Nazi occupation forces, they chose the second course. They decided to continue fighting for the cause of an independent Ukraine and to defend the gains made by the Ukrainian independence movement, to perish in defence of their honour rather than consent to slavery under the rule of Bolshevik Moscow. The Ukrainian people chose the second course in the full knowledge that it would entail an extraordinarily fierce struggle and demand great sacrifices. In the face of these grim prospects, tens of thousands of the finest Ukrainians entered the UPA and the underground. When it came to Ukrainian independence and the nation's honour, death was not too great a risk. Zealous devotion to the concept of national independence has enabled the Ukrainian people to wage their very difficult struggle against Bolshevik Moscow over a period of several years. The Ukrainian revolutionary movement has had thousands of heroic members who chose to perish as free men, preferring to shoot themselves with their last bullets or blow themselves to bits with their last grenades rather than fall into the hands of the Soviets.

Is all this not proof enough that the concept of the nation is now the highest ideal, one for which millions of people are prepared to die? When any nation's independence is threatened, when its life is threatened, all internal discord ceases, internal misunderstandings fade away and the people unite in a single effort to defend their threatened national freedom, the life of their nation. *The nation, national independence, are and always have been mankind's supreme values. People recognize them as such without any hesitation and are prepared to die for them.*

III

In order to gain a better sense of the direction of historical development during the last one hundred fifty years, let us examine the major contradictions of the contemporary world.

As long ago as the last quarter of the nineteenth century, it became apparent that the most fundamental and dangerous antagonisms of the prevailing social and political system were: (a) *the antagonism between the bourgeoisie or, more broadly, capital, and the interests of the working masses, who formed the overwhelming majority of the people; (b) the antagonism between subjugated and dominant nations; (c) the antagonism among the great competing imperialist countries.* (The antagonism between the democratic aspirations of peoples and the dominant feudal absolutist system, which was an important factor at the beginning of the nineteenth century and the cause of many revolutions in the first three quarters of that century, ceased to exist in Europe by the century's end, except in Russia. Attempts by the bourgeoisie of various countries to seize new colonial territories also ceased, for by the beginning of the twentieth century all free territories had already been colonized.)

For the concept of the nation, *the most dangerous contradiction was that between the capitalist system and the labouring masses.* This contradiction could have led to a denial of the concept of the nation by a desperate working class, especially as in almost every country the bourgeoisie had managed to turn the national state organization into a tool of its own class policy directed against the labouring masses. Times of war, which always place maximum strain on all the nation's resources, could have become convenient opportunities for class strife.

But this did not happen.

At the end of the nineteenth century, class conflicts between workers and capitalists began to abate. Concrete evidence of this abatement during the period of the First World War was, as already mentioned, the support extended by socialist parties to government war policies. In the period between the two wars, the abatement of class conflict was shown by the socialist parties' policy switch from revolutionary struggle to struggle for peaceful reform. During the Second World War, there was hardly any noticeable conflict between classes.

Why did class antagonism begin to subside toward the end of the nineteenth century?

The first reason was, undoubtedly, the improvement in the economic position of the working class. Different economists offer different explanations for this improvement. Economists from capitalist countries explain it in terms of the so-called "democratization of capital," which, they say, occurred as the result of the creation of joint-stock companies, increases in pay, general cultural progress and so on. The Bolsheviks explain it in terms of the admission by the bourgeoisie of the working class to a share in colonial booty and a temporary economic upswing in the last years of the nineteenth century.[26] Whatever the explanation, very few economists would deny that as of the end of the nineteenth century the economic position of the working class began to improve.

Another reason for recent decreases in class antagonism lies in the concessions granted the working class by the bourgeoisie, concessions it was compelled to make because of pressure exerted by the workers. Among these concessions are the social legislation that originated in Germany and spread to most other countries, as well as the social control measures that the Nazis and fascists used for their own purposes. To some extent, these measures served to protect the interests of the workers (we shall disregard, for the moment, the fact that the only reason the Nazis and fascists implemented such measures was to gain the workers' support for their own imperialist purposes).

It must be pointed out that *as the antagonisms between workers and capitalists diminished, the concept of the nation gained in strength*, patriotism increased, national solidarity grew stronger, and the consciousness of common national interests expanded. To support our claim we shall again point out the revision of socialist labour party platforms advocating social revolution to those of defence of the homeland during the First World War. We shall also mention the stubborn and heroic underground partisan struggle waged by the workers of France, Belgium, Britain, Holland and Poland as participants in anti-Nazi resistance movements. The workers fought side by side with intellectuals, peasants and representatives of the propertied classes; all perished together in the defence of their national freedom. The main motives for this struggle were patriotism, an understanding of the national interest and a high degree of national consciousness. Partisan struggle—like all other forms of struggle—requires that its participants be highly motivated by these very qualities, and the workers participating in resistance movements were so motivated.

Furthermore, we shall mention the fact that neither during nor after the Second World War was any revolution waged on social grounds, although such revolutions had occurred after the First World War. In 1918, after the war was lost, socialist revolutions broke out in Germany and Hungary,[27] as had happened in 1917 in Russia. Even the communists, who worked for the goal of communist revolution for fifteen years between the wars, are now forced to resort to tactics of parliamentary struggle and to emphasize national issues in their propaganda, in spite of the fact that present circumstances favour them (the national economies of many countries are shattered as a result of the war, everywhere there is post-war misery and politics remain unstable). The communists are pursuing these new tactics primarily because the idea of socialist revolution is less attractive to the working class today than it was after the First World War. At present, national sentiment has taken the place of distrust among classes.

The growth of patriotism, national consciousness and national solidarity in all social classes, especially in the working class, is the most notable development of our time. And it is no accident that it coincides with an improvement in the economic condition of the workers. *These two developments are closely linked; the decrease in class antagonism serves to strengthen the concept of the nation.*

When we say that class antagonisms have recently subsided, we do not claim that they have totally ceased to exist. Class antagonisms continue to exist and still remain strong. This is evident from the struggles waged by workers against capitalists in capitalist countries (the political struggle in France, strikes in Britain and the USA) and the hostility of the workers of the USSR toward the Bolshevik overlords, the new class of exploiters made up of leading members of the party, the administration and the army. We should stress that the class struggle will continue as long as classes exist. It will cease completely only when the very basis of class society is eliminated—that is, when in capitalist countries private ownership of the tools and means of production is eliminated, and when in the Bolshevik Soviet Union the political monopoly of the Bolshevik Party has been abolished and the dictatorial, totalitarian Bolshevik regime dismantled. Thus, while class antagonisms are now far less strong than they were in the 1860s and 1870s, they are still far from having been eliminated altogether. To diminish class antagonisms and to put an end to the exploitation of man by man and labour by capital—these are the most pressing problems confronting humanity at the present time. Only now are many nations taking the first steps toward their solution. What we meant to indicate was that even the slight lessening of class antagonisms that set in because of the partial improvement of the economic and political status of the working class has served to strengthen the concept of the nation. A full cessation of class antagonisms, the elimination of their very basis, will strengthen national unity to an even greater extent and increase national consciousness.

The second fundamental contradiction in the world today—*the contradiction between the few dominant and the many oppressed nations*—is moving in the direction of the liberation of subject peoples from foreign domination. This is shown by the many concrete political gains made by the concept of the nation in the process of its development. Let us consider these gains.

In 1821 the Greeks rose up against Turkish rule. In 1829 Greece was recognized as an independent country. At the beginning of the nineteenth century the Serbs began to rebel against the Turks. In 1829 Serbia became, for all intents and purposes, an independent state. In 1878 the Congress of Berlin recognized Serbia's independence. The same congress recognized the autonomy of Bulgaria and in 1908 Bulgaria proclaimed herself an independent state. The year 1870 brought total unification to the Italian and German states (although a certain number of Germans and Italians remained within the boundaries of Austria). The Belgians separated from Holland in 1880 and created their own national state. In 1905 the Norwegian Storing (Parliament) renounced allegiance to the Swedish king, severed the union with Sweden and proclaimed the independence of Norway. At the Paris Conference of 1858, the union of the Romanian principalities of Moldavia and Wallachia was proclaimed and the foundation laid for a Romanian state. In 1878, at the Congress of Berlin, the independence of Romania was recognized. The Philippines revolted against Spain in 1896 and were granted autonomy by the USA in 1902. During the First World War, Ireland was given the status of a dominion. In 1918, out of the ruins of the Austro-Hungarian monarchy, the Germany of the Kaisers and imperial Russia arose Hungary, Yugoslavia, Czechoslovakia, Finland, Latvia, Lithuania, Estonia and Poland. In the wake of the First World War some of the Arab states secured their independence. After the Russian revolution, peoples subjugated by the tsars—the Ukrainians, Belorussians, Georgians, Armenians and the peoples of Central Asia—fought for national liberation from 1917 to 1923. Some of them managed, for a short time, to establish their own independent states. These states were destroyed by the Bolshevik imperialists. During the Second World War, Slovakia and Croatia rose briefly as independent states. After the war, as already stated, great advances toward independence were made by India, the Philippines, Syria and Lebanon.

What does all this tell us? Above all, these facts indicate that the current period of history is *the period of the emancipation of hitherto subject peoples in Europe and around the world.*

These facts also tell us *that events in which the national factor plays the leading role constitute a major part of all the historical events taking place in the period under discussion.* The entire history of the German and Italian peoples in the first three-quarters of the nineteenth century is basically the history of their struggle for unification in their own national states. We are aware of the importance of the so-called Eastern Question in European politics during the nineteenth century. And it was in this context that the question of independence for Greece, Serbia, Bulgaria and Romania was resolved. After the First World War, which in Europe was clearly a war of national defence (the defence of Belgium and France against Germany, Serbia against Austria), there broke out on the territories of the former Austro-Hungarian, German and Russian empires a whole series of revolutions. They often developed into prolonged wars of national liberation, some lasting until 1921. We still clearly remember the underground struggle for national independence waged by almost all the European peoples subjugated by Hitler. That same struggle is now being continued by the peoples of Eastern and South-Eastern Europe against the Moscow Bolsheviks.

The facts listed above also tell us that *whenever a people begins a struggle for liberation from a foreign yoke, it always wages that struggle for the establishment of its own national state and this struggle always ends in complete victory; the subject people succeeds in establishing its own national state.*

We shall not discuss here the obvious prerequisites of victory—the development of national consciousness among the subject people, the need for politically experienced leaders, a favourable external and internal political situation. If these prerequisities are not met, the subject people, even if it sustains temporary defeat, never loses morally. The Greeks, the Serbs, the Bulgarians—none of these peoples achieved full independence all at once. For them, triumphs alternated with defeats. But in the end the idea of complete national independence always prevailed.

The year 1918 holds a special place in the history of the development of the concept of the nation. In his speech of 8 January of that year, American President Wilson advanced his famous Fourteen Points, *which proclaimed the principle of self-determination of peoples as the basic principle for the post-war organization of Europe*.

The idea of national self-determination was crystallizing in Wilson's mind at the end of the First World War. In his view, the right to self-determination was the most important right of any people, great or small. He felt that the Monroe Doctrine[28] should be made applicable to all peoples, with the understanding that peoples not be permitted to extend their rule over others or to interfere in the internal affairs of others (address of 22 January 1917). Along with their right to self-determination, all peoples, he believed, should have the right to their own national territories (address at Washington's tomb on 4 July 1918). All agreements and treaties of an economic or political nature were to be made only by the people whom they concerned; in no case were they to be made on the basis of the interests of other peoples (address of 4 July 1918). All peoples had the right to be free and no regime was to be imposed upon them against their will (message to Congress, 4 December 1917).

The proclamation of the right of all nations to self-determination by one of the most responsible world leaders was *the greatest ideological and political triumph the concept of the nation had known to that time. For the first time, the national principle was advanced as the fundamental principle for the political organization of the world*.

The ideological and political significance of this proclamation is not diminished by the fact that many "errors" have been made—some unintentional, most deliberate—in the practical implementation of the principle of self-determination. Such "errors" will inevitably occur as long as the application of the principle of self-determination of peoples is left in the hands of those forces which are least eager to see its full realization.

Wilson's proclamation of the right of nations to self-determination also shows *the ideological weakness of the imperialist world*. In order to keep themselves alive, the forces of imperialism are obliged to give up their own point of view and adopt that of their opponents; in this case, the forces of imperialism have had to adopt the point of view of the subject peoples. This is the best proof of the ideological bankruptcy of the imperialist world. *And ideological bankruptcy always marks the beginning of the end of any political or social system.*

Similarly, the third contradiction characterizing the present world—*the antagonism among competing imperialist nations—is hastening the total victory of the concept of the nation.*

To a considerable degree, the Balkan peoples are indebted for the creation of their independent states to the imperialist struggle between European states and Turkey. In order to weaken Turkey, Britain aided Greece in securing her independence. In order to destroy Turkey and gain support in the Balkans for her own imperialist struggle against Austria-Hungary, Tsarist Russia supported the Serbian and Bulgarian struggles for independence. Wilson's proclamation of his "Fourteen Points" had as one of its objectives to turn the peoples of Austria-Hungary against Vienna and toward the Entente. The First World War was waged basically between, on the one hand, Germany and Austria-Hungary and, on the other, Britain, France and Russia; it was a struggle over the distribution and division of colonies and spheres of influence, but it ultimately led to the creation of a number of new national states. It is now generally recognized that the Bolsheviks, intent on undermining the British Empire, are supporting or are prepared to support the liberation struggles of Egypt and India. It is also generally known that during the First World War Britain supported the Arabs against Turkey. *Obviously this type of support only works to promote the concept of the nation, regardless of the fact that the assistance granted to subject peoples by the great powers is not motivated by friendship. It is also well known that the weakening of the dominant state by war helps the subject people in its struggle for liberation.* The weakening of the dominant nation allows the subject people to begin its revolutionary struggle for liberation, which in many cases it wages with its own forces alone. During the Russo-Turkish War of 1828–9 Greece profited from Turkey's weakness to become a fully independent state, while Serbia too became practically independent.

Competition among imperialist powers is increasing. It will inevitably lead to new imperialist wars. *This will aid the subject peoples in their struggle for liberation. The imperialists themselves will often create opportunities for the victory of the subjugated.* We say this although we know how often in the past imperialist powers made agreements at the expense of subject peoples. But we believe that, given the present growth in national consciousness among subject peoples, imperialists will find it even harder to trade in territories that are not their own.

The principle of the self-determination of nations has become the most effective weapon of the subject peoples. But it has also—as shown by the facts cited above—become a menacing weapon in the hands of the imperialists, a weapon they have recently begun to use against one other. And this is another characteristic feature of our time—the imperialist bourgeoisie and the socialists, both of whom have often been forces directed against the concept of the nation, are compelled to adopt that concept as their own weapon. The bourgeoisie is using this weapon in its struggle against imperialist rivals whenever they subjugate other nations. The socialists, and especially the communists, use it in their attempts to win the confidence of the masses. This is yet further proof that *the concept of the nation is the dominant concept of the present historical era.*

Have the victories won by the concept of the nation come easily?

It must be admitted that these victories have been very difficult. We shall not speak of all the blood that has been shed by individual peoples for the realization of the concept of the nation, of the patriots who perished in the struggle for national liberation. We are concerned here with the theoretical and political aspects of the issue. The bourgeoisie of the ruling nations recognized the national principle in certain specific cases, but did not wish to admit it as a general principle that would form the basis for a new world order. The bourgeoisie simply accepted or rejected this principle in accordance with its own interests. Subject peoples had to struggle very persistently for their due right to an independent existence.

When the concept of the nation spread among the peoples of the former Austro-Hungarian Empire, a pseudo-scientific theory of "historic" and "ethnic" nations made its appearance there. Among the "historic" nations were those which at one time had had their own states either within or beyond the limits of the country in which they currently lived. The "ethnic" nations were those which supposedly had never had their own states. The former groups included the Italians, Germans, Poles, Czechs and Serbs; the latter, the Ukrainians and Croatians. On the basis of this theory, the idea developed that only "historic" nations should enjoy full national rights, while "non-historic" or "ethnic" peoples could not claim them. Obviously this theory represented a gross falsification of history with regard to Ukrainians; it was put forward by German historians who were hostile to the Ukrainian people. Ukrainians are as much a "historic" people as the Czechs and Serbs. The goal of these theories was clear—to deny certain peoples their due national rights as a way of dealing with the so-called national problem. But reality proved more powerful than the views of pseudo-scholars. Instead of solving the existing problem, denying certain peoples their proper national rights only complicated the situation.

In order to bring the national-liberation struggles of the subject peoples into harmony with the interests of the dominant states, all sorts of "scholars" of the ruling nations began to put forward the idea of "autonomy" (in some cases "cultural autonomy," in others "territorial autonomy"). The concept of autonomy was intended to limit the struggle to one for a few particular rights, for self-government alone. Thus, prior to the First World War, autonomous national units existed in the Austro-Hungarian Empire and, after the war, in Czechoslovakia. But history has shown that no nation ever ceases its efforts for independence when it obtains autonomy. Autonomy did not satisfy either the Poles or the Ukrainians in the former Austro-Hungarian Empire. They took up the struggle for complete independence as soon as circumstances allowed.

The victorious course of the concept of the nation could not be stopped by any mere theory or act of violence. With each passing decade it has spread further, winning over millions more people and becoming ever more clearly the fundamental motive force of history. This has become evident from the change in the face of Europe.

Negative attitudes of the imperialist circles of dominant nations to the national question and their attempts to prevent the national-liberation struggles of the subject peoples have always provoked determined national resistance which has sapped the strength of the dominant powers and often even caused wars among states or world-wide conflicts. It is generally recognized, for example, that the struggles among the peoples of the Hapsburg Empire helped weaken the power of Austria-Hungary. The negative attitude of the imperialist circles of Austria-Hungary toward the national aspirations of the Serbs and the attempts of these circles to annex Slavic lands in the Balkans were the immediate cause of the First World War. The unfavourable solution of the Ukrainian question by the Supreme Council in Paris in 1919 was the cause of the pitched battles between Ukrainians and Poles and between Ukrainians and Bolsheviks in 1919–20 and in the inter-war period. The struggle against the Bolshevik invaders still goes on and will continue until the Ukrainian people gain their own independent state. The weakness of the pre-1939 Polish state was due largely to its multinational character. Historical experience shows that denying the principle of the self-determination of peoples when establishing state frontiers leads to very serious and dangerous complications that often threaten the peace of the entire world. It has long ceased to be possible to establish frontiers with no consideration for the national aspirations of the peoples concerned. Since the beginning of the nineteenth century, the world has seen countless determined struggles for the full realization of the principle of national self-determination.

To what extent the national factor has played a key role in shaping the political face of the world (especially in Europe) during the last one hundred fifty years, to what extent the national principle has become the basic principle of world order, the general historical tendency of the last century and a half, can be seen from a comparison of the political maps of Europe at the beginning of the nineteenth and the beginning of the twentieth centuries.

On the political map of Europe after the Congress of Vienna in 1815 we find in Eastern Europe the Russian Empire; in Southern Europe, the Turkish Empire; in Central Europe, the Austrian Empire; and on the territory of Germany and Italy, a whole series of small states.

"The political order established by the Vienna treaties of 1815, based on total disregard for the national principle (the right of every nation to self-determination), proved very weak and very quickly began to collapse under the blows of the national-revolutionary currents."[29] Even Bolshevik historians write in this vein concerning the political system existing in Europe after the Congress of Vienna. The incongruity between the political boundaries established in Europe and existing national relations was the main cause of all the wars and revolutions that Europe underwent during the nineteenth century.

On the political map of Europe after the First World War, we find the Russian Empire replaced by the Soviet Union, which has been pushed eastward from the western and north-western borders of the former tsarist empire and divided into a whole series of so-called union republics. In addition, on former territories of the Russian Empire we see Finland, Estonia, Latvia and Lithuania. All these states arose as a result of the realization of the principle of self-determination of peoples. In place of the Austro-Hungarian Empire we see a number of new states — Austria, Hungary, Czechoslovakia and Yugoslavia. Between the Carpathians and the Baltic Sea we find a new state, Poland, carved out of the peripheral lands of the German, Austrian and Russian Empires and inhabited by Poles, Ukrainians, Belorussians and Lithuanians. On the territory of the former Turkish Empire, we see Romania, Bulgaria, Greece and Yugoslavia. In place of the divided Italian and German states we find a united Italy and Germany. The great dynastic empires which for centuries had been the basic systems of order in Europe have disappeared. In their place a number of new national states have arisen as a result of the implementation of the national principle. *A comparison of the political map of Europe of 1815 with that of 1920 demonstrates most clearly that history is evolving toward the idea of establishing independent national states for all peoples.*

Let us summarize what we have said so far about the concept of the nation:

1. The concept of the nation is currently the dominant idea among all peoples and all social classes.

2. In any struggle between the concept of the nation and forces directed against it, the concept of the nation emerges victorious. It is the most powerful force influencing the course of history at the present time.

3. At the end of the nineteenth century and particularly in the twentieth, class antagonism abated, and this served to increase support for the concept of the nation.

4. The concept of the nation was gaining ground to such an extent that in 1918 it was recognized as the fundamental principle of world political order.

5. The concept of the nation has already fundamentally changed the political face of the world and, in particular, of Europe.

All these facts clearly demonstrate that *the basic political tendency in the modern world is the creation of new national states. Social problems are being dealt with in the framework of individual national states. The goal of social change is to put an end to class antagonism and increase national unity.*

IV

To what can one attribute the power of the concept of the nation? Why did this idea come into the world? How can we explain its enormous vitality, its influence on the development of events?

An idea becomes a historical force only if it corresponds to the deepest aspirations of the broad masses. Only if it answers their true needs will the masses struggle and die for its sake. Any idea that fails to correspond to their aspirations remains just a dead theory with no influence on the flow of history. *The concept of the nation has become a decisive historical force because it corresponds to the deepest natural aspiration of all peoples* — their aspiration to an independent existence.

Marxists like to claim that "a current in the realm of ideas is a reflection of changes occurring in the real, objective world."

In this case, that assertion is totally true, however inconvenient it may be for Marxists, who generally dub all national ideas "metaphysical." That which objectively exists and has produced the concept of the nation is the organic human grouping we call the nation, the people. The nation and the people exist objectively. No one, not even the Marxists, can or does deny this. The most inherent desire of every people is the desire for national freedom. At the present time, national freedom can be secured only within an independent national state. A people's thirst for independent existence is also a real, objective fact. *And at present the reflection of this objective reality is the concept of the nation.* This concept was born in the nineteenth century, because at that time *the nation as a particular form of human society gained a great deal of strength.* The main factor in this process was the growth of national consciousness. National consciousness increased as a result of the following developments: a) a growing interest during the age of Romanticism in the historical past of nation and the way of life of the popular masses; history began to serve as a mirror in which, for the first time, people saw their own individuality, their national profile; b) improvement in the economy and communications; this enabled people from different parts of a given country who previously had lived in isolation to meet more frequently, exchange ideas and deepen their national consciousness; c) the rise of democracy, which drew the broad masses into active participation in their nation's political life; d) improvement in education for the masses and the introduction of compulsory universal military service; e) increased political and economic oppression of subject peoples by dominant nations. Because these developments resulted from the growth of capitalism, it can be said that capitalism has been largely responsible for the making of the modern nation. *But capitalism only strengthened the nation as a particular social grouping; it did not, as the Bolsheviks claim, create it.* ("The nation emerged and gained form only in the age of the growth of capitalism.") Nations were formed much earlier, and their emergence was not linked to capitalism as a particular system of social and economic organization. Even when slavery and feudalism were the reigning forms of social and economic order, nations existed. *In the age of capitalism, they simply grew much stronger* and became a greater motive force of history than ever before. Nor is it true that under capitalism "national differences and antagonisms between peoples" are reduced.[30] In terms of the concept of the nation, it would be desirable if antagonisms between peoples were to disappear and the right of all nations to independence were respected. However, the exact opposite is the case. Today, more than ever, antagonisms between peoples have increased as a result of the fact that a handful of nations rule over dozens of others.

Let us look at another Marxist assertion. If Marx's statement that "the most economically progressive capitalist states at present are prototypes of the future development of the most backward states" (we are citing from memory here)[31] is true, then logic and the Marxist conception of history would tell us that it is also the case that "the most advanced nations, those currently displaying the highest degree of national consciousness, are prototypes of the future development of the most backward nations." If it is true that capitalism is embracing more and more countries, then it must be equally true that more and more peoples that have not yet done so will form their own nations. History has shown this to be the case. Along with the industrialization of Eastern Europe and Asia, a process of national awakening is taking place in those regions. At present, the peoples of Eastern Europe and Asia are struggling for national liberation, just as those of Central and Western Europe did in the past. The current national-liberation struggle of peoples subjugated by the Bolsheviks is shaking Stalin's empire far more vigorously than liberation struggles shook Austria-Hungary or tsarist Russia in the past. In Austria-Hungary and, for a time, in Russia, this struggle took the form of an underground insurgent campaign. Now more and more peoples are declaring their desire for full national independence. *And the constant rise in national consciousness, the ever wider acceptance of the concept of the nation, is currently the most important law of history. Even the Marxists, if they apply their own theories with true consistency, cannot deny this.* Lenin's assertion that "capitalism does not necessarily rouse all nations to independence"[32] is false. History proves that capitalism does indeed rouse all nations to independence.

The continual strengthening of the nation as a human social grouping, brought about by developments in the political, social and economic spheres, is yet another reason why the concept of the nation has now become the most powerful and fundamental force of history.

When we say that the growth of capitalism has largely been responsible for the creation of the modern nation, we are thinking of capitalism's development of productive forces rather than of capitalism as an overall social and economic system. Relations of production under capitalism—i.e., the principle of private ownership of the means of production—have led to the emergence of class antagonisms between, on the one hand, the proletariat and the peasantry and, on the other, the proletariat and the bourgeoisie. As we have already pointed out, class antagonisms pose a danger to the concept of the nation. Thus it is obvious that, in general, capitalist relations of production hinder rather than help the process of nation-building. *The factor that hastens nation-building under capitalism is the development of productive forces, i.e., the development of industry, technical know-how and methods of production, as well as general cultural progress.* Thanks to the development of productive forces, conditions are created which hasten the process of nation-building. As mentioned above, these conditions are the development of communications, economic progress, expansion of the press and education and a general improvement in the level of culture. Given all these facts, we can see that the collapse of capitalism, by which we mean an end to the system of private ownership of the tools and means of production, or, in other words, socialization, would not threaten the existence of the nation as such. On the contrary, *socialization of the tools and means of production would bring about an even greater development of productive forces* than was the case under capitalism. It would also put an end to the class antagonisms that now exist by wiping out the very basis for the existence of social classes (in particular, the bourgeoisie and the proletariat). Both these occurrences would serve to strengthen the nation. *For this reason, the implementation of our concept of a classless society in the future Ukrainian state would strengthen the Ukrainian nation and raise it to a higher level of national consciousness and solidarity.*

V

As we stated at the beginning of this article, the concept of an independent Ukraine is a concept of a social and economic regime in which there is no exploitation of one man by another. We briefly outlined the basis of that social and economic order. The social and economic changes that took place in the period between the two world wars and continue to take place clearly demonstrate that, socially and economically, the world is moving toward the socialization of the major sectors of the national economy. We can mention here the nationalization of industry, banks and large estates in Poland, Czechoslovakia, Bulgaria, Yugoslavia and, to some extent, in Romania. At present, certain sectors of the economy are also being nationalized in such countries as Britain and France. In Britain the Bank of England, the coal industry and the railroads have been nationalized. In France, the large banks have been nationalized. In addition, the intrusion of the state into the economies of the fascist states—Nazi Germany and Italy—was very much akin to nationalization. The idea of a totally free economy is losing ground almost everywhere except in the United States. It is being replaced by the principle of state control or, in some cases, state ownership of the major sectors of the national economy. This development marks the beginning of the end of capitalism as a social and economic system.

Given these social and economic trends in the modern world, we can say that our concept of the social order in the future Ukrainian state *is fully congruent with present developments in the world.*

VI

In view of what we have said so far about the concept of the nation, it will not be difficult to answer the second question we posed at the outset of this article: is the Ukrainian national-liberation movement, which forms an integral part of the general process of emancipation taking place in the world today, a new phenomenon, a movement of the future?

Let us consider the following facts:

1. Although the so-called "national question" had been in the forefront for more than a century in Europe, it was only in 1918 that the concept of self-determination of peoples was advanced by responsible world leaders as the basic principle of world order. Until that time, although the national question had in some cases been positively resolved, the principle of self-determination of peoples was not regarded as the general, fundamental principle of world order. And even after this principle was formally recognized, it was not fully implemented even in Europe. Thus one can say that the idea of the nation is still very new. It is particularly new when applied to the peoples of Eastern Europe, the Caucasus and Asia. These peoples have only just attained or are only now attaining national consciousness and in most cases are just beginning their struggle for national liberation. The history of the modern era shows that any people which begins a struggle for national liberation continues that struggle until it wins its own independent state. Sooner or later, every people's struggle for national liberation ends in complete victory.

2. All the factors that caused the so-called "national question" to emerge are still as current as they were several decades ago. These factors are, on the one hand, the growth of national consciousness, the desire for independence among subject peoples and the dominance of the concept of the nation and, on the other, the attempts by a few great powers to maintain at all costs the status quo that allows the few largest and most advanced nations to live at the expense of the subject ones and exploit people all over the world. It should be pointed out that the factors which caused the national question to emerge in the past are even more operative today. National consciousness has increased. The adoption of imperialist views by socialists in the dominant nations — that is, the acceptance of imperialist views by those elements of the dominant nations which, at least in their official declarations, formerly opposed imperialism — has convinced the subject peoples that liberation can be attained only by means of independent struggle against the imperialists. When we look at the Soviet sphere of influence in Europe, we see that in the wake of the Second World War, the number of subject peoples has significantly increased. The exploitation and oppression of subject peoples by dominant nations have not diminished. In Bolshevik Russia, this oppression has sometimes taken the form of

overt genocide of particular peoples.[33] This means that in our age the national question will assume even greater proportions than in the recent past. Given the present state of the imperialist system and the readiness of peoples to defend their national freedom, it is evident that the subject peoples and the concept of the nation will be victorious. Furthermore, the imperialists are proving unable to deceive the subject peoples. For example, the Bolsheviks are trying to satisfy national aspirations to independence by granting formal independence to certain national states within the USSR. But people are well able to discern the difference between independence in form and in fact: they want real, not formal, independence. This is evident from the struggles waged by the non-Russian peoples of the USSR against Bolshevik Moscow. It is also evident from the anti-Soviet struggles of those peoples that have now been forced into the sphere of influence of Bolshevik Moscow. All these peoples have joined together to launch a common anti-Bolshevik struggle under the aegis of the Anti-Bolshevik Bloc of Nations.[34] They are all striving to overthrow the Bolshevik USSR in order to build their own independent national states on its ruins. The Bolsheviks themselves are well aware of this. They know very well that their claims about the ''moral and political unity of the peoples of the USSR'' are mere lies. If any of them still harbour illusions and actually believe in this ''unity,'' so much the worse for them. The subject peoples of the USSR will do their best to cure them of these illusions at the nearest opportunity. Bolshevism will be destroyed and the concept of the nation, the idea of the self-determination of nations, will score another great victory.

3. Any system for ordering the world which rejects the idea of the political independence of nations is totally unacceptable to people around the world. The best proof of this fact is the opposition that the Nazis encountered from the European peoples and the opposition that the Bolsheviks are encountering today. The only political system acceptable to all peoples is one which guarantees every nation political independence in its own national state.

The facts outlined above demonstrate that the tendency to establish national states—of which the present struggle of the Ukrainian people is a concrete manifestation—is a *new* tendency and one still far from being fully realized. Equally new is the movement away from capitalism as a form of social organization. Most nations are only now taking their first steps toward radical social reform. *The liberation struggle of the Ukrainian people thus represents the new tendency just coming into the world, the movement of the future.*

VII

Can the tendency to establish a national state for every people be realized without any hindrance?

Unfortunately, at present we have not yet reached such an ideal state of affairs. In any case, the difficulties are normal ones. The old order never yields willingly without a struggle. It always tries to prolong its existence by all possible means, if only for another year or two. This is the stage we are now passing through. History is shaking off the old imperialist world, in which a few developed nations rule over dozens of others as their enslavers and exploiters. And the old imperialist world is making its last stand, its final attempt to prolong its existence, if only for a short time.

One of the means used by the great powers to conceal their imperialist policies is *to fabricate "theories" about the need for large political groupings to deal with complex modern economic conditions.* Some imperialist "theoreticians" claim that, given current economic conditions, it is impossible to establish new states. According to their arguments, to divide the world into small states, which will inevitably move toward autarchy and attempt to isolate themselves with trade barriers, is to fail to recognize that a single world economy already exists. It is evident, these theoreticians tell us, that economically speaking, different countries and territories complement one another and thus should form a single political entity. These same "economic" arguments were used by Nazi "theoreticians" to justify their concept of a "New Europe" and advance the theory of "large-scale economy" (*Grossraumwirtschaft*). In 1922 Stalin used arguments of economic benefit to argue for "a close union of the Soviet republics in one federal state." Arguments of economic advantage also lie behind the "pan-European" concept or that of the "United States of Europe," advanced by some political leaders as early as the end of the First World War.

What Hitler's theory of "large-scale economy" meant in practice became all too apparent to most European peoples during the German occupation. It meant total economic plunder of raw materials and food supplies, as well as the total economic subordination of all countries to Berlin.

The peoples of the USSR also came to learn the economic advantages of "a close union of the Soviet republics in a single state." Experience has shown them that this union is advantageous only to the imperialist centre—Moscow—and not to individual union republics. Along with economic union came terrible economic exploitation of the so-called union republics.

Why is it that in order to support their anti-national, imperialist ideas the imperialists are now turning to economic arguments? The reason is that with the creation of a single world economy, the economic interdependence of nations has significantly increased. An economically isolated country would find it hard to survive. And imperialists are trying to take advantage of this fact to frighten nations and convince them of the necessity for political union. Such unions are most advantageous to the large, most developed nations. They would allow these nations to dominate smaller, economically weaker countries completely and easily. The fact is that the bourgeoisie of the great powers, acting in its own class interest, has overdeveloped its industry (to a degree exceeding the economic needs of the country) or developed it one-sidely. This industry must have guaranteed sources of raw materials and markets. The bourgeois classes of the great powers must seek these sources of raw materials and markets beyond the borders of their own countries. Naturally, national frontiers and the economic interests of other nations stand in the way of this search for raw materials and markets. As far as the bourgeoisie of the great powers is concerned, the ideal solution to this problem would be for national borders to disappear and for individual economic interests to cease to come into play. This is the basis for the concept of a "new Europe."

No one can deny that economic interdependence among nations has greatly increased. But the question arises: could not the ideal of close economic co-operation be realized in a system of independent national states of all peoples? Why must there be political union in order to realize the ideal of economic co-operation? There are no objective barriers to the implementation of the idea of close economic co-operation within a system of independent national states. Only within a system of that type could there be harmony between the interests of the large nations and the small ones. Only within such a system would it be possible to have true economic co-operation among nations.

The subject peoples must not forget that one of the most prevalent forms of economic dependence of one country upon another is the dependence of colonies upon metropolitan centres. This dependence is highly advantageous to the metropolis and most disadvantageous to the colonies. Because of this dependence, the ruling nations have attained the height of prosperity and development, while the subject peoples have sunk to the very bottom of economic misery. This situation calls for immediate and radical change. The opposition of nations to the idea of a "large-scale economy" in Hitler's "New Europe" most clearly demonstrates how most people regard such a concept.

The economic factor in no way negates the concept of the nation. The highest goal of economics is to maximize the development of a country's productive forces in order to assure the population the best possible living conditions. *As history has shown so far, productive forces have reached their maximum level in those countries where the people enjoy full political independence and have their own state institutions.* Only full political independence can guarantee a nation the maximum development of its creative spiritual powers. And the development of spiritual powers is the basic requisite for the development of productive forces in general. Only on the basis of full equality of nations, an equality protected by complete political independence, can economic co-operation among peoples yield truly positive results and help to raise the standard of living of all nations.

We know that the Bolsheviks—both as socialists and as representatives of Great-Russian imperialism—have always favoured a large centralized state and opposed the separation of non-Russian peoples from Russia. Nevertheless, Lenin, in his analysis of the economic basis for the aspirations of national states, was compelled to write in his article, "The Right of Nations to Self-Determination,"

> There is no doubt that most of Asia, the most densely populated area of the world, is made up either of colonies of the "great powers" or of states that are highly dependent and oppressed as nations. But does this well-known circumstance alter the indisputable fact that in Asia itself the conditions for the fullest development of commodity production and the freest, broadest and swiftest growth of capitalism arose only in Japan, i.e., only in an independent national state? ... It is an undisputed fact that capitalism, having aroused Asia, has caused national movements to spring up everywhere in that continent, too; that these movements all tend toward the creation of national states in Asia and that such states are the best guarantee of conditions favouring the development of capitalism ...
> The example of the Balkan states also shows that the most favourable conditions for the development of capitalism in the Balkans arose in conjunction with the establishment of independent national states on that peninsula.[35]

To Lenin's words we should add that a national state guarantees the maximum development of productive forces not only under capitalism. History shows that even under feudalism productive forces developed best within a national state. The example of "the first socialist country in the world," the USSR, in which the Bolshevik clique is hampering the economic development of the national republics by all possible means, shows that even under socialism productive forces can only develop within a national state.

After the First World War *there arose the idea of close co-operation among nations and peoples*. This idea has remained on the agenda of international politics ever since. After the First World War, in an attempt to implement this idea, the League of Nations[36] was established; following the Second World War, the United Nations Organization was set up.

What is the aim of this new international co-operation? In concrete terms, international co-operation aims at deciding all international political, economic, cultural and social problems by peaceful means, preventing wars among nations and furthering progress and civilization in general.

It is not difficult to see that in theory, *the idea of international co-operation is, objectively speaking, a progressive idea* that in no way contradicts the concept of the nation. However, experience shows that the international organizations established to implement and foster this idea are far from fulfilling their task. These international organizations are not really concerned with the full implementation of the lofty principles by which they claim to be guided. The United Nations Organization, like the League of Nations before it, has failed to ''develop friendly relations among nations based on respect for the principle of equal rights and self-determination of peoples'' or ''to achieve international co-operation . . . in promoting and encouraging respect for human rights and for fundamental freedoms for all.'' The Bolshevik USSR, a member of the United Nations Organization, is currently subjugating nations of Eastern and South-Eastern Europe and Asia. The Soviet Union is a great prison of nations in which not even minimal democratic freedoms exist. The Bolsheviks are attempting to turn the United Nations Organization into a tool of their own imperialist policy. They are attempting to turn it into an institution which would protect their imperialist conquests. Naturally, when the peoples of the world, especially the subject peoples, see what the Soviet imperialists are doing, they do not fully trust the United Nations Organization or the very idea of international co-operation. All the peoples of the world sincerely desire co-operation, but it must be co-operation that truly espouses the aims laid down in the charter of the United Nations. Since such is not the case, since individual members of the United Nations often totally disregard these aims, the peoples inevitably regard the United Nations as a mere tool of imperialist policy, controlled by only a few of its members.

The idea of international co-operation can be fully realized only with the implementation of the principle of self-determination of peoples. As long as there are dominant and subject peoples, as long as stronger nations enslave weaker ones, *there will be no trust among nations. And without such trust there can be no effective international co-operation.*

The Ukrainian people sincerely desire close and extensive co-operation with all other peoples of the world. But they will never accept the subjugation of Ukraine by Bolshevik Moscow and will struggle with all the means at their disposal for their full political and economic liberation. As long as the Bolshevik USSR, which has been brutally oppressing and exploiting Ukraine for almost thirty years, remains a member of the United Nations Organization, as long as the United Nations accept the subjugation of Ukraine by Bolshevik Moscow, the Ukrainian people will not have faith in the United Nations or in the very idea of international co-operation. When the Ukrainian people gain their own independent national state, *they will be in the forefront of the struggle for the greatest possible co-operation among all the nations of the world.*

If we examine the declared goals of the Allies during the Second World War, we see that *in fact they represent a step backward, even in comparison with 1918.* In that year, in his Fourteen Points, President Wilson very clearly and unambiguously put forward the principle of the self-determination of peoples as the basic principle for ordering the world. In the Treaty of Versailles of 1919, the victorious states made at least a formal declaration of their readiness "to establish order in Europe on the basis of the following principles: the liberation of subject peoples; the establishment of frontiers, so far as possible, on a national basis; and the creation of conditions that would allow every nation the opportunity for independent national and economic life." In the Atlantic Charter,[37] one of the first declarations by the Allies of their goals in the Second World War, what emerges as the chief goal is the restoration of the status quo that existed before the Nazi aggression began, even though that status quo was often based on a brutal disregard of the principle of self-determination of peoples and of the very concept of the nation. In the second declaration of Allied goals, a document which now forms the basis of the present world order, the Charter of the United Nations Organization, the chief aims outlined include: "to maintain international peace and security," "to reaffirm faith in . . . the equal rights . . . of nations large and small," "to develop friendly relations among nations based on respect for the principle of equal rights and self-determination of peoples." Thus, given the political order existing in the world after the defeat of the Axis powers and their satellites, the primary goal of the organization is the maintenance of international peace. The development of friendly relations among nations, "based on respect for the principle of equal rights and self-determination of peoples," is mentioned only secondarily. Clearly, to speak only of "respect for the principle of equal rights and self-determination of peoples" in 1945 is really to say very little. We particularly emphasize this point because, as a result of the Allied victory over Nazi Germany, the peoples of most of South-Eastern and part of Central Europe have come under the rule of Bolshevik Moscow, and all of them—not to speak of the non-Russian peoples of the USSR—have been deprived of independence. In its almost thirty years of existence, the Bolshevik USSR has shown itself to be the greatest enemy of the independence of peoples. Anyone who now demands no more than "respect for the principle of self-determination of peoples" is in fact giving a free hand to the Bolshevik imperialists.

There are other reasons for our claim that as far as the concept of the nation is concerned, current political leaders are going against the developmental tendencies of the modern world and taking a step backward even in comparison with 1918. Let us consider what happened at the recent post-war conferences held to decide state boundaries and thus the fate of many nations. What arguments have the diplomats been using? True, there was mention of the right of nations to self-determination, but at the same time, how openly have the Bolshevik diplomats, who cry out most vociferously for the self-determination of nations, also been talking of "spheres of influence" and the need to "safeguard state interests"! How openly have the Bolshevik diplomats been speaking of the Soviet Union's need to have "friendly countries" on its borders! What they mean by "friendly" countries are those which Bolshevik Moscow can control totally. How often the diplomats now speak of "strategic positions" and "strategic borders"! Can any of this be reconciled with a positive regard for the concept of the nation or the recognition of the national factor as the principle of world organization?

The present wave of resurgent imperialism can be compared to the wave of resurgent absolutism in Europe after the Congress of Vienna.[38] In 1815 the forces of feudal and absolutist reaction were triumphant over the idea of "liberty, equality and fraternity." Europe, awakened to new life by the French Revolution, now stood threatened by the Holy Alliance,[39] whose aim was to oppose "revolution," to maintain the "old order." Tsarist Russia came to play the role of policeman of this alliance. Today, in a world roused to new life by recent historical events and made up largely of subject and exploited peoples, there stands the Security Council, one of whose permanent members is the world's most vicious predator, the Bolshevik USSR. The aim of the Security Council, so far as can be gleaned from its current activities, is to preserve the political order that emerged after the Second World War and which, thanks to the actions of the Soviet imperialists, has reversed even the small gains made by humanity after the First World War. Just as tsarist Russia took on the role of policeman of Europe during the nineteenth century, so today the Bolshevik USSR, as a permanent member of the Security Council, is playing policeman to the entire world. The only truly just principle, that of the genuine self-determination of peoples, is now replaced by ideas of "spheres of influence," "state interests" and "strategic borders." But just as the Holy Alliance could not rescue absolutism or keep the political system created in Europe by the Congress of Vienna from collapsing (for in 1848 Europe was shaken by the "spring of nations"), so now the Security Council, which the Bolsheviks seek to turn into their own imperialist tool, will prove unable to maintain the present political order in the world. Already progressive people of many nations are recognizing what the Bolsheviks are attempting to do and are demanding changes in certain parts of the United Nations Charter. Already a number of states, including some permanent members of the Security Council, are demanding the abolition of the right of veto accepted by the Security Council. Already the peoples of Eastern and South-Eastern Europe are waging a struggle against the Bolshevik imperialists.

However much current political leaders may try, *they will never prevent the total victory of the concept of the nation*. This victory is inevitable given the present political tendencies in the world, and given the fact that *the masses now play an important role in the course of history*. During the last one hundred fifty years the masses have learned to exert their influence upon the flow of events and to determine their own fate in keeping with their own interests. It must be borne in mind that during the last one hundred fifty years more revolutions have taken place than ever before in the course of history, and thus the masses have become a motive force of history as never before. Anyone who now attempts to ignore the aspirations of the masses and tries to implement policies hostile to their interests will soon undoubtedly be reminded of their power.

VIII

The concept of an independent Ukraine stands in opposition to the USSR, the Bolshevik prison of nations.

When in 1917 the Bolsheviks seized power in Russia, the world underestimated the danger posed by this movement. Most of the world's politicians cared only to ensure that the Bolsheviks would honour the international obligations of the former tsarist regime and protect the economic interests of foreign countries. Bolshevism itself they considered an experiment inevitably doomed to failure. None of the leading statesmen of the day fully appreciated the danger posed to the world by the Bolsheviks' destruction of the independent national states established by various peoples on territories of former tsarist Russia in 1917–23. The Bolsheviks were allowed to suppress the national liberation struggles of the Ukrainians, Belorussians, Georgians, Armenians and the peoples of Central Asia. They were allowed to restore the tsarist empire. The subject peoples, among them the Ukrainians, were abandoned in their struggle against Bolshevik aggression. No one in the world then understood that only the partition of Russia into separate national states could permanently prevent the rebirth of that most reactionary Russian imperialism which for centuries had been a threat and a shame to the world.

Because world statesmen failed to recognize the danger posed by the Bolshevik seizure of the states established by the peoples of the former tsarist empire in 1918–23, the world is now faced with Bolshevik Moscow's seizure of half of Europe and the threat of Bolshevik expansion over all of Europe, Asia and beyond.

At present, most nations probably assess the Bolshevik danger correctly. Most of the world's people probably understand that in order to be free forever from the threat of Russian imperialism *they must reconstruct the present multinational Soviet state according to the principle of self-determination of peoples.* Only by partitioning the USSR into separate national states will the rebirth of Moscow's imperialism be prevented. *The concept of an independent Ukraine will form an integral part of the plan to destroy the Bolshevik prison of nations, the nest of the most shameful reaction and the most dangerous aggression in the world today. The concept of an independent Ukraine will form an integral part of the plan for the reconstruction of Eastern Europe and of much of Asia.* The establishment by the Ukrainian people of an independent Ukrainian state will be a great step toward the implementation of a true balance of power in the world and a lasting peace among nations.

*   *   *

History is clearly moving toward the full realization of the principle of self-determination of peoples and the abolition of capitalism as a social and economic system. The concept of an independent Ukrainian state, as it is viewed by the Ukrainian national-liberation movement, is fully congruent with these tendencies. The ideas of the Ukrainian national-liberation movement truly reflect the enormous changes taking place in the real world. This means that these ideas are viable, realistic and progressive and that the struggle will be successful. Such are the laws of history.

The concept of an independent Ukraine is also in accord with the historical development of the Ukrainian people. Let us recall that during the nineteenth century, the Ukrainian problem was simply one of culture—a problem of language, ethnography, literature and historical scholarship. Before 1918, the political aspirations of most Ukrainians did not go beyond the idea of autonomy. In 1918 the Ukrainian people established their own independent national state. Since that time, the idea of an independent Ukrainian state has remained alive among the Ukrainian people. With every year and every day it gains broader acceptance among the masses of the Ukrainian people. With every year and every day it mobilizes thousands more people to join the revolutionary struggle against the forces of occupation and for total national liberation. If the Ukrainian people's liberation struggle of 1917–20 experienced one battle at Kruty, then at present, in 1946, the liberation struggle involves thousands of such battles. Most of Ukraine has become a battleground. However paradoxical it may seem, the sacrifice of thousands *today* for the freedom of Ukraine means that victory will be ours *tomorrow*.

The Ukrainian national-liberation movement is not running counter to the flow of history. It is in step with all current developments in the world. It is an integral part of the tremendous force which is now destroying the old world and creating the new. It represents all that is new and objectively progressive, all that is just now being born. We, the members of the Ukrainian revolutionary movement of national liberation, are not representatives of the past, but heralds of the future. We who struggle for an independent Ukrainian state and for the right of every people to live a free life in its own independent state can say of ourselves, in the words of Ivan Franko[40]: *"We are the prologue, not the epilogue!"*

Source: This article was printed as a pamphlet in Ukraine in 1947. It was reprinted in 1948 and 1949 in Ukraine and in 1948, 1951 and 1959 in Germany. See P. Poltava, *Zbirnyk pidpilnykh pysan* (Munich 1959), 13–70.

NOTES

1. Kievan Rus' existed from the ninth to the thirteenth centuries.
2. Reference is to the Revolution of 1648 under the leadership of Hetman Bohdan Khmelnytsky and the establishment of the Cossack state that lasted until the third quarter of the eighteenth century.
3. The Ukrainian People's Republic was established on 20 November 1917 by the Third Universal of the Central Rada, an all-Ukrainian represent-

ative assembly. The independence of the Ukrainian People's Republic was proclaimed by the Fourth Universal of 22 January 1918.

4. L.M. Novychenko (1914–): Editor-in-chief (1943–6) of *Literatura i mystetstvo* (Literature and Art), later of *Literaturna hazeta* (Literary Gazette) and of the journal *Vitchyzna* (Homeland). The quotation is from Novychenko, "Maskaradne drantia ukrainskoho-nimetskoho natsional-izmu (Pro reaktsiinu romantyku mynuloho)" (The Shabby Disguise of Ukrainian-German Nationalism [On the Reactionary Romance of the Past]), *Radianska Ukraina*, 30 March 1946.

5. Jean Jacques Rousseau (1712–78): French philosopher.

6. Napoleonic Wars, 1803–15.

7. The Holy Roman Empire embraced most of central Europe from 962 to 1806. It was "Roman" because it claimed succession to imperial Rome and "Holy" because it originally claimed supremacy over Christendom.

8. Giuseppe Mazzini (1805–72): Italian patriot and revolutionist.

9. Giuseppe Garibaldi (1807–82): Italian patriot and soldier.

10. The Declaration of the Rights of Man and Citizen, originally drafted in 1789, was a preamble to the French Constitution of 1791.

11. Napoleon I (1769–1821): emperor of the French.

12. The uprising took place in 1817 under the leadership of Milos Obrenovič (1780–1860).

13. The July Revolution of 1830 resulted in the monarchy of Louis Philippe.

14. Chartism, 1838–48. The "People's Charter," drafted by William Lovett and Francis Place, advocated universal manhood suffrage and other reforms.

15. Louis Blanc (1811–82): French socialist. His *Organisation du travail* (1840) outlined a social order based on the principle "From each according to his abilities, to each according to his needs."

16. The International Workingmen's Association was established by Karl Marx in London in 1864. It was dissolved in 1874. In 1889 the Second or Socialist International was established at Brussels. It comprised most socialist parties and was torn apart by World War I. The Bolshevik Revolution led to the establishment of the Third International or Comintern. The Second International was revived in 1919, but its political significance was greatly reduced. Ukrainian socialist and communist groups maintained close ties with the Second International and with the Comintern.

17. Reference is to the Second World War, which is officially known in the USSR as the "Great Fatherland War of the Soviet Union, 1941–5."

18. Reference is to the Social Democracy of the Kingdom of Poland, organized in March 1893, and known from 1900 as the Social Democracy of the Kingdom of Poland and Lithuania. One of its leaders was Feliks Dzerzhinsky, the future head of the Soviet political police.

19. The author refers here to the commitment of Ukrainian socialists to feder-

alism in a democratic Russian state. This attitude changed as a result of the Bolshevik Revolution: the Central Rada, which was controlled by socialists, proclaimed Ukrainian independence in January 1918.

20. The author cites this as a quotation from *Novaia istoriia* (Moscow 1939), v. 1.

21. This quotation is taken from Friedrich Engels's "Revolution and Counter-Revolution in Germany," which Poltava mistakenly attributes to Karl Marx. See K. Marx and F. Engels, *Collected Works* (London 1975ff.), 11: 45.

22. Ibid., 11: 47.

23. Ibid., 11: 46.

24. Engels, letter of 23 May 1856, ibid., 40: 50.

25. Marx, letter of 18 August 1869, *Werke* ([East] Berlin 1965), 32: 368.

26. Reference is probably to Lenin's work, *Imperialism, the Highest Stage of Capitalism* (1916).

27. A sailors' mutiny at Kiel touched off the German revolution of November 1918. The Hungarian revolution under the leadership of Bela Kun lasted from 21 March to 1 August 1919.

28. Monroe Doctrine (James Monroe, 1758–1831): statement of United States policy with respect to the activities and rights of European powers in North and South America, made in a message to Congress by President Monroe in 1823, and the modified and expanded version of that policy which evolved through subsequent interpretations and applications.

29. Cited by the author as a quotation from *Novaia istoriia*, v. 1.

30. A quotation from Part 2 of "The Communist Manifesto." See K. Marx and F. Engels, *Collected Works*, 6: 503.

31. Marx, "Preface to the First German Edition," *Capital*, ed. F. Engels (New York 1967), 1: 9. The translation in this edition reads: "The country that is more developed industrially only shows, to the less developed, the image of its own future."

32. Lenin, "The Right of Nations to Self-Determination" (1914), *Collected Works*, 20: 437.

33. Reference is to the forcible deportation of nationalities such as the Crimean Tatars, Chechens, Ingush, Karachais, Balkars, Kalmyks and others, during which nearly fifty per cent of some of them died of hardship, disease and starvation. See Robert Conquest, *The Nation Killers: The Soviet Deportation of Nationalities* (London 1970); Alexander Nekrich, *The Punished Peoples: The Deportation and Fate of Soviet Minorities at the End of the Second World War* (New York 1978); Peter J. Potichnyj, "The Struggle of the Crimean Tatars," *Canadian Slavonic Papers* 17, nos. 2 and 3 (1975): 302–19.

34. Anti-Bolshevik Bloc of Nations (ABN): a co-ordinating centre for the revolutionary national-liberation organizations of the peoples subjugated by

Bolshevik Russia. It was created as a co-ordinating committee on the initiative of the Ukrainian underground on 21–2 November 1943 in Rivne oblast at a secret meeting called the "First Conference of Subject Peoples of Eastern Europe and Asia." Thirty-nine delegates representing thirteen nationalities (primarily representatives of national legions within the UPA) took part in the Conference. The conference called for the establishment of a revolutionary committee to organize a simultaneous revolution on all territories of the USSR and create independent states. The First Congress of the ABN took place on 15 April 1946 in Munich. The President of the ABN since that time has been Iaroslav Stetsko.

35. Lenin, *Collected Works*, 20: 399.
36. The League of Nations, established after World War I, was intended to maintain peace, arbitrate international disputes and promote international co-operation. It was founded at the Paris Peace Conference in 1919. The League dissolved itself in April 1946 and transferred its services and real estate to the United Nations Organization, which was officially founded at the San Francisco Conference, 25 April–26 June 1945.
37. The Atlantic Charter was a program of peace aims jointly enunciated by Prime Minister Winston Churchill of Great Britain and President Franklin D. Roosevelt of the United States on 14 August 1941. These aims were incorporated in the so-called "United Nations Declaration" of 1 January 1942, in which 26 states pledged to continue the joint war effort and not to make peace separately.
38. Reference is to the Congress of Vienna (September 1814–June 1815), which was called to supplement the Treaty of Paris of 1814 with a general settlement of European affairs after the first abdication of Napoleon I.
39. The Holy Alliance, formed in 1815, was an agreement among Alexander I of Russia (its sponsor) and the rulers of Austria and Prussia. Its influence on the political climate lasted until the revolutions of 1848.
40. Ivan Franko (1856–1916): famous Ukrainian writer, poet and political activist.

III
STRATEGY AND TACTICS OF THE UKRAINIAN LIBERATION MOVEMENT

AT THE TURNING POINT

Iu.M. Khersonets

I

Currently in Ukraine we are witnessing a whole series of developments that will have far-reaching significance for the country's future destiny. One of them is occurring among the young people of Ukraine. It is sufficiently interesting and important to merit somewhat closer consideration.

Leading officials of the USSR have focused a great deal of attention on youth. This did not occur by chance; it was deeply grounded in the plans of the Kremlin leaders. What, exactly, were these plans?

Anyone who has carefully followed the inner evolution of internal relations within the so-called Union of Soviet Socialist Republics, anyone who has been able to see not their declared, but their true nature has realized that the Soviet Union is the new form of Russian imperialism, the successor of Muscovite tsarism and the Russian Empire. The last decade in particular has left not the slightest doubt in this regard. During this time, the remains of the autonomy of individual republics, which were not very extensive in any case, were totally suppressed and the process of centralization of power, which had begun during the phase of war communism, found its legal consolidation in the Stalin constitution of 1936. The USSR, one and indivisible, became a fact. But even this was not enough for the Kremlin overlords. Within the framework of a single state, they intended to meld dozens of nationalities into a single nation. Thus they formed the concept of the so-called Soviet people. The first step toward achieving this goal was the attempt to bring about the political and cultural unification of the peoples that populated the USSR.

There cannot be the slightest doubt as to what was entailed in the creation of the so-called Soviet people. This was simply Russification veiled by Bolshevik slogans. Millions of Ukrainians, Belorussians, Georgians and a whole series of smaller peoples were to perish once and for all in the Russian sea.

If we consider these plans, the Bolshevik emphasis on youth will become clear. It was the younger generation that was to decide the fate of the so-called Soviet people. Orphanages, children's organizations, the Pioneers, the Young Communist League and schools were to rear the new so-called Soviet man. Material means for the realization of this goal were not spared. Thus, young people were granted certain privileges, at least in comparison with the generally grey existence of the Soviet citizenry. This does not mean that the younger generation was given a sufficient quantity of all essentials; it means only that, given the niggardly capacities of the USSR, the needs of the young were satisfied more speedily and solicitously than those of other segments of society.

*   *   *

Did the Kremlin overlords attain their goal? Did they succeed in inspiring Ukrainian youth with their ideal?

We have deliberately formulated our question in this manner. For us, *the essential consideration is not whether there was a mechanical acceptance of Marxist philosophy, but to what extent the communist ideal became the driving force for these young people when "the sun of the Stalin constitution" ceased to shine*. For only in 1941 did the communism of Ukrainian youth begin to undergo trial in practice. And these last two years have manifestly proved that Russian communism has not become deeply rooted among Ukrainian youth.

How are the young people of Ukraine reacting to current circumstances? The answer to this question lies in the practical orientation of the present generation of young people and in the presence or absence of specific ideological impulses in their behaviour.

There are certain young people who do not involve themselves deeply in the current situation. Dejected by material difficulties, reared in a spirit of absolute obedience to authority, incapable of seeing the prospects for liberation, they passively accept the bitter reality as some sort of elemental misfortune, God's will or fate. Attuned to preserving their own individual existence, deprived of the social sense that would tell them to group together, for "unity is strength," they have been and continue to be tools of the occupying power, incapable of partaking in an organized struggle for a better future for themselves and their nation.

There is a second category. These young people are able to observe and are conscious of the great threat that looms over the whole nation, but are incapable of active struggle. Out of despair, they take the path of least resistance. Indulging in diversions of doubtful value such as dancing and drinking, they attempt to forget the brutal reality of the world around them. These gramophone and dancing types are spiritual descendants of the "drunkards" of Shevchenko's era; they are as unproductive and impotent as their spiritual ancestors.

There is a third group. These young people react, but their reactions are not always purposefully carried through; they are often arbitrary and unorganized. Thus, for example, according to a report in the *Visnyk Ukrainskoi Informatsiinoi Sluzhby* (Herald of the Ukrainian Information Service), last summer five girls in Dnipropetrovsk ended their lives because they did not want to go to work in Germany. They left behind notes saying, "We will never be slaves." Of course, we can feel proud of the fact that our girls prefer death to the moral and physical torments of the enemy, but how much more purposeful would their actions have been had they given all their strength and, if need be, their lives, to the revolutionary struggle. The enemy fears revolutionary struggle more than suicide.

A fourth group of young people is opposing existing conditions in an organized manner. Some of these are, unfortunately, still within Bolshevik ranks. Others have already found their way to the organized Ukrainian independence movement and are fighting in its ranks on both the main fronts of the Ukrainian national revolution—the anti-German and the anti-Bolshevik. And it is these young people, these former Pioneers and Young Communist League members, these zealous neophytes, these ever-ready soldiers of the Ukrainian revolution, who inspire us with the confident belief that in future all young Ukrainians will take the rightful path of struggle for the Ukrainian national idea, an independent, united Ukrainian state. The ranks of these young fighters are increasing, and this increase gives us the right to state that at present Ukrainian youth has reached the *turning point*. From this turning point, the road leads not to Soviet Moscow, but to our own Ukrainian Kiev, the symbol not only of our glorious past, but of the great future of the Ukrainian nation.

II

Let us not be surprised at the current spiritual Bolshevization of a segment of Ukrainian youth. We can be surprised only by the strong immunity that made it possible for young people, who had undergone so many years of the most refined psychological experiments of the Bolsheviks, at least partly to preserve their Ukrainian souls. For these young people were brought up in ignorance of the true history of those whose blood runs through their veins. The history of their nation was begun for them with the October Revolution. Everything that came before was either appropriated for Russia or spat upon by Russians such as Karamzin[1] and Ilovaisky.[2] So it was with the glorious era of old princely Ukraine; so it was with the heroic epic of the Cossack state; so it was with the liberation upheaval of 1917–20. The aim of Soviet education in Ukraine was the *destruction of the historical memory* of Ukrainian youth. Young people were to find their satisfaction in what was concocted in the studies of Muscovite historians with the obvious aim of Russification.

Another means of achieving this goal was the tendentious debasing of the value of Ukrainian culture and the orientation of youth toward the great "fraternal" culture of the Russian people. Cultural separatism was treated in the same way as political separatism and its propagators exterminated as "enemies of the people." Moreover, there were attempts to reduce our culture to the level of provincial primitivism. All this was done to the accompaniment of paeans in honour of this culture, national in form, socialist in content.

Soviet economic science was also harnessed to Russian imperialism. Contrary to all the principles of sound economics, Ukraine was designated part of the Eurasian economic zone so that she could more easily be represented as an "inseparable" part of Red Russia.

The main offensive, however, was waged on the ideological front. Here the Bolsheviks attempted, by a variety of means, to discredit the cause of Ukrainian sovereignty in general and the Ukrainian independence movement in particular. "Enemies of the people," lackeys of international capitalism, agents of foreign intelligence—these were some of the dozens of idiotic slanders that Bolshevik agitators, by means of the spoken and printed word, heaped upon members of the Ukrainian independence movement. Presented in contrast to "scientific" Marxism and its "progressive" adherents, the Ukrainian cause was stigmatized as regressive and its proponents vilified as yellow-and-blues, sentimentalists straight out of the nineteenth-century archives.

Young people who grew up under the incessant drumbeat of Bolshevik propaganda, hermetically sealed from the surrounding world, deprived of the opportunity to verify the assertions of Soviet "science" against true, objective scholarship, absorbed by participation in various campaigns, socialist competitions and other such Stakhanovite[3] drives, simply lacked the time to ponder the problems that confronted them. Is it surprising that a segment of this youth became Marxist in its philosophy? No! But we do not regard this as a tragedy, especially as we know the value of this Marxism. At present, it is a temple without God. Some of the youth adhere to it through inertia and from a lack of any other philosophy. *But there is no communist ideal which stirs the souls of these young people* (we speak of the mass, not about particular groups), which has a central motive core that would impel them to action. Young people in Ukraine await the proponents of an ideology new to them, the ideology of Ukrainian independence. This ideology is already being propagated by their own comrades, former members of the Pioneers and the Young Communist League, whose souls have been set on fire by the idea of an independent, united Ukrainian state, which is now successfully undergoing the most difficult trial, the trial of blood and iron, throughout Ukraine.

*   *   *

The present war has played a significant role in this process. The tumult of war made it possible for Ukrainian youth to place its Soviet upbringing and Soviet teachings under scrutiny. Every meeting with a Ukrainian who did not have the ''good fortune'' to grow up under the ''sun of the Stalinist constitution'' stimulates thought, gives birth to new problems, implants new ideas in the soul. As a result, young Ukrainians have begun to grow aware of the true face of Russian Bolshevism. They have had time to see, lurking behind the veil of internationalist rhetoric, the true face of the Kremlin overlords. The face is red in colour but white, Purishkevich-like[4] in design, the face of those capable of masking themselves behind anything, even rhetoric about combating imperialist Russian chauvinism. They have seen through the arguments claiming that the brotherhood of peoples and internationalism have been achieved in the USSR simply because the Georgian, Stalin,[5] the Russian, Molotov,[6] and the Jew, Kaganovich,[7] stand at its helm. The presence of individuals of foreign origin within the ruling stratum in Russia is a typically Russian feature which has been evident since the times of Peter I, Minikh,[8] Osterman,[9] Bagration,[10] Paskevich,[11] Loris-Melikov[12] and Dzerzhinsky[13]—all these Germans, Georgians, Ukrainians, Armenians and Poles had nothing in common with the nations from which they came, apart from their origins; they all served Russian imperialism in its white or red form. To regard this as internationalism is more than naive.

The young people of Ukraine have realized that the basic element of Russian policy has been and continues to be nothing more than predatory imperialism, the same imperialism that sent Bogoliubsky[14] to Kiev, Peter[15] to Poltava, Catherine[16] to the Zaporozhian Sich and

Lenin[17] to Donbas, Kryvyi Rih and the golden fields of Ukrainian wheat, each time with different slogans, but always with the same intent—imperialist plunder of Ukraine.

Yesterday's Pioneers and Young Communist League members are asking *why*, in the wealthiest country in Europe, millions of people died of hunger.[18] Why was there famine specifically in Ukraine and not somewhere amid the sands of the central Russian provinces?

Yesterday's Pioneers and Young Communist League members are asking *why* such people as Khvylovy[19] and Skrypnyk[20] had to end their lives with a revolver; why Shumsky,[21] Volobuev[22] and thousands of other fighters of the October Revolution were killed; why thousands of Ukrainians who were fanatically dedicated to the idea of communism were repressed. And they find only one answer, the one given by the immortal author of *Valdshnepy*[23] (Woodsnipes): because the Communist Party had quietly transformed itself into a red Ivan Kalita,[24] the "gatherer of Russian lands," and they did not want to serve Kalita.

Yesterday's Pioneers and Young Communist League members ask *why* Soviet historians vilify Mazepa[25] as a traitor. What does this have to do with Marxism? Why has Dmitrii Donskoi[26] remained a hero, in spite of the fact that he betrayed the khan? Let them explain why the betrayal of one is heroism, and of the other, treachery. Let them explain why there is such an amazing unity of opinion on this matter among Peter,[27] his priests, who anathemized the great Hetman,[28] Karamzin, Ilovaisky, Pokrovsky[29] and a long line of Soviet historians. Perhaps this is because Mazepa was a bourgeois, a feudalist? But what was Peter? A miner in the Urals or a farm labourer in some Russian village?

Young people are asking dozens of such "whys" and finding only one answer: Marxist ideology has become a mere tool of Russian imperialism, just as the slogans of the defence of Orthodoxy or protection of the Slavic world have been in the past.

We are not racial chauvinists and do not preach the destruction of the Russian people. Our motto is "freedom for nations and individuals." But the Russian people possess a great deal of space, much of which is not put to use. Let us only consider Siberia, which is well endowed with underground and surface wealth and is sparsely populated. We do not forbid anyone to live on his own land or to reap the fruits of his own labour, but at the same time, we do not want an eternal plunder of our land. We want to keep our coal and iron for ourselves; we want to consume our wheat ourselves, rather than see it used to feed one-sixth of the world or, as was done until recently, sold to the European bourgeoisie at dumping rates in exchange for cash needed to finance some coup in Mexico or Paraguay. We have had enough of these "benefits,'' and if our position does not accord with Marxism as interpreted by Stalin or Kaganovich, so be it. The Ukrainian people are not on this earth in order to serve as experimental rabbits for foreign doctrines, whether Marxist or fascist.

III

The young people of Ukraine are rediscovering themselves. From history, they are learning about the greatness of their own people. They are coming to the proud realization that we are not illegitimate sons, but one of the oldest nations of Europe, a nation which, having settled this land several thousand years ago, withstood invasions from the plains and would not be driven out by Goths,[30] Huns[31] or the hordes of Genghis Khan. It was our ancestors alone, without any foreign Varangian[32] aid, who established the great state which, for five hundred years, in a manner *worthy* of a great nation, defended the *true* values of European culture against the onrush of the East, thus fulfilling a global mission.

The young people of Ukraine are proud of such granite figures as Sviatoslav,[33] Volodymyr,[34] Monomakh[35] and Roman,[36] who built states, and of those, such as Ilarion,[37] Smoliatych[38] and the author of the "Song of Ihor's Campaign,"[39] who created works of cultural value. They are enthralled by the scope, exuberance, chivalry, energy and breadth of purpose of the heroes of the Cossack era, the era that gave birth to Vyshnevetsky,[40] Triasylo,[41] Hunia,[42] the iron cohort of Khmelnytsky[43] and the great Krychevsky,[44] Bohun,[45] Morozenko,[46] Kryvonis[47] and Nemyrych.[48] They regard with awe the titanic figure of the genius Khmel.[49] Their attention is riveted by the "last Cossack," Doroshenko,[50] and the last great hetman, Mazepa. Young Ukrainians note with pride the great vitality shown by the nation at a time when it appeared doomed to perdition. With deep emotion, they follow its rebirth as they study the century which, in one great leap, brought us near to the realization of our highest ideal.

But this is not all. From their own history, they learn that theirs is a leading nation with regard to the great ideals for which humanity has been striving for thousands of years, but which even now have not found their full realization; the ideals of liberty, respect for human dignity, freedom of thought and true democracy. Ukraine has never known slavery, tyranny or the caste system. Only in Ukraine was it possible to travel the dizzying path from serf to Cossack colonel; only in Ukraine was it possible for such figures to arise as Burlaiv,[51] Dzhedzhal,[52] Donets,[53] Tysha[54] and a whole host of others from the lower strata of society who occupied such high positions in the Cossack hierarchy. Let us not forget that this was in the seventeenth century!

*   *   *

The young people of Ukraine are also beginning to learn about their own culture. They look to Kiev not only as the oldest political centre, but also the oldest cultural centre of Eastern Europe. It was from Kiev that culture spread to all adjacent countries. It was from Kiev that Ilarion's "Slovo"[55] rang out; it was from Kiev that Boian sang his immortal song about Ihor's campaign.[56] It was here that the Mohyla Academy[57] drew thousands of students from Muscovy, Poland and the Balkans. It is true that we did not give the world Shakespeare[58] or Stevenson[59] or Pascal,[60] but what nation in our circumstances could have done so? For whole centuries we were compelled to defend ourselves or to stand with arms at the ready, at a time when the old Roman saying *inter arma silent musae* (in time of war, the muses are silent) still held its full force. Our historical circumstances allowed us, from time to time, to express the cultural and creative energies of the people in the form of great works of world stature, but they did not permit systematic, uninterrupted cultural activity, which is the *only* basis for the development of great writers, artists, philosophers and inventors. Nevertheless, the Ukrainian people produced the genius of world renown, Shevchenko,[61] and such widely known writers as Kotsiubynsky[62] and Lesia Ukrainka.[63]

The young people of Ukraine are beginning to shake off the influence of Russian geopolitical and economic theories. They recognize that their fatherland has the full natural potential for independent existence and development, and they are coming to the conclusion that only the establishment of an independent, united Ukrainian state will put an end to the colonial pillage of the country and the economic misery of its population.

And the result of all this is belief in their own nation, a belief that every plundering occupying power so persistently and relentlessly strove to destroy. This belief, which sounds with a mighty rhythm in Ilarion's "Slovo," which runs through the Cossack chronicles[64] and the *Istoriia Rusov*[65] and which is capable of moving mountains, is beginning to take root in the hearts of Ukrainian youth. It is sweeping away the feeling of inferiority which led them to feel ashamed of the Ukrainian language, or even of belonging to the Ukrainian nation, the feeling of inferiority which both the white Valuevs[66] and the red Khrushchevs[67] took such pains to implant in Ukrainians. This feeling of inferiority is being replaced in these young people by a proud feeling of their own worth and strength, by a belief in the great future of the heroic, industrious, richly endowed Ukrainian people, who have successfully withstood the greatest adversities known in the history of mankind. The belief in Ukraine is growing stronger, but this is not a belief in that "mother" figure, draped in embroidery, which is idolized by whiners and sentimental dreamers. No! It is a belief in the Ukraine of the Conqueror,[68] Monomakh, Khmelnytsky, Bohun, Petliura[69] and Konovalets,[70] the Ukraine which, by the blood of Myron,[71] Lehenda,[72] Sherstiuk,[73] Shchepansky[74] and thousands of her finest sons, demonstrates her unbreakable will *to live her own, free, human life*.

This is a belief in a Ukraine which struggles and will be victorious.

*   *   *

The young people of Ukraine have seen one occupying force and another. One wished to turn them into traitors, the other into slaves. The young realize that their only salvation lies in the struggle for a Ukrainian state. They know that only in a new, free Ukraine will they be able fully to manifest their powers. Only then will they have at their disposal elementary and secondary schools, universities and technical institutes, dormitories and stadiums without being required to commit treason, co-operate with the NKVD[75] or sacrifice the blood and happiness of those nearest to them. In the Ukrainian state, young people will live a truly free life; they will be cared for and will enjoy full rights to work and study. They will know no compulsion, violence, fear of the NKVD, concentration camps or execution walls. They will be able to spread their young wings to their full breadth and to manifest all their capacities, for their state will establish the preconditions necessary for a life free of national or racial oppression.

Young people are taking up the cause of Ukrainian sovereignty with fanatical devotion. For them, this cause is the symbol of struggle for a new world, a world of liberty, justice and well-being. They are eager to bring about this new world. In their struggle for it, they bind themselves to the illustrious traditions of previous generations of youth— those who went among the people; those who established the Revolutionary Ukrainian Party[76]; those who laid down their lives on the snow-covered fields at Kruty[77]; those who, in the ranks of the Ukrainian Army, travelled the difficult, glorious path to the Sun of Freedom and, finally, those who, in secret activity carried out under the aegis of the Ukrainian Youth Association[78] and other pro-independence organizations, struggled for this same ideal. Young people will not withdraw from this battle. The present state of devastation will not frighten them away! Cries about the impracticality of their dreams will not shake them; the bloody terror of the occupying powers will not break them.

They have decided to achieve that which the faint-hearted consider impossible. Their resolution is not some temporary passion, but the firm will of those who face *victory or death*. *Yesterday, these young people numbered in the hundreds. Today, they number in the thousands, and, when hundreds of thousands and millions take this path, ultimate victory will be ours! This we believe most firmly!*

Source: Ideia i Chyn 2, no. 4 (1943): 15–20. Original: Archive of the Foreign Representation of the Supreme Ukrainian Liberation Council. Photocopy: Archive, *Litopys UPA*.

NOTES

1. N.M. Karamzin (1766–1826): Russian historian.
2. D.I. Ilovaisky (1832–1920): Russian historian.
3. A.G. Stakhanov (1906–77): initiator of the Stakhanovite movement of so-called "socialist competition" designed to raise production norms.
4. V.M. Purishkevich (1870–1920): Russian monarchist and organizer of the Black Hundred chauvinist organizations, the Union of the Russian People and the Union of Michael the Archangel.
5. I.V. Stalin (Dzhugashvili) (1879–1953): Soviet dictator, General Secretary of the CPSU. Georgian.
6. V.M. Molotov (Skriabin) (1890–): member of the CPSU Politburo, Foreign Minister of the USSR (1939–49 and 1953–6).
7. L.M. Kaganovich (1893–): member of the CPSU Politburo, First Secretary of the Communist Party of Ukraine (1925–8 and 1947).
8. B.K. Minikh (Khristofor Antonovich) (1683–1767): Russian field marshal of German origin.
9. A.I. Osterman (Johann Friedrich Heinrich) (1686–1747): Russian statesman of German origin.
10. P.I. Bagration (1765–1812): Russian general of Georgian origin.
11. I.F. Paskevich (1782–1856): Russian field marshal of Ukrainian origin. Suppressed the Polish uprising of 1830–31 and the Hungarian uprising of 1849.
12. M.T. Loris-Melikov (1825–88): Russian statesman of Armenian origin.
13. F.E. Dzerzhinsky (1877–1926): head of Cheka and later OGPU (Soviet political police), of Polish origin.
14. Andrei Bogoliubsky (1111?–1174): Prince of Rostov-Suzdal and Vladimir. Sacked Kiev in 1169.
15. Peter I (1672–1725): Russian emperor. Defeated Ukrainian and Swedish armies at Poltava (1709).

16. Catherine II (1729–96): Russian empress. Destroyed the Zaporozhian Sich in 1775.
17. V.I. Lenin (1870–1924): Russian revolutionist, organizer and leader of the Communist Party.
18. Reference is to the famine of 1932–3 in Ukraine organized by Stalin and the leadership of the CPSU with a view to destroying the resistance of the Ukrainian peasantry to collectivization. Estimates of the death toll range from 4 to 10 million. See R. Serbyn and B. Krawchenko, eds., *Famine in Ukraine 1932-1933* (Edmonton: Canadian Institute of Ukrainian Studies, 1986).
19. M.H. Khvylovy (Fitilov) (1893–1933): Ukrainian writer who called on his colleagues to turn "away from Moscow" and toward "psychological Europe" and sources of world literature. Committed suicide. See M. Khvylovy, *The Cultural Renaissance in Ukraine: Polemical Pamphlets 1925-1926*, ed. and trans. M. Shkandrij (Edmonton: Canadian Institute of Ukrainian Studies, 1986).
20. M.O. Skrypnyk (1872–1933): Old Bolshevik. Premier of the Soviet Ukrainian government, 1918. Minister of Education of the Ukrainian SSR and member of the Politburo, Ukrainian CP. Member of the Comintern executive. Committed suicide.
21. O. Shumsky (1890–?): Soviet Ukrainian ambassador in Warsaw (1919). Minister of Education, Ukrainian SSR (1924–26). Removed in 1926 for "bourgeois-nationalist deviation" and sent to Moscow. Arrested in 1933; allegedly died in prison.
22. M. Volobuev (1900–?): Ukrainian economist of Russian origin. Defended the policy of independent economic development of Ukraine. Arrested in 1930, died in internal exile in the 1930s.
23. *Valdshnepy* (Woodsnipes): novel by M. Khvylovy.
24. Ivan I Danilovich Kalita (died 1340): Prince of Moscow and Grand Prince of Vladimir.
25. Ivan Mazepa (1644–1709): Hetman of Left-Bank Ukraine. Allied himself with Charles XII of Sweden against Peter I. Defeated at the battle of Poltava in 1709.
26. Dmitrii Donskoi (1350–89): Prince of Moscow and Vladimir. Defeated Khan Mamai at the battle of Kulikovo in 1380.
27. Reference to Peter I.
28. Reference to Hetman I. Mazepa.
29. M.N. Pokrovsky (1868–1932): Russian Communist historian. In 1936 his historical views were proclaimed "anti-Marxist" and "anti-Leninist."
30. Goths: old Germanic tribes that settled on Ukrainian territory between the second and fourth centuries.
31. Huns: Turko-Mongolian tribes that reached Ukrainian territory at the end of the fourth century.

32. Varangians: old name for Scandinavians who appeared on Ukrainian lands in the ninth century.
33. Sviatoslav I Ihorevych (died 972): Grand Prince of Kiev.
34. Volodymyr Sviatoslavych (The Great) (died 1015): Grand Prince of Kiev. Made Christianity the state religion.
35. Volodymyr Monomakh (1053–1125): Grand Prince of Kiev.
36. Roman Mstyslavych (died 1205): Prince of Galicia-Volhynia.
37. Ilarion: first non-Greek metropolitan of Kiev. Consecrated in 1051 during the reign of Iaroslav the Wise (978–1054), Grand Prince of Kiev.
38. Klymentii Smoliatych became the second Ukrainian metropolitan of Kiev (1147–54). The Byzantine patriarch refused to sanction his election by the local hierarchy.
39. The author is unknown. Various scholars assume that he was either from Kiev, Chernihiv, Halych or even Transcarpathia.
40. Dmytro Vyshnevetsky (died 1563): First known Cossack leader (otaman).
41. Taras Fedorovych (Triasylo): Hetman of Zaporozhian Cossacks and leader of the anti-Polish uprising of 1630.
42. Dmytro Hunia: one of the leaders of the anti-Polish uprisings in the first half of the seventeenth century.
43. Bohdan Khmelnytsky (1595–1657): Hetman of Ukraine.
44. (Stanyslav) M. Krychevsky (died 1649): Cossack colonel. Captured at the battle of Loiev with the Lithuanians. Committed suicide.
45. Ivan Bohun (died 1664): Cossack colonel. Executed by the Poles.
46. Stanyslav (Mrozovytsky) Morozenko (died 1649): Cossack colonel. Died in battle.
47. Maksym Kryvonis (died 1648): Cossack colonel, allegedly of Scottish origin.
48. Iurii Nemyrych (1612–59): At first fought against Khmelnytsky but returned to serve the Cossacks in 1657. Killed in battle with insurgents against Hetman Ivan Vyhovsky.
49. Khmel: reference to Hetman Khmelnytsky.
50. Petro Doroshenko (1627–98): Hetman of Ukraine. Died in "honorary exile" near Moscow.
51. Burlaiv: either a Cossack colonel who died near Zbarazh in 1649 or Kindrat, Cossack otaman, Khmelnytsky's envoy to Moscow in 1653.
52. Dzhalalii (Dzhedzhalii) Filon: Cossack colonel of Tatar origin. Khmelnytsky's envoy to the Porte (1648).
53. Hryhorii (Zakharzhevsky) Donets (died 1691): Cossack colonel.
54. Ivan (Tyshyk) Tysha: leather worker, later Cossack colonel.
55. Reference to his *Slovo pro zakon i blahodat* (Word on Law and Grace), allegedly written between 1037 and 1050, which defended the political and cultural independence of Kievan Rus'.

56. Boian: legendary poet mentioned in the "Song of Ihor's Campaign," not its author.
57. Kievan Academy established in 1632 by Metropolitan Petro Mohyla. Closed by the Russian government in 1817.
58. William Shakespeare (1564–1616).
59. Robert Louis Stevenson (1850–94).
60. Blaise Pascal (1623–62).
61. T.H. Shevchenko (1814–61): greatest Ukrainian Romantic poet.
62. M.M. Kotsiubynsky (1864–1913): Ukrainian writer.
63. L. Ukrainka (L.P. Kosach-Kvitka) (1871–1913): Ukrainian poetess and writer.
64. Cossack chronicles (*litopysy*) of the seventeenth and early eighteenth centuries describe the revolution of 1648 and other events in Ukrainian history of the period.
65. *Istoriia Rusov* (History of the Rus' People): historical work of an unknown author widely circulated in Ukraine at the beginning of the nineteenth century.
66. P.A. Valuev (1814–90): Russian minister of internal affairs. In 1863 he forbade the use of the Ukrainian language in scientific and scholarly publications. Further restrictions on the Ukrainian language were introduced in 1876 in the Ems Ukase.
67. N.S. Khrushchev (1894–1971): First Secretary, Communist Party of Ukraine, 1938-49, responsible for Russification measures. Became First Secretary, CPSU, in 1953. Purged in 1964.
68. Reference to Sviatoslav I Ihorevych (see n. 33 above).
69. Symon Petliura (1879–1926): Supreme Otaman of Ukrainian armed forces in 1917–19 and Head of the Directory of the Ukrainian People's Republic. Killed in Paris by Shalom Schwarzbard, allegedly a Soviet agent.
70. Ievhen Konovalets (1891–1938): Head of the Ukrainian Military Organization and later of the Organization of Ukrainian Nationalists (OUN). Killed in Rotterdam by a Soviet agent.
71. Dmytro Myron (1911–42), pseudonym "Orlyk": member of the OUN leadership and one of its ideologues. Arrested in Kiev and killed by the Nazis during an attempted escape from jail.
72. Ivan Klymiv (1915–42), pseudonym "Lehenda": member of the OUN leadership and active in anti-Polish, anti-Soviet and anti-German resistance. Tortured to death in Lviv jail by the Gestapo.
73. Serhii Sherstiuk: born in the Kharkiv region. OUN activist killed by the Gestapo in Kryvyi Rih in 1942.
74. Petro Shchepansky: political activist in the Kiev region. Killed by the Gestapo in Kremenchuk.
75. NKVD: People's Commissariat of Internal Affairs.

76. Revolutionary Ukrainian Party: first Ukrainian political organization in the Russian Empire, established in Kharkiv in 1900.
77. The battle of Kruty, 29 January 1918, at which 300 students died defending Kiev against Bolshevik-led forces.
78. Ukrainian Youth Association: allegedly organized in 1925 as an arm of the Union for the Liberation of Ukraine. It was liquidated in 1929 with the arrest of its leaders.

INTERNAL OBSTACLES TO THE UKRAINIAN NATIONAL-LIBERATION STRUGGLE

P.T. Duma

This is not the first time that we are pondering the reasons for our statelessness. A number of works exist in our literature which thoroughly analyze our people's history, searching for the reasons and the primary causes of the nation's rise and fall. They boldly point out all the illnesses of the national organism and portray, often in exaggerated colours, all the problems that either brought about our state of subjugation or prevented us from freeing ourselves from this state. Obviously, the nation's internal readiness for liberation is insufficient for the attainment of statehood, since international events also play a significant role. But for us, perhaps the most important factors have been, and still are today, internal obstacles. Of course, it is difficult and inexpedient to speak extensively of these obstacles, for in doing so, one runs the danger of turning, or encouraging others to turn, from a sound, positive outlook to a psychosis of weakness and morbid hopelessness generated by the awareness of a large number of negative qualities in one's nation. If we choose here to point a finger at the obstacles that currently hinder the process of our liberation, it is because we are compelled to do so by our awareness of the onset of important and decisive times and by the blindness of many of our countrymen, who fail to see these obstacles or choose not to see them. It has been our lot to live in a great era of world wars, a time when the military forces of empires are moving across the map of history. In the struggle between these empires, there are times when one state collapses in the course of a day and a new one arises on the next. We should expect that at the end of the present war there will be many such opportunities, particularly for stateless peoples. However, if we fail to make use of these opportunities at this time, if we do not establish our own state, then we should be aware of the consequences in advance. It is already obvious that in that case we may have to wait another century for a new set of decisive events to occur, that is, if any place at all is still left for us on this earth. And if this is how things stand, if today we are confronted with the question to be or not to be, then let us draw the proper conclusions and search immediately for a way to deal with this situation. Whoever fails to take account of these things now should at least consider the fate of those of our countrymen whose lot it was, in the winter and spring of this year, to change "liberators" several times (on the left bank of the Dnieper). In such circumstances, there is no longer any use for cunning machinations or any hope of foreign assistance; all that we can do is defend ourselves, and defend ourselves in common, as a nation.

What, then, are the obstacles that hinder the Ukrainian people's national-liberation struggle at the present time?

The first and most important obstacle is the sickness that has become chronic among a segment of our intelligentsia: *an orientation on foreign powers*. We have witnessed this throughout our history and seen all the tragic results that inevitably follow. At one time, this was a device employed in the struggle for power; at another, pure servility on the part of "collaborators"[1]; finally, it was the cultural and national assimilation of noblemen, princes and officers. But always it resulted in a political orientation on powers foreign and hostile to Ukraine. Although the tradition of political independence has been preserved and continues to exist among the Ukrainian people, it is not a strong enough cementing factor to be able to unite the whole nation and lead it to rely only on its own resources, as is the case with other nations recently deprived of statehood. A large segment of the population eagerly sways with foreign winds and constantly searches for something more, something in addition to its own ideas, something to be found only beyond the borders of its own country. At present, this is particularly evident on territories formerly held by the Russians. Russia, whether White or Red, "took care" of the Ukrainian people with particular diligence. Whoever was not swayed by the Orthodox faith, the Slavic oak, the dictatorship of the proletariat or Great Russian culture in all its aspects was undoubtedly swayed by deportation, prisons and executions—in a word, by terror. Hermetically sealed from any breath of ideas opposed to Moscow, the Ukrainian people, in spite of desperate struggles for independence, grew up deformed. And this deformation is a great obstacle to political self-reliance. Having lived for generations in the Russian Empire, some of our countrymen fell in love with its vast expanse, with the grand style of a multinational state, with an area covering one-sixth of the globe, and now they are unable or do not wish to think in terms of political independence for their own land. This is the reason for their avid search for international, cosmopolitan and all-union concepts; it is the reason for their belief in doctrines, theories and utopias. This is also the source of the process of denationalization, which is so pronounced, particularly in the large urban centres of Ukraine. In their search for all-embracing, universal ideas, they lost themselves or forgot their own fatherland and unconsciously came under Russian influence. In this way, Moscow became for them the centre with which they associate their meagre hopes, on which they orient themselves politically and with which they also associate their social and economic plans. Lack of faith in one's own powers, lack of belief in the national-liberation struggle and a deeply rooted impotence of the will are the symptoms of the political sickness still common among Ukrainians. It is found not only in areas formerly held by Russia but, unfortunately, in western and émigré circles as well. For these circles, the radiant centre has so far been Berlin or some other world metropolis that in future may become interested in Ukrainian territory. People belonging to such circles link the nation's efforts to achieve political liberation with these foreign centres and the fate of Ukraine with their strength. Thus they base all practical political thinking on foreign power or foreign intervention. They disdainfully dismiss all who pursue an autonomous path to liberation as "dreamers," "visionaries," and "knights of the absurd," reserving to themselves the epithet of "realistic" politicians. Such was the origin of the various opportunistic groups and movements now active in Ukraine, which have gone over entirely to the side of the enemy. The shouts emanating from these groups against those who strive for independence become all the louder as the downfall of their protectors draws nearer and becomes more obvious. These opportunistic individuals have no concept of the possibility of autonomous national liberation, for they have no faith in the nation's capacities or in the strength and justness of its cause. Instead of concentrating on building up a solid, autonomous force within the nation, they delight in the panzer divisions of imperialist pillagers and stand ready to fortify these divisions with the blood of their countrymen, simply in order to maintain their superficial way of life. And this usually lasts until such time as their master is ruined. Then those who only yesterday took no notice of the nation, still less of its strength, begin to seek shelter and protection in its midst. But even then, it is not for long. A new master arrives and, with him, a new orientation on another, equally foreign, power.

This is the great sickness that blocks our way to liberation. Were we to remove this hindrance, the cause of establishing our own state would proceed by leaps and bounds. For the moment, this is still the fundamental obstacle.

A further impediment to the Ukrainian national-liberation struggle is the attitude of some of our political groupings. We speak here of the remnants of political parties now terminating their vegetative existence or restricting their activity to the external political front. Their traces can be seen to some extent in western Ukraine and, even more, in the emigration. In central and eastern Ukraine, they are not carrying on any activity; they are not organizing the masses or leading the Ukrainian people to battle for an independent Ukraine. For where today, on the Ukrainian plains, are there any signs of the existence or activity of once clamorous Ukrainian political parties? They do not exist. All that exists is the mass of the people; of these, some are sinking into dull hopelessness, while others, of necessity, are orienting themselves on the Bolsheviks or on Moscow generally. Still others are answering the call of the Ukrainian independence movement and joining the ranks of those fighting for an independent, united Ukrainian state.

It would be normal if the situation abroad corresponded to that in Ukraine; if corresponding to the united front of the independence movement on Ukrainian soil there were also such a front abroad. Such, however, is not the case. While on the wide expanses of the Ukrainian plains we see no representatives of party groups carrying on any significant activity and organizing the masses against the occupying power and its merciless terror, beyond the central and eastern regions, that is, primarily in émigré circles and to some extent in western Ukraine, dozens of party groups and little gatherings are preparing to "represent" Ukraine and protect her interests in foreign state antechambers. While in those regions of Ukraine an implacable struggle is being waged for independence, while in Ukraine, and nowhere else, the fate of the Ukrainian people is being decided in their struggle against the German occupying power and the Muscovite one, which is even more dangerous because of its ideology, no assistance is forthcoming from the above-mentioned parties and groups to those who have had the courage to take up this struggle under the most difficult conditions.

And this is one of the major obstacles to the liberation struggle of the Ukrainian people, for it allows the occupying powers to play a capital game. On the one hand, they mercilessly stifle every manifestation of the independence movement in Ukraine and, on the other, they make use of small political groupings for their own purposes. Under the protection of the occupying powers, and whenever their interests so require, these small groups grow into "serious representations of the nation"; they "protect" its interests in the world and help the occupying powers manufacture all kinds of fictions intended to deceive the Ukrainian people and cover up the true aims of the imperialists. Cut off from their home ground and lacking any autonomous organized strength, "representations" of this sort must soon become playthings in the hands of the occupying powers. At the same time, by toying with these groups in order to impress the outside world, the occupying powers gain an excellent opportunity to strike another blow to the cause of independence.

How different the situation would be if the independence struggle of the Ukrainian people were represented externally by a single collective body! Then all attempts by the occupying powers to interfere in Ukrainian affairs would be opposed by the resolute will of this body, which would have all of Ukraine behind it, for it would represent her will. If such a body existed, it would put an end to the games played by various speculators who, representing absolutely nothing, enable foreigners to meddle in Ukrainian affairs. At the same time, the internal front of the Ukrainian independence movement would also be greatly strengthened.

Finally, it would appear that the most entrenched obstacle to our liberation is the division of the Ukrainian masses into two spiritual-philosophical and socio-cultural mentalities, a division brought about by the conditions of our subjugation. We cannot conceal this misfortune: to do so would be inexpedient. It exists and must be discussed.

One mentality is that of eastern Ukraine; the other, that of western Ukraine. Each has its positive qualities, which we shall not discuss. But each also has its negative qualities that must be identified, so that by tempering them the two sides may create a sound synthesis in the form of a single, united spiritual and social entity. What are the faults of the East? When we considered the reasons for the political orientation of a segment of the Ukrainian population on Moscow, we indicated the spiritual and philosophical deformation that resulted from the long, one-sided influence of Moscow on Ukraine. This deformation is also apparent in another sphere. Its most evident symptom is what might be called the Moscow complex, which is particularly prevalent among the urban Ukrainian intelligentsia. However it may have come about, a rather pronounced Russification is evident among these people at present, particularly in their way of thinking and appraisal of events, but also in their day-to-day life, language of conversation, ethical and moral outlook and domestic customs. The spirits of Tolstoy,[2] Dostoevsky,[3] Gorky[4] and a long succession of others have weakened and even totally emasculated the principle of national primacy; they heaped derision on the sacred values of the nation. As a result, the circle of spiritual cripples has constantly widened. For some of our countrymen, Moscow and its territory gradually became the ''fatherland''; the Russian nation came to be regarded as a joint patrimony, first because it was Russian, then Orthodox, Slavic and proletarian, and now Soviet. The sense of belonging to one's own nation was reduced to a narrow, territorial, regional feeling and thus deprived of all its political force. Included among the symptoms of this state of mind is also the desire, which exists primarily among the lower strata of society, to reduce everything to their own level—the level of nothingness. We see here not the healthy endeavour, traditional among the Cossacks, to raise oneself higher, to equal others on the social scale, to strive nobly to be first, but rather an egoistic levelling downward, a gravitation to the lowest point, simply so that there not be anyone richer, better, more intelligent.

One could go on and on pointing out and analyzing the negative symptoms of this mentality, which unfortunately has permeated rather large segments of society.

Western Ukraine is not free of negative qualities either. Here, the chief problem is parochialism, that narrowly provincial patriotism which makes it impossible for many to restructure their thinking to fit the wider sphere of an all-Ukrainian liberation front. This is above all a lack of faith in the capacities of people in other parts of the country and their ability to form a state; it is a narrowness of concepts, plans and organizations which leads those who suffer from it to jostle one another within a small, confined space in a limited environment; it is egoism played out in one's own back yard; the limited ambition of small people afraid to take the high road of history. If any model is imitated in these circles, it is primarily the West, and not always in its positive aspects. The people belonging to these circles evaluate the East incorrectly; they underestimate it; they close their eyes to what is happening there, although in their plans they always situate themselves precisely in the East. Unlike the East, the population here is devoid of that elemental, subconscious dynamic force which can erupt in a sudden volcano. Here, everything is categorized and confined within the rigid framework of a narrow system. Of course, the West, like the East, is not homogeneous, and these qualities should not be generalized. Only in harmony, in a select synthesis of these two mentalities that eliminates extreme, negative qualities can a sound, organic, new type of Ukrainian statesman be shaped.

Despite all obstacles, the Ukrainian national-liberation struggle is developing systematically and producing ever greater results. To demonstrate this fact, it will suffice to compare the current situation with that of 1939. The cause of the Ukrainian independence movement is not a dream; it is becoming the rallying point of the broadest masses of the Ukrainian population. In the furnace of the Ukrainian people's struggle for liberation and independence, all shortcomings are melted down. Only in a common struggle waged by the whole nation and all classes of society can the differences among individual segments of the nation be eradicated. And only in revolutionary struggle, rather than in petty political speculation, can all the obstacles that block the path to our liberation be swept away. One of the basic preconditions for the attainment of Ukrainian sovereignty is internal solidarity, the ideological and organizational consolidation of the nation, particularly of its leadership. This means that we must eliminate all internal impediments to the national-liberation struggle of the Ukrainian people.

Source: Ideia i Chyn 2, no. 4 (1943): 6–9. Original: Archive of the Foreign Representation of the Supreme Ukrainian Liberation Council. Photocopy: Archive, *Litopys UPA*.

NOTES

1. In the original *tatarski liudy* (Tatar people), peasants of eastern Podillia who surrendered to the Tatars in 1240 and undertook to supply them with grain. King Danylo of Halych mounted several successful campaigns against them in 1241 and 1244–5.
2. L.N. Tolstoy (1828–1910): Russian writer and proponent of the philosophy of "non-resistance to evil".
3. F.M. Dostoevsky (1821–81): Russian writer who opposed the revolutionary transformation of society.
4. M. Gorky (A.M. Peshkov) (1868–1936): Russian writer noted for his anti-Ukrainian attitudes.

OUR BATTLE PLAN FOR THE LIBERATION OF UKRAINE UNDER THE PRESENT CIRCUMSTANCES

P. Poltava

In 1946 the Ukrainian revolutionary liberation movement in the USSR began to change its tactics from those of large-scale partisan warfare to those of underground struggle. In practice, this change of tactics manifested itself in the following manner: 1) according to circumstances and needs in different regions, UPA detachments were gradually disbanded and their participants, both commanders and soldiers, entered the ranks of the underground, the underground network; 2) all the work and activities of the underground were veiled in the utmost secrecy; 3) in contrast to the period of large-scale UPA activity intended to prevent the enemy from extending his control beyond the provincial and regional centres, priority is now being given to political propaganda and organizational activities. At present, the Ukrainian revolutionary liberation movement in the USSR is making use of the armed underground to wage its struggle, operating under conditions of the utmost secrecy.

*   *   *

Given this change in the form of the struggle being waged by the Ukrainian liberation movement, as well as the existence of "peace" in the world, Ukrainian citizens who are not members of the underground would undoubtedly like to know our battle plan in the present circumstances. What is our goal in the current underground struggle? What do we in fact hope to achieve in these very difficult circumstances, which constantly take such a great toll in human lives?

In brief, these are the major tasks in our present battle plan for the liberation of Ukraine:

1. At all costs, to maintain our underground organization on Ukrainian territories of the USSR and to extend it in accord with existing needs and possibilities;

2. Through our underground organization, as well as by all other means, to conduct political, educational and propaganda activities among the Ukrainian people and all the peoples of the USSR;

3. To organize large-scale resistance of the Ukrainian people and, as far as possible, of other peoples of the USSR to the Bolshevik oppressors and exploiters;

4. To conduct the military operations needed to prevent the occupying power from consolidating itself in our country to the extent that it would wish and to show the Russian-Bolshevik criminals and all their hirelings that they cannot commit crimes with impunity against the Ukrainian people and the Ukrainian liberation movement.

This, briefly, is the present plan for our liberation struggle.

The liberation of Ukraine, the liberation of the Ukrainian people in the near future depends upon how successful we are in implementing this plan.

It might be asked why this is so. The reasons are as follows:

All of history demonstrates that a subject people liberates itself only when its most dedicated members establish a sufficiently strong liberation organization. Such an organization is essential above all for preparing a nation-wide liberation uprising or any other decisive act of liberation. As is well known, it is only by way of a nation-wide uprising that the rule of an occupying power in a subjugated country can ultimately be overthrown. Furthermore, an organization of this type is essential in order to ensure that at the appropriate moment there is someone to call the people to an uprising (or any other act of liberation), to organize the uprising, to lead the people in it, to march in its front ranks, to be its support and its vanguard. *If, when the right moment arrives, a people lacks an organization capable of leading such a struggle, that people will not attain liberation even under the most favourable conditions.*

It is particularly important that a people have such an organization on its own territory rather than abroad. Those members of a people who live abroad can return to their native land only in the wake of foreign armies, or at best as unimportant elements of those armies, permitted, perhaps, to march under their own flags. This means that at decisive moments, as in time of war against the power occupying their native land, the influence of those living abroad on the fate of their people is negligible, almost non-existent. This is particularly true if the attitude of the warring states to the given subject people is one of *indifference*. And if the attitude of the warring states opposing the occupying power is one of hostility to the given subject people, then those living abroad can have no influence at all on the fate of their own nation. *The liberation of a subject people almost always depends solely upon what that people can attain on its own soil, in its native land, and not abroad.*

In light of what has been said, it becomes clearly apparent that the existence of the present underground organization in Ukraine, the existence of our present organized revolutionary underground, has an enormous significance for the Ukrainian people.

Many Ukrainians tend to think as follows: "Everything depends on war against the USSR. Our people (i.e., the underground) cannot do much on their own."

It is perfectly true that at present our revolutionary movement in Ukraine is still too weak single-handedly to overthrow Bolshevik rule in Ukraine. It is also true that war against the USSR, and particularly a war of the type now being prepared, would greatly assist our liberation efforts. This we do not deny. *Nevertheless, anyone who thinks that war alone will suffice for the liberation of Ukraine is very much mistaken. Without the existence in Ukraine of a suitably experienced and developed liberation organization, the Ukrainian people will not be liberated even if a war takes place.* Considering what we have already said about the role and significance of a liberation organization for a subject people, this should be perfectly understandable. The conclusions we have drawn are confirmed by the information we receive about the current status of Ukrainians living abroad. Generally speaking, the world is totally indifferent to our liberation efforts at the present time. Because we have been a stateless nation for such a long time, it is now difficult for us to gain a place on the international stage.

At present we have an experienced and well-developed organization in Ukraine that will be capable of leading the people at the appropriate moment in a decisive liberation campaign, of organizing such an action and heading it. That organization is the underground OUN, the revolutionary underground as a whole. The fact that such an organization currently exists in Ukraine is an enormous advantage to us as a subject people; it is our great national achievement. It is the most important guarantee of our liberation at the earliest appropriate moment.

For this reason, we naturally make the preservation of this organization and its further development the major task in the plan for our liberation struggle under the present circumstances. As we have in the past, we will continue to strive to fulfill that task at any price, even at the price of great losses in lives. For we are fully aware that should we choose to abandon our plan or should the enemy succeed in destroying the underground, all hopes for the liberation of the Ukrainian people in the near future would be dashed.

But in order to make it possible for our liberation organization to carry out its goal when the appropriate moment arrives, that is, in order for it to attain the liberation of Ukraine as a national state, *it must be assured of the support of the broadest Ukrainian masses, of the whole Ukrainian people, particularly at the decisive moment of battle.* Our liberation organization will enjoy this support when, on the one hand, our program suits the needs and desires of the broadest masses of the Ukrainian people and, on the other hand, the Ukrainian masses are fully acquainted with our program and goals.

With regard to the first requirement, our position is quite good. Our program truly reflects the yearnings and needs of all strata of Ukrainian society, of the broadest masses of the people. That this is so is confirmed by the innumerable comments on our program that come to us daily from people of all classes and all walks of life in all regions of Ukraine. And this is not surprising, for our revolutionary liberation movement, the OUN in Ukraine, has always paid great attention to the desires of the Ukrainian people and has always kept track of their needs.

There still remains the second requirement: to make our goals known to the broadest masses of the Ukrainian people. *In this regard, it must be said that our position is less than fully satisfactory.* This is of course most true in the eastern regions of Ukraine. Even today the majority of eastern Ukrainians either know very little about our true goals and the true character of our underground organization and the liberation movement as a whole, or they continue to believe the Bolshevik lies about us. In addition, many eastern Ukrainians, particularly members of the intelligentsia, are still influenced by Bolshevik ideas in general.

This unfortunate state of affairs can be altered only by means of a large-scale political and educational and propaganda program: our underground publications—leaflets, brochures, press publications, appeals and the like—must be widely disseminated among the people of eastern Ukraine and educational work of an oral nature must be conducted. This work must be carried out not only by members of the underground but by all patriots, all nationally conscious Ukrainians.

Because of its great significance for our liberation struggle, waging a campaign of political propaganda among eastern Ukrainians and the people of the Soviet Union in general is considered the second most important task in our present plan for liberation. The strength with which the Ukrainian people are able to act at the earliest appropriate opportunity will depend on the fulfillment of this task. And as we know, the strength of that action will determine whether we are victorious in our liberation struggle, whether we attain our liberation.

Also included in our battle plan for the liberation of Ukraine is the task of organizing general resistance on the part of the Ukrainian people to the Bolshevik oppressors and exploiters. *This type of resistance is essential in order to prevent the Soviets from easily implementing their plans in Ukraine, whether these be political plans (building up the party, the Young Communist League, etc.), economic plans (collectivization, recruitment to the FZN,*[1] *deliveries of provisions, etc.), plans for Russification, propaganda plans or any others. Resistance is essential in order to hinder the fulfillment of these plans, to shake the foundations of Bolshevik rule in Ukraine.* It is not difficult to envision what a mighty blow a courageous, nation-wide, general resistance would constitute to the Muscovite-Bolshevik occupying power.

But it is obvious that such a task cannot be accomplished by the underground single-handedly. It can be accomplished only with the participation of the broadest masses of the Ukrainian people. The Ukrainian people must put up such resistance to the Muscovite-Bolshevik invaders. The struggle for the liberation of Ukraine, the struggle against the Bolshevik subjugators, cannot be limited to the struggle of the underground alone. Their resistance definitely is not sufficient. *The whole nation must join in this struggle.* Only then will the liberation of Ukraine be guaranteed. In spite of the terrorist character of the Bolshevik regime, it is still possible for the broad mass of the people to put up resistance. The opportunities for resistance must be perceived and courageously exploited as much as possible. Above all, there must be determined resistance to Moscow's policy of Russification of the Ukrainian people. That policy threatens us with complete destruction as a separate nation.

The struggle, the courageous, nation-wide resistance against the Muscovite-Bolshevik occupying power, will not only seriously undermine Bolshevik rule in Ukraine; it will also serve to prepare the people to take resolute, courageous action when the appropriate time comes. Above all, it will develop in the people such qualities as the courage to oppose and even advance upon the enemy, self-sacrifice, national solidarity, active patriotism, a militant spirit and the like. *History shows us that without this type of preparation, a subject people is not able to vanquish the hostile occupying power.*

There is a separate, well-defined place in our present battle plan for military action, in which our revolutionary underground is currently engaging on its own initiative (we are now engaging in many such actions, being compelled by the enemy's terrorist offensive against us to defend our existence as an organized liberation movement). The primary goal of these actions is to punish those most actively working against us and their servitors for the crimes they are committing against the Ukrainian people and the Ukrainian liberation movement—terrorizing the Ukrainian people and subjecting them to all kinds of other torments, plundering them, persecuting Ukrainian patriots, engaging in armed actions or acts of propaganda against the Ukrainian liberation movement and so on. By striking fear into the hearts of the Bolsheviks and their hirelings and cooling their ardour to serve the Bolshevik oppressors faithfully, we are doing a great deal to defend the Ukrainian population against these people's high-handed and unrestrained behaviour. Many heads of village Soviets and collective farms and other Bolshevik officials have been restraining their behaviour simply because they fear the just punishment of the underground! Thus, in the regions where we are waging our military actions, we are making it much more difficult for the Bolsheviks to implement their plans for domination of the Ukrainian masses. Furthermore, we are instilling the spirit of revolutionary struggle in the Ukrainian masses. Every successful assassination or surprise attack on the enemy raises the revolutionary spirit of the masses, increases the Ukrainian people's courage, strengthens them in their opposition to the Moscovite-Bolshevik invaders and activates them at the front of this resistance. *All this is extremely significant in the plan for the development of the revolutionary liberation struggle. It is, in fact, the only sure path to victory.*

However, it must be stated that we are now conducting far fewer military operations than we did, let us say, in 1944—6, the period of large-scale action by the UPA and of a massive armed underground. This is a result of the change in our battle plan. At present we are adopting as our major tasks the preservation and further extension of our underground organization and the continuance of political education. Military operations are now the last priority in our battle plan.

Regardless of all the difficulties in waging the liberation struggle under the conditions created by the totalitarian and terroristic Soviet regime, regardless of the great sacrifices in human lives we are constantly compelled to make, we are successfully implementing the battle plan we have set ourselves.

We have preserved and in some cases even extended our underground organization. With the aid of our underground network, we have gained almost total sway over approximately one-third of the territory of Ukraine.

We have attained a good deal of success in our political propaganda activities. An ever growing number of eastern Ukrainians, and even people from other parts of the USSR, are learning about our true aims, about the true nature of our movement and its goals of national and social liberation. Our literature is reaching every corner of Ukraine, as well as other republics of the Soviet Union. In 1948 alone, our underground printing presses turned out about 70 titles—brochures, leaflets, press and artistic publications—printed in editions of many thousands. Almost all this literature was intended for the masses of the people in the Soviet Union and, above all, for the eastern Ukrainian masses. We are continually receiving a great deal of enthusiastic praise for our struggle from eastern Ukrainians and people from all parts of the USSR. We often receive letters from Ukrainian patriots living in all regions of Ukraine. These people express their total solidarity with us and their readiness to take part in the struggle. We encounter generous support throughout Ukraine for our practical revolutionary activities.

The underground has also been successful in organizing the resistance of the Ukrainian masses to the Muscovite-Bolshevik invaders. Let us single out the Ukrainian people's boycott of all the Bolshevik elections held so far in regions of UPA and underground activity—in particular, the elections of 1946; the resistance to collectivization; and the refusal of Ukrainian youth to join the Young Communist League, the special NKVD units formed to fight the UPA,[2] the FZN and so on. Examples are too numerous to mention. In the regions of UPA and underground activity, a pitched battle between the Bolshevik oppressors and the Ukrainian masses has been going on continually since 1944. And this is largely the result of the struggle and other activities waged by the UPA and the underground.

Our military actions are also yielding success. A significant number of Bolshevik bandits and their servitors are falling under assailants' bullets or in ambushes organized by the underground. By its military actions, the underground has provided a great deal of assistance to western Ukrainian peasants in their struggle against collectivization. Because of the military actions waged by the UPA and the underground, the Bolsheviks have had very little success in their attempts to organize special NKVD units to fight the UPA. We shall not even mention the fact that these actions have a revolutionizing effect on the Ukrainian masses, and particularly on Ukrainian youth, for this is obvious.

*   *   *

What will determine whether we fully realize our battle plan for the liberation of Ukraine? In other words, what will determine whether our struggle is ultimately successful?

Obviously our success depends upon a number of factors. *But one of the most important factors determining our success is the degree to which Ukrainian citizens who are not part of the underground support the revolutionary underground in its struggle to fulfill the plan.*

What kind of support does the revolutionary underground currently require? Let us state at once that the support must not devolve to mere sympathy, to mere ideological agreement with the underground. The struggle does not hinge on sympathy; it is not strengthened by mere sympathy. For the people to be in agreement ideologically with the underground is not sufficient for winning our liberation struggle. *The support must be real, concrete, active.*

Members of the underground must have somewhere to stay. The demands of battle, and in many regions climatic conditions as well, require that hiding places for the underground be in populated places, inside buildings.

It is the duty of every nationally conscious Ukrainian, every Ukrainian patriot, to be willing to provide such hiding places in his home. Naturally, there is a certain risk involved. But there can be no struggle without risk. When some Ukrainian patriots risk their lives daily—not because they "don't care" about the risks they are taking, but because this is required for the sake of liberation—then other patriots should be prepared to risk at least their goods or their personal freedom for a certain period of time. Without sacrifice there will be no victory. And victory will be ours when not merely individuals, but the mass of the people are prepared to make sacrifices. Furthermore, given the deep secrecy in which the underground is operating at present, it is difficult for the MGB[3] to uncover their places of hiding.

The underground requires material help in the form of money, food and, at times, clothing, shoes, drugs and the like.

There is a particular need for money. Money is required primarily for running the printing presses and buying all the needed materials—paper, typewriters, office supplies; for acquiring necessary books, drugs, clothing and shoes; and for meeting a number of other expenses which for security reasons we shall not mention here. Without money, the underground would be incapable of conducting its political propaganda activities and perhaps of surviving at all. All financial assets are under the strict control of higher authorities.

The underground needs assistance from the public at large in the form of all types of information from institutions, factories and workplaces of all kinds in different regions of the USSR regarding all aspects of Soviet life. Because of the kind of struggle being waged (necessitating an insurgent way of life and deep secrecy), the underground itself cannot gather all the information it requires. Yet for a political organization to conduct its business properly, such information is vital.

The underground also needs more members. It is generally known that during the last few years of struggle, tens of thousands of insurgents and underground activists have died heroic deaths. Lives continue to be lost. That is inevitable in battle. Here and there, the underground needs to fill out its ranks. This is essential if the underground is to exist as a broad, integral organization. All Ukrainian patriots must be aware of this. Should the need arise, everyone should have the courage to take the difficult but noble path of underground struggle; no one should hesitate to allow his son or daughter to enter the underground.

We address ourselves above all to Ukrainian youth of high school and university age! The underground is a political organization that engages in political revolutionary work of every kind. It is deeply mistaken to think that there is no work for educated people in the underground. Our underground, our liberation movement, requires the greatest possible number of educated people. We can offer people enormous potential for growth and individual development. Hundreds of talented youths have gone through our underground and become first-class political revolutionary leaders with large stores of political and general knowledge and a great deal of all-round experience in practical political revolutionary activity. There is at present no higher calling for young Ukrainian patriots than to enter active revolutionary struggle for the liberation of Ukraine within the ranks of the underground. Only in the ranks of the underground can one serve Ukraine in the best possible way—with one's knowledge, one's courage, one's enthusiasm and determination. For this reason, when you are called to serve, do not hesitate even for a moment!

Yet another way of supporting the underground is to conduct educational work among those who are unaware of our movement's true character and true goals. It is not true that it is impossible to conduct work of this type in the USSR. We know from experience that opportunities for such work do exist. Naturally, it must be done with great care. One must always assess other people carefully and choose the appropriate moment for conducting one's work. It is also important that one not be overly fearful and that one not assume that every Soviet citizen is an agent of the MGB. While there are undoubtedly very many such agents, we have not yet reached the point where everybody is an agent. Many people in the Soviet Union might initially adopt a hostile attitude to our movement simply because they lack information about us. They may, in fact, be honest people, perhaps even secret opponents of the Bolshevik regime. What a loss it is for us, for our liberation movement, when a Ukrainian patriot meets such a person, works with him, lives with him, yet somehow does not dare to say a few words of truth about us. The framework in which our political propaganda work is carried out is thus greatly narrowed, and our success is diminished as well. For this reason it is the duty of every Ukrainian patriot to aid in every possible way in disseminating the truth about us, the Ukrainian liberation movement. The Ukrainian intelligentsia and student youth are particularly capable of accomplishing a great deal in this regard. It is generally known that at present our underground finds it difficult to reach the cities, particularly the larger ones. And that is precisely where we find most of the people to whom our educational work should be directed: eastern Ukrainians and citizens of the Soviet Union in general. Someone has to give these people our underground literature, send them explanatory letters (needless to say, written anonymously with the handwriting disguised), give them patriotic books published in western Ukraine before 1939 that will help raise their national consciousness, and so on. Our underground publications are often in short supply; it is often difficult to lay one's hands on more than one copy of any given work. When this happens, people must copy these publications, particularly leaflets, by hand and disseminate them in that form.

Only if all nationally conscious Ukrainians assist us in our political propaganda activities will our work in this area be successful. Every nationally conscious, politically aware Ukrainian intellectual, worker and peasant should take as great a part as possible in educational work of this type.

Finally, to support the underground not only in word or sentiment but in deed requires a constant readiness to carry out all the proposals and directives of the underground, to give it practical support in whatever situation may arise.

When, on the one hand, all Ukrainian patriots—peasants, workers and intellectuals—who do not form part of the underground give it the practical support it needs and, on the other, they offer courageous resistance to the Muscovite-Bolshevik invaders, then we will succeed in our liberation struggle!

April 1950

Source: This article was issued by the ''Volia Narodam'' press in Ukraine in 1951 as a 12-page brochure in octavo format. Outside Ukraine it was reprinted in *Suchasna Ukraina* (Munich), no. 5 (1951) (in condensed form); in *Ukrainskyi samostiinyk* (Munich), nos. 5 and 6 (1954); and in P. Poltava, *Zbirnyk pidpilnykh pysan* (Munich 1959), 265–76.

NOTES

1. FZN (*Fabrychno-zavodske navchannia*): factory and plant training.
2. In the original, *strybky*, a corruption of the Russian *istrebitelnye otriady* (extermination units).
3. MGB: Ministry of State Security, the Soviet political police.

PREPARATORY STEPS TOWARD THE THIRD WORLD WAR AND THE TASKS OF THE UKRAINIAN PEOPLE

P. Poltava

We are rapidly approaching a new world war. International developments over the past year clearly point to this fact: the outbreak of war in Korea; the failure of peaceful attempts to resolve the Korean conflict; the implacable, provocative, aggressive policy pursued by the Muscovite-Bolshevik imperialists in all parts of the world; the great increase in armaments in almost all countries; the total failure of all diplomatic moves aimed at reducing international tensions.

Given these circumstances, the Ukrainian people must determine their position with regard to the major international problems and events of the day and clearly define their own tasks for the present moment and in the event of the outbreak of a third world war.

The Ukrainian People's Position in Principle on War and Peace

Preparations for the Third World War are proceeding to the accompaniment of a particularly loud and large-scale propaganda campaign in favour of peace and against war. All the major blocs of countries, all governments, even all eminent statesmen are attempting to put themselves forward as the most resolute opponents of war and the most sincere supporters of peaceful co-existence among nations. The Russian-Bolshevik bloc in particular is making strenuous efforts in this regard.

The issue of war and peace has become one of the central political and ideological issues in the world today.

The Ukrainian people's position in principle on the issue of war and peace is best reflected by the ideology of the Ukrainian revolutionary liberation movement, which has the active support and sympathy of tens of millions of Ukrainians throughout Ukraine.

One of the major goals of the Ukrainian revolutionary liberation movement, with the Supreme Ukrainian Liberation Council (UHVR) at its head, is to rid international relations of all forms of imperialism. (The Ukrainian revolutionary liberation movement defines imperialism as any policy on the part of the dominant group of stronger nations to subjugate or deliberately subordinate weaker nations in order to attain territorial, strategic, economic, political or other advantages. It does not matter which social classes or segments of society are used to implement this policy or which ideas—no matter how apparently progressive they may be—are used to conceal its imperialist character.) The Ukrainian revolutionary liberation movement regards imperialism as the main source of all the international problems and armed conflicts that have been causing mankind so much misfortune since time immemorial. The ultimate effects of all forms of imperialism are negative, not only for subject peoples, but for dominant ones as well. The Ukrainian revolutionary liberation movement believes that all the peoples of the world should see their objectives not in conquest, not in imperialism, but in a peaceful effort to achieve the best in the realms of material and spiritual culture and to conduct the internal affairs of their own countries in the best possible manner. If only mankind were to pursue this policy, it would be well on its way to achieving true progress of a kind unparallelled in human history.

The most pronounced, most terrible and thus most shameful manifestation of imperialism, its very source and constant companion, has always been the almost incessant pattern of war between nations. In the past and particularly in our own era, wars have been mankind's greatest source of misfortune. They take their toll in millions of deaths and injuries and bring in their wake unparallelled destruction of human achievements and objects of spiritual value, material devastation and indescribable suffering to hundreds of millions of people. In this regard, mankind has not made the slightest progress. Today, just as thousands of years ago, relations among nations are governed by the brutish law of physical force, which states that might makes right. The Ukrainian revolutionary liberation movement regards war as the most shameful remnant of barbarity in the world today, the darkest stain on our civilization, the greatest evil in our world. The Ukrainian revolutionary liberation movement most resolutely condemns and rejects war as a means of conducting national policy. All nations, all the progressive forces of humanity, should make every possible effort to put an end to this tragic, shameful practice. The Ukrainian liberation movement will always be in the front ranks of the forces fighting to rid the world of war. The Ukrainian revolutionary liberation movement regards the prohibition of war, its condemnation and rejection by all nations of the world, as the first and most important step toward the suppression of imperialism in general.

Since it opposes all forms of imperialism and war, the Ukrainian revolutionary liberation movement supports unconditionally the idea of peaceful co-existence, sincere, profound friendship and the closest possible co-operation among all the peoples of the world in the context of independence for all national states, universal respect for sovereignty and complete equality of all peoples. The Ukrainian revolutionary liberation movement believes that lasting peace is inextricably linked to the concept of independence for all the nations of the world. A peace of this type is the goal for which the Ukrainian liberation movement is striving. The Ukrainian liberation movement regards this type of peace as a truly great achievement, mankind's true source of happiness.

The stand of the Ukrainian revolutionary liberation movement on the issue of war and peace has met with great approbation from the broadest masses of the Ukrainian people—peasants, workers and the working intelligentsia. And for good reason. The centuries-old national subjugation of Ukraine, the age-old oppression and exploitation of the Ukrainian people, the brutal torments which they have had to endure throughout their history are all the direct result of the dominance of imperialism in international relations and, more specifically, the direct result of the imperialism of Ukraine's neighbours—Russia, Poland, Austria-Hungary, Germany, Romania and others. Nowhere in Europe, and perhaps in the whole world, has a subject people suffered as much from imperialism as has the Ukrainian people. Imperialist wars, in particular, have inflicted great suffering on the Ukrainian people. Ever since Cossack regiments were compelled to take part in the wars of Muscovite tsars (in the second half of the seventeenth century) to the present day, the Ukrainian people have been dying and suffering injury by the millions every ten or twenty years for the imperialist interests of their oppressors. And what devastation those wars have inflicted upon Ukraine! During the past half-century alone, Ukraine has twice been the major battlefield of world imperialism: in 1914–20 and in 1941–5, during the First and Second World Wars. Ukraine emerged from both these wars more devasted and pillaged than any other country on earth. Several more decades will be required to heal the wounds inflicted on the Ukrainian people by the Second World War. And now another war is looming. The Ukrainian people know, perhaps better than anyone else, what war is and what horrors it brings. That is why they condemn it so strongly; that is why they are so determined to struggle for the prohibition of war, for the rejection of war as a means of conducting national policy. They will continue their struggle until that noble cause gains total victory, until that progressive idea of modern mankind is totally victorious.

The Stand of the Ukrainian People on the Issue of Peace and War under Current Historical Conditions. Just and Unjust Peace. Just and Unjust War

While in principle the Ukrainian people resolutely oppose imperialism and war and fully support the ideas of peaceful, friendly co-operation among peoples and a strong and lasting peace throughout the world, they are fully aware to what extent existing conditions permit them to take such a principled approach to *every* war and *every* peace.

Current international relations are still largely characterized by the following two qualities. First, many countries continue to pursue imperialist goals in their policies, although, for purposes of propaganda, they diligently mask these goals with seemingly lofty and progressive ideas and a clamorous, very subtly elaborated ideological and propagandistic phraseology. Second, many nations are still subjugated in various ways by other nations.

More specifically, relations in Eastern and South-Eastern Europe and in a large part of Asia are characterized by the brutal enslavement of old, civilized nations by the Muscovite-Bolshevik imperialists. Since 1920 Ukraine, Belorussia, Georgia, Armenia, Azerbaidzhan, the peoples of Central Asia and the Volga region have been groaning under the Muscovite-Boshevik yoke in the so-called Union of Soviet Socialist Republics. In 1940 the nations of the Baltic region also came under the Soviet yoke. As a result of the Second World War, Poland, Czechoslovakia, Romania, Bulgaria, Hungary and East Germany have, for all practical purposes, come under Muscovite-Bolshevik occupation. In all these countries, the Muscovite-Bolshevik imperialists are pursuing a policy of brutal national oppression and plunder, savage terror and merciless extermination of all patriotic and freedom-loving individuals. The peoples of this part of the world and their toiling masses are deprived of all freedom; they are placed into the heavy shackles of national, political and social slavery and thrust into extreme economic misery. Under the guise of socialism, a new oppressive and exploitative system has been established or is being established at a rapid tempo, a system whose like has never been known in human history. Many peoples are facing the threat of total national destruction.

This lamentable, reactionary system of relations among nations is the basis of the present peace in the world, particularly in Europe. This peace, so typical of imperialism, is based not on the lofty principles of freedom for all nations and international justice, but on the brutish principle of naked physical force, on the right of the strong to treat the weaker however he chooses.

The Bolshevik bloc claims to be fighting for the preservation of this peace. And the Western bloc, too, is not loath to maintain it.

Clearly, a peace built upon such unjust and reactionary foundations is an extremely unjust peace, a reactionary peace. It does not protect the interests or satisfy the needs of *all* nations, but only of *some* nations, of the dominant nations, or, more precisely, of the ruling circles of those nations. It denies and tramples upon all the lofty ideas and watchwords of the progressive segment of humanity.

In particular, the present peace is extremely unjust to Ukraine, this large European nation of forty million people. This peace *legitimizes* and *preserves* the Muscovite-Bolshevik imperialists' domination of Ukraine and gives them a *free hand* in implementing their oppressive, exploitative policy with respect to Ukraine and the Ukrainian people. Under the conditions engendered by the totalitarian, terroristic Bolshevik regime, the Ukrainian people have no opportunity to wage a peaceful, legal struggle for their own national, social and human rights. Neither can the Ukrainian people rely upon the peaceful measures of international diplomacy to put an end to their age-old subjugation. As all historical experience demostrates, such peaceful measures, even when applied, never produce the desired results. And certainly one cannot expect them to succeed with regard to the Muscovite-Bolshevik oppressors. To the Ukrainian people, suffering under the heavy yoke of Bolshevik Moscow, the present peace means only one thing: increased oppression and exploitation, continued extermination of millions of patriots and decent individuals, further persecution, misery and suffering, more extensive Russification and the total destruction of the Ukrainian people as a separate national entity.

For this reason, the Ukrainian people *cannot support* the peace that now exists. For this reason, the Ukrainian people are *opposed* to the present peace, for it is an extremely unjust peace, a peace which only serves to free the hands of the Muscovite-Bolshevik imperialists to implement their criminal policy of oppression and exploitation of Ukraine and all the other nations subjugated by them. It is a peace which stands as a cynical mockery of all the lofty ideals of modern humanity.

The Ukrainian people are categorically in favour of peace, but of a just peace, a peace built upon the principle of equal justice for all nations, including the Ukrainian nation. The Ukrainian people are categorically in favour of peace, but a peace based on the independence and sovereignty of the Ukrainian national state and of the states of all the nations of the world. Imperialist peace, a peace built upon violence, a peace such as the one that exists today, is condemned by the Ukrainian people now and always will be in the future.

Furthermore, as long as imperialism exists, not all wars are criminal or deserving of condemnation.

It is apparent to all that the imperialist war unleashed by Hitler in 1939 was an extremely unjust war, a truly criminal war, one which merited the most severe censure. All freedom-loving nations and progressive forces of the world branded it as such. But, on the other hand, the war launched after the end of the Second World War by the Indonesian people against Dutch domination for the purpose of attaining independence was of a totally different character. [1] The Indonesian people longed for independence. They had as much right to it as any other nation in the world. But the imperialist circles of Holland were not prepared voluntarily to satisfy the just demands of the Indonesians. No avenues of peaceful struggle yielded the Indonesians any significant results, nor did they promise to do so in the future. What were the Indonesian people to do in such circumstances? There was only one way out: to respond to Holland's imperialist policy, founded on brutal violence, with a violent struggle for the sake of gaining the rights they deserved, for the sake of establishing a better and more just national and social order in their part of the world. Can a war of this type be called criminal? Not at all. This is a just war. A war of this type, which is the only measure possible under the circumstances, hastens the destruction of the forces of reaction and the victory of the ideas of freedom, justice and progress.

The partisan and underground struggle now being waged by the Ukrainian people against the Muscovite-Bolshevik occupying power is another such war. Since no opportunity exists in the USSR to wage a legal, peaceful struggle, the Ukrainian people can fight for their rights, or the cause of freedom and justice, only by means of armed struggle, only by way of a partisan and underground war. This war is the only means by which Ukrainian patriots can protect themselves from death in Bolshevik prisons and concentration camps, the only means by which the Ukrainian people can oppose the criminal, anti-national, anti-popular Bolshevik policy, the only means by which they can prepare for the fulfillment, at the appropriate moment, of their age-old dream of national and social liberty. Furthermore, the Ukrainian people's war of liberation has had an enormous uplifting and revolutionizing effect, both morally and ideologically, on all the other peoples of the USSR, on all those subjugated by the Soviet Union. Through their partisan and underground liberation struggle against the Muscovite-Bolshevik oppressors, the Ukrainian people are rendering a great service to the human ideals of liberty, international justice and human progress in general.

As long as imperialism exists, each war must be judged according to its objectives. Any war waged for the purpose of subjugation of other nations is, undeniably, an unjust war and thus particularly criminal. Any war waged for national and social liberation, any war launched and waged by subject peoples that have exhausted all peaceful means of struggle or become convinced of the ineffectiveness of these peaceful means for the betterment of their fate, is undeniably just, as long as imperialism continues to exist. All the progressive forces of mankind welcome such wars and support them in every way.

Given the conditions of imperialism, anyone who condemns all wars only supports the forces of imperialism and reaction. Were the subject peoples of the world to be deprived of the opportunity to wage armed struggles, they would never be able to break the chains in which they are placed by brutal, savage and well-armed imperialist powers. Imperialism would reign victorious. Progress would be halted throughout the world; violence would hold full sway over justice.

Under the present circumstances, the Ukrainian people condemn and reject only unjust, imperialist wars. They regard wars of liberation as a completely legitimate means for subject peoples to defend themselves against oppression and plunder and to struggle for their just goals of liberation—the independence of their national states, sovereignty, equality with other nations of the world, the right to choose freely their own system of government, the destruction of imperialism and the reconstruction of the international order on a more just foundation.

The subjugated, forty-million-strong Ukrainian nation rejects Tolstoy's philosophy of "non-resistance to evil," a philosophy which condemns all violence.[2] The Ukrainian people refuse meekly to await their slaughter at the hands of their oppressors, like a herd of defenseless sheep. The Ukrainian people are convinced that a strong fist is a subject people's best defence against the rapacious claws of imperialists. When a bandit puts a knife to your throat, your only means of defence is to strike the knife from his hand. Anyone who refuses to use armed struggle as a form of defence only strengthens the dominance of imperialism in the world.

The Ukrainian people also reject Gandhi's[3] tactic of using only peaceful means of struggle. They reject it because, in the face of imperialist greed, it does not produce the desired results. They reject it because it is totally inapplicable in the conditions created by the Bolshevik regime in the USSR, where there are no democratic rights and no opportunity to wage a legal defence, a legal struggle.

The Ukrainian people will regard all wars as criminal only when the world is built on the principle of independence for all nations that desire it, when relations among peoples are truly based on friendship, mutual respect and equality and are governed by justice and civilized conduct. When that comes to pass, when the world is no longer divided into the subjugated and the subjugators, there will no longer be any reason for international wars. At that time, *all* wars between nations will be truly criminal.

At present, the Ukrainian people will gladly welcome any war waged against the Muscovite-Bolshevik imperialists if it is waged for the sake of the national and social liberation of the Ukrainian and other peoples subjugated by the Soviets and of their toiling masses, if it is waged for the sake of restructuring the USSR on the principle of independence for the states of the peoples subjugated by the Soviets and of their sovereign right to choose the system of government in their own countries. The Ukrainian people will welcome any war of this type as a just war of liberation waged by the freedom-loving peoples of the world against the most brutal oppressors and exploiters in the world, as a war waged by the world forces of progress for the destruction of the darkest forces of reaction to be found anywhere on earth. The Ukrainian people will gladly ally themselves with the forces waging such a war and co-operate with them in their struggle against the Bolshevik tyrants.

Any war against the Muscovite-Bolshevik oppressors which is waged for other purposes, any war in which the just national and social demands of the Ukrainian people and the other subject peoples of the USSR are ignored or denied, will be regarded by the Ukrainian people only as a new bloodbath conducted by imperialist powers opposed to liberation, a bloodbath from which the Ukrainian people can expect no positive results. The Ukrainian people will attempt to make use of a war of this type for their own liberation by developing and expanding *their own* forces. The attitude of the Ukrainian people to the opponents of the USSR in a war of this type will depend upon what position they assume with regard to the cause of Ukrainian independence.

The Ukrainian people are very much aware of all the horrors of the approaching war. They know that this war, like the others, will cause deaths in the millions at the front and even more terrible devastation. The blame for this new human tragedy will rest squarely on the Muscovite-Bolshevik imperialists. But the Ukrainian people are also aware that a peace entailing the continued subjugation of Ukraine by the Muscovite-Bolshevik oppressors brings them even greater tragedy: continued extermination of hundreds of thousands and millions of Ukraine's noblest patriots in Bolshevik prisons and concentration camps; continued terrible exploitation of their labour and physical strength; further misery and hunger and total national destruction. Unfortunately, the Ukrainian people do not have a choice between the joys of peace and the sorrows of war. Unfortunately, such is not the lot of the Ukrainian people. The Ukrainian people can only choose between the horrors of Muscovite-Bolshevik subjugation in conditions of peace or the horrors of war. For this reason, to the extent that the approaching war gives the Ukrainian people hope for liberation from under the Muscovite-Bolshevik yoke, *they await rather than oppose that war.* Since without war no hope exists in the foreseeable future for any betterment of the fate of the toiling masses and entire peoples subjugated by the Soviets, the Ukrainian people *are prepared to endure the horrors of another war* in order to liberate themselves as quickly as possible from the horrors of Muscovite-Bolshevik slavery. That is how much the Ukrainian people hate Muscovite-Bolshevik oppression; that is how much they love freedom and are filled with resolve to gain themselves a better future.

The Role of the Bolshevik USSR in Preparing the Ground for the New War

The Muscovite-Bolshevik imperialists are attempting to shift the full blame for the present international situation and, in particular, for the war in Korea, onto the Anglo-American bloc. Bolshevik propaganda is attempting to demonstrate in every possible way that only the ruling circles of Western countries desire and are instigating war, while the government of the USSR pursues a totally peaceful policy.

Instead, the exact opposite is true. The example of Korea clearly shows who is really endeavouring to unleash a new world war. Let us consider two facts.

Fact number one: on 25 June 1950, military action broke out in Korea. On the same day, North Korean armies occupied a significant portion of South Korean territory. During July and August, the North Korean army launched such a broad offensive that it almost succeeded in taking over all of Korea.

Considering this fact, can we really believe that the war was planned and launched by South Korea? Is is possible that North Korea could so quickly and successfully have repelled the enemy attack were it really, as it claims, "free of any desire for war" and "taken by surprise" while engaged in "peaceful work"? The experience of all past wars tells us otherwise. At the beginning of any war the advantage is always held by the attacker. The war in Korea is no exception to the general laws that have governed wars throughout history. The facts are far more convincing than any Bolshevik propaganda. The circumstances in which the Korean war broke out, the course of that war, the confusion and consternation that it evoked in the West, the widely recognized mendacity and cynicism of Bolshevik propaganda—all point to the fact that the war in Korea was planned and unleashed by the Muscovite-Bolshevik imperialists through their North Korean hirelings.

Fact number two: in the winter of this year, the Asian member states of the United Nations put forward a proposal to call a conference of seven states for the purpose of finding a peaceful solution to the Korean conflict. The Western states agreed to this proposal on one condition: that all military operations in Korea be suspended before the conference begins. The Muscovite-Bolshevik imperialists and their satellites rejected this Western condition. While they pretend to accept the proposal to call a conference, they refuse to agree that the cessation of all hostilities should be a precondition to the convening of the conference.

Again the question arises: is it possible that the side which truly desires a peaceful solution to the conflict would reject the possibility of such a solution for such an insignificant reason? Is it possible that the side desirous of peace would make such a provocative, obviously unacceptable demand as the demand that the conference be called without suspending the war itself?

The stance of the Bolshevik imperialists and their satellites with regard to the Korean conflict proves only one thing—that the Bolshevik criminals not only do not wish a peaceful solution to the Korean conflict but, on the contrary, are attempting to fan the flames of war. For this reason, they have sent their Chinese puppets into the Korean war. For this reason they are, for all practical purposes, rejecting all attempts to find a peaceful solution to the Korean problem.

These facts clearly demonstrate the following points:

1. The chief instigators of war at the present time are not the ruling circles of Western countries—not Truman, not Acheson,[4] not Marshall,[5] not even Churchill—but the Muscovite-Boshevik leaders—Stalin, Molotov, Malenkov[6] and the whole Kremlin Politburo.

2. The most reactionary, brutal and aggressive, and thus the most menacing force in the world today is the imperialism of Bolshevik Moscow, which seeks to dominate the whole world.

3. The chief enemy of the Ukrainian people, of all the peoples of the Soviet Union and all the peoples of the world is Muscovite-Bolshevik imperialism, which seeks to place the whole world in the fetters of na-

tional, political, social and economic subjugation and is prepared, for the sake of achieving this goal, to precipitate a new world-wide blood-bath.

The war in Korea has unmasked the Muscovite-Bolshevik tyrants and exposed their true predatory nature to the world. It has exposed them as instigators of war who lust for new blood in total disregard of the suf-ferings and misfortune of humanity.

Spurred on by their victory over Nazi Germany and Japan and by their present military superiority over a weakened West, they now want to extend their regime of terror, violence, oppression and exploitation throughout Europe and Asia.

This is the true role of the Muscovite-Bolshevik clique in the prepara-tion of the new world war; these are the true aims of their policy.

The Mendacity of Bolshevik Peace Propaganda

In the light of our earlier statements about the true role of the Bol-shevik imperialists in preparing the ground for a new war, it becomes clearly apparent that all the Bolsheviks' loud hue and cry in favour of peace and against war is simply a treacherous, brutally cynical attempt to deceive the toiling masses and the peoples of the USSR and of the whole world. Like all aggressors, the Muscovite-Bolshevik instigators of war wish to shift all the blame for it onto their opponents. Because the Muscovite-Bolshevik oppressors know how much all people hate imperialist wars, they take great pains to mask their intentions. All their hue and cry in favour of peace serves as a smokescreen to conceal their bloody, criminal intentions.

But the Ukrainian people will not allow themselves to be duped. Nei-ther, we believe, will the other peoples of the USSR or those of the so-called people's republics. We are equally certain that the free peoples of the world will also resist this deception.

All the peoples of the world can see how, behind the symbol of the in-nocent dove used by the ''peace-lovers'' of the Kremlin to mask their true intentions, lurks the Muscovite-Bolshevik predator, with its sharp teeth and wide-open, bloodthirsty jaws ready to grab the whole world by the throat. In this case, it seeks to bathe in fresh blood—not only the blood of its subject peoples, but the blood of all the peoples of the world.

The Probable Anti-Liberation Character of the Western Bloc's Involvement in the Third World War

The war being prepared by the Bolshevik aggressors, and already unleashed by them in Korea, will be totally imperialist in character. On this score the Ukrainian people have not the slightest doubt. As indicated earlier, the Muscovite-Bolsheviks' goal in this war will be the subjugation of new countries, particularly in Europe and Asia.

What has not yet been clarified is the role that will be played in this war by the Western opponents of the USSR.

The precise, official plans of the Western countries for their struggle against the Russian Bolshevik bloc are not yet known. There are, however, certain indications which allow us to draw some conclusions on this matter.

The first such indication is the generally negative attitude of American, as well as British, political thought to the concept of independence and sovereignty for all the peoples of the world. Most American policy-makers oppose the division of the world into independent national states. Many of these policy-makers regard President Wilson's assertion in 1918 of the principle of self-determination for all peoples as a tragic mistake.[7] The ideal of American and British politicians is the creation of large blocs of states—for example, a United Europe, or even simply a United States of the whole world. For this reason, the idea of restructuring the USSR into independent national states is not especially popular in American or British political circles. These circles tend to favour maintaining the integrity of the present-day Soviet Union. They wish to transform the internal political, social and economic order inside the USSR, but not to restructure the Bolshevik prison of nations into national states.

We shall not, at present, take the time to prove that this view is greatly mistaken and, given the concrete conditions in the USSR, downright reactionary. Readers of our underground literature can find discussions of this subject in many of our other underground publications. We shall only point out that the chief error of the American policy-makers lies in the fact that, viewing the world with American eyes, they underestimate the importance of the national factor in Europe and Asia, that is, in those regions where this matter is most urgent and where it cannot be ignored or shunted aside by anyone who wants to see his policy succeed.

The second indicator which allows us to draw certain conclusions with regard to the goals of the Western countires in a future war with the USSR is the active support given by American leaders to those Soviet émigré groups,[8] particularly Russian ones, whose programs are most in line with current American ideology, that is, groups whose stated goal is to transform the internal political structure of the USSR (replacing dictatorship with democracy and complete socialization with private initiative and private property) while preserving the territorial integrity of the present-day Soviet state. These groups oppose the idea of restructuring the USSR into independent national states. Kerensky,[9] who is well known from the days of the Russian Revolution of 1917–18, is receiving particular sympathy and support from the present ruling circles of the United States. Kerensky's position with respect to the national question in the USSR is as follows: after the overthrow of the Soviet regime, an all-Russian (that is, representing all the territories of the USSR) Constituent Assembly should be convened and given the power to decide the fate and legal status of individual non-Russian peoples in the USSR. Obviously Kerensky, a Russian great-power imperialist well known to the Ukrainian people from the period of 1917–18, does not envisage this all-Russian Constituent Assembly approving the separation of Ukraine, Belorussia, the Caucasus and other non-Russian territories from Russia. By putting forth a seemingly democratic formula which grants the assembly the exclusive right to determine the future regime of the present-day USSR, Kerensky hopes to conceal a new Russian occupation of non-Russian territories or to gain sufficient time for such an occupation. In 1917 Kerensky agreed to recognize the Ukrainian Central Rada and the General Secretariat as autonomous governing bodies in Ukraine only under the pressure of internal difficulties in Russia and after waging a protracted political battle with the Rada. And now American leaders would like to see this same Kerensky as leader of all the peoples and political forces striving to put an end to Muscovite-Boshevik domination in the USSR. They would like to see the Ukrainian liberation movement come under his leadership.

Given this thrust in present-day Anglo-American policy, the Ukrainian people have every reason to expect that in the future war between the Muscovite-Bolshevik and Anglo-American blocs, the Anglo-American bloc will also be a force opposed to liberation.

It may be true that the Anglo-American bloc has no aggressive intentions toward the Soviet Union or, more specifically, toward Ukraine. But if it supports forces that take a hostile attitude toward the liberation of Ukraine and strive to maintain, in one way or another, Russia's colonial rule over non-Russian territories and peoples, then its policy toward the peoples of the USSR and, above all, the forty-million-strong Ukrainian people, automatically takes on an anti-liberation character. If the Ukrainian people and the other peoples of the USSR cannot expect that during the next war the Anglo-American bloc will take a sympathetic view of their struggle for independence, if they can expect only that the Anglo-American bloc will abet their renewed subjugation by a new breed of Russian great-power imperialists, then they can only assume that the stance of the Western bloc in the coming war is likely to be anti-liberation in character.

In such an event, the Ukrainian people and all the other subject peoples of the USSR will not welcome this war as a war of liberation; they will not regard the Western opponents of the USSR as their true friends.

In such an event, the Ukrainian people, and, we expect, all the other non-Russian subject peoples of the USSR, will regard this war as another war of world imperialism, a war in which the national and social aspirations of the peoples subjugated by the Soviet Union will be attained only to the extent that they themselves bring these things about.

The Main Tasks Facing the Ukrainian People at the Present Time

The main tasks facing the Ukrainian people at the present time are as follows:

1. To resist being deceived by any form of imperialist propaganda and particularly that of the Muscovite-Bolshevik occupying power; to develop and maintain their own independent view of current international relations; always to ground that view in the just liberation interests of the Ukrainian and other peoples subjugated by the Soviets.

2. To resist being turned into mere tools of the imperialist policies of either of the competing blocs; to resist being turned into mere cannon fodder or labour power exploited by the forces of imperialism for their own victory.

3. To preserve the *independent* character of Ukrainian liberation policy and its *pre-eminence*.

4. To continue their efforts to preserve and extend their own liberation force on their native soil, in the knowledge that it is the very basis of Ukrainian liberation policy, the only hope of victory in the liberation struggle. In this regard, first and foremost to continue their efforts to preserve and extend the Ukrainian liberation underground in the knowledge that it is the only active, independent political and military insurgent Ukrainian force in Ukraine; the sole organized, experienced, hardened political and military nucleus of the Ukrainian liberation movement in occupied Ukraine; the *only* force that can make use of *any* war to attain the full national and social liberation of the Ukrainian people.

The Task Facing the Ukrainian People at the Present Time with Regard to the Muscovite-Bolshevik Imperialists' Plans for War and Their Ostensible Peace Propaganda

The Ukrainian people must respond to the actions of the Muscovite-Bolshevik imperialists in preparing and unleashing a new world war by increasing their efforts to undermine the military and economic power of the Muscovite-Bolshevik empire.

This struggle should be waged by means of secret, individual sabotage of production. The Ukrainian people must do their best to hamper the fulfillment of production plans, to resist complying with agreements regarding socialist competition, to avoid participating in the Stakhanov movement, to resist committing themselves to above-normal production quotas, to disrupt the delivery of agricultural supplies, to sabotage the threshing of grain, to take the fullest possible advantage of food rations from collective farms and of other goods provided by the state, secretly to damage machinery and tools in industry, the transportation system and the like.

To the greatest possible extent, the Ukrainian people should create difficulties for the Muscovite-Bolshevik occupying power in order to prevent the Soviets from easily carrying out their criminal plans for preparing a new war. At present, this is the most urgent task of Ukrainian peasants, workers and intellectuals.

By means of this secret, individual resistance on the part of every nationally conscious Ukrainian peasant, worker and intellectual, the Ukrainian people can strike the Muscovite-Bolshevik oppressors a serious blow. The lesser the military and economic power of the USSR, the less bloody will be the future war, the fewer the losses the Ukrainian people will sustain on imperialist battle fronts and in their own liberation struggle.

To the Bolsheviks' false propaganda for peace and their "peaceful" activities, the Ukrainian people must respond with a similar kind of general, secret resistance. They should avoid taking part in any campaigns, particularly campaigns for "peace," and, so far as possible, avoid participating in "peace" meetings, conferences, congresses and the like.

Every nationally conscious Ukrainian man or woman who understands the falseness of Bolshevik "peace" propaganda should, within the circle of his or her most trusted friends and associates, expose the imperialist character of the policy pursued by the Muscovite-Bolshevik oppressors and their true role as the chief instigators of war at the present time. They should indicate the main tasks of the Ukrainian people with regard to national liberation.

Educational work of this nature, even if it is conducted exclusively in circles of most trusted friends, will aid immeasurably in nurturing an anti-Bolshevik consciousness among the Ukrainian people. As a result, it will assist in extending the active struggle for Ukraine's national and social liberation from the Muscovite-Bolshevik yoke.

To prevent the Bolshevik oppressors from deceiving the people, to expose the true nature of the "peace-loving" Bolshevik aggressors, is the other urgent task facing Ukrainian patriots at the present time.

The Tasks Facing the Ukrainian People in the Event of the Outbreak of the Third World War

In the event of the outbreak of the Third World War, or any other war involving the Bolshevik USSR, the historic task facing the Ukrainian people will be to make use of this war for the purpose of attaining their complete national and social liberation and overthrowing Muscovite-Bolshevik rule in Ukraine and in the whole of the USSR.

The chief responsibility for making use of the Third World War to attain the complete national and social liberation of the Ukrainian people rests on the shoulders of the Ukrainian liberation movement in Ukraine and its leading body, the Ukrainian liberation underground. For this reason, the chief tasks of the underground at the present time are to preserve its ability to function and to prepare for the decisive events that are approaching. At present the Ukrainian people should give the Ukrainian liberation underground even greater and more generous support than they have in the past. Given the status of the cause of Ukrainian liberation in the international arena, the only realistic guarantee that our liberation struggle will succeed in the context of a new world war, even if it should be a war that is imperialist on both sides, is a sufficiently strong and capable underground in Ukraine.

The complete overthrow of Muscovite-Bolshevik rule in Ukraine, the complete national and social liberation of the Ukrainian people from the Muscovite-Bolshevik yoke, should be the goal of every Ukrainian who finds himself in the ranks of the Soviet armed forces—every Ukrainian soldier, sergeant, officer and general, every Ukrainian man sent by the occupying power to the imperialist battle front. The success of the liberation struggle waged by the Ukrainian people in the context of the next world war will depend in great measure on what Ukrainians in the ranks of the Soviet army, navy and air force are fighting for. Ukrainians fighting in the Soviet army will be in a position to strike a decisive blow at the Muscovite-Bolshevik war machine, the Muscovite-Bolshevik empire.

In order to attain the complete overthrow of Muscovite-Bolshevik rule in Ukraine and the complete liberation of the Ukrainian people from the Muscovite-Bolshevik yoke in the context of the new world war, it will be necessary for every Ukrainian man and woman working on the Soviet home front to struggle with courage and dedication. This includes every Ukrainian worker in factories, pits and mines, the transportation and communication systems and the system of supply; it includes all engineers and office workers, all collective workers and the whole Ukrainian intelligentsia. A massive, secret and—should conditions prove favourable—even open resistance on the part of Ukrainian workers will constitute a blow to the Muscovite-Bolshevik military and state machine no less powerful than that of Ukrainian men in the ranks of the Soviet army.

As the leading body of the Ukrainian revolutionary liberation struggle, the Supreme Ukrainian Liberation Council, along with other leading bodies of the Ukrainian liberation movement, will issue the Ukrainian people precise instructions at the appropriate time on how to conduct their struggle in the context of the next world war. Every Ukrainian should respond to all the appeals of the leading bodies of the Ukrainian liberation movement with precision, courage and dedication. This is one of the major preconditions of our victory.

Every Ukrainian man and woman should stand ready to respond to the call of the Supreme Ukrainian Liberation Council for a nation-wide uprising to bring about the ultimate overthrow of Muscovite-Bolshevik rule, to oust the Bolshevik oppressors from Ukraine once and for all.

The Ukrainian people should give a resolute and fitting response to any Russian political force which attempts to keep Ukraine in ''federation'' with Russia. The Ukrainian people must not forget that any federation with that rapacious, intrinsically imperialist country will always mean the occupation of Ukraine by Russia, colonial oppression and exploitation of the Ukrainian people by Russian imperialists. All our historical experience has shown this to be so.

*   *   *

The approaching world war will probably be waged in conditions more favourable to the Ukrainian people than either of the two previous wars. The question of partitioning the Russian-Bolshevik empire will *inevitably* arise. The Western powers, which in both previous wars were allied with the Russian imperialists and thus defended the Russian empire of the day, now find themselves mortally threatened by that same Russian imperialism; they are now the objects of its expansionist aims. The source of Soviet Russian imperialism, its very basis, lies in the fact that Russia is a conglomerate state. For this reason, the problem of *putting an end* to aggressive Russian imperialism must inevitably, sooner or later, bring up the issue of *partitioning* the conglomerate, centralized, despotic, totalitarian Russian state. In addition, with regard to their national renaissance, and particularly their political development as a nation, the Ukrainian people are now at a much higher level than they were in 1917–20, or even in 1939–44. All these facts make the goal of liberating Ukraine in the context of the new world war completely realistic.

Nevertheless, the Ukrainian people must not allow themselves to become complacent. Our fate lies in our own hands. Whether we achieve liberation in the context of the new world war will depend entirely upon our own ability to wage a sufficiently extensive and determined struggle against the Muscovite-Bolshevik occupying power for the achievement of our own aims. This struggle alone will determine whether we continue to exist as slaves or attain our freedom.

We believe in the freedom-loving spirit of the Ukrainian people, in their hatred of the Muscovite-Bolshevik yoke. We believe in the true desire of the Ukrainian popular masses for national and social liberation and a truly liberated, prosperous and happy life, free of any ''guardians'' or ''liberators,'' foreign masters or overseers.

We believe that the Ukrainian people will acquit themselves with honour in a test which history may set them in the near future.

Source: This article was written after the outbreak of the Korean War and published in Ukraine in the bulletin *Biuro Informatsii Ukrainskoi Holovnoi Vyzvolnoi Rady (UHVR)* 4, no. 9 (May 1951): 2–25. It was reprinted abroad in the following publications: *Suchasna Ukraina* (Munich), nos. 24 and 25 (1953); *Ukrainskyi samostiinyk*, Munich, nos. 47, 48, 49, 50 (1953); and P. Poltava, *Zbirnyk pidpilnykh pysan* (Munich 1959), 221–41.

NOTES

1. The Republic of Indonesia was established in August 1945. This led to warfare with the Netherlands which lasted until December 1949, when Indonesian sovereignty was finally achieved.
2. Leo Tolstoy (1828–1910): Russian writer and philosopher. About 1876, he underwent a conversion to belief in Christian love, non-resistance to evil, and the simple faith of the peasants.
3. Mohandas Karamchand Gandhi (1869–1948): Indian leader called the Mahatma (great-souled). He was so widely revered that he could exact po-

litical concessions by threatening "fasts unto death."

4. Dean Gooderham Acheson (1893–1971): U.S. Secretary of State (1949–53).

5. George C. Marshall (1880–1959): American general, Secretary of State (1947–9), author of the "Marshall Plan," and Secretary of Defence (1950–51).

6. G.M. Malenkov (1902–): Soviet premier, immediate successor to Stalin in 1953.

7. Reference is to Wilson's "Fourteen Points," which he considered necessary for implementing a peace settlement. At the Paris Peace Conference Wilson worked for a new world society governed by "self-determination of peoples." One of his strongest opponents was Henry Cabot Lodge (1850–1924), U.S. Senator from Massachusetts.

8. Reference is to *Sovet Osvobozhdeniia Narodov Rosii* (Council for the Liberation of the Peoples of Russia), headed by A.F. Kerensky; the American Committee for the Liberation of the Peoples of Russia (AKONR); and the Co-ordinating Centre for Anti-Bolshevik Struggle (KTsAB).

9. A.F. Kerensky (1881–1970): Premier of the Russian Provisional Government (July–November 1917).

OUR TACTICS WITH REGARD TO THE RUSSIAN PEOPLE

D. Shakhai

This article is Chapter Two of the author's work, "Problems Relating to the Struggle for an Independent United Ukrainian State," written in 1943. The work was a memorandum intended for the leading cadres of the underground; above the title was written, "Not for general publication." The article is interesting for two reasons. First, it is a rare document of the discussion that took place at this time among the leading circles of the Ukrainian underground concerning the re-evaluation of the liberation movement's policy and the determination of its strategy and tactics. Second, in terms of its theoretical basis, the article is generally consistent with later writings by leading publicists of the underground, particularly those of O. Hornovy, U. Kuzhil, P. Poltava and others. Thus, the author was among those who influenced the formation of the political thought of the Ukrainian underground.

The memorandum begins with the following words: "The Russian people are the human framework that supports the whole structure of the USSR. To shake this framework, to pierce it by creating ideological and political diversion, to confound it, disorienting some, turning others against Bolshevism and immobilizing the rest, is to pull it down. This is what we must do first of all. This is essential to us in the first, decisive stage of our struggle. To bring down this framework is the goal of our tactics under the present circumstances." (Sh. D., Shliakh, 1943)

Our first goal is to fulfill the basic tactical requirement which we examined in Chapter One, that is, the establishment of a single, all-Ukrainian non-partisan leadership to represent the United Ukrainian Popular Front (we stress, popular). Without this, the attainment of our goal through an autonomous struggle of the Ukrainian people for their own state is unthinkable at the present time (earlier, while discussing the first precondition for the attainment of this goal, we spoke of the absolute necessity of a strong, creditable party to direct the struggle). The second basic requirement is to develop *a just and adroit policy with regard to the Russian people*. This policy must be based on the following principle: *we are not pursuing a constructive goal with regard to the Russian people, but a destructive goal with regard to the Muscovite-Bolshevik empire*; in the destruction of that empire, the Russian people must play out their historical role. This principle requires that we take a suitable political approach to the Russian people, the approach of making use of the Russian people to achieve our goals. If we fail to do this, our struggle will be either totally impossible or doomed to failure.

To begin, we must examine the problem in principle, look at the internal and external situation of the USSR and consider some historical analogies.

On the basis of a sober assessment of existing conditions and relative strengths, we must, first of all, determine for ourselves (and not only for ourselves) the basic direction of our policy (taking into account all past and present developments and their consequences and foreseeing and anticipating those of the future). Are we to continue along the narrow path of inflaming Ukrainian-Russian and Ukrainian-Polish national antagonisms and act as a purely nationalistic and narrow, local force, regardless of our slogan about "the peoples of the East," or do we think in terms of a struggle having a "USSR-wide" significance from the ideological and political (tactical) point of view, in terms of an orientation on and support for a socio-political and national revolution in the entire USSR, and Russia first of all, basing ourselves on all the conditions favouring this? Do we choose a course that will allow us to make use of all the social, political and national contradictions in the USSR and base our strategy upon all the antagonistic forces, ideas and inclinations existing there, thus taking on the role of an initiative (tactically destructive) force of USSR-wide significance?

Since we are dealing with Bolshevism, we must choose the latter course in the interests of an independent, united Ukrainian state—the path of socio-political struggle, socio-political (and this means national as well) revolution *in the entire USSR*.

Fire must be fought with fire. The Bolsheviks have been striking at us throughout the Soviet Union, primarily with their ideology. We must turn their methods and ideology against them and that, too, throughout the country (at least in ideological and political terms), making use of all the Soviet Union's abundant contradictions and disparities and mobilizing the broadest masses, above all, the Russians, against Bolshevism by using its own methods, just as the Bolsheviks have always mobilized them against us. The enemy is beaten with his own weapons.

It might be argued that Bolshevism itself has jumped astride the nationalist horse. Yes, it has, but this very fact is a good indicator of its weakness and its ideological and political bankruptcy among the masses—the Russian masses most of all. This nationalist horse will throw off the Bolsheviks (it must throw them off), for they themselves have pounded a different philosophy into the heads of the people over the last twenty-five years. By all its recent shifts in policy, Bolshevism has definitively weakened its ideological position among the masses, and its "nationalistic," pro-Russian policy has spurred the growth of national antagonisms. But at the critical moment, the Bolsheviks or, more precisely, the ruling clique, had no other choice, and here lies the weakest point of Bolshevism, both as an ideology and as a political system. These national antagonisms, as well as all other contradictions, must be turned against Bolshevism as the source of animosity among nations (an animosity essential to Bolshevism, stemming from party policy).

In contrast to this, we offer not a "zoological" nationalism, for which the Bolsheviks have taught the masses to hate us, nor internationalism, which the masses have learned to hate after all the practices of Bolshevism, but *the progressive idea of national co-operation, peace and unity based on the principle of freedom, independence and friendship among peoples living as equals with equals.* The Bolshevik cudgel, with which they drubbed us as representing "national fascism," we will turn against them as the organizers of a monstrous "neo-national fascism." The Bolsheviks have sown animosity among nations, not in the interests of the Russian people, but in the interests of the plutocratic, international ruling clique, the new class of usurpers, which lives by the principle of "divide and rule."

Thus we take on the role of restorers and propagators of the greatest ideal of friendship and brotherhood of peoples, an ideal which, although not realized by the October Revolution, was its most powerful motive force. (We remind the reader that we are dealing here with the question of tactics.) We are not implanting this ideal in our own ideology. (This ideal, incidentally, is one for which all the peoples of the USSR yearn as the unfulfilled dream which inspired and impelled them to the first destruction of the empire, the revolution of 1917. Thus, it would be wise to raise this ideal once again.) No, we will turn the Bolsheviks' weapons against them, orienting ourselves toward a socio-political struggle, not with slogans of national animosity but with those of *unity among nations in a struggle* against a regime of massive pauperization, social inequality, brutal exploitation, disenfranchisement and the sacrifice of the people to the interests of the ruling party clique. In every case it must be stressed that the Russians themselves are a people equally exploited and deprived of rights.

In short, we must amend the major line of Ukrainian policy and action, at present and for the future, and in accordance with this change of course, we must deal directly with a series of questions (questions raised by the reality of our situation) and answer them clearly:

1. Against whom, in fact, are we struggling (that is, from the point of view of tactics)—against Bolshevism or against the eternal northern enemy, "the Russian people," "Muscovites," "primitive Russian peasants," "Muscovite imperialism," and so on?

2. What is the primary aim of our struggle? Is it to rush headlong toward some dreamt-up, problematical Ukrainian empire stretching from Khust[1] to Kazakhstan, or is it first to demolish the USSR, destroy Bolshevism, bring down the Bolshevik empire and then to establish a concrete Ukrainian state within the greatest possible limits determined by the concrete possibilities existing within the specific conditions that will arise? Do we look to the near future or do we begin our plans with the distant future; do we deal first with the bird in the hand or the two in the bush? And in relation to this, do we go round and round, relentlessly and tirelessly, within the circle of purely Ukrainian problems and standards (like a squirrel on a treadmill), or do we take a wider view and head first for the destruction of the USSR, for revolution (or anarchy, if you prefer) as the first and foremost precondition for the establishment of an independent, united Ukrainian state?

3. How do we struggle?

Do we do this solely by awaiting external intervention, in accordance with the dominant view in leading Ukrainian circles whose members believe that without external intervention the Ukrainian state will not be established? Or do we take the position that the "East[2] will produce the necessary forces and leadership" to begin and complete the task, a view with which many lull themselves to sleep?

Or do we struggle by taking the path of autonomous, large-scale (in the strategic and political sense) action, without awaiting any external intervention or making the fate of the Ukrainian state dependent upon it?

And finally:

4. With whom do we ally ourselves? With whom do we struggle

shoulder to shoulder? Is it together with all the subject peoples against the Russian people, Muscovite culture, Russian aggression and so on? That is, do we oppose the Russian people? Or on the contrary, do we include the Russians (and the Russians above all) in a united front against Bolshevism as a political and social system and a totalitarian regime which the Russian people hate as much as do other peoples (they must hate it); do we include the Russians, keeping in mind that the existence of the Ukrainian state depends upon the attitude of the Russian people to Bolshevism?

Paradoxical as it seems, this is the case.

These are the questions we face. And we must answer them clearly and resolutely:

1. We are struggling at present not against the "eternal northern enemy," "Muscovites," "primitive Russian peasants" and so on (all this cheap, patriotic drivel must be deleted completely from our propaganda and our political terminology, as well as all overt emphasis on militant nationalism, for what we need is not nationalist clamour but a nationalist goal for the sake of which we are ready to confront anything). *We are struggling not against the Russian people but against Bolshevism. Our aim is to bring down not Russia as a symbol of Russian patriotism*, not Moscow (reminding the Russians of all historical injustices and particularly Bolshevik injustices, and holding the whole Russian people responsible for them), and not Muscovite Russian culture, but the totalitarian Bolshevik regime, Bolshevik culture (which is anti-popular and anti-Russian), the red Kremlin as the organizer and leader of the grandiose totalitarian imperialist machine whose destruction is essential for us. For the empire was established and is maintained not by the Russian people and Russian culture, but by Bolshevism and its doctrine, by the Bolshevik party (whose membership is international), the Bolshevik regime, ideology (which is international), and the totalitarian state apparatus (which is international), without which the empire would not exist. Were this not so, the question of our relations with the Russians would be posed in entirely different terms.

2. We wage our struggle not in a narrow, exclusively Ukrainian nationalist context, but in the context of the United Ukrainian Popular Front and the United Front of Subject Peoples. We give this struggle the widest possible ideological and political scope, keeping in mind that "internationalist" Bolshevism counters Ukrainian nationalism not only in a narrow Ukrainian context, but on a USSR-wide and world scale, quashing even the slightest manifestation of this or any other type of nationalism. In countering Bolshevik practice (which stems from its ideology, its weapon), we must oppose Bolshevism in a suitable manner, that is, not by means of a provincial ideology and slogans, but by

means of an ideology and slogans which would strike at its very heart, at the milieu in which Bolshevism is most secure. These must be slogans which are the most progressive and which the USSR itself can supply: slogans concerning the broadest kind of true democracy; the restructuring of the "prison of nations" on the basis of democratic principles; social and political reorganization; the completion of the "class struggle"; the destruction of the most parasitic class of the international plutocracy (which has made itself felt all too painfully in the USSR); the abolition of state capitalism, and so on; in a word, slogans of *social, political and national revolution*, a revolution in the very heart of the USSR, *in Russia* first of all. In this way, we must provide a stimulus to those internal forces which have acted there and still exist at the present time, but are held in check for a variety of reasons, which we shall discuss later.

We are struggling for a concrete independent democratic Ukrainian state, but we are also struggling for a *Russian* state, and for the democratic states of other peoples of the old and new USSR. The slogan, "freedom for nations, freedom for individuals,"[3] must also apply to the Russians. This must be stressed particularly. We must make intensive efforts to implant this slogan in the Russian masses.

3. We do not make our struggle with the Bolsheviks (our struggle for an independent, united Ukrainian state) ultimately dependent upon external intervention. We will follow our course, which is correct regardless of the presence or absence of external intervention, because it is based on the following reasoning: external intervention may not take place (what if it does not?), but the USSR will collapse, for it must collapse. And an independent, united Ukrainian state will arise, for it must arise. And this is not because we *wish* it to be so, but because it will be *the logical result of all events*, all the social and political developments and revolutionary struggle in the East. It must be so. We hold this to be inevitable.

The harmful theory—one that is, alas, widely held at the present time—that Bolshevism cannot be destroyed without external intervention (and thus that the Ukrainian state cannot be established) cannot withstand critical analysis. This is a dangerous theory, for it leads to passivity. Is it truly impossible to destroy Bolshevism? Well, and what if no intervention occurs?

But what about the interesting fact that one empire (far mightier from every point of view than the Bolshevik) collapsed in 1917? And it collapsed without any external intervention aimed at destroying it but, on the contrary, with intervention which attempted to save it. What about this fact?

And the internal contradictions of the Romanov empire in 1917 were no greater than those which exist in Stalin's empire today, contradictions which have been shaking it from within for twenty years and must be all the stronger now, after five years of war . . . But we shall come to this, and a whole series of other questions, later.

Thus, at this stage, we do not make our struggle for an independent, united Ukrainian state in any way dependent upon external intervention (which at best could only ease the problem, and at worst make it more difficult, as was the case with the German intervention). We have reason to expect that British intervention would do more for an independent Ukrainian state than did the German. But it is possible that if British intervention proved contrary to the interests of the Russians, eastern Ukrainians and other peoples (if it proved incapable of creating a cleavage between the people and the party, for which armed intervention alone is insufficient), it would only produce a counter-effect in the struggle against Bolshevism, as did the German intervention or the intervention of these same allies in the struggle against Bolshevism in 1917–20. But we shall now turn our attention not to this, but rather to the following:

It was the Russian people who brought down the Romanov empire. They not only destroyed the empire by rupturing the social and political order, but also ground to dust their native—that is, Russian—ultranationalism, as represented by Denikin, Kolchak,[4] Iudenich,[5] Kappel, Wrangel and so on. This is an interesting fact which merits our attention. The roots of these events lie not in rhetoric, but rather deeper, *and we must understand this*. They are to be found in a whole range of important reasons (which exist even now) and in the characteristics of the Russian people, whom we do not understand and do not wish to understand, but whom we must understand, for we must profit from the qualities and inclinations of that people, whose deportment will determine the fate of Bolshevism. Without entering into unnecessary details, we emphasize the fact that Bolshevism owes its entrance onto the stage of history above all to those characteristics of the Russian people. It will also owe its death to them, as did the Romanov empire.

For tactical reasons, we desire a repetition of that which took place in the previous revolution.

Taking account of the particular characteristics of the Russian people, as well as all the contradictions within the USSR and the conditions existing at the present time, we state categorically that the fate of Bolshevism and its empire depends *in greater measure* upon the Russian people than upon external intervention. The Bolsheviks themselves understood this better and earlier than anyone and therefore made a 180-degree turn in their tactics with regard to the Russian people five years before the approaching events. For they understood that their fate would depend upon whether they had support among the broadest masses. And because other peoples were unreliable, since the national "Gordian knot" still remained tightly bound, the Bolsheviks chose the Russian people as a nation whose masses would support Bolshevism, elevating and raising them up in a variety of ways. If one wages a struggle from without against the Russian people, identifying them with Bolshevism (or, more precisely, failing to separate them from it completely), then no external intervention will topple Bolshevism, for the Russian people are the framework that supports the entire USSR. And the contrary is also true. If the Russian people stand with other peoples against Bolshevism and take the path of social and political revolution (to which they have aspired on numerous occasions), then not even external intervention will save Bolshevism, just as it failed to save the Romanov empire.

We do not say this because we feel any pious sentiment toward the Russian people, but rather because the Bolsheviks themselves, with all their characteristic ability to see into the heart of the matter, have shown that they are more aware of this than anyone else. And the heart of the matter lies in those internal social and political contradictions which have repeatedly threatened to throw the Bolsheviks from their horse in mid-course and came close to throwing them off at the most unexpected moment—at the moment in which the "sacred war for the fatherland" was declared. Only Hitler's external intervention saved them.

Thus, looking into the heart of the matter, we must answer (and declare not only to ourselves) the question, with whom do we fight shoulder to shoulder on the revolutionary front?

4. We are struggling alongside the Russian people against Bolshevism. This is what we strive for. To struggle above all with the Russian people. This is our tactical aim and the guarantee of our success. We have no dealings with political Philistines, ultra-patriots who "build Ukraine" with intransigent dreams while standing on their heads. Nor does it concern us how, after the destruction of the USSR, the Russians build their own national state or what it will be like. *This concerns us least of all.* Our principle is the following: we have *not a constructive goal* with regard to the future Russian state, but a *destructive* one with regard to the Bolshevik empire, the present-day "Russian" state. (The constructive mission we leave to Vlasov;[6] while we justly apply our tactics, let him attempt to deal with this.) At the present time, our interests do not extend to internal Russian national affairs. At present, they stop at the point where the common anti-Bolshevik front ends. What matters to us is that in the destruction of Stalin's totalitarian regime, the Russians help to recreate the situation of 1917. If not completely, then

at least in part, and the more, the better. In one way or another, they have already endeavoured to repeat it on numerous occasions (let us recall all the political trials which have taken place in the USSR, not only judicial trials, but others as well). This is what matters to us.

We must make use of the perpetual inclination of the Russian people toward social struggle, social revolution (an inclination which has been strengthened by much experience and failure), demagogical anarchism and meretricious "freedom," this morbid elemental penchant for nihilism and destruction.

Thus, in applying the tactic of creating the broadest possible united front in the struggle against Bolshevism, we must state clearly whether we regard the Russians as a subject people and include them in the united front or whether we exclude them and consider them the aggressor. We speak here of the Russian people.

Do we identify the Russians with Bolshevism and draw all the conclusions appropriate to this view or do we separate them from the state, the government and the party and include them in the ranks of other peoples opposed to Bolshevism?

So far, our propaganda has at best ignored the Russian people, giving them no distinct designation. In general, we have gone to the opposite extreme—we have stressed unequivocally that our enemy is the Russian people, that we are struggling against the Russian people, Muscovite Russian culture, Russian imperialism and the like. *Although essentially this is correct*, from the tactical point of view, particularly at this time, it is sheer stupidity to identify the Russian people with Bolshevism or to avoid this ticklish question by resorting to vague generalities. All those generalities and obscurities have a concrete political significance which does not bring us any benefit. The most progressive slogans in the East, "freedom for nations, freedom for individuals," and "a united front of subject peoples," when coupled with slogans against "Russian imperialism" and "Muscovite culture," exclude the Russian people from the front of subject peoples; this appears self-evident in the cluster of political concepts which form the basis of all our political propaganda and organizational undertakings. For example, the slogan about the front of subject peoples, although not stating this directly, seems to imply that the subjugation is perpetuated by the Russian people, for it is never stressed that the Russian people are not to be identified with Bolshevism. On the contrary, everything has been done and continues to be done to confuse these two concepts. And we will not even speak here of the long-standing past and present ultra-nationalist, anti-Russian propaganda, both written and spoken, which has traditionally marked Ukrainian politics.

We do not intend to hob-nob with the Russians. But neither do we intend to hob-nob with our own political "adolescents."

The danger, the threat to our existence, the strength of our "northern enemy" are currently contained in Bolshevism, in its state apparatus, and not in the Russian people. Bolshevism's ideology, its organization, its apparatus of control and subjugation are the root of our troubles (for Bolshevism is supported not only by Russians, but by millions of Ukrainians as well. In the past, this was for ideological reasons; now it is from inertia, from a lack of anything better and more credible to support). The root lies here, and not in the Russian people. And here we must strike.

Among the Russians, on the contrary, important or even decisive conditions exist for the destruction of Bolshevism.*

These conditions have existed and continue to exist. And this must not be forgotten.

Bolshevism is attempting to eliminate these contradictions in order to gain the support of the Russian people in its struggle against everyone, including us.

We must ground ourselves in these contradictions and make use of the Russian people in the struggle against Bolshevism. Under these circumstances, is it wise for us to raise the question of national antagonism between Ukrainians and Russians at the present time? This problem is for the future. We leave it to Dontsov[7] to brandish a paper sword. At present, we have a different goal. There are two stages in the struggle for an independent, united Ukrainian state. The first stage is the destruction of the Bolshevik empire. This is the beginning. Only a fool begins at the end.

Whatever the circumstances, the success of this first stage depends upon the participation and collaboration of the Russian people. Under no circumstances does the path lie through inflaming mutual antagonisms. In any case, the Bolsheviks have already inflamed them to the limit, for it was necessary for them to do so. Were we to take this same approach, which is so necessary to the Bolsheviks, we would be not only asses, but actual enemies of the Ukrainian cause. The complex set of steps and manoeuvres of our policy, which is demanded by the concrete struggle for a concrete Ukrainian state in a concrete reality, must be ideally planned and carried out if we, in our position, are to win the struggle.

---

*Since these lines were written, some changes have occurred, but not to such an extent that we need to alter our thinking. The tactics of Bolshevik propaganda have changed, but not the existing state of affairs.

We must therefore destroy this mutual antagonism and work out the tactics that we require.

Politically, the Ukrainian people (if one speaks of the whole) are more mature than the Russians. In addition, the whole Ukrainian people has a powerful ideal. The Russian people *do not have an ideal of equal value*, except, perhaps, the ideal of a new social revolution, the signs of which have repeatedly manifested themselves. Stalin's bluff with Russian international messianism has exasperated the people and it is not the idea of the masses. The new Stalinist nationalist idea is also a fiction of short duration, a dose of political opium which has only tactical significance. A breath of healthy wind will quickly blow this stupor out of the minds of the hungry and debilitated Russian "Soviet" masses. The true proponents of Russian nationalism—the émigrés—are generally isolated. The only ideal capable of rousing the masses can be and is that of social-political revolution. That ideal exists; it must only be supported in every way.

And here the political leadership of the Ukrainian people must play a leading, initiatory role, rather than take a position limited by a narrow "ism."

Our local, territorial, national struggle does not correspond to the goals of the Russian people (it is, rather, obviously hostile and mobilizes them to resistance). The idea of a socio-political struggle of USSR-wide (all-national) significance is totally in accord with their goals, and propaganda, as well as all other measures aimed in this direction, cannot fail to be effective.

The mere suggestion of co-operation with the Russians will drive many of our ultra-patriots into a state of frenzy and terrible indignation; they will accuse the author of Bolshevism and the devil knows what else. But we are not entering into polemics with political Philistines. In any case, there is nothing here to enter into polemics about.

Simply to await external intervention is both dangerous and harmful.

To imagine that we can contend with Bolshevism if we declare war on the whole Russian people is courageous, but stupid.

Simply to ignore or avoid the question of the Russian people is naive and equally harmful (as if to say, somehow things will turn out; of course they will turn out—that is certain—but how will they turn out with regard to our interests?)

We must choose one of two courses of action. Do we wage the struggle? If so, that means we must wage it, and wage it first and foremost against Bolshevism; first we must bring down the empire and then build a state. Or do we say "pass," fold our arms and wait until that state builds itself, wait for "external intervention"?

But again, we can state with certainty that no external intervention will ever support the idea of an independent, united Ukrainian state; there is no hope of that. External intervention will support a Poland stretching "from sea to sea"; it will support the Caucasus; it will support Russian nationalism, as represented by some Russian Badoglio[8] or some new version of the old Denikins and Wrangels. But it will not support an independent, united Ukrainian state for a number of political reasons. Providing we skillfully use the proper tactics, the idea of an independent Ukrainian state will more readily be supported by the Russian masses (they will support it at least objectively, like other peoples of the USSR) than by someone from Berlin (we have already had this lesson, and it was a brutal one), or London (in our time, we have also learned this lesson), or anywhere else. Above all, we ourselves must support this idea, opening all the paths to its fulfillment.

One way or another, Berlin, London and Washington will rely upon the Russian émigré imperialist rabble, which was thrown out by its own people and will not be permitted to return without a fight. It is wiser for us *to support* this stance of the Russian people, as well as all their anti-Bolshevik tendencies and movements, than to depend upon external intervention.

It must be said that the Russians, like the Ukrainians and all the peoples of the USSR, have in twenty-seven years produced sufficient cadres to deal with Stalin and his clique, should it come to that, as well as with the outdated émigré trash; sufficient cadres to enable them to march forward, and not backward, resuscitating the deceased. It is true that eventually these cadres will bring about a collision between Russia and Ukraine, but they will not do so immediately. As long as we have a common goal, we also have a common path. Our paths will diverge, but at that point it will be clear how Russia will conduct herself.

As long as the Bolshevik-Muscovite empire remains undestroyed and unvanquished, it is laughable to speak of a future struggle between an independent Ukraine and Russia; to do so would be to resemble that anecdotal gypsy with his future colt.

Thus, we fight side by side with the Russian people against Bolshevism.

And finally:

5. As to expectations with regard to "the eastern regions and their decisive role": it is true that the eastern regions, that is, Greater Ukraine, will produce a leadership, political cadres and armies. But a great danger lies in passively awaiting this.

What if they do not produce them? We do not say never—this would be impossible. But what if they do not produce them in time? What if they do not produce in sufficient time that beginning and that hope—

people of great breadth and potential strength, the sort of people whom Stalin shot by the thousands (not to say tens of thousands) during the last ten years? And it may be so. We must not forget that the eastern regions and their population are at the disposal of the Bolshevik totalitarian system, which prevents not only any organized anti-Bolshevik activity, but also any organizational and preparatory work.

The eastern territories[9] have great powers at their disposal, but history (with our help) may do us a bad turn—those powers may be prevented from playing any role. For having been dispersed by the cunning Stalin to all corners of the "unbounded fatherland," disunited and subjected to surveillance, they will be unable to carry out any preparatory work. These forces never had the opportunities which have been available to Ukrainian forces outside the boundaries of the USSR; the opportunities for preparatory organization and action. For this reason, these latter forces will have to fulfill a historical mission, that of drudges, perhaps, but they will have to be the ones on whom a great deal depends, those "first brave souls" whom "millions will support," those who chart the first path, who begin the great act, who take the helm and place the landmarks which will set the course for others, who are, perhaps, stronger and more talented, but also more subdued.

Whoever brandishes a knife must slash the first available ganglia on the giant's shoulders.

Perhaps this analogy is inappropriate. In any case, those Ukrainian forces (and they are quite impressive) which are beyond Stalin's reach must begin that course of Ukrainian policy which is capable of countering the Bolshevik political school and which will guarantee a swift disintegration within the enemy's camp, transposing a significant proportion of his forces objectively to our (the Ukrainian people's) side.

*   *   *

The internal contradictions in the USSR as a guarantee of its collapse.

The nature of Bolshevism and its paradoxical change of course as a tactic of self-preservation. The blind alley, the search for an outlet through expansion into Europe and the like.

The Vlasov forces, their strengths and weaknesses. The idea of the Vlasov forces as a restoration of the greatest motive ideal of the October Revolution in the Romanov empire, and as an idea of international leadership. The prospects of the Vlasov forces and their threat to us.

Our tactics with regard to the Vlasov forces: the UPA's idea of a united front of the subjugated as the best tactical move of Ukrainian policy toward the achievement of this endeavour.

The idea of "easterners" (eastern Ukrainian nationalism), the idea of

*a USSR-wide, international, revolutionary leadership as the path to
our goal.*

*The lack of any ideal among the Russian people. An ideal to be given
to the Russian people.*

*The watchword—the creation of a united front of the peoples of the
USSR; the creation of a USSR-wide, all-national resistance to Bolshevism and the Vlasov forces as the only correct path to our goal.*

Earlier, we stated that the existing theory of orientation on external intervention (that is, on a conflict between the allies and the USSR) is
harmful at the present time; that now we cannot and must not make the
cause of an independent, united Ukrainian state dependent upon external intervention; that the path to the creation of an independent, united
Ukrainian state lies not through external intervention, but through the
destruction of the Bolshevik empire; and that this destruction of Bolshevism is essential regardless of whether any external intervention
takes place, because it depends upon a number of other preconditions,
upon what one might call internal intervention.

However paradoxical this may appear to political Philistines, it is so.

It is true that external intervention can speed up the fall of Bolshevism.
But it could also fail to speed it up, or have the contrary effect. Germany's external intervention not only failed to speed up the fall of Bolshevism, but strengthened its position, primarily among the Russian
people. But let us say that external intervention does speed it up.

Will this intervention speed up and bring about the establishment and
consolidation of an independent, united Ukrainian state in the absence
of other preconditions which depend on the political leadership of the
Ukrainian people, the scale on which the struggle is waged and the tactics of that struggle? This is the first point. And the second is this: what
if that external intervention does not take place? What then? And it
may not take place for at least ten to fifteen years. Then, what about
the independent Ukrainian state? Then it is finished.

That is why this and all similar theories are harmful. They are harmful
because they distort perspective and demobilize us, improperly making
dependent upon problematical factors that which cannot be made dependent upon these things, for the fate of the Ukrainian state depends
upon other factors; it depends in large measure upon our own, subjective factors.

In short, today (after five years of war) we can no longer make the fate
of Bolshevism dependent upon external intervention; even less can we
make the independent, united Ukrainian state dependent upon it, for
external intervention may or may not take place, but the USSR is crumbling, for it must crumble. And the independent, united Ukrainian state

will arise, for it must arise. And there is no absolute necessity for external intervention in order to make this happen.

We have already seen the collapse of one empire without any external intervention, and that a mightier one than the Bolshevik from every point of view. And if the Ukrainian state that arose at that time was unable to maintain itself, it was only because of stupid leadership (God forbid that this should now be repeated). The Bolshevik empire is subject to the same laws as Nicholas's empire and will be treated no more kindly by history than its predecessor.

This is not because we wish it to be so (just as external intervention will not depend upon our wishes), but because, regardless of our wishes and those of the Bolsheviks themselves, other laws, other forces exist and act inside the Bolshevik empire, laws and forces which even the "legendary" and "devilishly clever" Bolsheviks (as our politicians refer to them) lack the power to eliminate or hold in check.

These laws were discovered in part by Marx, in part by Bakunin[10] and Trotsky[11] (in the Russian people) and in part by Lenin. In their time, the Bolsheviks rode into the historical arena on their knowledge and profound understanding of these laws. And it is not by chance that they rode out in Russia. And it will not be by chance that Bolshevism will perish in Russia, thanks to the same laws that gave it birth. Were we to analyze this according to the Bolshevik dialectical mode of thinking, we would be able to argue this point in an interesting and perspicacious manner. But we shall not resort to this extreme, for we do not wish to offend the sensibilities of representatives of the "idealistic" worldview.

Trotsky's theory of "permanent revolution" merits particular attention at this time—politically speaking, Trotsky was a "genius" compared to the dull-witted Stalin—for reality has proven him correct. But what interests us here is not so much the theory (for to dissect it would prove too disagreeable to our way of thinking) as the fact that it was the Soviet and, more precisely, the Russian reality which gave it birth and ensured its appeal to the Russian people. This theory and the laws discovered through it (which were, incidentally, so well learned, taken into account and later used by Stalin) stem from a deep knowledge of the activity, course and nature of the socio-political processes that take place in the Russian reality. And it is precisely in the Russian reality, which Trotsky knew so well, that these laws emerged. It is no wonder that Trotsky enjoyed such enormous popularity in Russia and that the ideological and political opposition which he spawned had so many adherents and caused Stalin so much trouble.

What interests us here is not so much Trotsky's theory as its background (for this theory was not some sort of demagogic fabrication, but concrete conclusions derived from the study of concrete reality and, on this basis, also a proper conception); what interests us is the reality which gave it birth, that potential inclination of spontaneous social and political forces toward permanent revolutionary action which is rooted in the Russian people and in all the peoples of the Soviet Union. The root of this theory, according to which the logical result of the development of historical social relations must finally be the negation and abolition of Bolshevism itself (if one carries Bolshevik dialectics to their conclusion), is found in those eternal, indestructible inner tendencies that have always stood and will always stand in opposition to any socio-political regime. These stem, first, from the psyche of the masses and, second, from the tangle of persistent social, political and national contradictions which have not been rooted out in the conglomerate that forms the USSR and which can be transformed, but never eliminated. So we must take an interest in those laws which, beneath all the specific subtleties of Trotsky's theory, are in fact a description of the characteristics of the Russian people themselves and were established before Trotsky's time.

We do not wish to pose political conundrums, so we shall leave Trotsky aside and limit ourselves to ascertaining those things which result from the action of these laws inside the USSR.

The whole twenty-five-year history of Bolshevism is the history of continual political instability, trials, executions, deportations and immense repressions—in a word, ceaseless struggles and ceaseless changes of direction. What has been happening?

Those laws have been slipping out from under the control of the greatest theoreticians and practitioners of revolutionary struggle and knocking Stalin and his party from side to side. It was under the pressure of these laws that Lenin and, later, Stalin so skillfully manoeuvred, changing course in every possible way, moving from extreme internationalism to extreme fascism, to religion and whatever else one can think of, from "absolute dictatorship of the proletariat" to "the greatest democracy in the world" and so on. The Bolsheviks made all these changes simply in order to maintain themselves in power.

Bolshevism has followed the path of propagandist half-measures and paradoxical compromises; if it did not, it would have to negate itself. But compromise does not save the situation.

The whole cluster of socio-political and national contradictions has not only failed to diminish, but has grown even more complex since it brought down the Romanov empire. And so greatly has it increased that one can say with certainty that never in the world has there been a state beset by greater internal contradictions than the USSR, with its massive contradiction between the people and the state, between the terrorized and defrauded society and the ruling international clique of mendacious and brutal social experimenters.

Only from this point of view can one begin to understand all the colossal struggles against "enemies of the people" in which those "enemies," put into prisons and camps, shot and murdered, numbered in the millions (in 1939, there were eleven million people in prisons and camps in the USSR; these figures do not include those who were shot). And how many people living in "freedom" were also touched by these repressions? Family members, brothers, sisters, near and distant relatives all entered the orbit of antagonism to the state (to Bolshevism). The whole "struggle against the enemies of the people" is the struggle of the system with these antagonisms, with the people; it is the struggle of the state-capitalist system with the subjugated and mercilessly exploited masses, with millions of pauperized, disenfranchised people.

Having eradicated one set of contradictions, Bolshevism created others that proved even more difficult, particularly in the social relations between the state as capitalist and the industrial proletariat and the state as landowner and the pauperized ("proletarianized") peasantry. In addition, there are the terrible contradictions in nationality policy, not to mention political sore spots. When it comes to the nationality problem, the Bolsheviks cynically defrauded the peoples. In recent years, they have displayed the ultimate cynicism in this regard. But in this, as in all matters, they present their cynicism to the masses in perfect propaganda form, concealing themselves beneath a mantle of divinity. To tear off that mantle, to reveal Bolshevism naked to the peoples of the USSR, is one of our major tasks. Not in the way the Germans and all the "politicians of the German school" have done this, but in the way in which it is done by those who know Bolshevism through and through, who know its essence, practice and tactics and who are equally familiar with the Soviet masses.

Thus the cluster of contradictions has become more complex since it toppled the Romanov empire, particularly after years of war.

The Romanov empire owed its collapse to the action of certain laws. Bolshevism owes its appearance on the historical arena to these same laws. They begat Bolshevism at that stage in history, both in Russia and in Ukraine. To these laws, Bolshevism owes its life. It will also have them to thank for its death, both in Russia and in Ukraine.

For having learned these laws, Bolshevism used them, but did not master, subjugate or eliminate them. As the product of socio-political experimentation, the new order, the new system was not successful. The Bolshevik phase turned out to be the most difficult, the most terrible; in comparison, even the tsarist "prison of nations," with all the attributes for which it was cursed, now appears like a dream. The contradictions have become more complex. The discrepancy between theory and practice is so great that it can hardly be dealt with. Disillusionment is so extreme that the Bolsheviks have had to make breakneck tactical leaps, including a leap to Russian ultra-nationalism, in order somehow to remedy the situation by hurriedly implanting a "new ideal" in the most populous nation—this despite the glaring incongruity between the ideal and their twenty-five-year-long social-international practice, as well as the risk of sowing national discord in the USSR. But they are choosing the lesser of two evils. Better to have at least one (the most populous) nation on their side than to have all the nations against them.

Better to give that nation at least some sort of ideal, even if it is incompatible with Bolshevik doctrine, than to face the terrible fact that this nation is devoid of any ideal and that it can suddenly take as its ideal that of destroying Bolshevism, that it can take its place in the ranks of other nations that have already adopted this idea, for the Russian people, too, are now ready for it.

The essence of the matter is that Bolshevism has failed in the struggle against those internal contradictions whose strength and significance it knows so well. All the "most radical" measures, including massive extermination of socially and politically active people under the banner of the "class struggle," produced nothing but contrary results.

Anyone who knows how Bolshevism scrambled from one side to another, anyone who saw all those "grandiose," desperate initiatives and concrete steps toward the so-called "reconstruction of humanity," anyone who knows the true motives of all those grandiose vivisections, also knows the immensity of the catastrophe that must come.

For no reconstruction of the individual (as a subject) can eliminate the main problem, that is, the social and political contradictions, particularly when these contradictions are manifestly coupled with the birth of a new parasitic class of state plutocrats, the birth and consolidation of the worst form of capitalism—state capitalism—and the fundamental disenfranchisement of the masses. The Bolsheviks knew this very well (otherwise they would not have been Bolsheviks), but to attempt honestly to eliminate these contradictions would have meant to eliminate themselves and their doctrine, to give up their positions, to capitulate at the time when they undertook—contrary to the teachings of Marx himself—to build "socialism in one country." For this reason, they took the approach which, although incorrect, was the only one acceptable to them—the approach of permanent social and political vivisections, terror, compulsion and sacrifice. Later, it took the form of paradoxical strained interpretations and grandiose window-dressing—what one might term political sorcery—reassuring the masses (like the naked king in the fairy tale) with loud, deceptive propaganda, asserting that socialism already exists, that "life has improved" and so on. Whoever denied this was declared an enemy.

This "worked" on the masses, driven to apathy and madness (this is rather like the hypnotized chicken: you lay it on the ground, draw a line with chalk right in front of its eyes, then say to it, "This is a piece of rope. Lie still, for you are tied up." And the chicken lies still). But none of this will save Bolshevism as a system and an ideology doomed to inevitable collapse.

The laws are working. And tomorrow they will emerge with unprecedented force, for the war is already bringing the end, as it did in 1917.

The Bolsheviks themselves, more than anyone, have been and continue to be aware of this fact; as many as ten years ago they began an intensive, radical preparation for the *future*.

Any unequal force which takes up the struggle with Bolshevism must be all the more aware of this and base its tactics upon it, rather than simply look to external intervention.

And that force must be the political leadership of the Ukrainian people, the people which is politically most mature and most endowed with potential in the USSR. And it must form its policy on the basis of all the contradictions in the Bolshevik empire (and, above all, in Russia); on the basis of a proper assessment of these contradictions; on the basis of a profound understanding of the essence of Bolshevism and its crisis among the masses, its theory and practice of "class struggle," all the paradoxes of its policy, the discrepancies between Bolshevism and the people and all the nations; on the basis of a detailed knowledge of the effects of Bolshevik ideology on the masses after twenty-five years and the philosophy, way of thinking and spiritual qualities of those masses. And this in particular with regard to the Russian masses. We must not simply avoid this issue, as many do, regarding those masses either as degenerate *Untermenschen* or, on the contrary, as a monolithic nation which is highly patriotic and ideologically faithful to Bolshevism, supporting it and sharing its "diabolical qualities" (look occasionally at *Krakivski Visti*).[12] This is not a true picture of the Russian masses. In general, they have quite extensive political training, are capable of thinking critically and are prejudiced against Bolshevism, which they know very well in all its aspects, better than many of us. Thus, if our propaganda attempted to combat Bolshevism according to the methods of the German political school, we would only make people laugh. But if we were to give these same people the opportunity to criticize Bolshevism openly, they would tear it to shreds.

The ideological attack on Bolshevism must be carried out in a different manner, one which at least equals that of the Bolshevik school. We must turn Bolshevism inside out, unmask its very essence, strike at it with its own theory and make use of its plentiful weaknesses, contradictions and paradoxical incongruities.

Only an attack which makes evident its ideological and political superiority and, most importantly, the integrity of the attacker, will have great success; anything else will only produce contrary results.

It must be kept in mind that we are dealing not with a horde of savages (at least when we consider eastern Ukrainians, Russians and even Tatars), but with a trained and educated mass (we are speaking of its most active members, those who are important to us) which has been steeped in all the Bolshevik theories and social sleights of hand and has, for the most part, lost confidence in them; some are entirely disillusioned; others in part; while still others are on the brink of disillusionment. To drive a wedge into these crevices is the tactical aim of our propaganda, but not in the manner of the German school. Propagandists of this sort are regarded as fools by the masses (and rightly so); they lead the masses to conclude that "obviously that Stalin cannot be caught hold of, if they jabber all this nonsense."

And this when for a decade the Bolsheviks, with all their floundering about in the spider's web of contradictions, have made the people laugh at their breakneck stunts and terrified them with their unparallelled and unmerited terror, eliciting condemnation and aversion from Vladivostok[13] to Bukhara.[14]

During the last years and months in particular, the Bolsheviks have unleashed all possible preventative measures, applying all their political and tactical dexterity and experience (one must admit that these are first-class) in a desperate attempt to avoid the inevitable downfall, to strengthen their iron regime.

But will they avoid the fate of the Romanov empire's iron regime? That depends upon who will oppose them throughout their empire as they themselves opposed the bankrupt, reactionary Romanov regime and its palliative, the Kerensky[15] regime, with Lenin and Trotsky at their head and with their revolutionary idea, which was progressive for its time in the Russian Empire (we stress the latter, for it is important).

Who will oppose them and with what idea—everything will depend upon this.

Whoever is capable of making use of the contradictions that exist within the USSR; whoever gives the proper stimulus, in accordance with the laws that are acting there, and rises to the occasion; whoever manages to arouse the Russian people and include them in the struggle against the regime of the emperor Dzhugashvili[16] (or at least exclude them from active struggle against the liberation front of all other peoples) will decide the fate of Stalin's social empire, regardless of whether external intervention takes place.

We have already stated that history has seen one example of the collapse of an empire, a powerful police state, without any external intervention (unless we consider the half-baked idea that this collapse was due to the Germans' bringing Lenin to Russia in a sealed carriage. But they did not bring in Kerensky, and it was Kerensky who gave Nicholas II the act of abdication to sign). And not only did the empire fall without intervention—when it began to collapse, there was external intervention aimed at saving it. But no external intervention saved it. The empire collapsed. The Russian Empire collapsed, pulled down by the Russian people, first and foremost.

Some will say that it did not collapse, that it only regenerated itself, as certain politicans like to maintain. We shall not argue against such manifestly amateurish analyses. The empire of the Romanov dynasty, with its particular social order, regime and immense state apparatus, crumbled like a sand castle. A number of independent states were being established. The Bolsheviks prevented this with their militant idea of creating a communist society. They found the key to the psychology of the masses, above all, the Russian masses, and threw them into battle against the Russian Empire and Russian nationalism, whose leaders were Denikin, Kolchak, Krasnov[17] and others. The Bolsheviks prevented a total separation of peoples, uniting them by means of the communist ideal and calling for the creation of a classless and nationless proletarian state, which was to be the "outpost of world revolution." At that time, this was not a hollow, illusory slogan, as some imagine. It was a powerful motive force that moved enormous masses to action; it was a gospel in which they believed. Otherwise, there is no way to explain the fanaticism with which the hungry and naked masses fought against modern armies and won. Serfs won against strategists of the bluest blood, the whitest bone. Because of this, the goal was realized; in place of the Romanov empire there arose a federation of separate republics.

It is well known that today this federation has become the same empire. That is true. The Bolsheviks have reduced it to that. But they did this because they had to, and herein lies one of the greatest contradictions in the USSR, a contradiction that the Bolsheviks inherited from the Romanov empire or, more precisely, not so much inherited as were compelled to restore. *They were compelled* to do this by their attempt, in creating a "single proletarian state," to reconcile the irreconcilable: since Marxism does not recognize nations, but only classes, the centrifugal gravitation of separate nations toward independence forced them to attempt to reconcile implacable internationalism with implacable nationalism.

This contradiction of a national order is so deep and threatening that even those "brilliant" Bolsheviks have proved incapable of dealing with it, all the more because it is interwoven with contradictions of a social order. For twenty-five years, Bolshevism struggled incessantly to eliminate this national contradiction by attempting to solve the social (class) and national problems at the same time. But this was a Sisyphean labour. The contradiction deepened. Coupled with other, perhaps even more important, social contradictions which stem from the socio-political structure of the USSR as a form of state capitalism, the national contradiction is destroying the Bolshevik empire from within. The social contradictions are of enormous significance for us when it comes to our tactics with regard to the Russian people. We emphasize these contradictions for the following reason.

The destruction of the Romanov empire was begun by the action of these social contradictions. And it was the Russian people, in the very heart of that empire, who began the struggle for its destruction. While on the periphery of the empire the acting motive forces were national as well as social, in Russia they were exclusively social. These social forces smashed the old reactionary social order and, together with it, Russian nationalism, represented by Denikin and the other imperialist heroes we mentioned earlier, which propped up that order. The contradictions in the old empire were no greater than those in Stalin's empire. Thus, logic tells us that Stalin's empire can expect no better end, regardless of whether any intervention occurs at the present time. The USSR has reached the present with twenty-five years of brutal vivisections and five years of war behind it; the people have suffered terrible misery and debilitation; countless unsettled accounts exist between the ruling clique and the people, who today hold the weapons.

For the Bolsheviks, an armed Russian people is as much a double-edged sword as an armed Ukrainian, Georgian or other people. One side strikes the Germans, but at any moment the other may strike the Bolsheviks, should the people suddenly recall everything at once. It is no accident that those all-powerful Bolsheviks are now betraying their internationalism, doing all they can to stress Russian patriotism and Russian history and appealing to the pride of the Russian soldier (who was brought up in an internationalist spirit). The Bolsheviks are hastily realigning themselves; they want to have, even in their "multi-national" state, a nation that is privileged, that is, at least formally, a hegemonic nation (in place of the former hegemonic class), so that they will have its support in their struggle with the internal revolution, which is constantly expected. And they not only appeal to the Russians' pride, but give them practical support, easing their wartime conditions and preserving their numbers by assigning them to armoured and mechanized units, where there are fewer losses than in infantry units, which are composed of men of other nations. All this is done in order to gain support among the Russian people. But even the Bolsheviks themselves are not convinced that they will succeed.

Tukhachevsky,[18] Kamenev,[19] Bukharin,[20] Piatakov,[21] Rykov,[22] Zinoviev,[23] Pilniak,[24] Bedny,[25] Koltsov,[26] Bliukher,[27] Bezymensky,[28] and countless other Russians who were Stalin's and Lenin's companions-in-arms were more than privileged, but did not they all, even in peacetime, work one way or another to bring down Stalin's regime? We are not concerned about the significance of every deviation in relation to the struggle for a Ukrainian state. What concerns us is that those currents existed and acted, objectively speaking, for the destruction of the USSR and, by extension, in our favour. What also concerns us is the fact that those currents not only existed in the past, but continue to exist. On the surface, they have been eradicated, but below the surface, have those ideas been eradicated? No, they have simply been held in check (thanks to Hitler, in particular).

To act across the line of Stalin's tactics in relation to the Russian people is the tactic of those who want to wage the struggle and win it.

What do we mean by acting across Stalin's tactical line?

One can howl, as some do, about the Russians' responsibility for the famine[29] and all the misfortunes in Ukraine, about the enslavement of other peoples by the *Russians*, about *Russian* imperialism, the *Russian* Stalin, the *Russian* empire, the *Russian* army, and so on. But this is idiocy.

Stalin is attempting to inject the largest nation in the USSR with a spirit of patriotic heroism and self-sacrifice, a readiness to fight and die "for the fatherland" (or, as all the so-called "anti-Bolshevik" propaganda would have it, for the "Russian empire," "Russian culture," "Russian hegemony," and so on); he is attempting to instill in that nation a spirit of national pride (for he knows that the spirit of Stalinism is not sufficiently strong), ambition and patriotism, to inject that most populous nation with a dose of tactical opium in order to gain its support.

Given this fact, for us, or anyone else wishing to struggle against the Bolsheviks, to shout about the "Russian empire," "Russian imperialism" and the like, and thereby to declare war on the Russian people, is to assist Stalin. To take this approach would be to help him pound the Bolshevik tactical hodgepodge into the heads of the masses and strengthen their artificial patriotism, which Stalin regards as a means of mobilizing the masses for a purpose entirely different than the creation of a "Russian empire."

Even if Stalin truly wished to create a Russian empire, such an approach would be wrong. It would be all the more mistaken because it is simply laughable even to suppose that having annexed Germany, France, England, Spain and so on to the USSR, the Bolsheviks would expect to implant Russian culture and civilization in these countries. They would implant Marxist-Leninist ideology, but never Russian culture. On the contrary, in a union or an "empire" of this type, "Russian culture" and even orthodox Bolshevik ideology would be threatened. In such an "empire," Russia would never be the hegemonic nation (it is laughable even to think this), and nobody knows this better than the Bolsheviks and Stalin himself. But this does not worry them at all. They are quite conscious of this and strive for a "union" of this sort not for the sake of exalting Russian culture, but for the sake of exalting Marxist-Leninist-Stalinist doctrine, for the sake of the so-called political and economic "dictatorship of the proletariat"—in other words, the Communist Party—that is, Stalin and his henchmen.

This is not even the same thing as German fascism. Fascism aimed at German supremacy. Stalin aims for party supremacy, party domination "on a world scale," and the cult of Marx-Lenin-Stalin "on a world scale." It goes without saying that he does not care in which language the psalm readers of world internationalism sing their hymns to him, or whose blood he sacrifices in order to achieve his goal. (And the Russians are aware of this.)

So far, time has worked in his favour. And all the fools, his "chum" included, have been working for him. The laws of the social "class struggle" have been and still are Stalin's strongest weapon. They assist him, but . . . only in the West. These same laws are the guarantee of his downfall in the East. Stalin knows this and is attempting to slash this Gordian knot, hoping to go as quickly as possible into Europe in order to find new communist cadres and reserves in those nations that have not yet learned the true price of Bolshevik social experimentation.

It is interesting to note, by the way (although we are straying here), that in relation to Marx's thesis about the impossibility of building socialism in one country under conditions of capitalist encirclement, a long-running discussion took place among the Bolsheviks on the possibility of building socialism in one country. This is probably the only point at which the Bolsheviks revised Marx, parted company with him and, in defiance of all, decided to build socialism in one country. And it was Stalin who made this decision. Whereas even Lenin entertained doubts and chose to compromise, instituting the so-called NEP, Stalin introduced a correction to the theory and decided to build socialism in spite of all. For the question faced him point-blank: is Bolshevism to exist, is the party to exist? And since the life or death of Bolshevism itself was at stake, Stalin, as leader, decided not to allow any paradoxes to stand in his way.

He did not build socialism (only proclaimed that it existed), and, having massacred millions of people, found himself where he had been before—on the edge of the abyss. Reality itself introduced a corrective to the previous discussion, and it was a corrective that not only proved the impossibility of building socialism in one country, but also completely destroyed any desire for socialism in the whole of that "one country," in its whole population, turning it into the gravedigger of any kind of socialism, and probably put social-communism out of fashion throughout the world. While Stalin was conducting his experiments, the world passed him by; it outgrew the social-communist idea, which by now had become an anachronism.

But the maniac, Stalin, takes no account of this. He continues to drive his one hundred seventy million disillusioned people toward the "beacon of world revolution," injecting them now with an additional (tactically significant) national-patriotic ideal, a mobilizing ideal whose purpose is to serve as a dose of opium in the attempt to drive them to this same goal. To Europe he carries his old idea at the point of a bayonet, never asking whether Europe wants it or not. And he cannot choose not to go to Europe; he must go. And since he must, he has nothing to take there but the old idea. So he must take it. He must, for today war is more dangerous to him than peace. The war, the campaign against Europe, is rechanneling the energy of the masses, the energy that had always shaken the ground under him and threatened to overturn everything. In addition, the campaign against Europe provides him with new support, new international cadres, which he intends to use to save Bolshevism from collapse at home (that is, in Moscow), employing them first of all to strengthen the regime of the old USSR. And if, in peacetime, Stalin's personal bodyguards were Chinese or Ingush (for he did not trust Russians), then, after the annexation of Italy or Spain, they will be Italians, Spaniards or Frenchmen. And the organs of the NKVD will again be manned by Latvians (as they were in 1917—25) or Hungarians, Zulus or Papuans, who will instill an "iron revolutionary order" in Ukraine and Russia, crushing that revolution at home which Stalin has always feared and continues to fear, which he has always fought and continues to fight.

Between 1920 and 1930, Bolshevism shouted loudly about "world revolution" and spurred the masses toward it with the communist idea. Now, when it would seem that the time has come to effect that goal,

Bolshevism is driving the masses forward with nationalism and rushing not to the achievement of world revolution but to self-preservation. Having entangled himself in contradictions, Stalin has no way out but to go into Europe, to create socialism on a "world scale." But to go into Europe to establish socialism is inconvenient when he has at his disposal a population that is exhausted, decimated and driven to despair. Stalin is now taking the risk of realizing Marx's theory of socialism in the entire world because his counterfeit "socialism in one country" will not withstand the collision with the capitalist world. Not to go into Europe is even more inconvenient, for that population (driven to despair) holds the weapons and, if it stops and recovers from its patriotic stupor, may use those weapons in the least desirable manner, attacking everything at once.

Thus Bolshevism has reached its most critical point. Either it goes into Europe, wins, and holds on a little longer—for as long as it takes the masses in Europe to recover their senses—or it stops and flies into the abyss under the pressure of its internal forces, its internal contradictions.

In short, one way or another, Stalin will have to take Marx's examination: was it possible to "build socialism in one country"?

And the examiners will be the peoples who were used as the basis for social experiments, among them the Russian people. The Russians must realize (for they realized long ago, but are now beginning to have doubts) that they are not the hegemonic people, that they were used first as experimental rabbits and now as cannon fodder in Stalin's struggle, which he wages not for Russian hegemony but for Stalin's hegemony, for the "dictatorship of the world proletariat," for the dictatorship of the "leader of the world proletariat," that is, Stalin himself. The Russian soldiers must realize that Stalin will reward them for their heroism, their blood, their mutilation, at best by giving their widows and orphans a kilogram of salt without requiring that they wait their turn, or by dubbing them, in the name of world revolution, honorary "Stalinist" widows and "Stalinist" orphans. Or, as was done in the past with those homeless children of the heroes of the October Revolution who died for the dictatorship of Lenin's and Stalin's party, by giving them a place, without requiring that they wait their turn, in corrective labour colonies and jails [*Buppry*][30] somewhere in the new English, German or Hungarian SSR. And their lands and factories will be managed by an English, German, Hungarian or Chinese "world proletariat" which will have its party cards, just as in the past, in Ukraine and Russia, lands and factories were managed by Latvians, Jews and other international "builders of socialism." "The proletariat has no fatherland": Marx's first commandment is also that of his apostle, Stalin, who will be faithful to it until the grave, for he has nothing in common with the Russian people.

Here is one of the directions that we must take in our propaganda.

The Russian soldier and the whole Russian people must think as they thought before, as they were taught to think for twenty-five years. They must think that there is no Russian empire and that nobody wants one; that the Russian people themselves, having destroyed the tsarist empire, do not want one; that they want no foreign land (they do not want even an inch of foreign land); that they must not permit any subjugation of the masses; that all these things are the attributes of capitalist or fascist systems, which are ruled by a caste that is accustomed to dealing in the blood of the people and has never cared for their interests; and that those who drive them to massacre are not fighting for their interests.

And as a result of all this analysis of Bolshevism and recent world events, a slogan must emerge which comes from the heart of the masses themselves and has great appeal among them: enough of Stalin's and Hitler's socialism (the two must always be coupled. Bolshevism besmirched itself by hob-nobbing with Nazism, and it must pay for this). At the same time, the following idea must be propagated:

The Ukrainian and Russian people worked side by side to smash tsarism in 1905 and 1917. Side by side they will also crush Stalin's bloody regime, for the sake of *peace, freedom and justice*, for the sake of a human way of life rather than a miserable, shackled subsistence. National liberty, the existence of free, independent states, cannot stand in the way of friendship between these two largest Slavic peoples; on the contrary, it is the guarantee of true co-operation and friendship between equals, a friendship based not on lies and dissimulation, not on compulsion, but on the principle of free, neighbourly co-operation. The Russian and Ukrainian peoples are not interested in subjugating each other; this was the goal of the ruling clique of agents provocateurs and speculators who aspired to world dictatorship at the price of the people's blood.

While the peoples of the USSR were suffering and sacrificing all their toil, sweat and blood to the Stalinist band "in the name of world revolution," the peoples of the world lived happily, nurturing themselves and their children. They gave no thought to the peoples in the "stronghold of world communism—the USSR" who suffered hunger and misery, went without sleep and nourishment, were ridden with lice and raised sickly, deprived children, sacrificing all so that Stalin might liberate that well-fed world. Liberate it from whom and from what? Only now have the peoples of the USSR realized that the world had no need of their self-sacrifice; that only Stalin and his international gang required it; that all those sacrifices were a cruel injustice; that the vital interests of a whole generation have been trampled by Stalinist liars and blood-suckers, who wish to live and luxuriate at the expense of the people.

It is not the world but themselves that the peoples of the USSR must liberate in order to live as the peoples of Europe and America have lived. The path to this goal is through the national freedom of every people, including the Russians. The people in whose name others are subjugated is not and never can be free.[31] The well-being of a people does not depend upon the size of its empire: Denmark, Sweden, Finland, Norway, Holland, Czechoslovakia and Switzerland are not great empires (they are not empires at all), but can one compare the life of these peoples with that of the Russians?

The lie which the ruling caste has pounded into the heads of the Russian people, telling them that they will find paradise when the whole world is in the tsar's or in Stalin's hands, must be severely punished by that people itself. For that expansionism, the people have paid and continue to pay with terrible, bloody sacrifices, deprivation of rights and misery.

The Russian people have never profited and will never profit from the Ukrainian people's enslavement by tsarism and by Dzhugashvili-Stalin's dictatorship. For they have always been the same kind of object of merciless exploitation, the same kind of subject of social experiments and a tool in the battle for imperialist ends, for the "glory" either of the little father, the "white tsar," or Stalin and the international Politburo of the VKP(b).

This is our basic approach, aimed at driving a wedge between the masses and the party and effecting a revolutionary mobilization of the Russian masses.

To declare war on the Russian people would mean to strengthen Bolshevism by identifying it with a nation of sixty millions. It would be impossible for the debilitated and decimated Ukrainian people to wage their struggle once they had mobilized against themselves the Russian people, a people endowed with an excellent state apparatus, an ideally trained leadership and a huge armaments industry. And although that people, or that "Russian state," is wrenched from within by contradictions, those contradictions would not prevent our defeat, for as long as the problem remains in the realm of national struggle, as long as it concerns the national honour, pride and vital interests of the Russian nation (and not the empire), or rather, the Russian people, the contradicitons between the people and the state, between the masses and the party, will be stilled. This is what happened in the struggle against the Germans. In addition to their zoological ultra-nationalism, the Germans also had an extremely powerful army. And at first they were helped even more by the action of those internal contradictions in the USSR which demobilized the masses and caused them to regard the Germans as saviours. This enabled the Germans to advance as far as the Volga. They had already reached the Volga. But when the tactics of the Germans revealed the true face of these "liberators," when it became apparent that what what was at stake was not the life or death of the Stalinist regime, but rather the life or death of the whole people, its very existence and its honour, then what occurred was not the expected collapse of the USSR, but the exact opposite. For the Germans had everything, but lacked one thing—political wisdom.

What, then, could we expect if we took a similar approach? The Germans themselves have already changed their approach, but too late (or perhaps not too late).

Political maturity is measured not by the degree of hatred for the enemy and readiness for sacrifice, but by sound, judicious reasoning and an ability to influence one's own and foreign masses skillfully and consistently as required by one's interests. This lesson must be learned from the Bolsheviks themselves; at present, they represent the highest school of political skill. All the same, even the Bolsheviks have not attained perfection in this regard. Within its school, Bolshevism has produced its standard-bearers, but also its gravediggers, those who work against it. We have already stated that the seeds of Bolshevism's destruction are contained within itself, in the results of its twenty-five years of activity among the masses and that, having understood this, the Bolsheviks are scrambling to save the situation, hurriedly grafting ideas which before they had always uprooted and uprooting those which they had grafted. This is true not only of the Russian national question, but of other questions as well.

To prevent those grafts from taking, to tear them away, is one of the tactical aims of anyone who wishes to struggle against Bolshevism. All the more so since, after all that has happened, those grafts are not taking well.

This is not surprising, for the tactics of the Bolsheviks in grafting Russian nationalism onto the people are being pursued in a particular manner, that of Bolshevik ideological duplicity. This new nationalism is not presented overtly and bluntly as Russian nationalism, for this would elicit opposition from the leading party cadres of other republics in the union; instead, it is draped in the mantle of "Soviet patriotism." The Bolsheviks realize that overt nationalism would be too incongruous with the ideological drilling to which they earlier subjected the masses, who have, in any case, been deprived, over two and one-half decades, of any feelings of national patriotism. It is particularly noteworthy that before they resorted to grafting even that disguised form of Russian nationalism onto the people, the Kremlin operators executed many of the old party members who might have opposed their plans. Thus, they reduced resistance from the most progressive political circles to a minimum. This price was not too high to pay in order to salvage the situation; in order to inject an ideal into the terrible void that existed in the Russian people.

In an attempt to elude contradictions of a deep ideological order, they opted, as we have said, for a particular form of Russian patriotism—"Soviet patriotism."

If one closely examines this policy, one can easily see that it is glaringly paradoxical, that it is a deceptive attempt, unfavourably perceived by the masses, to reconcile "USSR-wide internationalism" with extreme Russian fascism. The tactic is clever, but risky. With their propaganda, the Bolsheviks continue to give full support to internationalism; in practice, they use all possible means to support Russian nationalism. And at first sight it is difficult to perceive which is more important to them.

Nevertheless, if one pins an intelligent Bolshevik to the wall, he will argue, with some pride, that Bolshevism has not changed its course, but that this is simply a manoeuvre aimed at assuring the successful achievement of its original—and essential—goal.

The glaring cynical discrepancy between Bolshevism's true policy, which is rooted in its changeless ideology, and its tactics in relation to the Russian people must be fully exploited. And to do this we must approach the Russians not as a "wild mob," but as a society which, in spite of its split personality, has certain deeply rooted revolutionary traditions and inclinations; we must strike at Bolshevism's ideological heart, attack it for its brutal, anti-popular social practice and turn it inside out like a glove, just as the Russians themselves have done, constantly subjecting it to savage unofficial criticism.

The masses must think as they have been taught to think for twenty-five years and must regard Bolshevism as they have learned to regard it in that time, and not as Stalin now wants them to do. And not as the politicians of the German school want them to do either. For in all this time, these politicians' propaganda has not succeeded in supplying that people with any ideal, but has only pushed it closer to Bolshevism. The masses were waiting for a great motive ideal with which to oppose Bolshevism, but all that came was dejection and despair.

The Bolsheviks are grafting a new "great" ideal onto the Russian people. We must base our approach not on the fact that this new ideal exists, but on the fact that the Russian people are devoid of any ideal. In attacking and unmasking Bolshevism and its false ideal, we must supply the Russian people with a different ideal, one that will counter the Bolshevik scheme, an ideal that will stem from the deepest contradictions in the USSR.

We must remember that a true, deep nationalism as we understand it is not characteristic of the broad masses of the Russian people, particularly now that they have undergone a quarter-century of internationalist training, in spite of the fact that the Bolsheviks have killed countless numbers of the best representatives of the Russian people. We must remember that the Russians think not in terms of national struggle, but of political and social struggle—class struggle. The inclination toward national struggle has not been characteristic of the Russian people, for they have never experienced national oppression. They are characterized, instead, by an inclination toward social struggle and anarchy. This has been demonstrated countless times. It will be demonstrated yet again. The ideal that we should give the Russian people is that of *socio-political revolution*, the ideal of a struggle of the classless people against the class of exploiters, the party, the international gang, whose members are not true Russians. We should supply them with the ideal of a struggle waged by enslaved, pauperized peasants and industrial workers against state capitalism, against modern serfdom, against the whole totalitarian apparatus of exploitation, which is controlled by an army of idlers, parasites and social drones. Our slogans should be those of broad democracy, freedom of conscience, of the press and of speech, freedom of trade and of professions—all those things for which the people have yearned.

It is all the more important that we do this since, given the upbringing and philosophy of the Russian masses, it will not be mere empty demagogy. It will be hitting the mark directly.

And to top all this, we should suggest the ideal of co-operation and friendship among peoples, which is to be achieved by way of national liberty and national independence, the sole guarantees of true peace and neighbourly co-existence.

And this, too, will not be mere demagogy, for it will hit the same mark. Over a quarter-century of Soviet rule, the Russian people have been taught to think in terms of the so-called "Stalinist constitution," to recognize every people's right to independence. Thus, the demand for the honest implementation of a point of the constitution that has not been implemented by Stalin will not only be "within the law," but will serve as a powerful tool for propaganda purposes. Merely raising this question will result in a certain dislocation among the masses, alienating some, weakening the opposition of others, paralyzing the rest. It will bring about a state of disorganization and thus knock the ground from under Bolshevik propaganda, for the Bolsheviks themselves have been doing this with their many years of demagogy.

The enemy is beaten with his own methods and his own weapons.

Bolshevism's best and strongest weapon—the theory of class strug-gle—must be turned against it, particularly because this is a very flex-ible and convenient theory which offers inexhaustible possibilities.

If the Bolsheviks managed to raise to the rank of heroes of the prole-tarian state the great despots of all nations, including the Russian na-tion—tsars and various heroes of reactionary Russian imperialism, then we should have no difficulty in proving to the Soviet masses that the so-called "socialism" in the USSR is nothing more than the most bru-tal form of capitalist exploitation—state capitalism, in which even trade unions are unable to protect the interests of workers in the face of all-powerful capitalism. It will be easy to prove that the party and the whole servile state apparatus of social bureaucracy (where for one wor-ker there are two overseers, three informers, five red [bloodstained] gendarmes, party members or not, and a dozen NKVD agents and jail-ers) is the new grandiose class of idlers and exploiters, an intricate hierarchy of drones and bloodsuckers, in a word, a class of parasites. And it will be easy to prove that the road to well-being and to true hu-man existence leads through the destruction of the usurping totalitarian regime.

In addition, it must be emphasized that as long as this regime exists, there will be incessant wars caused by its senseless struggle for "world revolution." This, too, should be presented from the point of view of the class struggle, which we have just discussed.

Whether and to what extent this will diverge from Marx's teachings about class struggle is of little interest to us. In fact, even Marx himself would be unable to raise any objections to the assertion that the USSR is a system of state capitalism, in which the means of production (abso-lutely all of them) belong to the state capitalist while workers are re-duced to absolute subservience and deprived of any rights. In fact, this theory has always been current in the USSR, even in higher party cir-cles, and was the cause of many grumblings and complaints.

Thus we must mobilize the Russian people to struggle against this re-gime.

What matters to us is not what form that struggle may take, but only that it last, and on as large a scale as possible. We will even give it as much concrete support as we can. It is important for us to separate the people from the party, and the more we can do this, the better. In any case, they never were very tightly linked. It is important to us that as many of the Russian people as possible be at least ideologically ex-cluded from Bolshevism's struggle against us. It is important that the Russian people at least passively support those peoples that will fight for independence. The ideal is to obtain their collaboration in the destruction of Bolshevism. Not in the struggle for the Ukrainian state, but in the struggle for the destruction of Bolshevism.

When it comes to the Ukrainian state, we have nothing to discuss with the Russian people, except perhaps the fact that we will guarantee the Russian national minority in Ukraine equal rights, including the right to their own language and schools, as long as the Russians guarantee the same rights to Ukrainians in Zelenyi Klyn[32] and Kazakhstan.[33] At this point, our attempt to focus Russian attention on the Ukrainian problem ends. The focus of attention becomes the struggle against Bolshevism. The struggle of the Russian people against the Stalinist regime will objectively promote our cause, and that is sufficient. Here lies the essence of our tactical plan, of our united front with the Russian people.

We cannot take into account any rebukes or hysterical cries from "ultra-patriots" about our "eternal, implacable northern enemy." At present, we must define the enemy not in terms of geography, but in terms of the extent of his activity against us, our cause and our tactics. Under these criteria, even our "ultra-patriots" may fall into the category of enemies. Our "northern enemy" can and *must* play out his role in the struggle for the destruction of Bolshevism (and this means also for the establishment of an independent, united Ukrainian state).

If it were not for the existence of those contradictions and laws that we discussed earlier, the question of our relations with the Russian people would be posed differently. Then a struggle against the Russian people would be essential. But fortunately for us, this is not how matters stand.

Source: Typewritten copy in the Archive of the Foreign Representation of the Supreme Ukrainian Liberation Council; reprinted in *Litopys UPA* (Toronto 1980), 8: 203–56.

NOTES

1. Khust: city in the Transcarpathian oblast of the Ukrainian SSR.
2. Reference is to the central regions of Ukraine.
3. Slogan of the Ukrainian underground.
4. A.V. Kolchak (1874–1920): Russian admiral.
5. N.N. Iudenich (1862–1933): Russian general.
6. A. Vlasov (1900–46): Soviet Russian general captured by the Germans; leader of the German-sponsored "Russian Liberation Army" (1944–5).
7. Dmytro Dontsov (1883–1973): Prominent journalist and political activist. Contributed greatly to the ideology of inter-war Ukrainian nationalism.

Strongly anti-Russian in his orientation.

8. Pietro Badoglio (1871–1956): Italian field marshal. Succeeded Mussolini as premier (1943–4). Signed an armistice with the Allies (1943).
9. Reference is to the east-central regions of Ukraine.
10. M.A. Bakunin (1814–76): Russian revolutionary, proponent of anarchism and populism.
11. Leon Trotsky (Lev Davidovich Bronstein) (1879–1940): Russian revolutionary. Killed in Mexico, allegedly by an agent of Stalin.
12. *Krakivski Visti* (Cracow News): Ukrainian daily published in Cracow (1940–44) by the Ukrainian Central Committee.
13. Vladivostok: capital of the Maritime Territory, RSFSR, on a peninsula in the Sea of Japan.
14. Bukhara: city in the Uzbek SSR.
15. A.F. Kerensky (1881–1970): Premier of the Russian Provisional Government (July-November 1917).
16. Reference to Stalin's real name.
17. P. Krasnov (1869–1947): Russian general and otaman of the Don Cossacks. Extradited in 1945 by the British and hanged in Moscow.
18. M.N. Tukhachevsky (1893–1937): Marshal of the Soviet Union, executed by Stalin.
19. L.B. Kamenev (Rosenfeld) (1883–1936): Soviet communist leader, executed by Stalin.
20. N.I. Bukharin (1888–1938): Chief party theoretician, executed by Stalin.
21. G.L. Piatakov (1890–1937): Russian revolutionary, leader of CP(b)U (1918–19), executed by Stalin.
22. A.I. Rykov (1881–1938): Russian revolutionary, executed by Stalin.
23. G.E. Zinoviev (1883–1936): Russian communist leader, executed by Stalin.
24. Boris Pilniak (B.A. Vogau) (1894–1937?): Russian writer who opposed urbanization and mechanized society.
25. Literary pseudonym of E.A. Pridvorov (1883–1945), Russian writer who criticized the Russian national character. Expelled from the Communist Party in 1938.
26. M.E. Koltsov (1898–1942): Russian journalist; arrested by the NKVD in 1938, died in a prison camp.
27. V.K. Bliukher (1889–1937?): Marshal of the Soviet Union, executed by Stalin.
28. A.I. Bezymensky (1898–1973): Russian poet.
29. Reference is to the famine of 1932–3 deliberately created by Stalin.
30. Buppry (*Budynky prymusovoi pratsi*): buildings of forced labour, the Soviet Ukrainian term for jail.
31. Cf. Marx's statement: "A nation that enslaves others forges its own chains." Karl Marx, "Confidential Communication, Including Circular

of January 1, 1870, to the Swiss Romansh Council," *On the First International*, ed. Saul K. Padover (New York 1973), 174.

32. "Zelenyi Klyn": literally, the "Green Wedge," a large area of Ukrainian settlement in the Maritime Territory on the Pacific.

33. There are large Ukrainian settlements in Kazakhstan known as the "Siryi Klyn" (Grey Wedge).

OUR ATTITUDE TOWARD
THE RUSSIAN PEOPLE

O. Hornovy

Any discussion of our attitude toward the Russian people must begin by pointing out that we are addressing ourselves to two distinct problems: 1) our attitude toward the mass of the Russian people; and 2) our attitude toward Russian imperialists. Toward each of these groups our attitudes differ.

Our attitude toward the Russian people is indistinguishable from our attitude toward all other peoples. It is based upon our ideological and political principles, which call for freedom for nations and individuals.

The Ukrainian revolutionary movement of liberation, which arose in reaction to the subjugation and colonial oppression of the Ukrainian people and which embodies the nation's desire for liberation, regards all notions of chauvinism, and especially of imperialism, as foreign and repugnant. Since we are struggling for the liberation of our own people, we long for all peoples to be free and independent. All forms of subjugation and imperialism are abhorrent to us. We firmly believe that Ukrainians, like all other peoples, can attain their fullest development as members of an international family of free and independent states. We want to build our national life within our own independent state, in close co-operation with all other peoples. We believe that true world peace can be ensured only in a system of free, independent states of all peoples on their own ethnic territories.

The Third Extraordinary Grand Assembly of the Organization of

Ukrainian Nationalists expressed our position on this matter as follows:

"The Organization of Ukrainian Nationalists is fighting for an independent, united Ukrainian state and for the right of every nation to live a free life in its own independent state. The only way to effect a just solution to the national and social problem in the world is to bring an end to the subjugation and exploitation of one nation by another and to establish a system of free peoples living in their own independent states."

This basic philosophy determines our attitude toward the Russian people. *The OUN's struggle is not directed against the Russian people. It aims at liberating Ukraine from oppression by the Russian-Bolshevik invaders. The OUN maintains that the Russian state should correspond to Russia's ethnic territory and should not extend beyond those boundaries. We aspire to the closest possible co-operation with the Russian people as long as they live in their own national state as defined by their ethnic boundaries, as long as they do not oppose the Ukrainian people's efforts to attain freedom and as long as they renounce imperialism and fight for the destruction of their own imperialist cliques.*

Having adopted this position as fundamental to our movement, we are striving for the destruction of the Russian Bolshevik prison of nations and for the restructuring of the USSR into independent national states, including a national state for the Russian people. We are fighting for the separation of Ukraine from Russia, for this is the only way to bring to an end the colonial subjugation of the Ukrainian people, the plunder of their wealth and the brutal exploitation of their labour by the Russian-Bolshevik imperialists. This is the only way to fulfill the Ukrainian people's desire for freedom and independence, which is, after all, natural to every people.

The destruction of the colonial, exploitative Soviet regime, the destruction of the imperialist class of Stalinist overlords, is in the true interest of all the peoples of the USSR. A restructuring of the USSR into independent states would bring the most just and progressive solution to the national problem, for it would strike at the very root of Russian imperialism and enable each people to develop fully. It would lead not to provincialism and isolation, but to broad co-operation and friendship among peoples, based on principles of true independence, equality and voluntary participation. The restructuring of the USSR into independent states would liberate the constituent peoples from colonial oppression by the Russian-Bolshevik imperialists and would thus create the best possible conditions for the solution of each people's social problems with an eye to the true interests of the working masses. It would constitute not a regression to the old and the obsolete, but an enormous step forward.

The separation of Ukraine from Russia is in no way an act of hostility to the Russian people, as it is represented by Russian propaganda.

In the first place, the struggle for the separation of Ukraine from Russia is a struggle for the legitimate and long recognized right of every people to live a free and independent life in its own land. Can any rational and objective person regard this struggle as hostile to any other people? In addition, the struggle for Ukraine's separation from Russia is totally legal, even from the standpoint of Bolshevik law, for the Soviet constitution guarantees every so-called union republic the right to secede from the USSR.[1]

In the second place, the Russian people have no need of Ukraine; only the Russian imperialists need it. The claim, made by both Lenin and Stalin, that Russia cannot do without Ukraine is clearly an imperialist fabrication of the kind employed by all imperialists and promulgated for the purpose of deceiving the masses. (The German imperialists acted in the same way when they cried out that Germany was overcrowded, that its people were threatened by starvation, that they needed "living space," and so on.) Furthermore, such a claim cannot be taken as any kind of rational argument and cannot give any people the right to subjugate others. Arguments of this sort are used only by imperialists in order to justify imperialist wars and the seizure of foreign territories.

Russia is sufficiently wealthy and its people sufficiently industrious to survive alone. All that is required is that Russian land, resources and industry be controlled by the people rather than by the Bolshevik overlords. The Russian people should work for their own benefit, not simply to fulfill the imperialist plans of the Bolshevik exploiters. If the Russian people need Ukrainian coal, ore or grain, they can obtain them by means of trade, by exchanging for them goods produced in their own land (for example, lumber or manufactured goods) needed by Ukraine, rather than by seizing Ukraine and exploiting her wealth.

First the tsarist and now the Bolshevik imperialists have deliberately centred basic industries not in regions where raw materials are located, but in those regions of Russia in which no raw materials exist (the non-black–earth zone and Leningrad region). To these regions they transport raw materials pillaged from the so-called union republics. Given this fact, the separation of Ukraine and other "union republics" would obviously alter the existing Russian economic system. However, it would not harm the whole Russian economy, but only those branches of Russian industry that are engaged in meeting the imperialist and military needs of the Bolshevik conquerors. The Russian economy would suffer only those temporary problems which are an inevitable part of the process of national recovery and reorganization into non-imperialist national structures. Once it had been rebuilt on a national basis, the Russian economy would establish a firm basis for its successful development, strengthen itself and, most importantly, work for the benefit of the Russian people rather than for the Bolshevik exploiters. For what do the Russian people gain—we speak here of the whole people, not a corrupt minority—by having a developed industry (developed, incidentally, at such enormous cost in human life, labour and wealth) when this industry works not for them, but for armaments and for war; when profits from it are used by the Bolshevik overlord class for its own anti-national goals; when, for the great majority of workers (with the sole exception of the party official-Stakhanov[2] stratum), it provides not rewarding work, but hard penal servitude, inadequate wages and unbearable exploitation; and when workers are deprived of the slightest say in its administration? Given this situation, the destruction of the Soviet Union's imperialistically oriented industry is in the interest of Russian workers.

Its destruction is also essential if the just interests of the subject peoples of the USSR, who are not willing to accept their colonial status, are to be served. We cannot permit Ukraine's riches to be had for a song by the Russian-Bolshevik invaders in order to meet the requirements which have been deliberately developed in regions lacking raw materials. We cannot consent to a one-sided development of the Ukrainian economy (mainly in agriculture and extractive industries). We cannot accept that Ukraine, a country well endowed with all essential raw materials, should fail to develop all branches of industry. We cannot look on while millions of Ukrainians starve to death for the sole reason that their bread has been seized by the Kremlin plunderers. We cannot permit Ukraine to remain only a source of raw materials, a market for Russian industry and a source of wealth for the Bolshevik overlord class. For these reasons, we are struggling for the separation of Ukraine from Russia.

The separation of Ukraine from Russia is thus directed not against the Russian people, but solely against the Russian-Bolshevik imperialists, whose overthrow is also in the interests of the Russian people.

In conjunction with our struggle for the separation of Ukraine and the restructuring of the USSR into independent national states, we are striving for the closest possible political, economic and cultural co-operation with the Russian people, as with all other peoples. Since the Russians are our immediate neighbours, we share many common interests and could co-operate very fruitfully if our relations were based on true friendship and equality rather than imperialism.

The Russian imperialists are crying far and wide that the Russian people have provided "assistance" to Ukrainians. But this is totally untrue. This is a shameless lie, a lie twice over.

First of all, in the tsarist period, the Russian masses exerted no influence on either internal or foreign policy. The Bolsheviks know this very well, better, perhaps, than anyone else. Tsarist rule was autocratic. As there were no democratic institutions in Russia, the policies of the tsarist government were in no sense a reflection of the will of the Russian people. Thus, the tsarist government's policy toward Ukraine cannot be considered the policy of the Russian people. Living under autocratic rule, the Russian masses were given no opportunity to express their true attitude toward the Ukrainian people. To the extent that the Bolsheviks claim otherwise, they contradict the position that they have held until now, for they deny their own previously held view that under tsarist autocracy the Russian people were deprived of all political rights. Just as under tsarist autocracy the Russian people were unable to express their will, they are unable to do so now, under the totalitarian dictatorship of the Soviet Union. Thus, the Soviet government's policy toward Ukraine cannot be taken as a true reflection of the views of the Russian masses.

In the second place, the policy of the Russian-Bolshevik imperialists toward Ukraine, like the policy of Russian tsarism, has never been one of "assistance." It has been, instead, a policy of national oppression and exploitation, of annihilation and of brutal suppression of all attempts at liberation. This, unfortunately, has always been the substance of Russian-Ukrainian relations. But we lay the blame at the feet of the tsarist and Bolshevik imperialists rather than with the Russian masses.

We must here affirm, in all sadness, that the Russian people have allowed their imperialist leaders to use them as tools for implementing their policies of oppression and exploitation in Ukraine. For what did the Russian people do to prevent the tsarist imperialists from betraying the Treaty of Pereiaslav (by means of the Vilnius agreement with Poland in 1663 and the Treaty of Andrusovo in 1667)? Or to prevent them from destroying the Cossack Republic and devastating the Zaporozhian Sich, introducing serfdom into Ukraine and prohibiting the use of the Ukrainian language? What did the Russian people do to prevent the Bolshevik imperialists from conquering Ukraine in 1917–20, from oppressing the Ukrainian people after 1920 and continuing to do so up to the present? What are they doing today to prevent the Muscovite-Bolshevik oppressors from stifling the Ukrainian revolutionary struggle for liberation? What kind of "assistance" from the Russian people can one speak of?

Could such things as the payment for Shevchenko's freedom[3] by a group of progressive Russians, or the close friendship between Shevchenko and Chernyshevsky,[4] be considered assistance from the Russian people to the Ukrainian people? No, because it is only individual Russians who have striven to grant dignified treatment and legitimate rights to the Ukrainian people. No, because these individuals have always been lone voices crying in the wilderness. The positive attitude manifested toward the Ukrainian people by progressive Russian individuals cannot be regarded in general terms as "assistance" from the Russian people to the Ukrainian. These individual examples simply enable us to envisage real co-operation in the future between Ukraine and Russia as two free and totally independent nations; they prove the possibility of such co-operation even today, based on a joint struggle against the common enemy—the Russian-Bolshevik imperialists—who oppress not only Ukrainians but also the Russian working masses, brutally exploiting them and driving them to their deaths to meet goals that do not serve their interests.

Although we long for close co-operation with the Russian people, we totally reject the notion that the Russians are a people with nobler, higher qualities, destined to play a "leading role" and to take on the duties of an "older brother" (i.e. "the Russian people is the most eminent"; it has a "clear intellect, a stable character, and endurance"),[5] for such concepts are simply a cover for Russian imperialism, racism and chauvinism.

We take the position that there are no superior or inferior peoples, or peoples more eminent than all others. There can only be more or less developed peoples. But when undeveloped peoples emerge from their backward state, they show themselves to be in no way inferior to the developed ones; in fact, they often surpass them. How much "proof" have we seen put forward regarding the inferiority of the Slavs? Yet today, how vain these proofs appear in the face of reality! What a shameful end has met Hitler's assertions that the German nation is the most capable and the only one fit for imperial rule, that it is a master race. Every people has its particular qualities and talents, but these do not make any people the "most eminent" in the world. The claim that any one nation is more eminent than all others is pure racism and as such deserves only contempt and condemnation.

For this reason, we do not recognize in the Russian people any "higher qualities" which would endow them with the right to place themselves in a position superior to that of other, non-Russian peoples ("the older brother," "the great," "the most eminent nation" and so on). Nor will we ever accept the "theory" of the Russians' "leading role" in relation to non-Russian peoples, a role which, the Bolshevik imperialists so often tell us, the Russians have assumed throughout their history and continue to assume today in the Soviet Union because of their "higher" qualities. These "theories" have been fabricated by the Stalinist overlords in order to justify their imperialism, to disguise the colonial, oppressive nature of their regime and to stupefy the Russian people with racist ideas.

As Ukrainians, we are led further to reject these "theories" because they are created by absorbing the brightest periods of our history (the whole period of Kievan Rus' and the Principality of Galicia-Volhynia) and culture (for example, the "Rus' Justice,"[6] the "Song of Ihor's Campaign"[7]). Our own achievements are deliberately undervalued (all that we have achieved has been attained with "assistance" from the Russians) and historical facts are hideously falsified (for example, the Treaty of Pereiaslav, Mazepa, accomplishments of the liberation struggle of 1917–20, etc.) with the aim of Russifying the Ukrainian people and instilling in them feelings of inferiority. We reject the racist propaganda which attributes a higher worth to the Russian people, because it stirs up chauvinistic feelings among Russians and stands in the way of true co-operation between the Ukrainian and Russian peoples, thus making it easier for the Bolshevik imperialists to use the Russian working masses for their own anti-national ends.

Thus, we repeat that the *OUN's struggle is directed not against the Russian people, but against Russian imperialists, against all those who subjugate, or help to subjugate, Ukraine.*

The present-day champion of Russian imperialism is the Bolshevik Party, the VKP(b),[8] which has already turned into a new class of exploiters, headed by the Stalinist clique. Although not all members of the VKP(b) take an imperialist stance, this does not alter the imperialist character of the class as a whole. Among the aristocracy, too, there were many who opposed tsarist autocracy (for example, the Decembrists,[9] Herzen[10] and others), but these individuals did not alter the essentially exploitative nature of their class. The Bolshevik overlords constitute a purely imperialist class which has subjugated millions of non-Russians; having conquered its rival, Hitler's Germany, it has seized countries in Central and South-Eastern Europe and is now preparing to conquer the whole world. It has nothing in common with socialism or communism, but merely uses them as a cover for imperialism and as a means of establishing networks of agents in all countries of the world. The Bolshevik imperialists are the direct heirs of the tsarist imperialists, whose bloody activities they continue to this day. For this reason, we are struggling not only against the upper crust in the Kremlin, not only against the Stalinist clique, but against the entire imperialist, exploiting class of Bolshevik overlords.

The fact that Ukrainians, Belorussians, Georgians and others can be found in the ranks of the Bolshevik overlord class does nothing to alter its Russian imperialist character. Some of these "foreign" members— the Voroshilovs,[11] the Korotchenkos[12]—have turned their backs entirely on their national origins and become totally Russified. They have entered the Bolshevik overlord class along with Russians, in the same way as the Kochubeis[13] once entered the Russian nobility and the Vyshnevetskys[14] the Polish. Although the rest of the "foreign" members—the Hrechukhas,[15] the Tychynas[16]—have not become assimilated, they have become part of the ruling class on the basis of their long service, as have all the great and small Kysils[17] and Barabashes.[18] All serve with the devotion natural to renegades, and we are struggling actively against them.

The ruling class exploits the Russian people in the same way as landowners and capitalists exploited them in the past. The Bolshevik overlords have imposed a new serfdom on the Russian labouring masses, oppressing them with the heavy yoke of Stalinist despotism and exploitation and divesting them of all political and social rights. The Russian people have no say in the direction of the state; for them, democracy is only a dream.

But it would be a grave error to assume that the Russian people are generally opposed to the Bolshevik exploiting class or to Russian imperialism. Perhaps it should be so; one might wish it were so, but this is not the case. The Bolshevik overlords have won a significant portion of the Russian people to their cause *by appointing them to positions of imperialist officialdom (in the army, the MVD*[19] *and MGB,*[20] *administration, the economy, the cultural and educational fields and professional associations), thus letting them share in the rewards of imperialist pillage. The unenlightened Russian masses are deceived by false racist propaganda, demoralized by chauvinistic ideas and thus put at the service of the ruling class.* The Bolshevik overlords are all the more successful in implementing these policies because they mercilessly crush all those who might have the courage to open the eyes of the masses and show them the significance and the goals of all the propaganda about the "greatest eminence" and the "special role" of the Russian people.

In the case of the Germans, we have seen what a devastating and ruinous effect imperialist propaganda has upon the masses. The German masses, stupefied by racist ideas, enthralled by imperialist plans for mastery over other peoples and encouraged by initial military successes, chose to follow Hitler and his bandit gang. The Russian people are in an analogous situation. (If they keep following the chauvinist path that is now being taken and lend their full support to chauvinist

Soviet policies, they will meet the same fate as the Germans met in their support of Hitler.)

Thus, although we do not wish to identify the Russian people with Russian imperialism, we cannot disregard the fact that the Bolshevik overlords are acting on a broad front. Their ranks include hundreds of thousands of Bolshevik officials (the majority are Russians) and a significant part of the Russian population, which has been confused by chauvinist Soviet propaganda. To fail to take account of this fact would be to succumb to an illusion and to underestimate the strength of our enemy. In addition, we must bear in mind that the roots of imperialism go deep, not only in the imperialist classes, but also in the mass of the people. We must remember that the Russian people have been accustomed for centuries to oppress other peoples, that they have always been demoralized—and are so today, more than ever before—by their imperialist cliques. The result is a fertile soil in which to sow the seeds of imperialism among the masses, where they can take root.

One should not underestimate the significance of the fact that the Russian people have never in their history led a free existence, that they have never had a taste of individual freedom or civil rights. This, too, has been a factor favourable to imperialism. Russia, as Herzen wrote, "has neither any passion for equality nor any *capacity* for freedom (Herzen's italics). Thus it has carried on from Arakcheev's[21] imperial rule to Pugachev's[22]."[23]

We can add that this has led to Stalin's imperial rule. The Russian people's struggle against autocrats, landowners and capitalists for social liberation, their revolutionary surge in 1917, did not end with the attainment of freedom; they did not succeed in breaking the shackles of despotism, social exploitation and slavery. From exploitation by landowners and capitalists they fell into exploitation by the Bolshevik parasites. Instead of an emperor-tsar, they now have an emperor-generalissimo. If the Russian people had not for centuries known only despotism, if they had had any democratic traditions, they would not have fallen so readily into subordination to their imperialist classes; they would not have permitted themselves to be harnessed so easily to the imperialist cart. We must bear these traditions in mind, for even today they enable the Bolshevik imperialists to make ready use of the Russian masses to fulfill their own imperialist plans.

Imperialism and chauvinism are so deeply rooted that even progressive people are often unable to free themselves of these notions. For example, Belinsky,[24] who hated tsarism with all his soul, never modified his hostile stance toward the Ukrainian language and Ukrainian literature. He attacked Hrebinka[25] and Shevchenko in a most shameful manner for writing in Ukrainian. Given this fact, what can one say about the unenlightened mass of the people who are deeply demoralized by imperialist ideas? How much more difficult it is to counter the influence of imperialism among them! This influence makes itself felt in a variety of ways, in all aspects of national and individual life. Any Russian is an imperialist or a lackey of imperialism if he opposes the restructuring of the USSR into independent national states; denies Ukrainians the right to establish an independent state; opposes the separation of Ukraine from Russia; denies the colonial character of the present-day Ukrainian SSR; opposes the Ukrainian people's revolutionary struggle for liberation; fires at Ukrainian insurgents and revolutionaries; refers to them as "bandits"; tyrannizes the Ukrainian population; or terrorizes Ukrainians or murders them for their participation in the liberation struggle. Any Russian is an imperialist or a lackey of imperialism if he applauds and supports Bolshevik colonial exploitative policies in Ukraine; pillages Ukraine's riches; exploits the labour of the Ukrainian working masses; goes to Ukraine in order to colonize it and to procure for himself the best positions at the expense of Ukrainians; behaves in a colonialist manner, as an "older brother," toward Ukrainians or treats them as a conquered and subject people. Any Russian is an imperialist or a lackey of imperialism if he supports the policy of Russification; agrees with the present racist, chauvinist course of Bolshevik policy; regards the Ukrainian people as inferior and attempts to instill in them feelings of inferiority. *Against such people we obviously have to struggle, for they reveal themselves to be Russian imperialists or servants of Russian imperialism.*

Imperialism is deeply rooted. We must bear this in mind not only today, while we are still struggling for its destruction, *but even after it is destroyed, for the danger that the Russian people will revert to imperialist ideas will remain with us for a long time.*

This danger should be kept in mind not only by Ukrainians and all the other subject peoples of the USSR, but also by *the Russian people.* They must come to realize *that Russian imperialism has been the cause of the problems they have encountered throughout their history.* Russian imperialism has always been the root cause of the enormous poverty and backwardness of the Russian working masses, for it has caused all the nation's energy, labour and material wealth to be directed toward aggressive military pursuits and for the luxurious maintenance of members of the exploiting classes, rather than toward the full development of the material and spiritual life of the nation. The Russian imperialists have driven the Russian masses to take part in countless invasions and wars and to oppress other peoples. They have disgraced and continue to disgrace the Russian people. Until the Russian people rid themselves of the imperialists in their midst and free themselves from imperialist influences, they will never live as a free people, but will doom themselves instead to a life of slavery and cruel exploitation; they will be ruled by brute force and be deprived of all rights. Russia will thus continue to be the only nation in the world that has never known at least some measure of democracy.

In 1851, when Russia was living under a despotism similar to to-day's—only the despots and the forms were different—the great Russian patriot, Herzen, wrote: "If Russia accepts the existing order, she will not have the future we would wish her to have. *If she continues to follow the Petersburg path, or returns to Muscovite traditions, she can have no other destiny but to fall upon Europe like a half-barbaric, half-degenerate horde, laying waste civilized countries and perishing finally amid the general devastation"*[26] (Our italics).

How relevant are Herzen's profound words today! How close are his fears to realization! The Bolshevik imperialists are leading the Russian people further along the imperialist Petersburg path, having returned them, at the same time, to Muscovite traditions. In this way, they are leading the Russians ever more surely toward the ruin foreseen by Herzen. Stalin is preparing an even worse fate for the Russian people than Hitler brought to the Germans. This must be realized by all Russian patriots and by the Russian people as a whole.

June 1949

Source: This article was written in 1949. It was reprinted in *Suchasna Ukraina*, nos. 15–16 (1951), and in English translation in *The Ukrainian Quarterly*, no. 4 (1950) and in *The Ukrainian Insurgent Army in Fight for Freedom* (New York 1954), 165–77.

NOTES

1. Ukraine's right to secede was guaranteed in the 1936 USSR constitution (Article 17) and the Soviet Ukrainian constitution (Article 14).

2. Stakhanovism: movement begun in the USSR in 1935 to speed up industrial production. Stakhanovite workers received higher pay and other privileges.

3. The freedom of the poet Taras Shevchenko was bought for 2,500 rubles realized from the sale of a portrait painted by K.P. Briullov.

4. N.G. Chernyshevsky (1828–89): Russian writer, journalist, historian, economist and literary critic.

5. Reference is to Stalin's famous toast at the end of the Second World War.

6. The most important collection of laws compiled in Kievan Rus' in the eleventh and twelfth centuries on the basis of the common law.

7. Heroic epic written at the end of the twelfth century.

8. VKP(b): All-Union Communist Party (Bolsheviks).

9. The name given to those who rebelled against the Russian government in December, 1825.

10. A.I. Herzen (Iakovlev) (1812–70): Socialist, revolutionary, émigré radical publisher, author, thinker, memoirist.

11. K.E. Voroshilov (1881–1969): Marshal of the Soviet Union.

12. D.S. Korotchenko (1894–1969): Premier of the Ukrainian SSR (1947–54) and Chairman, Presidium of the Supreme Soviet, Ukrainian SSR.

13. Famous Ukrainian Cossack family. V. Kochubei (1640–1708) was General Judge in Mazepa's government. Betrayed Mazepa to Peter the Great but was not believed and, as a result, was executed.

14. Ukrainian noble family that became totally Polonized.

15. M.S. Hrechukha (1902–76): Chairman, Presidium of the Supreme Soviet, Ukrainian SSR (1939–54).

16. P.H. Tychyna (1891–1967): Ukrainian poet, academician, and politician.

17. Adam Kysil (1580–1653): Polish statesman and diplomat descended from an old Ukrainian noble family.

18. Ivan Barabash (died 1648): in Polish service as commander of the so-called "registered" Cossacks. Executed by the Cossacks who went over to Khmelnytsky.

19. MVD: Ministry of Internal Affairs.

20. MGB: Ministry of State Security.

21. A.A. Arakcheev (1769–1834): Artillery general who played a major military and political role under Paul I and Alexander I. His name became a synonym of despotism.

22. E.I. Pugachev (1742–75): leader of a peasant uprising (1773–5). Executed in Moscow.

23. Aleksandr Herzen, "Pisma k protivniku" (Letters to an Opponent, 1865) in A.I. Gertsen, *Sobranie sochinenii* (Collected Works) (Moscow 1954–66), 18: 289.

24. V.G. Belinsky (1811–48): One of the most important and influential figures in Russian intellectual and literary history. Leading proponent of a democratic but "one and indivisible" Russia, and a strong opponent of the development of the Ukrainian language.

25. Ie.P. Hrebinka (1812–48): Ukrainian writer.

26. Aleksandr Herzen, "O razvitii revoliutsionnykh idei v Rossii" (On the Development of Revolutionary Ideas in Russia, 1850), *Sobranie sochinenii* (Collected Works), 7: 243.

IV
PROGRAMMATIC DOCUMENTS
AND APPEALS

RESOLUTIONS OF THE THIRD EXTRAORDINARY GRAND ASSEMBLY OF THE ORGANIZATION OF UKRAINIAN NATIONALISTS 21–5 AUGUST 1943

Two Years of Struggle

In the spring of 1941, shortly after the completion of the deliberations of the Second Grand Assembly of the OUN, significant changes occurred in the course of the imperialist war. The German and Russian imperialists abandoned all diplomatic activity and entered into an open military conflict. With the outbreak of the German-Bolshevik war, the focus of world events shifted to the territories of Eastern Europe. Thus, Ukraine became not only the object of imperialist aspirations, but also the arena of the greatest and most brutal battles in history. As a result of the German army's military successes in 1941–2, all Ukrainian territory came under German occupation for some time.

The arrival of the new occupying power brought great political change to Ukraine. It is true that political oppression, economic exploitation and the extermination of the Ukrainian people remained a constant fact, but their forms had changed. The undisguised Nazi program of enslavement and the Germans' brutal colonial practices immediately thrust the whole Ukrainian nation into a very difficult position. The new reality compelled the whole nation and every individual to consider their position seriously.

The German policy of mass pillage and violence created a singular atmosphere for the growth of political consciousness among the broad masses of the people.

If the USSR had been destroyed and the Ukrainian people faced only with the threat of consolidation of the German occupation, the development of its political consciousness would have followed an unbroken line, proceeding logically and without any divergence to a clearly formulated national program in theory and a single front of all political forces in practice. However, this process of political growth was complicated by the advance of Russian-Bolshevik imperialism. The mere existence of the USSR and the Red Army has constituted a substantial danger of a return of the Bolshevik regime to Ukraine. Claiming that it penalizes only certain strata of society, the Russian-Bolshevik regime offers the rest of the population the fiction of a peaceful and tranquil life and the false prospect of happiness and well-being in the future. The Bolshevik system of occupation, in counterbalance to the German, is hindering the political activization of the masses and the creation of a single front composed of all the political forces of the nation.

It is characteristic of German Nazism and Russian Bolshevism that, politically, they did not destroy each other on Ukrainian territory. By going their separate ways and pursuing their individual goals, in practical terms each only lightened the task of the other. Some of the weaker segments of society, frightened by the prospect of a return of the Bolsheviks, saw salvation in the Germans' strength; others, crushed by the German colonial boot, chose what they considered the lesser evil and awaited salvation from the Bolsheviks. If in Ukraine, as in other countries of Eastern Europe, a part of the population has looked and continues to look to the Bolsheviks, this is due primarily to the German colonial system.

The double German-Bolshevik onslaught created very difficult conditions for spreading the idea of Ukrainian sovereignty. The problem was also complicated by the fact that, in 1941–2, both the occupying forces in Ukraine were great military powers. To take on the program of Ukrainian sovereignty in such conditions meant, in the words of Mikhnovsky,[1] to believe "contrary to reason." It would appear that no subject people has ever faced such a difficult and complex situation in its history. Only the vital strength of the Ukrainian people made it possible to pass through this period victoriously. Of course, this does not mean that the political campaign of Ukrainian revolutionary ideas proceeded easily, that political successes were gained at a small price. This is not the time to discuss the practical development of our political and organizational work and all the difficulties that went with it. In the most arduous conditions, hounded and pursued by the powerful apparatus of the occupying forces, deep in the underground, perpetually watchful, in ceaseless movement and activity, the cadres of the OUN held their political positions, took the offensive and spread their ideas.

The path travelled in the last two years has been marked by great sacrifices. Dmytro Myron-Andrii,[2] Ivan Klymiv-Lehenda,[3] Mykola Lemyk,[4] Serhii Sherstiuk,[5] Shchepansky[6] and hundreds and thousands of other political fighters laid down their lives in the unequal struggle, attesting with their blood to the nation's unshakable desire to live a free life in its own land.

The arrests and executions near Zviahel, in Kiev, in Iaholnytsia near Chortkiv, in Rivne and Lviv, executions in Kryvyi Rih, Kremenchuk, Zhytomyr, Dzhankoi and other towns covered Ukraine with new graves which, alongside the graves of the Cossacks, will speak for eternity of the indomitable heroism of a great nation.

During these difficult years, the OUN not only maintained the moral position of the Ukrainian people and the Ukrainian national revolution, but also created all the practical preconditions necessary for taking the offensive and gaining ultimate victory. In addition to propaganda work, a good deal of attention, time and energy were devoted to expanding the organizational apparatus. As a result of this organizational work, Ukraine is completely covered by an organizational network. Thus, the political leadership has at its disposal a powerful executive apparatus which makes it possible to carry out political actions and fulfill political plans on all Ukrainian territory.

While expanding its organizational network and bringing the active segments of society into its organized ranks, the OUN constantly kept a finger on the pulse of world political events. The period of relative stability on the fronts was used for more than just strengthening the organization. While forming an organized political force on all territories of Ukraine, the OUN leadership closely observed developments in Ukraine and reacted to each event in the manner demanded by the good of the broadest masses of the Ukrainian people. It could not be otherwise, for the ranks of the OUN were being filled by the best and most active representatives of the people themselves. For this reason, in spite of the sacrifices of its cadres, the leadership maintained the organization in a state of constant struggle for the people's most elementary rights.

The defence of the people against the terror imposed by the occupying power centred on two problems: the transport of people to Germany for hard labour and the pillage of food. The OUN regarded both these actions as conscious and planned attempts by the enemy to exterminate the people, and it immediately launched a strong counteraction. The degree of organized resistance and the form that it took depended upon the strength of the organized network in a given region, the extent to which the population understood the threat posed by enemy action and was psychologically prepared to give battle and, finally, the tactical requirements of waging our struggle on particular territories of Ukraine. For these reasons, the practical results of the action varied from one region to another. The greatest successes in this regard were attained in the north-western provinces of Volhynia and Polissia, where the deportation of workers was halted completely at the very beginning, that is, in the spring of 1942. The peasants of those regions also refused to allow themselves to be robbed of food products. Apart from these two problems, which were prevalent throughout Ukraine, the programme of struggle and self-defence also encompassed other problems encountered to a greater or lesser extent in individual regions.

Thus, in constant movement and struggle, the nation was activated and its organized political force, the OUN, grew and gained strength. The OUN's sacrifices did not go to waste: in the place of the fallen, numerous new detachments arose.

And for the mass of the people, active struggle brought only success. In those places where the people immediately took up the struggle against the occupying forces, the results were beneficial and significant. The resistance to deportation for hard labour in Germany obviously claimed some victims, but these sacrifices allowed the young to remain in place, in Ukraine. In this manner, the organization succeeded in greatly reducing the number of people who were taken forcibly to Germany, where many are dying every day from air attacks and the artificially induced famine and epidemics in German camps. For this reason, after a certain time, the people understood the correctness of the OUN's decision and responded to its new appeals with complete confidence. At the same time, the people became aware of the harmful work done by all the institutions, staffed by opportunists or agents, which were established in Ukraine by the Germans and have been calling on the people to go to Germany, to their certain deaths. It is clear that our liberation struggle would become impossible if the occupying power succeeded in depriving the nation of those of its members who are fit for battle, in particular, its youth.

By the spring of 1943, the OUN's political campaign was being executed in a perceptibly more uniform manner. During their spring attempts to recruit workers into "captivity," the Germans encountered massive resistance in Volhynia, Polissia, Galicia and in the central and eastern provinces. Chyhyryn, Kryvyi Rih and Novomoskovsk stood at the forefront of a unanimous and complete resistance. German attempts to pillage food have been met in a similar way.

The spring of 1943 brought new changes in the distribution of world political power. The German and Russian imperialists experienced great changes. The process of destruction and decline of the warring imperialists' strength had been proceeding systematically and incessantly during the last few years, but the results of this process did not manifest themselves until the spring of 1943. Defeats suffered by the German army at the fronts signalled the approach of catastrophe. And it was not only at the front that the harbingers of this catastrophe appeared. At this time, the whole system of German imperialism began to crack, revealing countless threatening gaps. Since that time, it has continued to totter and, because of the contradictions that lie at its very foundations, it is heading for inevitable collapse. Similar problems are evident on the Bolshevik side. The command of the Red Army was incapable of taking advantage of the extraordinary chance offered it as a result of the total collapse of the southern part of the Germans' eastern front. It became evident that neither the Red Army nor the economy of the USSR was capable of undertaking any serious military action. The desperate cries for assistance from the Allies in the form of a second front grew even louder. Since that time, the successes of the Red Army have been due in large measure to the weakening of Germany, which has been accelerated by the Allies' active offensives in Africa, Sicily and European air space.

Events have again vindicated our thesis regarding the destructive character of both the Russian and German forms of imperialism and the contradictions that lie at their centres, causing them to collapse when seriously shaken. The war became the shock that revealed the weakness of the German and Muscovite-Bolshevik empires. The subject peoples were given a real possibility to strike successfully from within at those things which, in contradiction to mankind's constructive tendencies, are generated by criminal elements overcome by the lust for power and easy gain. At the beginning of the war, our decision to look to our nation's own strength appeared utopian to the weaker segments of society. The thesis which we constantly emphasized, that by means of revolution we would decide the outcome of the war and determine the fate of Ukraine and her future regime, seemed to many a "hope against hope." Our practical work of political organization was dubbed belated quixotism both by our enemies and by some of our countrymen who were blinded by false splendour, particularly that of German imperialism. But the development of events during the last two years and our intense political work confirmed in practice our basic political thesis, which for us has been one of the most essential truths, serving us in our campaign as both a beacon and a helm.

Correct political thinking, planned and well-thought-out political campaigns, strict adherence to principle and determined, consistent practical efforts have resulted in significant successes. For the eastern provinces, the spring months of 1943 were critical. At that time, the growth of political consciousness and increase in activity among the masses began to proceed at a rapid tempo. The idea of an independent Ukrainian state was now attracting not only individuals, not only communities, but the whole population of the region. At about the same time, the populations of the north-western provinces of Volhynia and Polissia began to manifest their readiness for military action.

At its Third Conference in February 1943,[7] the OUN leadership considered the state of our internal strength and the strength of the enemy, examined external political conditions and ascertained that they had become favourable for military action. After this, the first armed detachments of the Ukrainian Insurgent Army (UPA) appeared in Polissia and Volhynia. From that time on, the defence of the Ukrainian population of Polissia and Volhynia was assumed by a Ukrainian military force. In addition to its duties of self-defence, the UPA also immediately took on the task of organizing the framework of a future Ukrainian People's Army.

News about the UPA, about the armed defence and struggle in Polissia and Volhynia, evoked enthusiasm and aroused the fighting spirit of those living in other provinces of Ukraine. Discussions about the possibility or impossibility of establishing our own forces, about the possibility or impossibility of forming an independent Ukrainian state, ceased. Having cast off their doubts, vacillations and discussions, the masses longed for only one thing: to fight actively, to take the offensive. The Ukrainian giant raised his shoulders; the spirit of revolution made itself felt.

The UPA movement spread rapidly from the Brest, Pinsk, Volhynia and Rivne oblasts to the Kamianets-Podilskyi, Vinnytsia, Zhytomyr and Kiev oblasts. At the beginning of July 1943, armed detachments of the Ukrainian People's Self-Defence (UNS)[8] appeared in Galicia. The UNS was formed in response to the people's need for protection from the terror imposed by the occupying forces, but it soon began to organize itself into regular army divisions. Thus, by July 1943, twelve oblasts of Ukraine had taken the path of armed struggle against the occupying forces for the establishment of an independent, united Ukrainian state. This fact brought enormous changes to the political struggle of the Ukrainian people. The struggle entered a new, higher phase. In addition to a radical change in tactics, the circumstances necessitated a change in the OUN's organizational structure and programme. Because the necessary changes went beyond the official competence of the leadership, it convened an Extraordinary Grand Assembly of the OUN in August 1943.[9] This completed the two-year period of political struggle which, because of its form and content, forms a separate epoch in the history of the OUN.

*   *   *

Reports and discussions at the Assembly revealed that many new problems were resolved in action. In that regard, the leading cadres of the OUN displayed a great deal of elasticity and political discernment. It is characteristic that the decisions made were correct, that is, they conformed to the basic ideological and political theses of the OUN. The transition to new tactics was made in the course of the struggle and was dictated not by theoretical reflections but by the demands imposed by circumstances. There has been sufficient time for practice to demonstrate the correctness of these changes. The Third Extraordinary Grand Assembly of the OUN considered the tactics used in the past and recognized that the transition to armed struggle in all its forms was correct.

Circumstances made it necessary to consider questions regarding the programme. Linked to the programme were three basic questions of an ideological nature: the questions of nation, society and state.

Like all previous assemblies, the Third Extraordinary Grand Assembly takes as its fundamental principle the living historical truth that the nation—the highest organic human community—is indestructible. For this reason, it regards the national principle as the basis for political order in the world. Only that order can be just and durable which is founded not on doctrinaire theses but on the eternal laws of existence. A system of free peoples and independent states is the best and only solution to the problems of world order. Attempts to organize the world on other bases have never yielded positive results. All supra-national political creations—empires—have always been agents of historical reaction and decline. Within empires, one people always subjugates others and causes them to decline.

For this reason, the OUN stands for the right of every people to lead an independent life in its own state and to pursue full cultural and economic development, for only in this way can humanity progress.

While fighting for the liberation of the Ukrainian people, the OUN is already working to establish political co-operation with other subject peoples and will co-operate with all free peoples in the future. The basis of this co-operation is mutual respect and recognition of the right of all to lead a free existence. The OUN wishes to hasten the Ukrainian nation's historical evolution into a homogeneous society by removing all economic and social inequalities. We believe that the present historical era offers every prospect for the establishment of an economic order which will provide equal opportunities for work and earnings to all citizens. By abolishing all forms of exploitation of one class by another, we will create a just social order in Ukraine.

Only this type of social order can guarantee that government will not be at the service of any single class, but will, instead, serve as an organizing, planning and governing body for all the people.

Under such circumstances, the state itself will be more than just a mechanical, unifying framework; it will become a living organization of the whole nation.

The free individual represents the ideal of the new society. The fundamental moving force in society will be the free initiative of individuals. But this free initiative must follow the interests of society and never mere self-interest, which would result in the exploitation of other "free" individuals, as happens within the capitalist system.

These ideas form the basis of the programmatic resolutions of the Third Extraordinary Grand Assembly of the OUN. The resolutions represent the gains made by our political theory and practice during the last two years. They are a concrete formulation of the concept of the future Ukrainian state. Time and further struggle will bring new gains and will enable us to formulate an even clearer and more detailed programme.

In formulating its programme, the Third Extraordinary Grand Assembly of the OUN views it as more than just a goal which we are approaching in our present conditions of struggle. The programme must also serve as a mighty weapon which will help increase our strength and ease our victory.

The Third Extraordinary Assembly of the OUN also dealt with a whole range of problems arising from the current political situation. We shall mention here the question of the arrival of the Bolsheviks, the question of military strength and the question of unity. The decisions of the Grand Assembly have been expressed, in part, in the resolutions cited here and, in part, in the directions set for our work and the concrete indications given to the leadership of the organization. The accepted directions and instructions are already being put into effect and will continue to be applied in accordance with foreign and domestic developments.

One of the main issues on which the Grand Assembly had to take a position was that of the new Bolshevik occupation of Ukrainian territories. This is not the place to discuss the complete plan for our further struggle; we will only affirm that, in the opinion of the Grand Assembly, only a *politically and militarily organized* people will be able to protect itself against extermination by the Bolsheviks and continue the struggle for its own state. The practices of the Bolsheviks in their offensives in the spring of this year and at the present time demonstrate that they are intent on the conscious destruction of the Ukrainian people. It is not important whether they do this by means of merciless executions or by forcibly driving untrained men and women to the first line of the front to face German machine guns. What is important to us is the fact that in this manner the Bolsheviks are continuing the coercive mobilization of Ukrainians into the Red Army and are imitating the German tactic of removing from Ukraine those who are fit for military action.

The people must defend themselves against this danger. We say the people, for we are not speaking here about some particular segment of the nation, about those who favour independence or those who do not; we are speaking about every Ukrainian peasant, worker and intellectual. Let no one delude himself that he personally will remain unscathed by the Bolsheviks.

The Ukrainian people, who do not want to go defencelessly to the slaughter in the manner of the Jews,[10] must resist the rapacity of the Bolshevik imperialists in an organized, military fashion. This does not mean that we will seek all-out confrontations at every moment, regardless of external conditions. The moment of confrontation will be decided by the requirements of the goals and directions of the liberation struggle. But it does mean that the Ukrainian people will meet the Bolshevik occupation prepared and ready to defend their rights. The forms taken by the struggle waged under German and Bolshevik occupation have been and will continue to be determined by the conditions that exist at any given time and by the goals which, at any given moment, we wish to attain. Nevertheless, the preparation or, rather, the practical execution of our task is already under way. It is certainly not too soon, for the consolidation of a people's political and military force demands a great deal of time, and military units intended to form the nucleus of an army are always the products of long preparation and struggle.

Related to the current political situation and to our tasks is the question of participation by all the people in the struggle. This question was also thoroughly examined by the Grand Assembly. The Ukrainian state is the possession of all the citizens of Ukraine; for this reason, all must fight for it. Furthermore, at the present time, danger threatens the whole nation, so all its sons must take up the struggle. Even thousands of the most dedicated fighters will not liberate Ukraine if the whole nation does not take part in the struggle. Anyone who has not understood this, or who, having understood, withdraws from the struggle, is a deserter and a saboteur and will be treated as such by the people.

For this reason the OUN, as the leader of the revolutionary liberation struggle, summons all citizens to direct participation. The OUN is not fighting for Ukraine for its own benefit; it is not fighting to govern Ukraine or for a [particular] form of government. The government and its form will be chosen by the people themselves and by their finest representatives. But today, the OUN is the leading force in the nation's liberation struggle and, for this reason, it calls on others to join this struggle. No one can stand aside. The whole nation must take the burden of struggle onto its shoulders. Certain aspects of the current liberation struggle, particularly the military aspect, demand a whole range of experts. They exist among the Ukrainian people and they must hasten to serve their nation. The OUN believes that it is the duty of every Ukrainian citizen to serve the cause of Ukrainian liberation, and it will consistently fulfill this requirement. Thus, in the opinion of the Grand Assembly, conditions will also be created for unifying the whole nation; only in battle will this be accomplished. Accordingly, in developing particular forms of the liberation struggle and drawing the broadest masses into this struggle, the OUN also recognizes that ending party conflicts and unifying all Ukrainians is one of the fundamental tasks at the present moment.

August 1943

I. Programmatic Resolutions

The Organization of Ukrainian Nationalists is fighting for an independent, united Ukrainian state and for the right of every nation to lead a free life in its own independent state. The only way to effect a just solution to the national and social problem in the world is to bring an end to the subjugation and exploitation of one nation by another and to establish a system of free peoples living in their own independent states.

The OUN is fighting against imperialism and against empires, for within empires one ruling people culturally and politically subjugates and economically exploits other peoples. For this reason, the OUN is fighting against the USSR and against Germany's "New Europe."

The OUN is resolutely fighting against both internationalist and fascist national-socialist programmes and political concepts, for they are the tools of imperialist policies of conquest. Thus, we are opposed both to Russian-Bolshevik communism and to German National Socialism.

The OUN is opposed to any people, intent on fulfilling its imperialist goals, "liberating," "taking under its protection" or "into its care" other peoples, for these deceptive phrases conceal a repugnant reality: subjugation, coercion and plunder. For this reason, the OUN will struggle against the Russian-Bolshevik and German plunderers until it rids Ukraine of all "protectors" and "liberators," until it attains an independent, united Ukrainian state in which peasants, workers and intellectuals will be able to live and develop in a free, prosperous and cultured manner.

The OUN is for the full liberation of the Ukrainian people from the Muscovite-Bolshevik and German yoke; it is for the establishment of an independent, united Ukrainian state free of landowners and capitalists, as well as of Bolshevik commissars, NKVD agents and party parasites.

In the Ukrainian state, the governing power will regard serving the interests of the people as its hightest duty. Since it will have no plans for conquest, nor any subjugated countries or oppressed peoples within its state, the national government of Ukraine will not waste time, energy or financial resources on establishing an apparatus of oppression. The Ukrainian national regime will direct all economic resources and all human energies toward establishing a new political order and a just social system, toward building up the economy of the country and raising the cultural level of the people.

Within the ranks of the OUN, Ukrainian peasants, workers and intellectuals are fighting against their oppressors for an independent, united Ukrainian state, for national and social liberation, for a new political and social order.

1. a) For the destruction of the Bolsheviks' and Germans' exploitative system of serfdom in the organization of the rural economy. Since the land is the property of the people, the Ukrainian national regime will not impose on farmers any one method of working the land. In the Ukrainian state, both individual and collective work on the land will be permitted; the method will depend upon the will of the farmers.

b) For a free transfer to peasants in western Ukrainian oblasts of all lands held by landowners, monasteries and churches.

2. a) For state ownership of large industry and co-operative ownership of small industry.

b) For the participation of workers in the direction of factories; for directors to be chosen on the basis of expertise, rather than on the commissar-party principle.[11]

3. a) For a universal eight-hour work day. Overtime will have to be consented to freely—like all work in general—and will have to bring the worker additional wages.

b) For fair wages for work; for the participation of workers in the profits of commercial enterprises. Every worker will receive a wage sufficient to meet the material and spiritual needs of his entire household. During the period when annual financial reviews of commercial enterprises are carried out, every worker will receive the following: in co-operative enterprises—a dividend (his share of the yearly profits); in state-owned enterprises—a premium.

c) For freedom in work, a free choice of profession, and a free choice of the place of work.

d) For free trade unions. For the abolition of the Stakhanov[12] work method, socialist competition, increasing norms and other methods of exploiting workers.

4. For freedom in the trades; for the right of tradesmen to unite voluntarily in workmen's associations; for the right of the tradesman to leave the association in order to pursue his work on an individual basis and to dispose freely of his income.

5. For state ownership of large business; for co-operative and private ownership of small business; for free marketplaces.

6. For full equality of women with men in all the rights and obligations of citizenship; for free access for women to all schools and all professions; for the fundamental right of women to engage in physically lighter work, so that women will not be obliged to ruin their health by seeking employment in mines and other heavy industries. For state protection of motherhood. Fathers will receive, in addition to wages for their work, a supplementary payment for the support of their wives and of children who have not yet reached the age of majority. Only in these conditions will women have the opportunity to carry out their important, honourable and responsible duties as mothers and educators of the younger generation.

7. a) For compulsory secondary education. For raising the educational and cultural level of the population by increasing the numbers of schools, publishers, libraries, museums, cinemas, theatres and similar institutions.

b) For increased advanced and professional training; for a continual growth of cadres of highly qualified specialists in every field of human endeavour.

c) For free access by young people to all institutions of higher learning. For ensuring students' ability to pursue their studies by providing stipends, food, habitation and the equipment necessary for education.

d) For a harmonious, all-round development of the younger generation in the moral, intellectual and physical spheres. For free access to all the scientific and cultural achievements of mankind.

8. For respect for the work of intellectuals. For creating material conditions for intellectual work that will ensure the well-being of the intellectual's family, so that he can be free to devote himself to his cultural and creative work and constantly increase his knowledge and raise his intellectual and cultural level.

9. a) For protection of all workers in old age and in case of illness or handicap.

b) For the establishment of large-scale health care; for a broadening of the network of hospitals, sanatoriums, health resorts and rest homes. For expanding the medical cadres. For the right of workers to have access, without payment, to all health institutions.

c) For special state protection of children and youths; for an expansion of the network of nurseries, kindergartens, sanatoriums, recreation camps and sport organizations; for the inclusion of all children and youths in the programs of state institutions dedicated to care and education.

10. a) For freedom of the press, speech, thought, convictions, worship and world-view. Against the official imposition on society of any doctrines or dogmas with regard to world-view.

b) For the freedom to profess and practice any religion which does not run counter to the morals of society.

c) For the separation of church organizations from the state.

d) For cultural relations with other nations; for the right of citizens to go abroad for education, medical treatment or in order to learn about the life and cultural achievements of other nations.

11. For the full right of national minorities to cultivate their own national cultures.

12. For equality of all citizens of Ukraine, whatever their nationality, with regard to the rights and obligations of citizenship; for the equal right of all to work, remuneration and rest.

13. For a free, fully Ukrainian culture; for a spirit of heroism and a high moral standard; for civic solidarity, friendship and discipline.

II. Political Resolutions

A. The international situation

1. The present war is a typical war between competing imperialist powers for domination of the world, for a new division of material wealth, for the acquisition of new sources of raw materials and markets and for the exploitation of labour.

2. The warring imperialist powers are not bringing the world any progressive political or social ideas. In particular, Germany's so-called "New Europe" and Moscow's "Soviet Union" are a denial of the

right of peoples to free political and cultural development in their own states; instead, they bring political and social enslavement to all peoples. For this reason, a victory for the imperialist powers in the current war and the organization of the world according to imperialist principles would bring only a momentary pause in the war and would soon lead to new collisions between the imperialist powers over the division of the spoils of war and new conflicts. At the same time, the liberation movements of the peoples subjugated by the imperialist powers would become the seeds of new conflicts and revolutions. Thus, a victory for the imperialist powers in the present war would lead to chaos and further suffering for millions of people in the captive nations.

3. At this time, the present imperialist war has entered a decisive phase, which is characterized by:

    a) the exhaustion of the imperialist powers,
    b) an increase in the contradictions between the imperialist powers,
    c) the development of the struggle of the subject peoples.

At the same time, the present war is serving as an external auxiliary factor, bringing nearer the time of the outbreak of national and social revolutions in the captive nations.

4. The reactionary and anti-popular plans of German racist imperialism to enslave other peoples, the Germans' terroristic practices on occupied territories and the subject peoples' struggle against the so-called "New Europe" have hastened the complete political collapse of German imperialism. Now, as a result of the blows dealt by her imperialist opponents and of the liberation struggle waged by the subject peoples, Germany is also approaching inevitable military defeat.

5. Bolshevik Moscow, ideologically and politically compromised and materially weakened, is making use of the Germans' terroristic policy on occupied territories and of the provisions supplied by the Allies in order to continue the war.

Only the fear of German occupation and the internal Stalinist terror are compelling the soldiers of the Red Army to continue fighting. The enormous losses of human life and military equipment are deepening the internal crisis of the Muscovite imperialist regime. The shortage of food in the country, along with the landing of the Allies in Europe, and the threat posed as a result to Bolshevik plans, are compelling the Bolsheviks to accelerate their own offensive.

The aim of the Bosheviks, under the guise of their so-called "defence of the fatherland," revived Slavophilism[13] and pseudo-revolutionary rhetoric, is to pursue the goals of Muscovite imperialism, that is, to gain dominion over Europe, and eventually the whole world. The point of departure for the fulfillment of Moscow's imperialist plans is Ukraine, with all her natural wealth. Further bases for fulfilling the plans of Muscovite imperialism are the Balkans, the Baltic region and Scandinavia.

6. In spite of the differences that exist among the Allies, they are waging the war for the destruction of their rivals, above all, of German imperialism. The Allies' next task is the destruction of Japanese imperialism. In order to bring about the destruction of these opponents, the Allies are making use of Muscovite imperialism and will attempt to do so as long as possible. At the same time, the domination of Europe by the Bolsheviks is not in the interest of the Allies, and they are attempting in the present war to weaken, and eventually destroy, Muscovite imperialism. The continuation of the war on the eastern front and the mutual destruction of German and Muscovite imperialism are in accord with the interests of the Allies. The goal of the Allies—especially Britain—on the European continent is the defeat, or at least the substantial weakening, of all the imperialist states of Europe and the establishment of an order which would guarantee them a decisive voice in Europe and give free rein to Anglo-Saxon political and economic influence. In order to attain these goals, the Allies are gaining control or attempting to gain control of the most important bases around and inside Europe (Sicily, the Apennine and Balkan peninsulas, Scandinavia and the Caucasus).

7. The subject peoples and their struggle for liberation constitute one of the most important elements in the further development of the current political situation. The military superiority of the imperialist powers at the present moment still prevents a full manifestation of the powers of the subject peoples. But as the war crisis deepens, the strength of the subject peoples is increasing and the moment of national and social revolutions is approaching: the subject peoples are becoming a new, decisive political factor. Only on the platform of a new political concept with regard to the subject peoples, a concept which, in opposition to the imperialist powers, guarantees every people the right to its own national state and grants it social justice, can a just order be built and a lasting peace maintained among nations.

8. The approaching military collapse of Germany in the East and the complete ideological and political bankruptcy of Muscovite-Bolshevik imperialism have set the subject peoples of the East the task of fighting against imperialist oppressors in order to rebuild the East according to the new principles of freedom for peoples, autonomy in free, independent states and the liberation of nations and individuals from political oppression and economic exploitation. Only by way of national and social revolutions, waged by the subject peoples of the East for the sake

of new progressive ideas and the struggle against imperialism, can Muscovite-Bolshevik imperialism be destroyed.

9. Ukraine stands at the centre of the present imperialist war. Muscovite and German imperialists are fighting for the domination and exploitation of Ukraine. At the same time, Ukraine, as the bearer of progressive ideas to all the subject peoples, is becoming a decisive factor in the preparation of revolutions in the East. Ukraine is the first country in the East to have raised the flag of resolute struggle by the subject peoples against the imperialists, and she will begin the period of national and social revolutions. Only through a common struggle of the Ukrainian people along with those of other subject peoples of the East can Bolshevism be defeated. The re-establishment of an independent, united Ukrainian state will guarantee the re-establishment and permanent existence of the national states of other peoples of Eastern, South-Eastern and Northern Europe and of the subject peoples of Asia. Only with the existence of a Ukrainian state can permanent existence be guaranteed for those peoples which, in mutual understanding and co-operation based on the principles of the right of every people to its own state, a just social order and economic independence, oppose all the covetous plans of hostile imperialist powers. In this way, lasting peace and the peaceful national, social and cultural development of these peoples will be guaranteed.

B. The internal situation on Ukrainian territory

I. External factors

10. In spite of the blows sustained by Germany on all fronts, her policy on occupied Ukrainian territory continues to follow the line of total political subjugation and merciless colonial economic pillage of the Ukrainian people.

11. Bolshevik agents of Muscovite imperialism in Ukraine (Bolshevik partisans, the so-called People's Guard)[14] are preparing the Bolshevik occupation of all Ukrainian territories by spreading discord among the Ukrainian people, provoking German attacks on them and exterminating members of the Ukrainian independence movement.

12. The remnants of the White Russian imperialists (Vlasov,[15] the Union of Russian Officers) do not constitute an independent political force. Serving foreign imperialists and aspiring to re-establish a reactionary regime of landowners and capitalists, they exert no political influence among the Ukrainian people and are driving the Russians to Bolshevism.

13. The Polish imperialist ruling class is the hireling of foreign imperialists and an enemy of national freedom. It is attempting to harness the Polish minorities in Ukraine and the mass of the Polish people to struggle against the Ukrainian people and helping German and Muscovite imperialists to exterminate the Ukrainian people.

14. The national minorities in Ukraine, conscious of the fact that they share the fate of the Ukrainian people, are fighting together with them for a Ukrainian state.

II. The internal situation in Ukraine

15. The present period of the Ukrainian people's liberation struggle is marked by a great increase, on all territories, of national consciousness and political activity. This increase is manifesting itself in the following ways:

a) a linking of the masses with the revolutionary liberation programme and tactics of the Organization of Ukrainian Nationalists,

b) the direct participation of the masses in the struggle, particularly in its new self-defence and military actions.

16. All attempts by opportunists to steer the Ukrainian people's liberation struggle for an independent, united Ukrainian state onto the sideroad of co-operation with the imperialist forces of occupation and to link the cause of Ukrainian liberation to the imperialists' plans have been shattered by the determined resistance of the Ukrainian masses.

17. The fully autonomomous, pro-independence Organization of Ukrainian Nationalists is the sole leader of the Ukrainian people's revolutionary liberation struggle for an independent, united Ukrainian state (USSD).[16]

C. Our goals

18. The Organization of Ukrainian Nationalists is fighting for an independent, united Ukrainian state, for the right of every people to its own independent state, for the liberation of the subject peoples from imperialist powers and for the establishment of a just political and social order.

D. The methods and forms of our struggle

19. The only method of fulfilling our goals is a revolutionary struggle waged by the Ukrainian people and all other subject peoples against the imperialism of Berlin and Moscow. This struggle will hasten the defeat of both forms of imperialism and, by means of national revolutions among the subject peoples, will lead to the re-establishment of national states.

20. Only through united struggle will the Ukrainian people attain an independent, united Ukrainian state. For this reason, our task is to include the broadest masses of the people in a planned and active struggle. During the current pre-revolutionary period, the masses are to be included in the struggle by actively participating in:

    a) political actions,
    b) actions of self-defence,
    c) military actions.

21. The unification of the Ukrainian people will be achieved only through struggle. Aspiring to the unification of the Ukrainian people, we look at the present time to those who are capable of revolutionary struggle.

22. An armed force of the Ukrainian people is the basic precondition of victory in the struggle for an independent, united Ukrainian state.

23. We will attain our goals by going beyond the boundaries of Ukraine and linking our struggle for an independent, united Ukrainian state to that of other peoples subjugated or threatened by imperialist powers, in particular, the peoples of the East, the Baltic region and the Balkans, by propagating and putting into effect our motto of for freedom for nations and individuals and of the right of every people to an independent national state, and by countering the reactionary concepts and plans of the imperialist powers.

24. An organized military and political force of the Ukrainian people is the only guarantee of success on the external front of our struggle.

25. In leading the struggle against the imperialist oppressors of Ukraine, we stand for the exclusion of all secondary fronts. In our relations with our neighbours, we count on co-operation with their national masses and the revolutionary, non-imperialist segments of their societies. We fight against all sympathizers of the imperialist powers.

E. Our attitude to territorial and political changes in Ukraine

26. The Berlin and Moscow imperialists warring in the East are

headed for self-destruction. Territorial and political changes in the East and movements of the fronts and borders are and will continue to be nothing more than an expression of the transitory distribution of power between the imperialists. They do not demonstrate the internal capacities of the imperialist states permanently to rule over and organize the East. The only organic and durable forces in the East are the forces of the subject peoples, which are striving toward national and social revolutions and toward the reconstruction of their own national states. At the present time, their struggle is directed toward undermining the strength of Muscovite and German imperialism.

We will wage our struggle for the realization of our goals independently of any territorial and political changes that may occur in the East.

We are meeting the occupation of Ukrainian territories by the Bolsheviks with a planned and active struggle, waged in whatever forms will lead to a collapse of the state apparatus of Muscovite imperialism and contribute to the growth of the Ukrainian people's organized forces in its struggle for an independent, united Ukrainian state. Organized and planned participation by the masses in an active struggle under the new Bolshevik occupation is the only way to defend the Ukrainian people against extermination by the Bolsheviks and to attain an independent, united Ukrainian state. We will wage our struggle on all Ukrainian territories occupied by the Bolsheviks as well as beyond the borders of Ukraine, in close co-operation with other subject peoples.

Our attitude toward all external forces is dependent upon their attitude to the idea of Ukrainian sovereignty.

"In Eastern Europe, there are no colonies for anyone; whoever seeks them will find nothing but a grave."
M. Kolodzinsky,[17] *Ukrainian Military Doctrine*

Source: Ideia i Chyn 2, no. 5 (1943): 1–10 (partial text). Original: Archive of the Foreign Representation of the Supreme Ukrainian Liberation Council. Photocopy: Archive, *Litopys UPA*.

NOTES

1. Mykola Mikhnovsky (1873–1924): political and social activist and Kharkiv lawyer; author of *Samostiina Ukraina* (Independent Ukraine), published in 1900, one of the first works of Ukrainian nationalist literature.
2. Dmytro Myron ("Orlyk") (1911–42): a leading figure in the OUN, he

was arrested by the Gestapo in Kiev and killed during an attempted escape.

3. Ivan Klymiv ("Lehenda") (1915–42): leading figure in the OUN. Killed by the Gestapo.

4. Mykola Lemyk (1914–41): member of the OUN. In 1933 he assassinated A. Mailov, a staff member of the Soviet consulate in Lviv. Hanged by the Germans.

5. Serhii Sherstiuk: member of the OUN. Killed by the Gestapo in Kryvyi Rih in 1942.

6. Petro Shchepansky: killed by the Gestapo in Kremenchuk.

7. Third Conference of the OUN, 17–21 February 1943. Important for changes introduced into the political programme and organizational structure of the OUN.

8. Ukrainska Narodnia Samooborona (Ukrainian People's Self-Defence): organization that preceded the UPA in Galicia. Most of its members were incorporated into regular units of the UPA. In several areas the UNS continued to exist parallel to the UPA in the form of irregular units of the underground.

9. The same as the Third Extraordinary Grand Assembly of the OUN, 21–5 August 1943. It abolished the position of "leader," replacing it with a collegial organ, and revised the OUN programme by introducing progressive social and economic ideas.

10. The Ukrainian underground did not come out with an explicit defence of the Jews as a people.

11. Reference is to the *nomenklatura* system, one of the main instruments of political control in the USSR—the list of positions in state, economic and social institutions and organizations which are filled exclusively on the recommendation of party organs by persons from special lists compiled for that purpose.

12. Stakhanov movement: a form of "socialist competition" representing an attempt to establish high records of productivity. Formally it was considered a voluntary expression of workers' initiative, but in reality it was organized by directives from above.

13. Slavophiles: representatives of the conservative Russian intelligentsia of the nineteenth century.

14. Narodnia Hvardiia im. I. Franka (I. Franko People's Guard): a small pro-Soviet underground organization established in Lviv in the autumn of 1942.

15. Andrei Vlasov (1900–46): Soviet general taken prisoner by the Germans; organized the Russian Liberation Army, which fought with the Germans against the USSR. Extradited by the Americans, Vlasov was executed in Moscow.

16. *Ukrainska Samostiina Soborna Derzhava* (USSD): Ukrainian independent united state.

17. Mykhailo Kolodzinsky (1902–39): member of the Ukrainian Military Or-
    ganization (UVO) and leading figure in the OUN. Chief of Staff of the
    Carpathian Sich. Killed in battle with the Hungarian army.

GENERAL PROCLAMATION OF THE SUPREME UKRAINIAN LIBERATION COUNCIL

People of Ukraine!

In 1917–18, by a revolutionary upheaval, the armed struggle of your finest sons, you erected on the ruins of the empires that had enslaved you for long ages *a temple of freedom—a Ukrainian state*.

Fierce winds scattered your victorious flags over all of Ukraine. The Dnieper's moaning, the roar of the Black Sea waves, the rustle of the feather grass in the plains and the secret murmur of Carpathian and Polissian forests harmonized in one symphony, singing the joyous song of *freedom's victory*. Your age-old enemies destroyed this holy temple of yours, but you, the Ukrainian people, preserved it in your souls as the sacred *vision of your forefathers*.

And for two decades you guarded this vision, resisting its destruction; you fought to defend it. For the idea of a free Ukraine, for your own independent state, you gave millions in sacrifice.

Again the storms of war have been raging for five years and rolling across Ukrainian territory. Ukraine is shuddering under the heels of hordes of enemy soldiers.

It is not for your freedom, people of Ukraine, that they are engaged in this bloody and cruel struggle; they bring you only, devastation, enslavement and death. But you did not surrender. You took up a bloody struggle against all the occupiers of Ukraine. To guard your freedom, you placed—from the Carpathian peaks to the Don and the Caucasus—armed cadres of your sons—the *Ukrainian Insurgent Army*.

People of Ukraine!

The age of national revolutions of liberation is approaching. In their unceasing revolutionary struggle, the subject peoples of East and West are awaiting the moment when, on the ruins of enemy empires, free nations will begin to lead lives of freedom.

The Ukrainian people are entering the *decisive stage* of their struggle for liberation. The moment which generations of Ukrainians have awaited for centuries is approaching, the moment in which our fate will be decided.

The present generation of Ukrainians can be proud of the fact that it will fall to them to complete, by way of heroic struggle, *the establishment of the Ukrainian state and to fulfill the task left to them in legacy by their ancestors.*

The gigantic task of building a Ukrainian state demands even greater determination and even greater devotion; most importantly, it demands that all *the revolutionary forces struggling for independence be united under a single political leadership.*

And thus, in order to unite all the Ukrainian people's national forces of liberation, to direct our liberation struggle from a single centre, to represent the will of the Ukrainian people to the rest of the world and to counter the attempts by the enemies of the Ukrainian state to smash the single front of Ukrainian independence forces, we are establishing the *Supreme Ukrainian Liberation Council, which, from this moment, assumes leadership of the Ukrainian people's struggle for liberation.*

Within the ranks of the Supreme Ukrainian Liberation Council are gathered representatives of all the revolutionary forces of liberation currently active in Ukraine, as well as leading individuals from Ukrainian political circles who now acknowledge the *fully independent platform* of the Ukrainian people's liberation struggle for an independent, united Ukrainian state and who intend to bring it into reality.

All truly autonomous pro-independence forces in Ukraine are eligible to join the Supreme Ukrainian Liberation Council, regardless of their world-view or political and social orientation, as long as they are prepared to fight for a *sovereign Ukrainian state*.

The Supreme Ukrainian Liberation Council is the highest governing body of the Ukrainian nation during the period of revolutionary struggle, until the establishment of the government of an independent, united Ukrainian state.

We, *the Supreme Ukrainian Liberation Council,* pledge the following to you, the *people of Ukraine*:

Our goal is to establish an independent, united Ukrainian state on Ukrainian ethnic territory.

Our path is that of a revolutionary liberation struggle against all conquerors and oppressors of the Ukrainian people.

We will fight for your right *to rule over your own land.*

We will fight to guarantee the whole Ukrainian people the right to participate in determining the future political order and the constitution of the independent, united Ukrainian state. We will fight for *a just social order*, free of oppression and exploitation.

On the altar of this struggle we dedicate our efforts and our lives.

We believe in your strength, people of Ukraine; it is *the guarantee of our victory.*

We salute the struggles of other subject peoples for their liberation. With them and, in particular, with our neighbours, we seek to enjoy good neighbourly relations and to co-operate in common struggle, as long as they respect the liberation struggle of the Ukrainian people.

We call on all the national minorities living in Ukraine to take part in the Ukrainian struggle for liberation. We guarantee them full rights of citizenship in the Ukrainian state.

People of Ukraine!

We are conscious of the fact that the coming struggle will demand of you even greater determination and heroism and, above all, an unshakable belief in *the justness of your cause*.

We believe that you *will not disgrace your land*!

We believe that you will show yourselves to be worthy heirs of the princely retinues and the glory of the Cossacks!

Your ancestors' heroic struggle for a Ukrainian state stands as an order for you to fight!

For this reason we call on you.

United in your struggle, grow stronger in your faith!

Glory to Ukraine!

Supreme Ukrainian Liberation Council

Headquarters of the Supreme
Ukrainian Liberation Council
June[1] 1944

Source: Original: Archive of the Foreign Representation of the Supreme Ukrainian Liberation Council, Folio Y1–2. Photocopy: Archive, *Litopys UPA*.

NOTE

1. This document was adopted by the First Grand Assembly of the Supreme Ukrainian Liberation Council on 11–15 July 1944 and not in June 1944. The earlier date was given in order to mislead the Soviet security organs and prevent them from pursuing the participants. There are various versions of this document in existence. The translation was made from the official version.

PLATFORM OF THE SUPREME UKRAINIAN LIBERATION COUNCIL[1]

1. The Ukrainian national-liberation movement, the establishment of an independent Ukrainian state and the struggle for its consolidation in the years 1917–21 deepened the national consciousness and increased the political activity of the Ukrainian masses.

The collapse of the Ukrainian state as a result of foreign conquest, which was the result of insufficient internal unity of Ukrainian national forces, made it easier for foreigners to gain dominion over Ukraine. This foreign domination has been marked by unprecedented oppression, massive plunder of the Ukrainian people, a return of peasants and workers to a state of true serfdom, merciless exploitation and the extermination of millions of people by means of famine and terror. These terrible and bloody times, twenty-five years in duration, have taught the Ukrainian masses that no foreign political and social system will benefit them and that only the establishment of their own national sovereign state will guarantee the normal existence and development of the nation and its culture and the material and spiritual well-being of the masses.

2. The present war between two huge imperialist powers, Muscovite-Bolshevik and Hitlerite-German, is being waged primarily for dominion over Ukraine as a point of departure to dominion over Eastern Europe and even all of Europe. Both these powers have as their policy the total colonial exploitation of Ukraine and her population. Having seized all the material and economic resources of the Ukrainian people,

they mercilessly exterminate the leading national forces in Ukraine, destroy the national culture and national consciousness of the masses and colonize the country with foreigners, while exterminating great masses of the Ukrainian people or transporting them beyond the boundaries of Ukraine.

3. Nevertheless, this war is also debilitating our enemies and reducing them to a state of social and political disintegration. As a result, conditions are favourable for liberation struggles on the part of the subject peoples and their ultimate victory is facilitated.

4. Under these circumstances, it is essential that

a) in the vortex of the present total war, the Ukrainian people and their leading cadres be protected from extermination,

b) the Ukrainian people be led to battle for their liberation and for their own sovereign state.

For the fulfillment of these tasks, it is necessary that there be a single, pan-Ukrainian national front, organized by uniting all the active national Ukrainian forces endeavouring to establish a sovereign Ukrainian state, and that there be a single governing centre.

For this reason, on the initiative of the Ukrainian Insurgent Army (UPA), which was formed in the process of the Ukrainian people's armed struggle against the plunder and coercion of the peaceable Ukrainian population by the forces of occupation, a pan-Ukrainian governing centre has been established, including representatives from all regions of Ukraine and all Ukrainian political circles, under the name:
Supreme Ukrainian Liberation Council.

I. The Goals and Duties of the Supreme Ukrainian Liberation Council

1. To unite and co-ordinate the activities of all the pro-independence liberation forces of the Ukrainian people on all the territories of Ukraine and beyond these territories in a national-liberation struggle against all the enemies of the Ukrainian people, in particular, against Muscovite-Bolshevik and Hitlerite-German imperialists, for the establishment of an independent, united Ukrainian state.

2. To determine the ideological programme of the Ukrainian people's liberation struggle.

3. To direct the whole Ukrainian national-liberation struggle until the

attainment of sovereignty and the establishment of organs of independent government in the Ukrainian state.

4. To represent, in its capacity as the highest pan-Ukrainian governing centre, the current political struggle of the Ukrainian people, both inside the country and abroad.

5. To bring into being the first government of the Ukrainian state and to convene the first nation-wide Ukrainian representative body.

II. The Fundamental Principles of the Ideological Programme of the Supreme Ukrainian Liberation Council

The preservation of a nation's life, national unity and culture constitutes the primary and highest goal of any sound national organism. A sovereign national state is the chief guarantee of the preservation of a nation's life, its normal development and the well-being of its citizens.

For this reason, the Ukrainian nation should, at this time, dedicate all its powers to the establishment and consolidation of its own state.

All politically active Ukrainian agencies should consolidate their forces in the struggle for an independent Ukrainian state, laying aside all disputes of a social and political nature, for until the attainment of an independent state, these disputes remain in the realm of theory.

The struggle for an independent national state can be successful only if it is carried out independently of the political influences of foreign powers.

Accordingly, the Supreme Ukrainian Liberation Council bases its activity on the following principles:

1. The Supreme Ukrainian Liberation Council aspires to the re-establishment of an independent, united Ukrainian state on all Ukrainian territories by means of revolutionary struggle against all the enemies of Ukrainian sovereignty, in particular, against the Bolshevik and German forces of occupation. The Supreme Ukrainian Liberation Council endeavours to work in co-operation with all those who favour such independence.

2. The Supreme Ukrainian Liberation Council is founded on the principle of complete political independence of the influences of foreign powers and agencies.

3. The Supreme Ukrainian Liberation Council unites all the leading political groupings that favour political sovereignty for the Ukrainian state and political autonomy in the Ukrainian struggle for independence, regardless of their ideological world-views or political and social orientation.

4. To achieve the union of Ukrainian national-liberation forces in the struggle for an independent, united Ukrainian state, the Supreme Ukrainian Liberation Council adopts the following political and social platform:

a) guarantee of a popular, democratic method of determining the political order in the Ukrainian state by means of universal popular representation,

b) guarantee of freedom of thought, world-view and belief,

c) guarantee of the development of Ukrainian national culture,

d) guarantee of a just social order in the Ukrainian state, free of class exploitation and oppression,

e) guarantee of the genuine rule of law in the Ukrainian state and of the equality of all citizens before the law,

f) guarantee of citizenship rights to all national minorities in Ukraine,

g) guarantee of the right of equal educational opportunity for all citizens,

h) guarantee in the labour sector of the right of all citizens to free exercise of initiative, regulated by the demands and needs of the totality of the nation,

i) guarantee of freedom in methods of working the land; designation of a minimum and maximum size for individual farms,

j) socialization of the basic natural wealth of the country: the land, forests, water and underground resources; transfer of arable land to farmers for permanent agricultural use,

k) nationalization of heavy industry and heavy transport; transfer of light industry and the food industry to co-operatives; guarantee of the right to free large-scale co-operation on the part of small producers,

l) guarantee of free trade within limits set by legislation,

m) guarantee of the free development of trades and of the right to establish individual workshops and enterprises,

n) guarantee of the right of freedom in work for workers engaged in physical and intellectual occupations and a guarantee of the protection of the interests of workers by social legislation.

5. The Supreme Ukrainian Liberation Council will wage its struggle for an independent, united Ukrainian state in alliance with all the subject peoples of Europe and Asia which are fighting for their own liberation and which recognize Ukraine's right to political independence.

6. The Supreme Ukrainian Liberation Council is striving for accommodation and peaceful co-existence with all of Ukraine's neighbours on

the basis of mutual recognition of the right of every people to its own state on its ethnic territory.

Source: Original (carbon copy of a typescript): Archive of the Foreign Representation of the Supreme Ukrainian Liberation Council, no. 7–2. Photocopy: Archive, *Litopys UPA*.

NOTE

1. This document was adopted by the First Grand Assembly of the Supreme Ukrainian Liberation Council on 11–15 July 1944.

PROVISIONAL ORGANIZATION OF THE SUPREME UKRAINIAN LIBERATION COUNCIL[1]

I. General Principles of Organization of the Supreme Ukrainian Liberation Council

1. The Supreme Ukrainian Liberation Council is the highest governing body of the Ukrainian people in its revolutionary liberation struggle for an independent, united Ukrainian state.

2. The Supreme Ukrainian Liberation Council's power stems from the will of the Ukrainian people as manifested by the efforts of all the people's active forces to achieve independence.

3. The Supreme Ukrainian Liberation Council:

a) consolidates pro-independence social and political groupings,

b) co-ordinates the activities of active political circles,

c) heads the liberation struggle, sets the line of Ukrainian pro-independence policy and directs that policy,

d) represents the Ukrainian people and their independence efforts to the world.

4. Nationally active Ukrainians who support Ukrainian sovereignty, accept the political platform adopted by the Assembly of the Supreme Ukrainian Liberation Council and are ready at all times to put its programme into practice are eligible for membership in the Supreme Ukrainian Liberation Council.

5. The Supreme Ukrainian Liberation Council is composed of twenty-five members.[2]

The number of members can be increased by co-optation. Co-optation is carried out by:

a) the Grand Assembly of the Supreme Ukrainian Liberation Council,

b) the Presidium of the Supreme Ukrainian Liberation Council, on a motion by the General Secretariat.

6. Individuals cease to be members of the Supreme Ukrainian Liberation council if they resign voluntarily or are expelled by the Supreme Ukrainian Liberation Council.

7. A member of the Supreme Ukrainian Liberation Council can be expelled only by a two-thirds vote of the Grand Assembly.

Between sessions of the Grand Assembly, the Presidium of the Supreme Ukrainian Liberation Council has the right to suspend an individual's membership rights until such time as the matter is resolved by the following session of the Grand Assembly.

8. The Supreme Ukrainian Liberation Council carries out its activities through the following bodies:

a) the Grand Assembly of the Supreme Ukrainian Liberation Council,

b) the Presidium of the Supreme Ukrainian Liberation Council, headed by the President,

c) the General Secretariat, headed by the chairman,

d) the General Court, headed by the General Justice,

e) the Board of Control, headed by the General Comptroller.

9. The Supreme Ukrainian Liberation Council also acts through Conferences of the Supreme Ukrainian Liberation Council, which are chaired by the President of the Supreme Ukrainian Liberation Council.

10. The activities of individual bodies of the Supreme Ukrainian Liberation Council will be subject to internal regulations, ratified by the President in consultation with the General Justice.

11. All bodies of the Supreme Ukrainian Liberation Council can summon separate commissions, boards and bureaus for the purpose of dealing with specific matters.

12. The Supreme Ukrainian Liberation Council exists on Ukrainian territory. It can send its delegates abroad.

II. The Grand Assembly of the Supreme Ukrainian Liberation Council

1. The highest Ukrainian legislative power during the period of the revolutionary liberation struggle for an independent, united Ukrainian state is the Grand Assembly of the Supreme Ukrainian Liberation Council.

2. The Grand Assembly of the Supreme Ukrainian Liberation Council:

a) enacts fundamental laws,

b) examines and resolves fundamental political questions, sets the line of liberation policy and defines the programme and tactics of the Ukrainian people's liberation struggle,

c) receives reports on the activities of all bodies of the Supreme Ukrainian Liberation Council,

d) sets guidelines for the activity of all bodies of the Supreme Ukrainian Liberation Council,

e) elects: the President, seven members of the Presidium, the Chairman of the General Secretariat, the General Justice and the General Comptroller,

f) accepts the President's oath,

g) co-opts new members and confirms those co-opted by the Presidium,

h) expels members.

3. The regular Grand Assembly of the Supreme Ukrainian Liberation Council is convened by the President not less than once a year.

4. The extraordinary Grand Assembly is convened by the President:

a) on his own initiative,

b) on a motion by the Presidium,

c) on a motion by the General Secretariat,

d) on a motion by the General Comptroller,

e) on the request of one-third of the members of the Supreme Ukrainian Liberation Council.

5. The Assembly is opened by the President. The Assembly is chaired by an elected Chairman of the Grand Assembly, who appoints the other members of the Assembly Presidium.

6. For decisions made by the Grand Assembly to be legally binding, at least one-half of the members of the Supreme Ukrainian Liberation Council must be present.

7. All matters are decided by a simple majority of votes, except for the

expulsion of a member and the enactment of changes in the organization of the Supreme Ukrainian Liberation Council, which require two-thirds of the votes of those present. The dissolution of the Supreme Ukrainian Liberation Council requires three-quarters of the votes of all active members of the Supreme Ukrainian Liberation Council.

8. In exceptional cases, the Supreme Ukrainian Liberation Council can pass a resolution without convening the Assembly, on the basis of individual voting.

III. The President and the Presidium of the Supreme Ukrainian Liberation Council

1. The President stands at the head of the Supreme Ukrainian Liberation Council and represents it externally.

2. The powers of the President of the Supreme Ukrainian Liberation Council are as follows. The president:

a) convenes and prorogues the Grand Assembly of the Supreme Ukrainian Liberation Council,

b) chairs the Presidium of the Supreme Ukrainian Liberation Council and the Supreme Ukrainian Liberation Council Conferences,

c) confirms the General Secretaries appointed by the Chairman of the General Secretariat,

d) confirms the two members of the General Court appointed by the General Justice,

e) confirms the two members of the Board of Control appointed by the General Comptroller,

f) confirms the external delegates of the Supreme Ukrainian Liberation Council, who are proposed by the Chairman of the General Secretariat, on a motion by the General Secretary of External Affairs,

g) on a motion by the Chairman of the General Secretariat, removes General Secretaries from office,

h) accepts the oaths of members of the Presidium, the Chairman of the General Secretariat, the General Secretaries, the members of the General Court and the members of the Board of Control,

i) has the right of clemency.

3. The President makes his oath to the Grand Assembly; the oath is administered by the Chairman of the Grand Assembly of the Supreme Ukrainian Liberation Council.

4. The Presidium, headed by the President, is the body of the Supreme

Ukrainian Liberation Council which acts between sessions of the Grand Assembly of the Supreme Ukrainian Liberation Council.

5. The Presidium is composed of:

a) the President,
b) three Vice-Presidents,
c) four members of the Presidium.

6. The Presidium of the Supreme Ukrainian Liberation Council examines the political line and tactics and their practical execution by all the bodies of the Supreme Ukrainian Liberation Council, gives these bodies its evaluation and makes proposals to them.

7. The powers of the Presidium of the Supreme Ukrainian Liberation Council are as follows. The Presidium:

a) makes proposals with regard to convening the Assembly,

b) co-opts new members of the Supreme Ukrainian Liberation Council, on a motion by the General Secretariat,

c) suspends individuals in their rights as members of the Supreme Ukrainian Liberation Council,

d) receives reports from the Chairman of the General Secretariat, from individual General Secretaries, from the General Court and from the Board of Control.

The time and method of rendering reports is established by the Presidium by means of separate orders passed in consultation with individual bodies of the Supreme Ukrainian Liberation Council.

8. The Presidium of the Supreme Ukrainian Liberation Council acts as a body composed of no fewer than one-half of the members of the Presidium, excluding the President.

9. In the event of the non-functioning of the Presidium, its powers, excluding the right to dismiss the Chairman of the General Secretariat, pass to the President until the convening of the next Grand Assembly of the Supreme Ukrainian Liberation Council.

10. The Presidium passes its resolutions by a simple majority of votes. In the event of a tie vote, the vote of the Chairman shall be decisive. In the event of a constitutional or political conflict, the Presidium has the right to demand the resignation of the Chairman of the General Secretariat; for this motion to pass, two-thirds of the members of the Presidium must be present and the motion must receive three-quarters of the votes.

11. During the absence of the President, his duties are carried out by a member of the Presidium designated by him.

12. In the event of resignation, death or any other permanent hindrance

to the fulfillment of the functions of the President, his powers pass to the Presidium Board, which is formed automatically from the three members of the Presidium of the Supreme Ukrainian Liberation Council closest in succession.

13. The Presidium Board is provisional in character and is obliged to convene the Grand Assembly of the Supreme Ukrainian Liberation Council as soon as possible.

14. The President and Presidium of the Supreme Ukrainian Liberation Council are responsible to the General Assembly of the Supreme Ukrainian Liberation Council.

IV. The General Secretariat of the Supreme Ukrainian Liberation Council

1. The executive body of the Supreme Ukrainian Liberation Council is the General Secretariat.

2. The General Secretariat is composed of:

   a) the Chairman of the General Secretariat,
   b) the Secretary of Internal Affairs,
   c) the Secretary of External Affairs,
   d) the Secretary of Military Affairs and the Commander of the Armed Forces,
   e) the Secretary of Economic Affairs,
   f) other Secretaries.

3. The Chairman of the General Secretariat is elected by the Grand Assembly of the Supreme Ukrainian Liberation Council.

4. The General Secretaries are appointed by the Chairman of the General Secretariat and confirmed by the President of the Supreme Ukrainian Liberation Council.

5. The posts of the General Secretaries can be held jointly.

6. The General Secretariat renders reports of its activities to the Presidium of the Supreme Ukrainian Liberation Council.

7. The General Secretariat and individual General Secretaries are responsible to the Grand Assembly of the Supreme Ukrainian Liberation Council and report to it on their activities.

8. On matters of discipline, the Secretaries are responsible to the Chairman of the General Secretariat and the President.

9. On a motion by the Chairman of the General Secretariat, the President removes Secretaries from office.

10. The General Secretariat acts as a body and makes decisions by a

majority of votes. In the event of a tie vote, the vote of the Chairman of the General Secretariat is decisive.

11. The Chairman can appoint one of the General Secretaries to take his place temporarily in fulfilling the functions of Chairman of the General Secretariat.

12. In the event of resignation, death or any other permanent hindrance to the fulfillment of the functions of the Chairman of the General Secretariat, the President and the Presidium, the General Justice, the General Comptroller and the General Secretaries elect a temporary chairman of the General Secretariat.

13. Legislation is binding only if it bears the signatures of the President and the Chairman of the General Secretariat.

V. The General Court

1. The executive judicial body of the Supreme Ukrainian Liberation Council, responsible for the establishment in its name of law and order, is the General Court, which is composed of the General Justice and two members of the General Court.

2. The General Justice is elected by the Assembly of the Supreme Ukrainian Liberation Council; two other members of the Court are appointed by the General Justice and confirmed by the President of the Supreme Ukrainian Liberation Council.

3. The General Court is responsible for the fulfillment of its duties to the Grand Assembly of the Supreme Ukrainian Liberation Council.

4. In the event of the resignation, death or any other permanent hindrance to the fulfillment of the functions of the General Justice, the President and the Presidium, the General Comptroller, the Chairman of the General Secretariat and the members of the General Court elect a General Justice.

5. The General Justice has the right to interpret questions concerning the organization of the Supreme Ukrainian Liberation Council and to render his observations to the President during the ratification of the internal regulations of the bodies of the Supreme Ukrainian Liberation Council.

VI. The Board of Control

1. The executive controlling body of the Supreme Ukrainian Liberation Council is the Board of Control, which is composed of the General Comptroller and two members of the Board of Control.

2. The General Comptroller is elected by the Grand Assembly; the two other members of the Board of Control are chosen by the General Comptroller and confirmed by the President of the Supreme Ukrainian Liberation Council.

3. The Board of Control examines the economic activities of all bodies of the Supreme Ukrainian Liberation Council and, in particular, oversees the economic policy of the General Secretariat.

4. In the event of resignation, death or any other permanent hindrance to the fulfillment of the functions of the General Comptroller, the President and the Presidium, the General Justice, the Chairman of the General Secretariat and the members of the Board of Control elect a General Comptroller.

Source: Original (carbon copy of a typescript): Archive of the Foreign Representation of the Supreme Ukrainian Liberation Council, no. Y7–1. Photocopy: Archive, *Litopys UPA*. Reprinted in *Litopys UPA* (Toronto 1980), 8: 27–33.

NOTES

1. This document was adopted by the First Grand Assembly of the Supreme Ukrainian Liberation Council on 11–15 July 1944.
2. Members of the Supreme Ukrainian Liberation Council elected at the First Grand Assembly in July 1944:

    1. BAHRIANY, IVAN (1907–63). Born in Poltava oblast, Eastern Ukraine. Writer, poet, journalist and political activist. Arrested by security police in 1932, he spent several years in a concentration camp. Founder and leader of the Ukrainian Revolutionary Democratic Party (URDP). Consented to be a member but did not take part in the First Grand Assembly. Died in Germany.
    2. BILENKY, IAROSLAV (1883–1945). Born in Western Ukraine. Teacher, scholar and social activist. Editor of *Ukrainska Shkola* (Ukrainian School). Elected General Justice of the Supreme Ukrainian Liberation Council. Died in Ukraine.
    3. CHUIKO, PETRO (1893–1970). Born in Tavriia, Southern Ukraine. Teacher. Mathematician. Active in anti-Nazi resistance. Pro-monarchist in his political views. Died in the United States.
    4. DUZHY, MYKOLA (1902–55). Born in Western Ukraine. Political and social activist. Executive Secretary of Prosvita (Enlightenment) Society. Editor of *Studentskyi Shliakh* (Student Path). Member of the

OUN leadership. In Soviet concentration camp 1946–55. Died in Ukraine.

5. GALIANT, MYKOLA (1875–1945). Born in Western Ukraine. Catholic priest. Faculty member of the Lviv Greek Catholic Theological Academy and Chancellor of the Lviv Metropolitan Consistory. Consented to be a member but did not take part in the First Grand Assembly. Tortured to death in a Soviet prison.

6. HRYNIOKH, IVAN (1907–). Born in Western Ukraine. Catholic priest (Mitred Patriarchal Archimandrite), scholar, journalist and political activist. Faculty member of the Lviv Greek Catholic Theological Academy (1935–9) and currently of the Ukrainian Catholic University in Rome. Member of the OUN leadership. Elected Second Vice-President of the Supreme Ukrainian Liberation Council and President of its Foreign Representation. Lives in West Germany.

7. LEBED, MYKOLA (1910-). Born in Western Ukraine. Revolutionist and political activist. Member of the OUN leadership. Sentenced to death for his anti-Polish activities, but his sentence was commuted to life imprisonment. Escaped during the German-Polish war and became the leader of anti-German resistance and founder of the UPA. One of the founders of the Supreme Ukrainian Liberation Council and, from July 1944, Secretary of Foreign Affairs and General Secretary of the Foreign Representation of the Supreme Ukrainian Liberation Council (ZP UHVR). Lives in the United States.

8. LOGUSH, KATERYNA (1913–). Born in Dnipropetrovsk oblast, Southern Ukraine. Organizer of the OUN in Dnipropetrovsk oblast during the Second World War and active in organizing the First Conference of Subject Peoples of Eastern Europe and Asia, 21–2 November 1943, in Volhynia. Lives in the United States.

9. LOGUSH, OMELIAN (1912-). Born in Western Ukraine. Journalist. Member of the OUN leadership. Organizer of the OUN in Dnipropetrovsk oblast and of the UPA in Volhynia. Active in maintaining contacts between the Hungarian army and the Ukrainian underground. Lives in the United States.

10. MALYNOVSKY, OLEKSANDER (1889–1957). Born in Western Ukraine. Catholic priest. Vice-Rector of the Lviv Greek Catholic Theological Academy and Apostolic Administrator of the Lemkian region (1940–46). Rector of the Ukrainian Catholic Theological Seminary in Hirschberg, Germany, and in the Netherlands. Vicar-General of the Ukrainian Catholic Church in Great Britain from 1950. Consented to be a member but did not take part in the First Grand Assembly or in the work of the Supreme Ukrainian Liberation Council. Died in England.

11. MUDRY, VASYL (1903–66). Born in Western Ukraine. Journalist

and political activist in Galicia. Member and, from 1935, leader of the Ukrainian National Democratic Union (UNDO), and member of the Ukrainian Parliamentary Representation. Deputy and Vice-Marshal of the Polish *Sejm*. Elected First Vice-President of the Supreme Ukrainian Liberation Council. Died in the United States.

12. OKHRYMOVYCH, VASYL (1914–54). Born in Western Ukraine. Member of the OUN leadership. One of the founders of the UPA. In Western Europe from 1946, but returned to Ukraine in 1953. Arrested by the Soviets and sentenced to death by the Kiev Military Tribunal in May 1954.

13. OSMAK, KYRYLO (1900?–1945?). Born in Eastern Ukraine. Member of the Ukrainian Party of Socialist Revolutionaries (UPSR) and its representative in the Ukrainian Central Rada. Active in the Directory of the Ukrainian People's Republic. Arrested by the GPU and sentenced to five years in prison. Elected President of the Supreme Ukrainian Liberation Council. Arrested by the Soviets in the autumn of 1944 but probably not identified. Died in a Soviet prison.

14. PELENSKY, ZENON (1902–79). Born in Western Ukraine. Journalist and political activist. Member of the OUN. Editor of several newspapers and magazines. President of the Association of Ukrainian Journalists in Germany (1967–9). Elected member of the Presidium of the Supreme Ukrainian Liberation Council. Died in Germany.

15. POTISHKO, VASYL (1895–). Born in Zhytomyr oblast, Central Ukraine. Active in the co-operative movement. Secretary of the All-Ukrainian Military Committee and its representative in the Ukrainian Central Rada in 1917. Member of the Ukrainian Party of Socialist Revolutionaries (UPSR). Lives in the United States.

16. POZYCHANIUK, IOSYP (1911–45). Born in Vinnytsia oblast, Central Ukraine. Writer, journalist, revolutionary activist. Organizer of UPA units in Central Ukraine. Became Head of the Information Bureau of the Supreme Ukrainian Liberation Council in July 1944. Died in battle against Soviet security troops in 1945.

17. PROKOP, MYROSLAV (1913–). Born in Western Ukraine. Journalist and political activist. Member of the OUN leadership responsible for propaganda and head of its underground radio station. Editor of several newspapers and journals and author of many publications. Elected member of the Presidium of the Supreme Ukrainian Liberation Council and Vice-President of its Foreign Representation. Lives in the United States.

18. REBET, DARIIA (1913–). Born in Bukovyna. Journalist and political activist. Member of the OUN leadership. Elected member of the Presidium of the Supreme Ukrainian Liberation Council and of its Foreign Representation. Lives in West Germany.

19. SHANKOVSKY, LEV (1903-). Born in Western Ukraine. Educator, journalist, scholar and military historian. Author of many books. Consultant of the Supreme Military Command of the UPA. Chairman of the Preparatory Committee for the convocation of the First Grand Assembly of the Supreme Ukrainian Liberation Council. Lives in the United States.

20. SHUKHEVYCH, ROMAN (TARAS CHUPRYNKA), (1907–50). General. Born in Western Ukraine. Member of the OUN leadership, active in anti-Polish, anti-German and anti-Soviet resistance. Leader of the OUN in Ukraine (1943–50). Commander-in-Chief of the UPA (1944–50). Elected Chairman of the General Secretariat of the Supreme Ukrainian Liberation Council and Secretary for Military Affairs (1944–50). Killed in battle against MVD troops on 5 March 1950.

21. SHUMOVSKY, PAVLO (1899–1983). Born in Rivne oblast, Western Ukraine. Scholar, teacher and social activist. Supporter of the Ukrainian People's Republic and sympathizer of the OUN. Studied in Kiev, Cracow, Berlin and Warsaw. Professor at the Sorbonne. Died in France.

22. TURULA, PAVLO (1909-). Born in Western Ukraine. Chemist. Member of the OUN. Lives in the United States.

23. VOLOSHYN, ROSTYSLAV (1911–46). Born in Volhynia, Western Ukraine. Revolutionist and political activist. Prisoner of Polish, German and Soviet jails. One of the founders of the UPA. Chairman of the First Conference of Subject Peoples of Eastern Europe and Asia, 21–2 November 1943, and of the First Grand Assembly of the Supreme Ukrainian Liberation Council, 11–15 July 1944. Elected Secretary of Internal Affairs of the Supreme Ukrainian Liberation Council. Killed in battle against Soviet troops.

24. VOVCHUK, IVAN (1900–79). Born in Kharkiv oblast, Eastern Ukraine. Teacher and agronomist. Member of the Kharkiv Institute of Plant Science. Elected Third Vice-President of the Supreme Ukrainian Liberation Council. Political and social activist. Editor of several newspapers and journals. Died in the United States.

25. VRETSIONA, IEVHEN (1905–75). Born in Western Ukraine. Leading member of the Ukrainian Military Organization (UVO) and of the OUN. Organizer of Ukrainian military units in Transcarpathia (1938) and of the UPA. Member of the Presidium of the Foreign Representation of the Supreme Ukrainian Liberation Council. Died in Switzerland.

Co-opted Members of the Supreme Ukrainian Liberation Council:

26. DIAKIV, OSYP (1921–50). UPA Captain. Born in Western
    Ukraine. Member of the OUN and major ideologue of the Ukrainian
    underground. Joined the UPA in 1942; co-opted in 1950 as member of
    the Supreme Ukrainian Liberation Council and made Vice-Chairman
    of the General Secretariat. Killed in battle against Soviet security
    troops.
27. KUK, VASYL (KOVAL), (1910–). UPA Colonel. Born in West-
    ern Ukraine. Member of the OUN leadership. In charge of Dniprope-
    trovsk *krai* in 1942–5 and later of Volhynia. Co-opted as a member of
    the Supreme Ukrainian Liberation Council after the death of General
    Shukhevych in 1950, he became Chairman of the General Secretariat
    of the Supreme Ukrainian Liberation Council and head of the Ukrain-
    ian underground. Captured by the Soviets in either 1954 or 1955, he
    was later employed in the Archives of the Academy of Sciences of the
    Ukrainian SSR.
28. LAVRIVSKY, M. (pseudonym). Probably a priest whose identity is
    not known. Co-opted as a member of the Supreme Ukrainian Libera-
    tion Council. Signed "An Appeal from Embattled Ukraine to All
    Ukrainians Abroad" as head of the underground Greek Catholic
    church.
29. POLTAVA, P. (pseudonym), (19?–52). UPA Major. Born in West-
    ern Ukraine. Journalist and leading ideologue of the Ukrainian un-
    derground. Member of the OUN leadership. Co-opted as a member
    of the Supreme Ukrainian Liberation Council and made Vice-Chair-
    man of the General Secretariat, Head of the Information Bureau and
    Chief of the Political Education Division, UPA General Staff. Killed
    in battle against Soviet troops.
30. ZELENY, H. (pseudonym). Identity unknown. Co-opted as a mem-
    ber of the Supreme Ukrainian Liberation Council. Signed "An Ap-
    peal from Embattled Ukraine to All Ukrainians Abroad" as "Mem-
    ber of the UHVR."

WHAT IS THE UKRAINIAN INSURGENT ARMY FIGHTING FOR?[1]

The Ukrainian Insurgent Army (UPA) is fighting for an independent, united Ukrainian state and for the principle that every nation should be able to lead a free life in its own independent state. The only way to effect a just solution to the national and social problem in the world is to bring an end to the subjugation and exploitation of one nation by another and to establish a system of free peoples living in their own independent states.

The UPA is fighting against imperialism and against empires, for within empires one ruling people culturally and politically subjugates and economically exploits other peoples. For this reason, the UPA is fighting against the USSR and against Germany's "New Europe."

The UPA is resolutely fighting against both internationalist and fascist national-socialist programs and political concepts, for they are the tools of imperialist policies of conquest. Thus, we are opposed both to Russian communist Bolshevism and German National Socialism.

The UPA is opposed to any people, intent on fulfilling its imperialist goals, "liberating," "taking under its protection" or "into its care" other peoples, for these deceptive phrases conceal a repugnant reality: subjugation, coercion and plunder. For this reason, the UPA will struggle against the Russian-Bolshevik and German plunderers until it rids Ukraine of all "protectors" and "liberators," until it attains an independent, united Ukrainian state in which peasants, workers and intellectuals will be able to live and develop in a free, prosperous and cultured manner.

The UPA is for the full liberation of the Ukrainian people from the Muscovite-Bolshevik yoke; it is for the establishment of an independent, united Ukrainian state free of landowners and capitalists, as well as of Bolshevik commissars, NKVD agents and party parasites.

In the Ukrainian state, the governing power will regard serving the interests of the people as its highest duty. Since it will have no plans for conquest, nor any subject countries or oppressed peoples within its state, the national government of Ukraine will not waste time, energy or financial resources on establishing an apparatus of oppression. The Ukrainian national regime will direct all economic resources and all human energies toward establishing a new political order and a just social system, toward building up the economy of the country and raising the cultural level of the people.

Within the ranks of the UPA, Ukrainian peasants, workers and intellectuals are fighting against their oppressors for an independent, united Ukrainian state, for national and social liberation, for a new political and social order:

1. For the destruction of the Bolsheviks' exploitative system of serfdom in the organization of the rural economy. Since the land is the property of the people, the Ukrainian national regime will not impose on farmers any one method of working the land. In the Ukrainian state, both individual and collective work on the land will be permitted; the method will depend upon the will of the farmers.

2. a) For state ownership of large industry and co-operative ownership of small industry.

b) For the participation of workers in the direction of factories; for directors to be chosen on the basis of expertise, rather than on the commissar-party principle.[2]

3. a) For a universal eight-hour work day. Overtime will have to be consented to freely—like all work in general—and will have to bring the worker additional wages.

b) For fair wages for work; for the participation of workers in the profits of commercial enterprises. Every worker will receive a wage sufficient to meet the material and spiritual needs of his entire household. During the period when annual financial reviews of commercial enterprises are carried out, every worker will receive the following: in co-operative enterprises—a dividend, in state-owned enterprises—a premium.

c) For freedom in work, a free choice of profession, and a free choice of the place of work.

d) For free trade unions. For the abolition of the Stakhanov[3] work method, socialist competition, increasing norms and other methods of exploiting workers.

4. For freedom in the trades; for the right of tradesmen to unite voluntarily in workmen's associations; for the right of the tradesman to leave the association in order to pursue his work on an individual basis and to dispose freely of his income.

5. For state ownership of large business; for co-operative and private ownership of small business; for free marketplaces.

6. For full equality of women with men in all the rights and obligations of citizenship; for free access for women to all schools and all professions; for the fundamental right of women to engage in physically lighter work, so that women will not ruin their health by seeking employment in mines and other heavy industries. For state protection of motherhood. Fathers will receive, in addition to wages for their work, a supplementary payment for the support of their wives and of children who have not yet reached the age of majority. Only in these conditions will women have the opportunity to carry out their important, honourable and responsible duties as mothers and educators of the younger generation.

7. a) For compulsory secondary education. For raising the educational and cultural level of the population by increasing the numbers of schools, publishers, libraries, museums, cinemas, theatres and similar institutions.

b) For increased advanced and professional training; for a continual growth of cadres of highly qualified specialists in every field of human endeavour.

c) For free access by young people to all institutions of higher learning. For ensuring students' ability to pursue their studies by providing stipends, food, habitation and the equipment necessary for education.

d) For a harmonious, all-round development of the younger generation in the moral, intellectual and physical spheres. For free access to all the scientific and cultural achievements of mankind.

8. For respect for the work of intellectuals. For creating material conditions for intellectual work that will ensure the well-being of the intellectual's family, so that he can be free to devote himself to his cultural and creative work and constantly increase his knowledge and raise his intellectual and cultural level.

9. a) For full protection of all workers in old age and in case of illness or handicap.

b) For the establishment of large-scale health care; for a broadening of the network of hospitals, sanatoriums, health resorts and rest homes. For expanding the medical cadres. For the right of workers to have access, without payment, to all health institutions.

c) For special state protection of children and youths; for an expansion of the network of nurseries, kindergartens, sanatoriums and recreation camps; for the inclusion of all children and youths in the programs of state institutions dedicated to care and education.

10. a) For freedom of the press, speech, thought, convictions, worship and world-view. Against the official imposition on society of any doctrines or dogmas with regard to world-view.

b) For the freedom to profess and practice any religion which does not run counter to the morals of society.

c) For the separation of church organizations from the state.

d) For cultural relations with other nations; for the right of citizens to go abroad for education, medical treatment or in order to learn about the life and cultural achievements of other nations.

11. For the full right of national minorities to cultivate their own national cultures.

12. For equality of all citizens of Ukraine, whatever their nationality, with regard to the rights and obligations of citizenship; for the equal right of all to work, remuneration and rest.

13. For a free, fully Ukrainian culture; for a spirit of heroism and high moral standards; for civic solidarity, friendship and discipline.

Ukrainian Insurgent Army

August 1943
Republished 1949

Source: An UPA leaflet. Original: Archive of the Foreign Representation of the Supreme Ukrainian Liberation Council, Folio of Leaflets. Photocopy: Archive, *Litopys UPA.* Reprinted in *Litopys UPA* (Toronto 1976), 1: 126–31.

NOTES

1. This is a revised edition of the document "What is the Revolutionary-Liberationist UPA Fighting For?" initially signed by the OUN leadership.
2. Reference is to the *nomenklatura* system, one of the main instruments of political control in the USSR—the list of positions in state, economic and social institutions and organizations which are filled exclusively on the rec-

ommendation of party organs by persons from special lists compiled for that purpose.

3. Stakhanov movement: a form of "socialist competition" representing an attempt to establish high records of productivity. Formally it was considered a voluntary expression of workers' initiative, but in reality it was organized by directives from above.

TO THE WHOLE CIVILIZED WORLD! AN OPEN LETTER FROM UKRAINIANS LIVING BEYOND THE CURZON LINE

"We the peoples of the United Nations determined to reaffirm faith in fundamental human rights, in the dignity and worth of the human person, in the equal rights of men and women and of nations large and small, and to establish conditions under which justice and respect for the obligations arising from treaties and other sources of international law can be maintained, and to promote social progress and better standards of life in larger freedom,

And for these ends to practice tolerance and live together in peace with one another as good neighbours, have resolved to combine our efforts to accomplish these aims."

Excerpt from the Charter of the United Nations Organization ratified at the conference in San Francisco.

We, Ukrainians, inhabitants of Ukrainian ethnic territories in the Carpathian Mountains in the region west of the River San,[1] north along the Rivers San and Solokiia[2] and west of the River Buh,[3] territories which, as a result of the decision taken at the Crimean Conference,[4] have been left within the bounds of the restored Polish state, appeal by this means to the embassies and governments of Great Britain, the United States of America, France, Sweden, Switzerland, Turkey and all other European and non-European states; we also appeal personally to President Truman,[5] Prime Minister Attlee[6] and their ministers of external affairs, who drafted, ratified and signed the Charter of the United Nations. Further, we appeal to all the heads and officials of the Christian churches, to the International Red Cross, to all progressive political and humanitarian organizations in all countries and to the conscience of all progressive humanity with this open letter on the terrible injustice and violence to which we are being subjected by the army and other agencies of the present Polish government, which is directed in this action by the [Soviet] Bolsheviks.

On the basis of the decision taken by the Crimean Conference, the above-mentioned territory lying to the north and west of the Curzon Line[7] is to remain within the bounds of the restored Polish state. In accordance with this decision, the Ukrainian population of approximately one million persons, which has lived on this territory since time immemorial, is to enjoy all constitutional rights and rights of citizenship in the Polish state.

However, the present Polish government, blindly obeying the directives of the Soviet authorities upon whom it is dependent, refuses to grant Ukrainians any human or civil rights and has decided to launch an enforced deportation of the whole Ukrainian population from its age-old, ancestral settlements.

The Ukrainian population in this region does not, under any condition, wish to abandon its lands and its settlements. There are a number of understandable human reasons for this, but the most important reason is that in the Soviet Union, where the authorities want to transport us and where all the rest of the Ukrainian population of more than forty million lives, our people have no guarantee of any national, political, religious or social human rights.

In the Soviet Union, the Ukrainian people are subjected to unparallelled national, political and social oppression. The Soviet regime, under which it has been the lot of Ukrainians and other peoples to live, is one of complete dictatorship and tyranny which deprives our brothers of all their human rights.

For this reason, out of the approximately one million Ukrainians living behind the Curzon Line, almost none have chosen to move voluntarily to the Soviet Union. The Ukrainians living on this territory have stated almost unanimously that they do not wish to leave, but instead want to remain where they have always lived, in their ancestral settlements, and to enjoy the civil rights that are their due.

Nevertheless, the present Polish government, under pressure from Moscow, which fears to leave any Ukrainians outside the immediate range of its inhuman assimilatory practices, has decided to eject the

Ukrainian population by force from its settlements.

The official government treaties proclaim this to be *voluntary* resettlement.[8]

We Ukrainians are adhering to this official decree concerning the voluntary nature of the resettlement. However, representatives of the Polish and [Soviet] Bolshevik governments are attempting to conduct not a voluntary resettlement but a forced evacuation. Throughout the past year, the Soviet-Polish resettlement commissions constantly announced new deadlines for our departure and launched an extensive propaganda campaign for this purpose, but almost none of the Ukrainians chose to leave. Then the representatives of the Polish and [Soviet] Bolshevik governments began to organize armed bands among the Polish population and ordered these bands to attack Ukrainian villages, intending in this way to drive the inhabitants out by means of terror.

As a result of this campaign, throughout the past year and particularly in the spring of 1945 Ukrainian villages were attacked by numerous armed bands of Poles, who were openly receiving assistance from the state militia and other government officials. Last year these armed bands, along with the militia and units of the army, burned scores of Ukrainian villages in this region and plundered and destroyed many more. Terrible crimes of mass murder were committed. In some villages, the armed bands and state militia killed one hundred, two hundred or more people in a single day. Even women, old people and children were severely beaten, tortured and murdered; living people, including infants, were thrown into fires.[9]

Supervising these cannibalistic terrorist actions were border units of the Bolshevik NKVD, which often crossed the newly drawn border between Poland and the Ukrainian SSR, stationed themselves on the Polish side and assisted the Polish terrorist bands in breaking the opposition and defence of the Ukrainian population against the terror and deportation.

However, even this long campaign of terror waged by organized bands of the state militia failed to break the Ukrainian population's determination to remain on its land.

Even under the pressure of this unprecedented terror, only a small percentage of the population registered for departure. And those who registered did so only under compulsion. They still did not wish to leave and often escaped and hid away. And in many cases, even those who were transported to the Soviet Union soon returned across the border to their native settlements, having succeeded in escaping from the concentration camps which await the Ukrainians who are resettled.

Driven to the extreme, the Ukrainian population drew on its own resources to organize an armed force for self-defence against these

Polish-Soviet bands. The whole population joined together to wage a determined defence. Armed units of the Ukrainian Insurgent Army (UPA) and self-defence units often succeeded in repelling the attacks of the bands and militia.

In addition, intelligent voices began to speak up among the Polish population, condemning the terroristic anti-Ukrainian attacks as shameful and harmful to the interests of the Polish people.

As a result of the determined self-defence waged by the Ukrainian population and the influence of the more intelligent patriotic Polish circles, it became possible eventually, in May and June of 1945, to bring an end to most of the terrorist activity of the armed bands and to suspend the bloody Polish-Ukrainian struggle.

The remnants of the terrorist bands have remained active only in those few places where the Polish population is under the influence of the official communist Bolshevik camp. In the great majority of the territories along the Ukrainian-Polish border, a state of complete peace descended in the summer of 1945. Peaceable citizens, both Polish and Ukrainian, turned for the first time in a long period to their normal work in the fields in an atmosphere of neighbourly harmony. With every passing day, relations on these territories improved. The earlier struggle, which had brought harm to both peoples, was being replaced by friendship and co-operation, from which important benefits would flow to both sides in the future. All honest and intelligent people rejoiced at this turn of events.

But the present Polish government, which is totally subject to the influence and directives of the red Muscovite imperialists, grew fearful that the new understanding and co-operation between Poles and Ukrainians would serve to strengthen significantly the anti-Bolshevik liberation front of subject peoples of the USSR, which are struggling for liberation and independence. For this reason, it was decided in official Bolshevik circles to eject the Ukrainians at any price in order to drive a wedge between the two peoples, for this is essential to Moscow's present imperialist policy.

The attempt to eject Ukrainians with the help of the terrorist actions of the military and organized civilian bands failed. Accordingly, in the month of September 1945, the Polish government assigned large army units to conduct an enforced deportation of Ukrainians. Thus, at the beginning of September, a new wave of terror was launched against the Ukrainian population. This time the terror was waged openly, rather than being attributed to irresponsible civilian bands, for it was conducted by army units. It should be pointed out that the commanders of these units of the Polish army are almost exclusively [Soviet] Bolshevik officers dressed in Polish uniforms.[10] Following the tactics used by the infamous Nazi murderers during the recent German occupation, the army surrounds Ukrainian villages by night and forces the population to leave.

Because the Ukrainians refuse to leave voluntarily, these Polish soldiers, following orders from above, plunder their goods, terrorize them with mass executions, beat them, rape the women, shoot innocent villagers, eject them by force from their homes and commit many other crimes and acts of violence.

In the city of Peremyshl,[11] the authorities have arrested the bishop of the Ukrainian Greek Catholic church, Kotsylovsky.[12] In this, they are following the example of the Bolsheviks, who arrested the Metropolitan of the Greek Catholic church, Iosyf Slipy,[13] in Lviv and sent him to Siberia. The Bolsheviks also arrested all the bishops and many priests and turned Greek Catholic churches over to the Orthodox church,[14] which currently is not at all a free religious organization but simply a tool of the [Soviet] Bolshevik police (the NKVD-NKGB). In our region, in addition to Bishop Kotsylovsky, many members of the Ukrainian intelligentsia were arrested in an attempt to terrorize the Ukrainian intelligentsia into moving to the Red Soviet "paradise," which our people hate and fear with all their souls, for they know, not from studying the theory of communism or reading books or propaganda, but from the terrible experience which the Ukrainian people have undergone during more than twenty-five years of Bolshevik rule, that the Soviet Union is one huge prison of nations, a system of endless concentration camps, executions and those dreadful forms of terror characteristic of all totalitarian dictatorships that have reached a state of complete degeneracy.

Our people are being subjected to all these injustices and crimes just at the time when the whole world has heard proclaimed the principles of the Atlantic Charter,[15] President Roosevelt's Four Great Freedoms[16] and the Charter of the new international organization of the United Nations, which Secretary of State Stettinius[17] has called a "magnificent institution of the new, free world," just at the time when President Truman is announcing the dawn of a golden age of liberty for mankind and the most eminent statesmen in Great Britian are proclaiming the same great principles and pledging their words and their honour that they will firmly stand guard for truth and justice in the world.

Meanwhile, with respect to the Ukrainian people as a whole and to us, the inhabitants of the territories beyond the Curzon Line, not only are the obligations imposed by the Charter of the new international organization of the United Nations being broken and trampled upon, but even the most basic principles of Christian morality and elementary humanity are being totally ignored. We are denied even those rights which in civilized, democratic countries are guaranteed to every animal and every living thing.

We are ejected by force from our homes and villages; women, children and old people are beaten to death; living people, even infants torn from their mothers' breasts, are thrown into flames; our priests and bishops are arrested; our goods are plundered; our poor village women have their last worn shirts torn from their backs; and we are forced to go against our will to the Soviet Union, to face a wretched existence or even death. There are many villages whose inhabitants have been spending months in damp forests with all their meagre possessions, with their wives and children, hiding in the ground, in woods and in water from the savage, inhuman terror, just as in the Middle Ages people hid from the attacks of nomadic hordes.

And these terrible crimes, reminiscent of Hitler and Nero,[18] are being committed by the very people who make so much noise throughout the whole world about how "progressive" they are, about "social progress" and "world revolution," and who are attempting to represent themselves as mankind's "saviours" from all misery and distress.

We, Ukrainians, inhabitants of territories located beyond the Curzon Line, are fighting with all our strength, along with the whole Ukrainian people, against these acts of violence; we do not spare our efforts or our blood, for we are deeply convinced that the great sacrifices we make in this brutal struggle will benefit all mankind, which stands threatened by the danger of totalitarian tyranny that has at present assumed a red guise.

At the same time, we appeal, by means of this open letter, to the whole civilized world, in the hope that all freedom-loving nations and all civilized, humane people who hear our voice will respond and support the heroic struggle of our people against the barbaric, cannibalistic destruction with which we are menaced by the [Soviet] Bolshevik and Polish Bolshevik tyrants.

Above all, we address ourselves to those representatives of the great Western democratic powers who proclaimed and signed the Charter of the United Nations Organization cited in excerpt at the beginning of our letter, in which they solemnly pledge to defend the rights of nations and the rights of people.

We turn to them with our protest, complaint and fervent appeal that they work with all their powers to implement the great principles they have proclaimed concerning human *freedom and justice*.

October 1945

Representatives of all strata of the Ukrainian
population beyond the Curzon Line[19]

Source: Original: Archive of the Foreign Representation of the Supreme Ukrainian Liberation Council. Photocopy: Archive, *Litopys
UPA.*

NOTES

1. San (Ukr. Sian): largest Carpathian tributary of the Vistula. Until 1946 the
   upper part of the river up to the city of Sanok flowed through Ukrainian
   ethnic territory, the middle up to Syniava served as the border between
   Ukrainian and Polish Galicia, and the lower part was on Polish ethnic territory.
2. Solokiia: left tributary of the Buh (Bug).
3. Buh (Bug): right tributary of the Vistula. Forms the border between
   Poland and the USSR, part of the Curzon Line.
4. Reference is to the Yalta Conference (4–11 February 1945).
5. Harry S. Truman (1884–1972): President of the United States, 1945–53.
6. Clement Attlee (1883–1967): British prime minister, 1945–51.
7. Curzon Line: eastern frontier of Poland as recognized by the Entente in
   1919–23, named after G.N. Curzon, First Marquis Curzon of Kedleston
   (1859–1925), British statesman, who proposed it in 1919.
8. On the basis of treaties between Poland and the Ukrainian SSR (9 and 22
   September 1944) and Poland and the USSR (6 July 1945), most of the
   Ukrainian population was forcibly removed from the Lemkian, Sian,
   Kholm and Podlachia regions to the Soviet Union. At the same time, the
   Polish population in the USSR was allowed to emigrate to Poland.
9. For example, in the village of Pavlokoma 365 men, women and children
   were killed on 5 March 1945, among them the Rev. Lemtsio, a Ukrainian
   Catholic priest. The rest were exiled; the village was then resettled by the
   Poles. The UPA burned the village in the fall of 1946.
10. The so-called *Popy* (*Pełniący Obowiązki Polaka*): a sarcastic popular ex-
    pression, "doing the work of the Poles."
11. Peremyshl (Przemyśl): city on the river San. The seat of the oldest Ukrain-
    ian bishopric in Galicia and, from 1691, the seat of the Ukrainian Catholic
    bishop.
12. Iosafat Kotsylovsky (1876–1947): Ukrainian Catholic bishop of Peremyshl
    eparchy. Died in a Kiev jail.
13. Iosyf Slipy (Slipy-Kobernytsky-Dychkovsky) (1892–1984): Archbishop
    Major of Lviv, Head of the Ukrainian Catholic Church and a Cardinal.

Spent 18 years in Soviet forced-labour camps and resided in the Vatican after his release from prison in 1963.

14. Reference is to the forcible liquidation of the Ukrainian Catholic Church on 8–10 March 1946.

15. Atlantic Charter: programme of aims for peace, jointly enunciated by Winston Churchill and Franklin D. Roosevelt on 14 August 1941. These aims were incorporated into the United Nations Declaration of 1942.

16. The Four Freedoms outlined in President F.D. Roosevelt's message to Congress (6 January 1941) were: freedom of speech and expression, freedom of worship, freedom from want and freedom from fear. These were substantially incorporated into the Atlantic Charter.

17. Edward R. Stettinius, Jr. (1900–49): U.S. Secretary of State (1944–5). Resigned to serve as U.S. representative to the United Nations (1945–6).

18. Nero (Claudius Caesar) (A.D. 37-68): Roman emperor (A.D. 54-68).

19. It is not known who wrote this document, which was widely circulated both in Poland and abroad. There were seven underground editions of the letter in Ukrainian, five in Polish, two in Slovak and French and one in Czech and English. It was written at the time of the forced deportation of Ukrainians from Poland.

AN APPEAL FROM EMBATTLED UKRAINE TO ALL UKRAINIANS ABROAD

Freedom for nations and individuals!
For an independent, united Ukrainian state!

To our brothers scattered far and wide:
Four years have passed since war ended in Europe. But it has not yet ended in Ukraine. For four years now you have seen the peoples of Western Europe and America living their lives in peace. But in Ukraine there is no peace! In Ukraine a savage struggle still goes on: the guns have not grown silent, the fires have not been extinguished. In plants and factories, on collective and private farms, in schools and other institutions, in forests and mountains, in Ukraine and distant Siberia and Kazakhstan, everywhere the Ukrainian people have mounted the barricades for liberty. They stand bloody but unbowed, unconquered and unmastered.

Filled with hatred for oppression and slavery, violence and disregard for human rights, they have declared war on Russian-Bolshevik imperialism. In full knowledge of the justice of their cause, they are reaching great heights of devotion and heroism.

They have taken their destiny into their own hands and have chosen to forge it to the end. And they are forging it now, ceaselessly, tirelessly, fearlessly.

As the advance guard of the holy war against the totalitarianism, despotism and terror of Stalin'S USSR, they are fulfilling their task manfully. They have raised high the banner bearing the words close to the hearts of all nations and peoples: *Freedom for nations, freedom for individuals!*

No Ukrainian can remain on the sidelines of this bloody struggle, which is unlike anything known in history. All Ukrainians must take part, regardless of where they may be. Your embattled homeland looks upon you, brothers scattered abroad, as part of the single front of our great struggle. Embattled Ukraine regards you as warriors for the great cause of liberation who have opened a new front in Western Europe, America, Australia—wherever there is even a single Ukrainian. *Embattled Ukraine sends its fraternal greetings to you at your posts.*

Your native land is paying heed to everything that goes on among Ukrainians abroad, whether they be recent immigrants or those who left long ago. The Ukrainian people are watching to see whether the Ukrainian front abroad is keeping step with that in the homeland. The people here have the right to expect that Ukrainians abroad will not abandon the struggle or the tasks assigned them by history.

Above all, Embattled Ukraine expects Ukrainians abroad to represent their people and their struggle for liberation in a worthy and responsible manner to the rest of the world.

Ukraine is only entering the international arena. The world still knows little about Ukraine, and what it does know is often confused and twisted. To change this state of affairs, to convey the truth about Ukraine and its struggle to all nations and peoples beyond the borders of the USSR, is your first duty, Ukrainians abroad. Ukraine is doing all she can in this regard. Her struggle has created a great store of capital and you, Ukrainians abroad, must use it in the interests of the cause of liberation.

Fate has scattered you in all countries of the world, to the most distant ends of the earth. But this is not the time to complain about your difficult fate. You must make use of the fact that you now live in all parts of the world for the good of the Ukrainian people as a whole; you must make use of your situation to inform people about Ukraine as much as possible, so that they will learn more about Ukraine, the Ukrainian people, their past achievements and their present heroic struggle.

Remember that today every Ukrainian abroad is a representative of embattled Ukraine.

Remember that in viewing each of you, foreigners view the entire Ukrainian nation; in judging you, they judge our whole nation.

Let each of you conduct himself in a way that will not dishonour his people; behave in a way that will add to their glory. Ask yourself each day: "What have I done for the good of Ukraine?"

Stay as close in spirit as possible to Ukraine. Live by her, by her efforts and her struggle. Never allow yourself to doubt the success of our great cause. Never doubt the justice of our struggle in the homeland, for if you do you will never convince your neighbours of the justice and ultimate success of our endeavours or gain their support for your nation.

Embattled Ukraine expects Ukrainians abroad to be ardent exponents of the ideas for which the Ukrainian people are fighting.

Inform foreigners of the need to partition the USSR into free national states of all its member nations. Demonstrate to them that all the subject peoples of the USSR are longing for independence and are struggling bravely to attain it. Explain to them that the interests of all the peoples of the world would be served by the dismemberment of the USSR, for this is the only way to prevent the possible rebirth of Russian imperialism, which in its present Bolshevik form is menacing the entire world.

Propagate the idea of building an international order founded on a system of free, independent states of all peoples. Only a system of this type can create the best conditions for true political, economic and cultural co-operation and unity among peoples, for it will build on true equality, good will, mutual respect and confidence. Only this type of system can prevent bloody wars and safeguard lasting peace in the world.

Explain to your neighbours that the Ukrainian people are struggling for the realization of the most progressive ideas of humanity—freedom for nations and individuals, true democracy and a just social order, where there will be neither exploiters nor exploited.

Embattled Ukraine expects Ukrainians abroad tirelessly to propagate the truth about Stalin'S USSR to all the peoples of the world and to mobilize them actively to struggle against Russian-Bolshevik imperialism, the greatest foe of all mankind.

The world is still woefully ignorant of the truth about the USSR. It still does not fully realize that it is itself threatened by Russian-Bolshevik imperialism. To expose the true face of Bolshevism, to tear away the mask of democracy and socialism that it uses to disguise its true intentions, to expose it in its hideous reality is your great task, Ukrainians abroad.

Strive to enlighten the millions of foreigners who still sincerely believe in the socialism of the USSR. Tell them about the terrible oppression of peoples within the USSR, the colonial plunder of their resources, the unprecedented exploitation and treatment of workers as slaves, the new form of serfdom on collective farms and the stifling of the intelligentsia.

Tell the whole world about the true nature of the world's "most democratic" country, where people are driven in terror to vote; where they are forced to elect their executioners and oppressors; where the courts are organs of coercion and deny all rights; where not only are people silenced, but even their thoughts are fettered; where men are turned into slaves and deprived of all rights; where millions are sent to prisons and concentration camps.

Tell everyone about the country in which religion is stifled, the church is dishonoured, freedom of conscience does not exist, all morality—not only Christian, but human morality in general—is trampled underfoot, while paradise is proclaimed, and a church is maintained that is but a puppet of the Ministry for State Security (MGB) and the Ministry of Internal Affairs (MVD). Speak of the suppression of the Ukrainian Autocephalous and the Ukrainian Greek Catholic churches, and of the murder and deportation of Ukrainian bishops, priests and faithful. Explain to foreigners that the present-day Russian Orthodox church has nothing in common with a free church and is simply a tool of the MVD. Call all believing Christians and the faithful of other religions to the struggle against the mortal enemy of humanity—Bolshevism.

Embattled Ukraine expects Ukrainians abroad to work actively to organize a single front of all peoples enslaved or threatened by Russian-Bolshevik imperialism.

The Russian-Bolshevik imperialists have already subjugated many peoples and are preparing to place their yoke over all others in the near future. All Bolshevik declarations about the peaceful co-existence of the two systems are only misleading propaganda. All the efforts of the Kremlin leaders are directed at preparing a new war in order to conquer the entire world. The whole existence of the USSR is directed toward that one goal. The hopes of the Western world that war can be averted are but vain hopes built on sand. *The world cannot escape war.*

You, Ukrainians abroad, must take every opportunity to make this truth known to the peoples of the West. This fact should serve as the starting point in all your practical political work among other peoples. Tell the people clearly that the entire world now faces a problem: not how to avoid a new war, for it is unavoidable, but how to preserve liberty, independence and culture, how to avoid the enslavement and ruin of mankind—that is not unavoidable. You must tell them clearly that the world's only hope is *the speedy and complete destruction of Russian-Bolshevik imperialism where it exists today.* And this can be done *only through an organized effort by a single front of all peoples subjugated and threatened by Russian-Bolshevik imperialism.*

You, Ukrainians abroad, must do more than just speak of the need for such a front and convince the world of its necessity. You must also do everything possible to ensure that the anti-Bolshevik front assumes a concrete form. In order to achieve this, you must arm yourselves with belief in the justice of your cause; you must also display a high degree of organizational skill, tolerance and endurance, for you must bring together all people who thirst for freedom, regardless of their race, nationality, religion or political orientation.

Above all, you must henceforth strive to bring together in one anti-Bolshevik front exiles from all the nations of Europe and Asia which are now under Bolshevik rule, as well as from the nations of Central and South-Eastern Europe recently added to that number.

Your country gratefully welcomes your successes so far in this regard. Build upon and enlarge these successes, Ukrainians abroad! Work tirelessly to overcome all difficulties and disagreements that stand in the way of a complete union of people from all nations of the USSR living abroad. Strengthen this union in its work both among the exiles and in the outside world.

Along with your work to unify exiles from all the subject peoples of the USSR, you, Ukrainians abroad, must work as actively as possible among the peoples of the West to form an anti-Bolshevik front composed of all the freedom-loving people of the world. Forge ties with all national and international organizations that fight for human rights and freedom. Strive to create an international organization which would aim at struggling against imperialism and totalitarianism and defending the rights of nations and individuals.

Remember, brothers living abroad, that the task of organizing a single anti-Bolshevik front of all peoples does not rest only with the leaders of political parties. It is your duty as well. Remember that the issue of forming an anti-Bolshevik front, like that of representing the Ukrainian people, is not to be raised only in political and diplomatic circles. It must be raised in the broadest possible arenas among all the peoples of the West—in factories, mines, farms, schools and other institutions. Only when the masses take part in the anti-Bolshevik front, when the movement has acquired so broad a base, will it be capable of destroying its foe.

Remember that disseminating the truth about the USSR and mobilizing and organizing peoples for the struggle against Bolshevism is a mission of universal significance. So be worthy of the great mission history has assigned you. Fulfill it with apostolic devotion and zeal, fulfill it with the sort of courage and dedication manifested at present by the revolutionary fighters. If you fulfill your mission, future generations of all peoples will gratefully remember you.

In order to fulfill all these responsible tasks, brothers abroad, you must be united. You must act in harmony. *Embattled Ukraine most defi-*

nitely expects Ukrainians abroad to be fully united, united in deed and not simply in words, united by the revolutionary struggle for the liberation of Ukraine.

The present situation cannot be allowed to continue. There must be no divisions on the basis of religious affiliation or belief; above all, there must be no "Easterners" or "Westerners." Divisions of this sort cannot be tolerated. Ukrainians living abroad must make every effort to heal the scars left on the living body of the Ukrainian nation by long years of subjugation and the imposition by occupying powers of artificial borders dividing the country. All differences between Ukrainians must be eliminated through common work and struggle. The more enlightened members of the Ukrainian community abroad must work to raise the level of national consciousness and political maturity of the less enlightened. That is now the major task of Ukrainians living abroad. And they must bear full responsibility for its successful completion.

At such a significant time, given the grave situation of the Ukrainian people today, Ukrainians abroad cannot allow themselves *any divisions or partisan disagreements. At present, all partisan disputes must be suspended for the sake of one goal, one task—the task of liberating the Ukrainian people.* People fall into two categories, not according to the party to which they belong, but according to whether they are patriots or traitors.

Your country does not object to the fact that different political parties exist abroad, but to the fact that these parties are incapable of co-existing and working with one another, or even achieving harmony within their own ranks. The homeland is incensed by the degeneration of political and civic morals in the emigration, which harms the whole cause of liberation; it shames the whole nation in the eyes of the world and creates a false impression of the struggle taking place in Ukraine. Embattled Ukraine is incensed by the fact that the values and achievements of the entire nation are being squandered in this partisan struggle. Embattled Ukraine most severely condemns all those unwilling to rise above their narrow party interests, all those who trade and deal in the idea of liberation.

Your country notes with sadness that among Ukrainians abroad are some who long refused to believe in the existence in Ukraine of the Ukrainian Insurgent Army, the Supreme Ukrainian Liberation Council and the Organization of Ukrainian Nationalists. There are even some who opposed these bodies. Only after the UPA carried out its march to the West, only after many living witnesses had come forward, only after the insurgents had fought their way across more than one thousand kilometers did these Doubting Thomases begin to accept that the

UHVR, the UPA and the OUN exist and act and struggle in Ukraine. And even after all that, there are still some people abroad who constantly try to minimize the significance of the struggle in Ukraine; they try to narrow the scope of the struggle and minimize its political importance. Your country calls on all these people to cease their attempts to denigrate the liberation struggle in Ukraine and to work instead for the interests of their embattled country. As for those who, because of their own narrow interests, fail to find the courage and desire to cease their attacks on the Ukrainian liberation movement, those who consciously continue to denigrate it—your country states unequivocally that their efforts will be regarded as crimes against the Ukrainian people and its struggle for liberation.

Brothers living in foreign lands: Your homeland has now attained complete unity; you abroad must follow that example. Anyone who truly feels his nation's sufferings, who truly desires its liberation, who sincerely wishes to devote himself to his people, who treasures the idea of a Ukrainian state, will enter into the joint effort for the achievement of our great goal. Establish a powerful single front and act in a resolute, united fashion. Let political differences among Ukrainians abroad be directed toward developing political thought, not toward partisan bickering. Demonstrate your understanding of the historical significance of the present moment and your devotion to the task before you. Serve as an example to others of unity and organization, for these qualities are required by all nations if the struggle against the Bolsheviks is to be successful.

Brothers abroad who are engaged in manual labour: Unable to return to your native land, you find yourselves in factories and mines and on farms in almost all the countries of the world. You work side by side with workers of all nationalities. The people with whom you work are those who have been most deceived by Bolshevik lies and propaganda. Help these millions of workers to free themselves from Bolshevik delusions. Convince them from your own long experience that no socialism exists in the USSR; that the USSR is a reactionary, totalitarian state. Rouse them to share your hatred for Russian-Bolshevik imperialism. In their souls these workers hate slavery, coercion and the denial of rights as much as you do. Make friends with them in your places of work. Create a basis for close friendship between their peoples and the Ukrainian people.

Take part in the activities of Western labour organizations and stand as an example of comradeship and solidarity. Establish Ukrainian labour organizations and stand up for your rights. Broaden your cultural and intellectual life.

Take part in the work of international anti-Bolshevik labour organizations and act as representatives there for the millions of Ukrainian workers unable to speak freely for themselves. Struggle with all other workers against imperialism and totalitarianism and for true democracy and social justice.

Ukrainian poets, writers, artists, scholars and journalists abroad: In Ukraine, all Ukrainian scholarship and culture are suppressed. Freedom of speech has been driven underground. Under these circumstances you have the important task of fostering Ukrainian culture and scholarship and enriching them with new achievements. Ukraine joyfully takes note of the current creative achievements of Ukrainians abroad in the fields of science and culture and calls for even greater efforts in those spheres.

Establish new centres of Ukrainian culture and learning and concentrate there all the creative forces that are now abroad. Make every effort to develop Ukrainian studies, for in Ukraine these things are corrupted and falsified by the Russian-Bolshevik occupying power. Bring up a new generation of scholars.

Make use of every opportunity to represent Ukrainian science and culture to the outside world. Work tirelessly to make Ukrainian achievements known. Bring Ukrainian music, singing and theatre to all. Establish contacts with cultural and scientific organizations and representatives of other peoples! Do not miss any opportunity to make a contribution to international scientific or cultural organizations. Let the world see Ukrainian culture in all its fullness and creativity.

Ukrainian women abroad: Ukraine is pleased with your achievements and your organizational abilities and with the successes you have attained. Increase the strength of your organizations, become even more active, both in emigrant and in larger circles. Work to preserve in your community and family lives the shining traditions of Ukrainian womanhood. Make use of every opportunity to work with women of the West. Enlighten them about the terrible danger of Bolshevism. Arouse the conscience of the women and mothers of the world by telling them how women in the USSR live as slaves, how the family is destroyed, how millions of children have died of hunger, been incarcerated in prisons and sent into exile, torn by force from their mothers and turned into homeless orphans. Let the women of all nations take their place in the general struggle against Bolshevism.

Ukrainian youth: While living abroad, you must enter the advance guard of the struggle for liberation, just like young people in Ukraine. You must devote yourselves entirely to the interests of Embattled Ukraine and be prepared to answer her every call, to stand alongside your comrades who are engaged in an armed struggle for liberation, for a happy, joyous and creative existence in a Ukrainian state. You must be well organized and active; you must constantly temper your idealism and unceasingly strive to increase your knowledge and your political skills. Profit from your residence among other peoples to learn from them all that is good and useful; learn from their experience in all spheres of activity, including that of building their states. But guard yourselves against any disruptive influences that might sap your idealism and resolution.

You, Ukrainian youth abroad, like all Ukrainians abroad, are faced with the task of acquainting others with the struggle of the Ukrainian people for liberation. Do this at every opportunity and in every way. Make use of your own personal relationships, as well as your links with young people of other nations and international youth organizations. Arouse the youth of all nations to the struggle against Bolshevism. They will quickly respond, for young people are easily aroused against injustice and violence and are always ready to fight against them.

Fighters and commanders of units of the UPA who marched to the West: You have bravely fulfilled the task assigned to you by the Supreme Ukrainian Liberation Council. Ukraine followed your progress with bated breath and rejoices at your success. The whole nation is glad that you reached beyond the outer wall of the Bolshevik prison of nations to protest to the whole world against the oppression of the Ukrainian people by the Russian-Bolshevik plunderers and to the tell the truth about the liberation struggle.

Your arrival in Western Europe as direct participants and living witnesses of the liberation struggle in Ukraine has had a significant effect upon the foreign view of our struggle. It has put an end to the falsification of the facts of this struggle. In this lies your great service to the whole cause of liberation. History will give you the credit you deserve.

Although you are now far from your native land, your struggle has not ended. The enemy who oppresses your homeland is also active where you now live, and you must struggle against him there just as you recently struggled in Ukraine. Continue to guard and foster the heroic traditions of the Ukrainian Insurgent Army and raise high its banner of glory.

Brothers living abroad: Soon you will be even more scattered around the world, even further from your homeland. But keep in mind that this is a temporary state of affairs; your stay abroad, your nostalgia for your country will not last forever.

When the bells peal to announce Ukraine's resurrection and she rises in a hymn of glory, you will all return once more to your country. Then, united ''in a new, free family,'' all the children of Ukraine who are now scattered around the world will come together to build a free, happy life. And the words of our great prophet, Taras Shevchenko, will be fulfilled:

> Ukraine will arise,
> Break the dark bonds of slavery,
> The light of truth will shine
> And the enslaved children will pray in freedom![1]

Believe this deeply and struggle bravely, so that that great day may come as quickly as possible.

Regardless of all the terrible difficulties, Embattled Ukraine will struggle as resolutely as she has done until now, without sparing her sweat or her blood.

Embattled Ukraine will do all in her power to enable the Ukrainian people to erect their great temple of freedom as quickly as possible and to enable you to return to Ukraine not as servants or hirelings but as your own masters.

In the name of Embattled Ukraine:

Rev. Prof. M. Lavrivsky, Member of the Supreme Ukrainian Liberation Council (UHVR), head of the underground Ukrainian Greek Catholic church.

General R. Lozovsky-Chuprynka, Chairman of the General Secretariat of the UHVR and Commander-in-Chief of the UPA.

V. Koval, Vice-Chairman of the General Secretariat of the UHVR, Member of the UHVR.

Prof. H. Zeleny, Member of the UHVR.

Captain P. Poltava, Chief of the Political Education Division, UPA General Staff.

Major D. Sokil, Member of the UPA General Staff.

Major M. Dubovy, Commander of UPA-North.

P. Maksymovych, Member of the OUN Leadership in Ukraine.

O. Hornovy, journalist, Member of the OUN Leadership in Ukraine.

Captain V. Khmel, Staff Member of UPA-West.

Major V. Hrim, Commander of the UPA-West Military District "Hoverlia."

Z. Savchenko, OUN leader in North-Western Ukraine.

J. Vasylenko, OUN leader in West-Central Ukraine.

Captain R. Ilnytsky, leader of the OUN underground youth organization.

A. Shybalynska, leader of the underground Ukrainian Red Cross.

Engineer K. Vladan, leader of the Western OUN District.

I. Budko, leader of the Eastern OUN District.

T. Iliian, leader of the North-Western OUN District.

S. Stal, leader of the OUN in Bukovyna.

Prof. S. Kuzmenko, editor of underground publications.

D. Bey, artist.

I. Fesenko, UPA physician.

In Ukraine, October 1949.

Source: Original: Archive of the Foreign Representation of the Supreme Ukrainian Liberation Council. Photocopy: Archive, *Litopys UPA.*

NOTE

1. Lines from Shevchenko's poem "Subotiv," written on 21 October 1845 in Marinske.

NOTES ON THE AUTHORS

Borovych, Ia. V. A pseudonym of Vasyl Mudry (1893–1966). Political activist and journalist. First Vice-President of the Supreme Ukranian Liberation Council. In 1921–5 he was Quaestor and Secretary of the clandestine Ukrainian University of Lviv. In 1926–35 he was a leading member of the Prosvita (Enlightenment) Society and of the Ukrainian National-Democratic Union (UNDO), of which he became leader in 1935. As an elected deputy he was one of the leading members of the Ukrainian Parliamentary Representation in Warsaw and became the Vice-Marshal of the Polish Diet *(Sejm)*. During the German occupation he worked closely with the Ukrainian underground and participated in negotiations on its behalf with the Polish underground and the Hungarian army of occupation. After migrating from Ukraine he was elected Chairman of the Central Representation of the Ukrainian Emigration (1949) and, upon arriving in the United States, became Executive Director of the Ukrainian Congress Committee of America. Died in the United States.

Brodovy, O. A pseudonym of an underground publicist who could not be identified.

Duma, P. A pseudonym (one of many) of Dmytro Maivsky (1914–45). Teacher, journalist and political activist. He was born in Kerlenets, Zhovkva raion, Lviv oblast, in the family of a teacher. He was jailed by the Polish authorities for his political activity. In 1941 he became a member of the OUN leadership. During the German occupation he was one of organizers of the anti-German resistance in Kiev. In 1942 and again in 1944–5 he served as editor-in-chief of *Ideia i Chyn* (Idea and Action), the official organ of the OUN. He was one of the chief promoters of the convocation of the Third Grand Assembly of the OUN and of the resulting evolution in the ideology of that organization toward democratic and socially progressive political goals. Under his direction, *Ideia i Chyn* became an important political publication on a high theoretical level. Maivsky was able to draw on the talents of such young publicists as P. Poltava, O. Diakiv, U. Kuzhil, R. Mokh and others who, like himself, developed and articulated the political programme of the Ukrainian underground. He was killed on 19 December 1945 in Czechoslovakia while on a foreign mission.

Hornovy, O. A pseudonym (one of many) of Osyp Diakiv (1921–50). Journalist, political activist, captain of the UPA and Vice-Chairman of the General Secretariat of the Supreme Ukrainian Liberation Council. He was born in the village of Olesyn, Koziv raion, Ternopil oblast. As a student at the University of Lviv, he was arrested by the NKVD in 1940 and later released, his health seriously damaged. During the German occupation he held various positions within the educational apparatus of the OUN youth organization. With the return of the Soviets he continued his journalistic activities and produced a number of important programmatic works and critical analyses of the Soviet system. He was made a member of the OUN leadership and, in 1950, of the Supreme Ukrainian Liberation Council. He died in battle against MVD troops on 28 November 1950 near the village of Velyke Pole in Ivano-Frankivsk oblast.

Iarlan. A pseudonym (one of many) of Iaroslav Starukh (1910–47). Journalist, political activist and, from 1945, leader of the OUN in *Zakerzonskyi krai* (Ukrainian ethnic territory in Poland). He was born in the village of Svoboda Zolota, Berezhany raion, Ternopil oblast. Under Polish rule he studied law and was active in the OUN, performing various important functions. He was arrested on several occasions and incarcerated in Polish and German jails. During the German occupation he worked on the staff of the underground radio station "Samostiina Ukraina" (Independent Ukraine). He was the author of many pamphlets, articles and proclamations. He was killed in battle against the Polish operational group "Lubaczów" near the village of Monastyrky, Tomashiv (Tomaszów) county, on 17 October 1947.

Khersonets, Iu. M. A pseudonym of an underground publicist who could not be identified.

Kovalenko, I. M. A pseudonym of the Rev. Dr. Ivan Hryniokh (1907 –), Catholic priest, scholar, journalist, political activist, Second Vice-President of the Supreme Ukrainian Liberation Council and Chairman of the Presidium of the Foreign Representation of the Supreme Ukrainian Liberation Council. He was born in Radekhiv raion, Lviv oblast, and completed his studies at the University of Innsbruck, Austria. An active member of the anti-German resistance, he contributed articles to *Ideia i Chyn* and conducted negotiations on behalf of the Ukrainian underground with the Poles, Romanians and Hungarians. He is the author of numerous underground publications.

Kuzhil, U. A pseudonym of an underground publicist who could not be identified. Some unconfirmed sources speak of him as one of the scholars from Eastern Ukraine working with the Ukrainian underground. His fate is unknown.

Poltava, P. (died in 1952). A pseudonym of a journalist, political activist, major of the UPA and Vice-Chairman of the General Secretariat of the Supreme Ukrainian Liberation Council. His real name and the place and date of his birth are unknown. It is known only that in 1940 he fought in the Soviet-Finnish War as a soldier in the Red Army, that during the German occupation he studied medicine in Lviv and that he was very active in the OUN underground. After the end of the war he wrote a number of articles and essays which make him, without doubt, one of the most important theoreticians of the Ukrainian underground. He was a member of the OUN leadership and served as Chief of the Political Division of the UPA Supreme Command, Vice-Chairman of the General Secretariat of the Supreme Ukrainian Liberation Council and Director of its Information Bureau. It is not known whether he held some of these posts concurrently. He was killed in battle with MVD troops in the Carpathian mountains in the winter of 1951–2.

Shakhai, D. A pseudonym (one of many) of Iosyp Pozychaniuk (1911–44). Writer, journalist, political activist, member of the Supreme Ukrainian Liberation Council and first Director of its Information Bureau. Born in Dashiv raion, Vinnytsia oblast, he was educated in Soviet schools. During the German occupation he was an organizer of UPA units in Central Ukraine and editor of the underground newspapers *Za Ukrainu* (For Ukraine) and *Za Ukrainsku Derzhavu* (For a Ukrainian State). Subsequently he headed the Political Division of the UPA Supreme Command in Volhynia. In addition he organized various underground presses and wrote many novels, articles, essays and proclamations. His contribution to the development of the political thought, programme, strategy and tactics of the Ukrainian underground was enormous. He died in battle against NKVD troops either in December 1944 or, according to a more reliable source, in the spring of 1945.